The Norm of Truth

THE NORM OF TRUTH

An introduction to the philosophy of logic

Pascal Engel

University of Toronto Press

Toronto   Buffalo

First published in North America in 1991 by
University of Toronto Press
Toronto   Buffalo

Translated from the French by Miriam Kochan and Pascal Engel
First published as *La norme du vrai* by Éditions Gallimard

Printed and bound in Great Britain at
the University Press Cambridge

Canadian Cataloguing in Publication Data

Engel, Pascal, 1954–
  The norm of truth

(Toronto studies in philosophy)
Translation of: La norme du vrai.
Includes bibliographical references and index.
ISBN 0-8020-2775-X (bound) ISBN 0-8020-6891-X (pbk.)

1. Logic.   2. Logic, Symbolic and mathematical.
I. Title   II. Series.

BCS0.E513 1991   160   C91-095379-1

To Claudine
To the memory of Henri Joly

Logic, we may agree, is concerned not with what men actually believe, but what they ought to believe, or what it would be reasonable to believe. . . . What however, would this ideal person's opinion be? . . . The highest ideal would be always to have a true opinion and be certain of it; but this ideal is more suited to God than to man.

Frank P. Ramsey

ACKNOWLEDGEMENTS

This book comes partly from courses given at the University of Grenoble between 1982 and 1987. The final version was written in 1987–8, thanks to a leave of absence from my teaching duties awarded by the Centre National de la Recherche Scientifique. The present publication is not simply an English translation of the original French book. It has undergone a number of revisions and changes, which were required both by the imperfections and mistakes of the first version, and by the fact that the French public is much less familiar with these topics than the English-speaking public. For better (I hope) or worse (I hope not), some of the French origins of the book can still be perceived, in particular in bibliographical references to French publications that I hope to see some day at the disposal of English-speaking readers.

I have had the occasion to present some of the themes of this book in various published articles and talks before various audiences, and I thank the participants for their remarks. I learnt a lot from a conference on formal semantics which I organised with Frédéric Nef in Grenoble in 1987 (proceedings in Cooper and Engel (1991)) and from Franco-British discussion groups from 1987 to 1990. Without the encouragement of my late colleague Henri Joly, to whom I dedicate the book, my work would have been much more difficult. Many people have helped me with their remarks on various drafts of the manuscript. I would like to thank Maurice Boudot, François Clementz, Claudine Engel-Tiercelin, Pierre Jacob, Daniel Laurier, Joëlle Proust, François Récanati, Mark Sainsbury, Dan Sperber and especially Gilles Granger, Frédéric Nef, and Jules Vuillemin. I received invaluable help from Tom Baldwin, who gave me detailed comments on a draft of Chapter 5 and on the whole book, and from Michel Seymour, who wrote a 70-page review article on the French version, which opened my eyes on many problems and implications of my views. I have often thought about Blackburn's (1984, p. vi) image of an army of snipers concealed behind every bush and ready to shoot the writer of such introductory works. Philippe de Rouilhan was one of the snipers, but it was for my benefit. I thank him for his detailed criticisms of Chapter 4 and other parts of the book, and François Rivenc and Jacques Dubucs. The published reviews of the French version have also helped me a lot to improve the present one: I am, of course responsible for all the mistakes that might remain. I thank my co-translator, Miriam Kochan. Without Eric Vigne, who asked me to write this book, and without Claudine Engel-Tiercelin, it would not have existed.

CONTENTS

LIST OF LOGICAL SYMBOLS

p, q, r	propositional variables
A, B, C	metalinguistic variables on propositions
Γ, Δ, Θ	metalinguistic variables on sets of propositions
( )	left and right parentheses
$-$	negation (not)
&	conjunction (*and*)
$\vee$	disjunction (*or*)
$\rightarrow$	material conditional (*if . . . then*)
$\equiv$	biconditional (*if and only if*; abridged: 'iff')
a, b, c	individual constants
x, y, z	individual variables
x/y	the result of the substitution of y for x
P, Q, R	predicate variables
ϕ, ψ	metalinguistic variables on predicates
$\exists$	existential quantifier (*some*)
$\forall$	universal quantifier (*all*)
$(\imath x)\, \phi\, x$	description operator
$\hat{x}\,[\, .\, .\, .\,]\, a$	abstraction operator
$=$	identity
$=_F$	relative identity (to a sortal term F)
$\{\, .\, .\, .\,\}$	set or class
$\langle\, .\, .\, .\,\rangle$	ordered n-uple of objects
$\vdash$	assertion-sign (theoremhood)
$\vDash$	'is a valid formula'
$A_1, \ldots, A_n \vdash B$	proof-theoretical consequence
$A_1, \ldots, A_n \vDash B$	semantical consequence
$\frown$	concatenation sign
$\Diamond$	*it is possible that*
$\Box$	*it is necessary that*
$\rightarrow\!\!\!\shortmid$	strict implication
$\triangledown$	vagueness operator (*vaguely*)
$\neg$	intuitionist negation
$\bullet$	intuitionist conjunction
$\Rightarrow$	relevant implication
$\varnothing$	null set

INTRODUCTION

This book is an introduction to the philosophy of logic. But 'philosophy of logic' is an umbrella term which covers a variety of different questions and styles of enquiry. I do not think that there is a single, well established, conception of the subject, and the one offered in this book does not pretend to represent them all. Although I shall not attempt to give a precise definition, it will be useful to indicate where my own treatment and choice of topics differs from other approaches.

By 'logic' I shall mean, in the usual sense, the theory of inferences that are valid in virtue of their form. It is in general admitted that this definition applies only to *deductive* logic, and that the theory of *inductive* inferences does not belong to 'formal logic' in the ordinary sense. A deductive inference is for instance: 'All Cartesians are dualists. Malebranche is a Cartesian. Therefore Malebranche is a dualist.' An inductive inference is for instance: 'All the swans observed so far are white; so if this animal is a swan, it will be white.' The first inference is such that if the premise is true, then the conclusion is true, and conclusively so. The second inference is such that the conclusion is only likely to be true, or probably true; in fact it could be false; so the conclusion is not certain. In the first case, we say that the conclusion follows from the premises; it is more difficult to say this in the second case. So the criteria by which we ascertain inductive inferences are less easy to specify in the inductive than in the deductive case. Although there are systems of inductive logic, there is no such system to which the term 'logic' can be applied in the same sense as for deductive logic, and many people even doubt that there is such a thing as inductive *logic*. Why it is so is in itself a very interesting question, and an important one for the philosophy of logic. But to answer it we need to ask first what deductive logic is, and this latter question is difficult enough to cope with here along with the question of the nature of inductive inference. So I shall leave aside inductive logic in this book.

In the narrower sense 'philosophy of logic' designates a set of problems about the *methodology* of formal logic, that is an analysis of the concepts and methods used by the logician. How does he delimitate the domain of his discipline? How does he codify the valid inferences with which he is dealing? How does he construct the formal languages in which these inferences are represented, and in particular how does he construct his central notions, such as those of logical consequence and of deduction? What are the properties of the systems that he builds? More generally, how is the territory of logic demarcated? Is it to be reduced to 'classical' logic, or must it include 'non-classical' systems such as, for instance, modal, epistemic or intuitionist logics? These questions are, so to say, internal to the logician's inquiry, and are not by themselves philosophical questions. But these cannot be separated from more general questions that are external to the analysis of the logician's methods, such as the following. What is the relationship between the intuitive validity of an informal argument and the formal validity of this argument according to the rules of logic? In what sense is logic 'formal'? If logic is a science, is it one of a number of sciences that would only deal with more general truths, or is it a foundation for all sciences, which would state the most abstract principles underlying all other sciences? What kind of knowledge is logical knowledge and what kind of truths are logical truths? Do the structures and categories of logical grammar mirror those of natural language, and do they reflect the concepts by which we think of reality, or are they independent from these concepts? Do they reflect the ultimate structures of reality? All these questions go beyond the strict domain of a methodology of logic, and raise problems that belong to the philosophy of language, to epistemology, to ontology and possibly to the philosophy of mind. Nevertheless they are usually taken to be central to the philosophy of logic.

But this is still vague. If the 'philosophy of logic' is a specific discipline, one would like to know when a certain question ceases to concern logic proper, and when it concerns the 'philosophy' thereof. In principle, the demarcation line seems clear enough: a certain question (for instance the question whether a logical system is consistent, that is does not lead to contradiction) is a properly logical question if it can be answered through methods and concepts that are sanctioned by logicians (for instance if the consistency of a given system is susceptible of being *proved* in a certain manner, recognised as a 'proof' by all practising logicians). A question is philosophical if it has a 'philosophical interest' and if it can be answered by means of a philosophical argument. For instance the concept of *a priori* knowledge is admittedly a philosophical concept from the theory of knowledge: there does not seem to be any 'purely logical' answer to the question whether logical truths are *a priori*, that is there is no logical proof of this claim. But this kind of characterisation seems question-begging: many problems that are *prima facie* 'purely technical' can have a philosophical interest, and the difference between a logical argument and a philosophical argument is sometimes difficult to spell out. Moreover, it has been supposed that there is a *specific* sphere of problems and methods intermediary between logic and philosophy, and a specific discipline dealing with these problems, called 'philosophical logic'.

Although the term 'philosophical logic' is of recent origin, the notion of such a discipline is, in a certain sense, rather traditional. For Aristotle, the term 'logic' did not denote only the theory of formal inferences that he had invented, namely syllogistics, but also a much wider kind of enquiry, dealing with the applications of his theory of formal inferences to scientific knowledge in general, and studied in his *Organon*. Later in the history of philosophy, 'logic' in this wider sense has been called sometimes 'the art of thinking', sometimes 'the doctrine of science' (*Wissenschaftslehre*), and the subject matters of the Aristotelian *Organon* have been accordingly modified to include either a theory of judgement, a theory of categories, a semiotic, or, more generally, the whole field of the theory of knowledge.[1] Thus Mill's *Logic* contains not only a theory of deductive inference, but also a theory of induction and of scientific inference in general. Today this use of the term 'logic' in the wide sense has almost disappeared as a result of the mathematisation of logic at the beginning of the twentieth century, but also because many philosophical topics that used to be associated with the term 'logic' as widely construed are now associated with the term 'philosophical logic'.

Our present use of the term 'philosophical logic' is mostly post-Fregean and post-Russellian. Frege called 'logic' not only his own formal system, but also his reflections about the nature of his formalism and about meaning and truth in general. Although Frege himself does not use the term 'philosophical logic', it is clear that these reflections are close to our contemporary understanding of that term. His insistence on the fact that 'logic' in the wide sense is concerned with language in general and should be kept separate from both psychology and the theory of knowledge justifies Dummett's claim that Frege's inquiries belong also to the philosophy of language and that this discipline holds for him the position of a primary philosophy.[2] Russell proposed explicitly the term 'philosophical logic' for a general enquiry into the nature of 'logical forms'. By this he did not mean only a study of the structure of logical languages, but also of the logical structures of natural languages, which would have both epistemological and ontological consequences.[3]

Our present conceptions of philosophical logic bear strongly their Fregean and Russellian heritages. Philosophical logic is taken to be continuous with the philosophy of language, and to use logic as a tool for the analysis of thought. But there are two main versions of what philosophical logic is, which differ in the respective weight or authority that is granted to logical analysis. One of them assigns precise limits to this authority, and can be called *informal philosophical logic*, whereas the other aims at conforting and extending this authority, and can be called *formal philosophical logic*.

According to the *informal* version of philosophical logic, formal logic is only a guide for the analysis of thought, and should not be allowed to have the last word. Ryle (1954) coined the phrase 'informal logic', to designate a 'logical geography' of our concepts, which would be to formal logic what cartography is to geometry: in the former the irregular features of the landscape must be adapted to the chosen scale, and the success of the enterprise depends upon the capacity of the cartographer to use the idealisations of the latter; just as the cartographer is a 'customer' of the geometer, the philosopher-logician is the customer of the professional logician, and adapts the logician's concepts for his own use, without adopting his full range of methods. Strawson (1969), following Ryle to some extent, has developed his own version of informal philosophical logic. He separates the whole field of logic into two parts: a 'formal' part and a 'philosophical' part. Formal logic proper studies logical truths and inference on the basis of the logical structures of sentences. The structural features of sentences can be studied through a small set of notions (reference, predication, generality) which constitute logical grammar and from which an account of the truth conditions of sentences can be given. Philosophical logic, according to Strawson, begins when we realise that all these notions raise problems that go beyond the study of formal systems, questions about the very nature of truth, of reference and of predication, or about the scope of logical grammar for elucidating the grammar of natural languages and our understanding of them. For Strawson, philosophical logic is a distinctive discipline not only because it poses specific questions, but also because it gives specific answers to them: formal logic in itself in unable to characterise the general features of our thought, and reflects only a small part of the set of categories that a complete description of our conceptual scheme must reveal. For this reason the logician's canonical notation has no particular authority over a description of our ontology. The usual logical categories are correct only in so far as they agree with a more general analysis of the fundamental categories of our thought as they are expressed in natural language and in the general conditions of our experience of the world. On this view, philosophical logic regains in part the field that it had left with Frege, namely a theory of judgement and an epistomology. Strawson's project is much closer to what Kant calls a transcendental analysis of judgement.[4]

Whereas philosophical logic in Strawson's sense is a kind of Kantian critique of formal logic, which sets limits to its philosophical applications, the second version, formal philosophical logic, aims at extending the applications of formal logic to philosophical analysis. The current reasoning underlying the philo-sophical logician's project is in general the following: logic can be a powerful tool for the analysis of philosophical concepts; but the expressive power of ordinary logic (classical predicate calculus) is too poor to serve that end; therefore an extension and a diversification of the logical tools is called for, and the development of non-classical logics, which have a greater expressive power, is required. Thus a number of extensions and revisions of classical logic have been envisaged for philosophical reasons. To give only a few examples, modal logics provide a formal analysis of the *prima facie* philosophical notions of possibility and necessity, the logic of time bears the promise of a formal analysis of time and temporal concepts, causal logic systematises analyses of causality, deontic logic does the same for the notions of obligation and of norms, epistemic logics are supposed to clarify our concepts of knowledge and belief, and 'free logics' intend to capture a number of philosophical views about existence.[5] Last but not least, one of the primary motivations of intuitionist logic is an analysis of the notions of proof and truth in mathematics which rests on different assumptions from those of classical logic. In this sense, 'philosophical logic' involves two complementary objectives. On the one hand, it is a method of formal analysis of concepts belonging to the classical repertory of philosophical concepts, which are represented by the various non-classical logical constants introduced in various systems (for instance the operators 'it is possible' and 'it is necessary' of modal logic, and the operators 'it is permitted' and 'it is obligatory' of deontic logic). On the other hand, the term 'philosophical logic' came to designate the non-classical logical *systems* that are supposed to serve the means of this kind of philosophical analysis. Thus epistemic logic is, in this sense, a part of 'philosophical logic'. As a *formal* system, it introduces two non-classical operators, B ('believes that') and K ('knows that'), and involves (for instance) such axioms as:

(1) $KSp \rightarrow p$ (*if S knows that p, then p*)
(2) $KSP \rightarrow BSp$ (*if S knows that p, then S believes that p*)

from which can be derived such propositions as:

(3) $BSp \& (BSp \rightarrow BSq) \rightarrow BS\,q$ (*if S believes that p, and if, if S believes that p, S believes that q, then S believes that q*)

(It should be noticed, however, that if S believes that p, and if s believes that *if p then q*, then it does not follow that S believes that q).[6]

As a *philosophical analysis* embodied in this formal system, epistemic logic is supposed to provide some insights into our ordinary inferential practices involving epistemic concepts, or about their 'logical forms'.

Formal philosophical logic pursues the same objective as informal philosophical logic – the correct analysis of philosophical and ordinary concepts – with different means: whereas formal logic is for the former only a limited tool for philosophical analysis, for the latter it is philosophical analysis itself, which tends to be a specialised branch of formal logic.

I believe that the philosophy of logic should not be reduced to 'philosophical logic', whatever version of it, informal or formal, one favours. Both versions have the effect of restricting the range of philosophically relevant questions that logic can raise. Informal philosophical logic in Strawson's sense limits the scope of these questions to elementary logic. Its formal counterpart limits this scope to non-classical logics. Both exclude from the outset a number of philosophical questions. I agree with Hintikka when he says:

> Is there a branch of logical studies especially relevant to applications to philosophy? Is there such a thing as 'philosophical logic'? Basically, my answer is 'no'. There does not seem to be much intrinsic difference in philosophical interest between the different conventional compartments of logic. Much of the recent work in the more esoteric parts of mathematical logic possesses, it seems to me, a great deal of relevance to philosophical inquiry. It is true that most of this work has not caught the eye of philosophers, or has done so only in those relatively rare cases in which logicians have themselves called philosophers' attention to their problems. However much of the work that has been done in such areas as recursive function theory, model theory, and metamathematics is concerned with the explication and development of concepts and conceptual problems which are of the greatest interest and relevance to a philosopher's pursuit.[7]

The idea that only certain parts of logic, such as its elementary part, would be of concern for the philosopher only, whereas other parts would be of mere 'technical' interest and of concern for the logician only, is wrong. The notion of a 'philosophically interesting subject' is eminently variable and relative to the kind of philosophical project that one has. To take up again Ryle's image, there are many ways for the philosopher to be a 'customer' at a logician's shop, and there is no reason to believe that only some logical goods are worth purchasing. A number of theorems in logic, such as Beth's definability theorem, or Craig's theorem about axiomatisability within a system, are not usually considered as relevant for 'philosophical logic', although they can have important implications for the philosophy of science.[8] Although it is true that some logical theories, such as Lesniewski's mereology (or Goodman's calculus of individuals), seem to have been conceived for purely philosophical reasons in the first place, there is no reason to believe that only these should be of interest for a philosopher. The specialists of many other disciplines can get an interest in such or such a branch of logic. Deontic logic, for instance, is of interest to jurists, and recently modal, temporal and epistemic logics have attracted the interest of computer scientists and of workers in artificial intelligence. To suppose that certain branches of logic or certain non-classical logics are limited to only one field of application is a category mistake: for the logical character of a system implies, in the ordinary sense of the word 'logic', that it is not about a particular subject matter and that it is (in principle) *universally* applicable. Of course the fact that a number of non-classical logics are classified as 'philosophical' indicates that, in some sense, their subject matter is less 'general' or 'formal' than classical systems, and that they seem to be 'logics' only *for a certain purpose*. But there is no *a priori* reason why these logics should be called 'philosophical', and not, for instance, 'logics for linguists', or 'logics for jurists' or 'logics for artificial intelligence'. The logical character of a system is one thing; its domain(s) of application is another thing.

The phrase 'philosophical logic' suggests also that there are not only properly *philosophical* parts of logic, but also that there are properly *logical* methods of philosophical analysis. In this sense the very notion of an informal *logic* is ambiguous and misleading. The distinction between a formal and an informal part of logic is reminiscent of the medieval distinction between a *logica docens* and a *logica utens*.[9] The former is the set of methods according to which one should reason correctly; the latter is the set of ways we in fact reason in ordinary life. The fact that one can apply the methods of the former to the latter does not mean that there are two kinds of logic at work, one formal, the other informal. On the other hand, when 'philosophical logic' is taken to be a part of formal logic, it is suggested that formalisation could, in some manner, be a substitute for philosophical analysis itself. But, to come back to the case of epistemic logic, it is difficult to see how such axioms or rules as (1) and (2) above can be more than a systemisation of some of our semantical intuitions about such notions as 'knowledge' and 'belief', and how they could replace a philosophical analysis of these notions. As a matter of fact, as the parenthetical remark about rule (3) above shows, standard epistemic logic has a very counter-intuitive consequence, namely that a believer should believe all the logical consequences of the propositions that he believes. But of course we are not such ideal or omniscient believers. This suggests that epistemic logic is not an analysis of our ordinary notion of belief, but an idealisation of it. In any case, the philosophical character of a logical theory is not, so to speak, written in its axioms and primitive vocabulary. These serve more as tools of clarification of different concepts than they define them or reveal their true nature.

I do not, therefore, believe that there is such a discipline as 'philosophical logic'. But there is no more a 'philosophy of logic', if it means a well specified and well delimited area of themes, concepts and methods. If, for lack of a better term, one still wants to use this label for a certain kind of enquiry, it should be kept in mind that the philosophy of logic is not a part of logic. It is not philosophy *about* logic either, if this means that it deals only with problems and concepts belonging to logic. It is philosophy *tout court*. Many questions in the philosophy of logic also belong to other areas, such as the philosophy of language, the philosophy of mathematics, or the philosophy of mind, and have links with ethics and ontology. As I shall try to illustrate in various ways in this book, many problems that arise in one or the other of these fields can be encountered in other, apparently foreign, areas. In this sense, as Grice said, there is a latitudinal unity of philosophy, which is, like virtue, entire.[10]

But to know what virtue is is one thing; to be virtuous is another thing. In the very oecumenical framework of a philosophical enquiry about logic that I have just indicated, one must choose, among the possible problems and approaches, some of them, at the price of excluding others that had an equal right to be included, or can be considered as central from another point of view. In the present case, it seemed to me more important to illustrate a certain kind of approach, rather than to elaborate an exhaustive panorama of the variety of problems that can fall under the heading of the philosophy of logic. The main guidelines of my approach are the following.

Although I believe that the philosophy of logic is not coextensive with the philosophy of language, I shall follow the lead of the majority of contemporary writers who tend to see the problems of the former in the light of the problems of the latter. Ideally an enquiry in the philosophy of logic can proceed through three different levels of analysis.

The first level is the level of a *semantical* analysis. Logicians build formal languages that have a syntax of formation rules for various expressions, and a semantics that interprets these expressions. A semantics is, in this sense, an analysis of the truth and reference conditions of the sentences of a formal language on the basis of analysis of their structure or of their 'logical form', or, in a somewhat technical sense of that term, a 'theory of meaning' for such a language (a formal theory specifying the truth conditions of all potential sentences of the language). The question arises whether we can apply the principles of such an analysis of truth conditions to a *natural* language. Although this project can, in a certain sense, be common to the philosopher and to the linguist, the philosopher is more concerned with the notion of a language in general than with a semantical analysis of natural languages. By trying to establish the semantic contribution of the various parts of the sentences of a natural language, such as quantifiers, names, descriptions, adjectives or adverbs, the philosopher aims to extract the main categories of a logical grammar, and to confront the formal criteria of the validity of inferences with our intuitive or informal understanding of this validity. He does not intend to replace a natural language by a formal one, but to understand both by comparing them. This first level overlaps much of the concerns of the 'philosophical logician'.

At a second level, the philosopher of logic analyses the theoretical concepts used at the first level: the concepts of meaning, truth, reference, structure, logical form or logical constant. He is led to compare the various 'theories of meaning' for a given language, and to set up the general criteria of adequacy of these theories. He is thus led to propose a theory of meaning in a more general, and philosophical, sense: a general theory of the constraints of a 'theory of meaning' (or semantics) in the more restricted sense based on an account of truth and meaning.

Finally, at a third level, questions can arise about the consequences of such a general theory of meaning for ontology, epistemology, and for the nature of logic itself, as a certain kind of language: what are logical truths? How do they get their meanings? Do they say anything about the world? How are they justified? Is logic a matter of truth at all? Is there a central concept on which a general theory of meaning is based, and how can we give an account of logic on the basis of this concept? Although there are many ways of formulating such questions, and many ways to put the emphasis on either one of them, they are the most general questions in the philosophy of logic.

Thus my conception of the philosophy of logic is much inspired by a conception of the philosophy of language made familiar by the writings of Davidson and Dummett, according to which the philosopher's task in this domain is to attempt to formulate 'theories of meaning' in both the narrower sense of a semantical account of language and the wider sense of an elucidation of the general form of such theories.[11] The problems of a philosophy of logic, as I see them, are continuous with those of a theory of meaning. A theory of meaning for logical expressions is a proper subset of a general theory of meaning for a language, and it can be presumed that both rest upon the same set of principles. Although the meaning and truth of logical sentences may not be accounted for in the same way as the meaning and truth of non-logical sentences (the question arises in fact whether they are the same), it would be surprising if one could not envisage these notions according to a common framework of notions. In this sense, an account of logical constants and of logical concepts serves as a kind of prototype for a more general account of meaning and concepts for language and thought in general, and both inform one another. In particular, one of the most interesting issues raised by the philosophy of language in the Davidson–Dummett style is the antagonism between the conceptions of meaning and truth of a *realist* and an *anti-realist*, namely the purported conflict between an analysis of meaning in terms of verification-transcendent truth conditions and an analysis of meaning in terms of conditions of assertibility. The realist/anti-realist debate in this sense has important consequences for the philosophy of logic, and in some sense rests upon a certain view of logic. A realist view of meaning and truth seems *prima facie* to involve a very different conception of the justification of logical principles and of the choice of logic than an anti-realist conception, and much of the current debate bears upon the respective commitments and consequences of both positions. Accordingly I have devoted a lot of space in this book to this debate as it arises in the philosophy of logic: the two central chapters (5 and 6) contain a presentation of the debate, and much of the remaining chapters of the book (in particular 11 and 12) develop it in various areas.

Although I believe that there is a deep continuity between the philosophy of logic and the philosophy of language in this sense, I do not think that the problems of a philosophy of logic are reducible to those of a philosophy of language. According to Dummett, the 'basic tenet' of analytical philosophy is that the philosophy of language and the philosophy of thought are more or less coextensive, because an analysis of language automatically yields an analysis of thought. Whether or not this assumption is correct – it has been contested by many philosophers – one of its consequences for the philosophy of logic has been that little attention has been paid to the relationships between logic and psychology, although much recent work in the psychology of reasoning is relevant to the problem of the nature of our thoughts involving logical concepts. Consequently, I have tried, in this book, to pay some attention to these issues in my treatment of the problems of the philosophy of logic (in particular in Chapter 13). The philosophy of language and the philosophy of thought (and of mind) seem to me to stand much more in a relationship of equilibrium rather than in a relationship of pre-eminence, and David Wiggins's advice seems to me to be wise, here as elsewhere:

> Where there is reciprocity or mutual presuppositions between concepts, analytical philosophy is often tempted into violence or arbitrariness. We find it hard to endure the thought that in the important substantive questions of philosophy there is rarely or never some unique and manifest starting place, or some single master thread to pull upon to unravel everything else.[12]

Two other criteria have guided the choice of the topics of this book. The first one has been my attempt to limit the amount of technicalities to a minimum. The philosophy of logic is a 'technical' subject in two respects. On the one hand it is technical because logic itself is technical, as soon as one leaves its elementary parts. It is also philosophically technical, because its problems are not, at least to the eyes of many of those who are foreign to this domain (including philosophers), immediately clear and transparent. Here Hintikka's recommendation quoted above, even if it is in general correct, encounters its limits: in an introductory work only a small amount of knowledge of logic can be presupposed from the reader. As a result, some of the problems that seem to me otherwise quite important for a philosophy of logic receive little or no attention here. It is in particular the case for those pertaining to the philosophy of mathematics, which could not be included in this book without changing much of its economy and style. It is also the case for many problems raised by non-classical logics, such as temporal logic, quantum logic or deontic logic, which would have required a separate treatment that is not given here. It is the case for the problems about existence, which, I believe, require a separate treatment too.

My second criterion has been to try to be myself. Although my first preoccupation has been mainly to deal with these matters in a neutral and expository way, I felt that it was very difficult to expose the themes of this book without taking sides on the issues and arguments of others, and without trying to give my own arguments. I have not done so on every occasion, but felt I was forced to in many cases. I am conscious, however, that my presentations and arguments do not always satisfy the criteria of prudence, of rigour and of care for details which is required by the usual style adopted by writers in this field. I have tried to privilege coherence over an attention to detail, in a domain where every detail counts. At every step of my progression into the various subjects, I felt that I had exposed myself to the firing of the machine-guns of experts. The reader will judge whether I emerge safely from this exercise.

I have said enough about what will not be found and about what one should perhaps have found in this book. Here is, in rough outline, what can be found in it.

The book is divided into four parts. The first three parts examine essentially the problems of the philosophy of logic that arise in the first and second levels of the hierarchy of questions presented above. In the first part, I follow the order imposed by the notions of elementary classical logic, that is the propositional and predicate calculi, which can be considered as the basis of modern logic. The first chapter deals with propositions, 'what they are and how they mean' (as Russell would have said). The second chapter deals with the propositional connectives of truth functional logic and in it are encountered two problems that will resurface later in the book: is the meaning of logical connectives conventional? Is it determined by psychological facts about speakers? The third chapter bears on the notions of subject and predicate, and compares their respective treatments in traditional logic and in modern logic. The fourth chapter analyses the notion of quantification, and confronts in particular two main interpretations of quantifiers: objectual and substitutional.

The second part bears on the notions of truth and meaning. The fifth chapter introduces various theories of truth in logic – in particular the Tarskian one – and confronts them with philosophical accounts of truth. Chapter 6 introduces Davidson's and Dummett's conceptions of meaning and the realist/anti-realist debate in the philosophy of logic.

The third part leaves the field of elementary logic and examines the limitations of the principles of extensionality and of bivalence of classical logic. Chapter 7 deals with modal logic and its philosophical implications. Chapter 8 is about the logical form of propositional attitude contexts. Chapter 9 bears on the notion of identity, and in particular on the question of the relationship between the formal properties of this notion and the conditions of individuation of things in the world. Chapter 10 is about the ubiquitous notion of vagueness.

The fourth and last part, the longest, deals mainly with the problems that arise at the third level characterised above, and contains an attempt to formulate a general conception of the nature of logic. Chapter 11 deals with the demarcation of logic, and offers various criteria for sorting out the class of expressions known as the 'logical constants', and examines in particular the conflict between a semantical conception of logic as a science of truths and a syntactical or proof-theoretic conception of logic as a science of inferences, a conflict that has important implications for the realist/anti-realist debate. Chapter 12 examines the notion of logical necessity, and here again are contrasted realist and anti-realist accounts of this notion. The last chapter, 13, contains an attempt to explain why logic is a normative discipline, principally through the conflict between psychologism, according to which logical truth and rules describe the laws of human psychology, and anti-psychologism, according to which logic is only prescriptive of what and how we ought to think.

Most of the questions examined here belong to the classical repertory of the philosophy of logic, although, as I said above, the book is far from being comprehensive and representative of the various kinds of approaches of the subject. I have tried, through the choice of topics and styles of presentation, to offer a somewhat different treatment from those that can be found in other books. I have tried to deal with the various problems in a relatively autonomous way, in order to allow a separate reading of each chapter. Nevertheless I hope that a general continuity can be perceived, and that various threads can be followed, in spite of the absence of a master thread. Such as, for instance, the problem of the nature of logical constants, the contrast between proof-theoretical and semantical accounts of logic, or the question of psychologism.

This book is not a manual of logic. I have introduced the logical notions and their formalism to the extent which seemed to me to be required for raising philosophical issues about them, trying to presuppose the minimum of logical instruction from the reader (that is not more than a small amount of knowledge of elementary logic). The reader is invited, in places where he or she would like to have more information and clarification, to consult the glossary–index at the end of the book for short definitions of technical notions, and the bibliographical indications at the beginning of the notes for each chapter.

— PART 1 —
Elementary structures

PROPOSITIONS

1.1 Four uses of the term 'proposition'

One of the most important problems of the philosophy of logic – if not of philosophy itself – is that of the nature of propositions. It is generally stated as an ontological problem: are there such *things* or *entities* as propositions and what is their nature? There is currently mistrust or hostility in respect of such entities; consequently the ontological question is often: do we need propositions and can we dispense with referring to such entities in favour of other entities which may be less 'compromising'? This way of posing the problem presumes that one has already identified what sort of entity propositions are: abstract entities, independent of language, which logicians and philosophers of a realist tendency are tempted to accept and which nominalist logicians and philosophers are tempted to reject. Put it this way, the ontological problem is obviously fundamental, and the answer it receives has a number of repercussions on the philosophy of logic. Nevertheless, before asking what sort of entities propositions are, and if they are entities, it seems preferable to set about finding out what they *do*, or what purpose they serve.

Traditionally, the notion of proposition has four distinct uses. (In everything that follows I will understand by 'proposition' any notion capable of serving any one of these uses, and not solely the proposition as an abstract entity; when I speak of it in that sense, I will follow Geach's use in 1968 and 'dignify' it by calling it a 'Proposition' with a capital 'P'.)

1. In the first place a proposition is *that which is capable of being true or false*, that is to say, of receiving a truth value. This use is obviously essential in logic, where the notion of truth is central. The notion of *deduction* or *inference* is no less central. It is said that a conclusion can be deduced or inferred from premises. The ordinary concept of deduction is a *semantic* concept, that is to say, that it calls on the semantic notions of truth, falsehood and validity: an argument or an inference is valid if, the premises being true, the conclusion is true, that is to say if the truth of the premises can be preserved in the conclusion. Let us call this use of the notion of proposition the *semantic use*.[1] In this sense, propositions are essentially 'truth-bearers', in the usual terminology. But propositions can equally receive a purely *syntactic* characterisation – parallel to the purely syntactic notion of deduction (cf. §2.2.2) – as entities capable of figuring as premises or as conclusions in inferences. It is doubtful whether propositions in logic can receive a *purely* syntactical characterisation. Suppose in fact that they are defined as entities, whatever they may be, which satisfy certain axioms of a system (for

example, axioms for the propositional calculus). In this case, it is presupposed that one knows what sort of entities the theorems and the axioms of the system represent, that is to say, the fact that the axioms and the theorems themselves are propositions.[2]

2. In the second place, a proposition is that which is capable of being the *linguistic meaning of a sentence*, that is to say, its literal or conventional meaning in the language. In this sense, propositions are fundamentally different from sentences. A sentence is a series of written or spoken signs, while a proposition is what a sentence expresses. Two distinct sentences can express the same proposition, if they are synonymous, such as 'an oculist amuses me' and 'an eye doctor entertains me', or when they are expressed in two distinct languages, such as 'Es regnet' and 'Piove'. The same sentence can express two distinct propositions if, for example, it contains an ambiguous term, such as 'He went to the bank'.

3. In the third place, a proposition is the *content of what is said* or conveyed by a certain act of language, such as an assertion, an order or a threat. This use must not be confused with the previous one: what a sentence says is not necessarily identical with its conventional linguistic meaning, because the same sentence, with a given linguistic meaning, can be uttered in such a way as to say different things in different contexts (if it is used metaphorically or ironically, for example). Let us call this use the *pragmatic* use. A distinction must also be made between what is said and the linguistic meaning when there are terms in a sentence which refer to different things in different contexts, such as personal or demonstrative pronouns (for example, 'I am fed up', said by me, can mean that Pascal Engel is fed up, and said by you, that the reader is fed up).

4. In the fourth place, a proposition is *the content of a certain psychological state* or of a 'propositional attitude' (cf. Chapter 8), such as a belief, a wish or a desire. Let us call this use the *psychological* use of the notion of proposition.

In the current meaning, we employ the notion of proposition in all these uses: the same term sometimes serves to designate something that is capable of a truth value, sometimes something that is capable of being the content of a sentence, an assertion or a propositional attitude, perhaps two or several of these things at the same time. These uses suggest the existence of one and the same entity which fulfils these four functions. But this is far from being obvious. It is not obvious, for example, that the contents of a speech act such as an order are capable of truth or falsehood: one obeys or one does not obey an order, but one does not say that an order is true or false. Likewise it is not obvious that the contents of a propositional attitude are true or false. Of course, they can be, if one maintains, for example, that this content is a certain 'intentional' content envisaged by a mental act. But if this content is (for example) made up of mental representations, and if these are states of mind, how can they be true or false? If we want to say that one and the same entity can serve more than one use, we need to say what the conditions of identity are. The ontological problem of propositions is precisely that of knowing if one and the same entity, and which, can play the four roles at the same time. In what follows I would like to show that it is extremely difficult to assign one and the same entity to these four roles, and that it is this difficulty which principally affects any unitary theory of propositions.

There are three major families of 'ontological' doctrines on the nature of propositions (families, because each doctrine can have different versions):

(A) Propositions are entities that are more or less similar to the sentences of a language, that is to say, like them, a series of symbols endowed with a certain syntactic structure.
(B) Propositions are abstract entities distinct from sentences: these are 'intension-al' entities that do not allow themselves to be reduced to a collection of signs, i.e. Propositions.
(C) Propositions are collections of objects or properties existing in the world ('facts', 'states of affairs' or 'situations').

Each of these doctrines has been invoked to account for the use of the notion of proposition as a truth-bearer. This use is the purely logical use, and it is difficult to see how an analysis of the nature of propositions in logic could disregard it. In each case, this involves a certain theory of truth because one of the principal questions of such a theory is this: what entities are capable of being true or false? Therefore the problems that will be dealt with in this chapter cannot be separated from those dealt with in Chapter 6 below. Apart from this, each of these doctrines aims to take account not only of use (1), but also of the others, or aims to show that some of them are illegitimate. For example, a supporter of propositions as sentences will be able to maintain that sentences take account of uses (1) and (4) (for example, he will say that propositions are entities made up of concrete symbols, and that the contents of our thoughts are written in a sort of mental language), but that it is not necessary to call on uses (2) and (3) (there are not 'meanings' or 'contents of what is said'). In fact, (A) is the doctrine whereby the notion of proposition intended in meaning (B) can be dispensed with. A supporter of the conception of propositions as intensional entities will be in a better position to put forward this notion as a candidate for the four uses simultaneously. Does this mean that this notion is adequate? A supporter of propositions as facts will have difficulties with use (4) (because how can the contents of thoughts be states of affairs?).

I will examine each of these theories of propositions in turn, without presenting all possible versions of them. But in this chapter, I will generally leave on one side any precise treatment of propositions in terms of contents of propositional attitudes, and I will not examine a fourth possible conception, whereby propositions might be reduced to mental or psychological states. This conception will be analysed in Chapter 8 below.

1.2 Propositions as intensional entities

1.2.1 A Fregean framework

A good part of modern orthodoxy in the philosophy of logic is derived from Frege's doctrines, or at least from doctrines attributed to Frege. I will follow the current usage which consists of calling 'Fregean' a certain conception of the nature of propositions, their relation to sentences, and their role in logic, without, however, entering into exegetic questions about what-Frege-really-said. Some of the implications of this conception will be examined further on in Chapter 8.[3]

Frege distinguishes the *sentence* (Satz) from the *thought* (Gedanke) that it expresses.[4] The second is the *sense* (Sinn) of the sentence. Apart from a meaning, sentences (like any expression) have a *reference* (Bedeutung), which is their truth value, that is to say, the true or the false (there is no need to elaborate here on Frege's doctrine whereby these latter are objects). According to Frege, it is not the sentence, but the thought that it expresses which is capable of receiving a truth value. Consequently, it is thoughts that are the subject-matter of logic.[5] Fregean thoughts are therefore a natural candidate for the notion of 'Proposition'. The question then is to know if their characteristics allow them to fulfil the different roles of the pre-theoretic notion of proposition.

1. As has been seen, thoughts are truth-bearers. If thought A is true, and if thought B is false, they are not identical thoughts.

2. Thoughts are the meanings of sentences. As such, they are certain entities.[6] The essential function of these entities is to ensure the cognitive meaning of sentences. This does not include the conventional meaning in natural language or the 'colouring' or the nuances of meaning that sentences can have in rhetorical, poetic or conversational uses. Consequently, when Frege identifies a proposition with the meaning of a sentence, he is only identifying it with its cognitive meaning, or, as he says, with the objective 'cognitive value' that the thought expresses (cf. § 8.1).

3. It is doubtful whether Frege concedes a pragmatic use (3) to thoughts because he is primarily interested in the expression of them in an ideal language or *Begriffsschrift*, independent of the contexts of utterance. Frege constructs the expression, by a sentence, of a Proposition, as independent of a context of utterance. The pragmatic use of the notion of proposition, on the contrary, requires the relativisation of this expression to the context of utterance. Natural languages, as Frege acknowledges, contain a number of expressions, such as indexicals, which force us to evaluate the truth value of the sentences that contain them in relation to a context.[7] The truth conditions of the sentences of an ideal language of logic are determined by assigning absolute meaning and reference to the expressions that compose them.

4. Lastly, are Fregean thoughts the contents of psychological acts like propositional attitudes? No, if that means that thoughts might be psychological representations. Frege is quite insistent on the non-psychological character of thought, which for him is the touchstone of a non-psychologistic conception of the logical laws (§ 13.2). The logical laws are thoughts that are true, independent of the knowledge and the representations that we have of them. These are the 'laws of being true'.[8] Nevertheless, a thought must be able to be 'grasped'. It must be able to come into contact with the mind of the person who thinks it. But Frege does not say how.[9]

Fregean thoughts again have two characteristics:

5. The existence of a thought is never dependent on the existence of the object that it concerns. This characteristic will not concern us here, but it will be discussed later (Chapter 8).

6. Thoughts, in so far as they are the meaning of sentences, are endowed with a certain structure. This structure is not identified with that of the sentence, but the various parts of the thoughts that it expresses must correspond to the various parts of the sentence. A thought is composed of the meanings of the expressions which compose the sentence that expresses it.[10]

The Fregean conception of propositions as thoughts is in close harmony with his philosophy of logic. Logic concerns a universe of thoughts, which are immutably true or false independently of our means of recognising them as such. A true thought, a logical law can never change from true to false. This universe has a reality that is distinct from but comparable with that of the physical universe. Logic must represent the nature of thoughts in an artificial language purified of the imperfections of natural languages, that is to say a language that adequately represents the logical structure of thoughts. The universe described by logic is not a different universe from the real universe: it is *the* Universe (logic is a language and not a calculus; it is universal, according to Van Heijenoort's phrase).

Are the propositions of logic Fregean thoughts? Most authors who have acknowledged the Fregean framework have not acknowledged all the doctrines that Frege associated with his conception of thoughts, such as what is called his extreme realism, or his identification of the reference of sentences with their truth values. Nevertheless, they do agree that the notion of thought, or a similar notion, is the best candidate, making it possible to account for uses (1) and (2) of the notion of proposition, once one agrees, with Frege, that logic is limited to these two uses.

The principal difficulty with the Fregean conception of thoughts or Propositions is that their identity conditions are imprecise. The few criteria Frege gives do not make it possible to say exactly when two sentences express the same thought, or when two thoughts are identical. He gives intuitive criteria such as the following: sentence S expresses a different thought from the one expressed by sentence S' if it is possible for someone to assert S without asserting S', or to have a different cognitive attitude *vis-à-vis* S than he has *vis-à-vis* S'. To go back to one of his favourite examples (a variation on the famous example which appears at the beginning of *Über Sinn und Bedeutung*, cf. § 8.1): someone who judges true the thought that a mountain, Ateb, is 5000 m high, is able not to judge true the proposition that a mountain, Alpha, is 5000 m high: even if 'Alpha' and 'Ateb' have the same reference, these names do not have the same meaning, and therefore not the same cognitive value. Consequently, the two propositions are different.[11] If it conforms to one of the notions that Frege employs to elucidate the notions of meaning (a meaning is a certain 'mode of presentation'), this criterion cannot totally determine the identity of the two thoughts: if a 'mode of presentation' is a certain way of thinking of an object, when is it possible to say that two individuals think of an object in the same way? If such a psychological formulation of a criterion is permitted, how can it be determined when two individuals grasp or understand the same thought? And can such a psychological criterion correspond to what Frege really intended by 'sense' (I will come back to this point in Chapter 8)? Elsewhere, Frege gives a criterion of identity of thoughts whereby two thoughts A and B are identical if and only if the biconditional '$A \equiv B$' can be established 'by purely logical laws'. But if this criterion were correct, it would follow that materially equivalent propositions, that is to say those that have the same truth value, would have the same sense, or express the same Proposition. For example, under the terms of Frege's logicism, the propositions '$2+2=4$' and '$2+1+1=4$', which are entirely expressible by means of logical concepts, and which can, solely by logical laws, be shown to be equivalent by showing the truth of the biconditional:

$$(2+2=4) \equiv (2+1+1=4)$$

would thus have the same sense. But Frege tells us again, apropos this type of example, that if the two sentences have the same reference (the same truth value), they do not have the same sense, and therefore do not express the same Proposition. Consequently, according to this criterion, one can no better give the individuation conditions of the sense that one can give those of the reference: all true sentences have the Truth as reference, and all false sentences have the False as reference (I will come back to this argument later, in § 1.3.2).[12]

Aware of these difficulties in the Fregean conception, supporters of theories that follow the same guidelines have sought to amend it by suggesting finer criteria of individuation of propositions.

1.2.2 Propositions as collections of possible worlds

Theories inspired by Frege redefine the notions of sense and reference by way of the traditional notions of intension and extension. A Proposition is the intension of a sentence; its truth value is its extension. But the difference between this distinction and the traditional distinction is that the intensions are conceived as functions (in the mathematical sense) determining the extensions. The basic ideas of the contemporary intensionalist conception were suggested by Carnap (1956), and by Church (1951). Using the notions of *intensional equivalence* and *intensional isomorphism*, Carnap formulated a precise criterion for the identity of propositions. However, the conception of propositions as intensional entities that I am going to set out here is not Carnap's, but a conception directly descended from it: that of propositions as *collections of possible worlds*.[13]

Analysis of propositions in terms of 'possible worlds' derives from the semantic treatment of modal logic, which defines necessity and possibility in terms of structures of possible worlds. I will deal with the application of these notions to the semantics of modalities later (Chapter 7). Only the general framework of the analysis concerns us here. One assumes the existence of a structure of possible worlds, that is to say situations in which the world might have been. This makes it possible to distinguish the intensions and the extensions of expressions. The extension of an expression is given in relation to a possible world: that is what this expression denotes in this possible world. The intension of an expression is the rule that determines the extension of the expression. Thus, if one assumes that the extension of a singular term (a proper name or description) is an individual, the extension (or reference or denotation) of a singular term is a function of the possible worlds to the individuals (that is to say an individual concept). The extension of a one-place predicate is a class of individuals, and its intension (the property it expresses) is a function of the possible worlds to classes of individuals. The extension of a sentence is its truth value. Its intension is the Proposition that this sentence expresses, that is to say a function of possible worlds to a truth value. The term 'function' here must be understood in the mathematical sense, that is as a rule which determines a certain value of the function in relation to the members of a certain family of arguments. According to this conception, a Proposition is therefore a *function* which takes as arguments a certain number of possible worlds, and which takes for values truth values. For example, the sentence

(1) John has passed GCSE

will receive as extension the value 'true' (will be true) in all possible worlds, or situations, in which John has passed GCSE. Its intension will be the rule that determines the assignation of these extensions, that is to say the Proposition expressed by the sentence in question. A Proposition is therefore a *collection of possible worlds*, the collection of possible worlds in which the Proposition takes the value 'true' as extension, in this case, the collection of possible worlds in which John has passed GCSE. According to this conception, the meaning of a sentence is therefore determined by its truth conditions relative to the possible worlds: to know the meaning of a sentence is to know in which situations that sentence is true, and in which situations that sentence is false, or again to know the rule that determines its truth value.[14]

The most distinctive feature of this conception is that it calls on a problematic notion, that of the 'possible world'. But what is a possible world? Is it, as supporters of this theory maintain, a convenient construction, postulated for heuristic purposes? Or is it, as its opponents suspect, a dubious abstract entity? If a possible world is a problematic entity, a *collection* of such entities seems even more so. However, it is neither this objection nor the ontological scruples that the notion of 'possible world' can arouse, that will delay us here (I will come back to the nature of possible worlds in Chapter 7). The objection that I will consider here does not concern the ontological reality of propositions or of intensions as entities, but their individuation conditions.

1.2.3 The individuation of intensional entities

Does the analysis of propositions as intensions make it possible to account for use (2) of the notion of proposition as the meaning of the sentences in a natural language? It is doubtful. As has been seen, according to this conception, the meaning of the sentences of a language is determined by their truth conditions in relation to a collection of possible worlds. But in a natural language these truth conditions are not only related to collections of possible worlds, but also to contextual factors with are so many coordinates making it possible to determine their truth values: the place, the time, the identity of the speaker, that of the hearer, and so on. These are pragmatic factors, but it is impossible to evaluate the truth value of a given sentence without them. These factors are indicated, notably, by indexical expressions, such as 'here', 'this', 'now', etc. For example, a sentence such as

(2) 'I am ill'

is true and expresses the same Proposition or intension: that the person uttering the sentence is ill. It is true in all the possible worlds in which the speaker is ill, and if two speakers voiced the same sentence and were ill they would be expressing the same Proposition. Nevertheless, it is insufficient for determining the truth conditions of the sentence, because these would depend on the identity of the speaker: the sentence is true for John, if it is John who is ill, but false if (for example) it is Paul who says it. Consequently, (2) does not only have its truth conditions as a function of the Proposition that it expresses, but as a function of contextual determinants. It follows that the intension only represents one part of the linguistic meaning of the sentences, in this case the part that is relevant to the determination of the truth conditions independently of contextual parameters. Supporters of analysis in terms of possible worlds therefore add to possible worlds other parameters, or *indices*, in relation to which the truth conditions are assigned to sentences. In most cases, this complicates the simplified image outlined above.[16]

To this one can reply that this difficulty only affects theories of propositions as intensions applied to natural languages. In a formal language, on the other hand, indexical expressions and, consequently, the parameters necessary to evaluate truth conditions, are absent. This is even one of the main characteristics of formal systems. In them, the semantic determinants of expression are, in some way, 'pure' and only involve reference to universes of entities fixed in advance. In them, in accordance with Frege's wish for a *Begriffsschrift*, the determination of truth conditions is actually in conformity solely with the logical form of expressions. Thus in them the truth conditions of a sentence of predicate calculus, for example

$$(\forall x)(\forall y)(Px \rightarrow Py)$$

are solely relative to the types of entities that are assigned to the individual variables 'x' and 'y' (individuals), to the predicate letters 'P' (properties) and to the meaning of the logical constants such as the universal quantifier '$\forall x$' and the sign for the conditional '$\rightarrow$'.[17] But this answer presupposes the reply that can be given to the question of knowing to what extent logical distinctions are independent of those of natural language. It also assumes that one has excluded the possibility that the entities that correspond to the symbolic expressions of a formal language (like the propositional letters 'p', 'q', 'r') might be sentences or 'propositions' of a natural language, or quite simply entities analogous to sentences, that is to say series of symbols endowed with syntactical structure. How, if this were the case, could one say that the expressions of a formal language, like the predicate calculus, can *represent* the 'logical form' of the sentences of a natural language?

But even if one decided not to take account of this objection, it would not be legitimate to assimilate the meanings of the sentences of a formal language to the intensions of its sentences. Depending on the analysis in question, two sentences have the same intension, or would express the same proposition if they are true in the *same* possible worlds. But in this case, two logically equivalent sentences, as, for example

(3) $(p \vee q)$

and

(4) $-(-p \mathbin{\&} -q)$

which are true in the same possible worlds (that is to say which are necessary, or true in all possible worlds), have the same meaning. In other words, all tautologies would have the same meaning. Wittgenstein had no hesitation in drawing this conclusion in the *Tractatus* when he maintained that all the tautologies of logic are identical in meaning, that is to say, they say the same thing.[18] But for all that, two sentences that are logically equivalent are not identical in meaning. There is, intuitively, a difference in meaning between the two sentences (3) and (4): to use the Fregean criterion referred to in the previous paragraph, someone who would acknowledge the truth of the first would not necessarily be able to acknowledge the truth of the second, and someone who believed that *the cat is on the mat or the dog in the kitchen* would not necessarily believe that *it is false that the cat is not on the mat and that the dog is not in the kitchen*. In what does this difference lie? It obviously lies in the fact that the *logical structure* of (3) and (4) are not identical. Note in passing that this difficulty affects also the application of the analysis of propositions as collections of possible worlds to the contents of propositional attitudes: if *S* believes *p*, and if *p* is logically equivalent to *q*, it does not follow that *S* believes *q* (cf. § 8.1). Here one finds the difficulty that Frege met, i.e. that the identity criteria of intensions are not more discriminant than the identity criteria of extensions. The correct response is therefore that although all tautologies really do have the same intension (the constant function that has the value *true* in every possible world), they do not have the same meaning. It must therefore be agreed that even in formal languages there are differences of meaning that are not accompanied by differences of intensions. The intension therefore can only serve as partial *analysans* of propositions as meanings of sentences.

This problem is closely connected to a second characteristic of this conception: propositions as collections of possible worlds are *non-structured* entities.[19] These are entities independent of language and the syntactic and semantic structure of the sentences. That is why the differences in logical form between (3) and (4) do not affect the identity of the intensions. Here there is an important difference between the theory put forward above and those that Frege and Carnap maintained. For them, the structure of the meaning and the structure of the intensions follow more or less in a parallel direction to the structure of the sentences and of their syntactical and semantical form. Carnap, for example, agrees that two sentences endowed with the same intension (here too, all true in the same possible worlds) such as

(5) A brother is a male child born of the same parents

and

(6) A brother is a brother

can nevertheless not have the same 'intensional structure'.[20] As Carnap says: 'The difference of meanings is here compatible with the identity of meaning in another sense'. There therefore really is a difference between the meaning as intension (which does not require consideration of the structure) and the meaning as intensional structure (which by definition requires it). But what then does determine the intensional structure? It can only be the logical form or the semantic structure itself of the sentences, which is not the same in the case of (3)–(4) and (5)–(6). If one accepts this, it is difficult to distinguish, on the one hand, the identity of intension from the identity of extension (that is to say from material logical equivalence), and on the other hand, the identity of intensional structure from the identity of logical or syntactico-semantic structure of the sentences. Propositions therefore seem hard to identify with the distinct intensional entities distinct from *sentences*, that is to say with series of syntactically and semantically structured symbols. This only makes the notion that propositions are entities independent of language all the more dubious.[21]

1.3 Propositions as facts

1.3.1 Propositions as collections of objects

The second great ontological conception of propositions is that of propositions as collections of objects or things existing in the world. In this sense, propositions are states of affairs that make sentences true, or exist if the sentences are true. While the intensional conception pulled propositions towards the Fregean dimension of sense, this pulls them towards the Fregean dimension of reference. Propositions are identified in a certain way with what sentences designate. But what sentences designate are not, as with Frege, truth values. They are *facts*, that is to say arrangements, collections of things in the world. In this sense, as in the previous conception, propositions are entities or collections of entities. But these are not abstract or intensional entities. These are very real entities which form part of the ultimate furniture of the universe.

The basic ideas are simple. They had their hour of glory in the twentieth century at the time of Wittgenstein or Russell's logical atomism, but they do not seem to have lost their attraction in contemporary philosophical literature. A recent expression of this theory (which moreover takes up the theses Russell developed in 1903) has been given notably apropos the representation of Propositions expressed by singular sentences, such as

(7) 'Socrates is snub-nosed'.

Several authors have suggested that sentence (7) can be represented as an *ordered pair*[22] composed of one individual, Socrates, and a property, being-snub-nosed:

(8) ⟨Socrates, being snub-nosed⟩.

In this case, it is neither the *name* nor the individual *concept* of Socrates that forms part of the ordered pair, but the real individual Socrates, and the real worldly property of being-snub-nosed. The Proposition expressed by sentence (7) is the ordered couple composed of the subject and the property (if one were dealing with a binary relation, this would be an ordered triple; with a ternary relation, an ordered quadruple, and so on). The ordered pair (8) represents the fact, or the complex corresponding to sentence (7). This is true if there is such a pair. Two sentences that can be represented by the same complex express the same Proposition. For example, if someone says to Socrates: 'You are snub-nosed', and if Socrates says to himself: 'I am snub-nosed', the Proposition expressed would be the same in each case, since it corresponds to the same individual and the same property, that is to say the same *fact*.[23] I am not going to get any further involved here in stating these doctrines (cf. Chapter 8), and will only discuss some of the basic difficulties they raise.

Like the one before, this analysis is capable of arousing suspicions as far as the nature of the entities thus designated is concerned. What is a fact? Do these sorts of things exist? There are a few well-known difficulties. If one says that a fact is something that makes a true sentence true, how can one say that a fact makes a false sentence false? Are there negative facts or objective falsehoods? How is error possible if judgement is a relation between a subject who knows and a fact? The theory of propositions as facts is a form of the theory of truth as *correspondence*. But what form of correspondence is required? Logical atomism required a form of isomorphism, or identity of structure, between the sentences and the corresponding facts. But up to what point? Most of the difficulties of the theory of propositions as facts are the same as those of the theory of truth as correspondence. I will discuss this in Chapter 5. Here, I will only raise one difficulty of this analysis, very close to those referred to above apropos the intensionalist conception of proposition: no more than propositions as intensions, propositions as facts do not have well-defined individuation conditions.

1.3.2 Frege's slingshot

The argument I will use is borrowed from Davidson and is one version of a famous argument of Frege's, taken up by Church, Gödel and Quine,[24] and known as the 'slingshot argument'.

In *Über Sinn und Bedeutung*, Frege notes that 'if the truth value of a proposition is its reference, all true propositions have the same reference and all false ones likewise'.[25] From this, he draws the conclusion that reference by itself is not sufficient to account for the 'singularity', that is to say the individuation conditions of sentences, in so far as they have a meaning. Church uses this statement by Frege to show that all true sentences in fact have the same reference or extension, and that consequently there is nothing against considering truth values as references of sentences. He invites us to consider the following sentences:

(9) Sir Walter Scott is the author of *Waverley*.

(10) Sir Walter Scott is the man who wrote all the twenty-nine *Waverley* novels.

(11) The number, just as Sir Walter Scott is the man who wrote this number of *Waverley* novels in all, is twenty-nine.

(12) The number of counties in Utah is twenty-nine.

(9) and (10) have the same references, (11) and (12) too, and (10) and (11) have the same reference by virtue of the principle of substituvity of expressions *salva veritate*: two expressions that have the same reference can be substituted for each other without changing the truth value of the sentences in which they appear (cf.

§ 6.2.2). (10) is derived from (9) by the substitution of the singular co-referential terms 'the author of *Waverley*' and 'the man who wrote all the twenty-nine *Waverley* novels'. (12) is derived from (11) by the same principle. The transition from (10) to (11) is more problematical. Church agrees that these two sentences are not synonymous, but that they actually have the same reference, which according to him is sufficient for the argument. The result is that one does not see what is the relationship between (9) and (12): although these sentences have the same denotation, they do not have the same meaning. This can be considered as a *reductio ad absurdum* of the thesis whereby all sentences with the same denotation have the same meaning, or are synonymous. Consequently, Church concludes, meaning and reference must be distinguished and reference and truth values identified in the case of sentences, which is in accordance with the Fregean approach.[26]

How can this argument now be applied to the theory of propositions as facts? If this theory is of any interest whatsoever, it must make it possible to give a meaning to sentences such as:

(13) *p* corresponds to the fact that *q*

(where '*p*' is equivalent to 'it is true that *p*', or to the assertion of that sentence). In other words, a sentence '*p*' is true if there is a fact to which this sentence corresponds. The fact in question is then the *Proposition* expressed by the sentence *q*. (13) is correct when '*p*' and '*q*' are the same sentence, for example the one that gives the following trivial instance of (13):

(14) 'It is true that it is a nice day corresponds to the fact that it is a nice day' (or again 'the fact that it is a nice day corresponds to the fact that it is a nice day').

But the difficulties begin as soon as one tries to substitute a different sentence, even though it expresses an identical fact, for '*q*'. Consider the following list:

(15) The fact that Paris is north of Grenoble.
(16) The fact that Grenoble is south of Paris.
(17) The fact that Grenoble is south of the capital of France.
(18) The fact that Grenoble is south of the city which is the capital of France and such that Clermont-Ferrand is in Auvergne.

Expressions (15)–(18) have the same reference by substitution, as in (9)–(12), co-referential singular terms. But, as before, the relationship between (15) and (18) cannot be seen. In other words, in the same way as all true sentences have the same reference, all the facts seem to designate the same one fact, the Great Fact, or again, if a sentence corresponds to the facts, it corresponds to all the facts, and if propositions are facts, all true sentences express the same Proposition.[27] It follows that the identification of propositions with facts does not provide us with better individuation conditions than their identification with intensions.

1.3.3 *Situations*

The slingshot argument, in one or other of its versions, has often been criticised. It rests on debatable hypotheses, notably concerning the semantics of singular terms (cf. §7.4). One of these criticisms, due to Barwise and Perry,[28] is particularly interesting for our thesis, because it is pursued in the name of a variant of the theory of propositions as facts, which also aims to remedy the defects in the intensional conception approached in §1.2. Barwise and Perry take their stand on our intuitive reaction to the slingshot argument: sentences (9)–(12) and (15)–(18) can actually have the same reference, but not be talking about the same thing. One can if necessary agree that (9) and (10), (11) and (12), (15) and (16), and (17) and (18) respectively designate the same *type* of facts, but it is out of the question to say the same of (9) and of (12), or of (15) and of (18). Instead of facts, Barwise and Perry talk about *situations*. These are collections of individuals, properties and relations like the former. But while the former conception only permitted a single type of fact, Barwise and Perry suggest distinguishing a variety of categories of situations. Situations pure and simple are complexes of real things or events: Garibaldi marching to Rome, Puccini composing *La Boheme*, myself walking in the Appenines in 1987. They must be distinguished from *types of situations*, which are abstract complexes of real situations. For example, the sentence

(19) Diana kisses Charles

designates a type of situation in which a person named 'Diana' embraces a person named 'Charles'. Many situations fall into this type, including one of those in which Princess Diana kisses Prince Charles of England. Types of situations are not possible worlds, but sub-collections of the collection of situations that compose the actual world. In the vocabulary of model theory (§ 4.2.1), these are 'partial sub-models',[29] that is to say, fragments of the world. A sentence is true if it is supported by a certain collection of types of situation, and a Proposition is a collection of types of situations. These, and not the truth values, are the references of sentences. This allows Barwise and Perry to block the inferences which go from (10) to (11) and from (17) to (18) in the slingshot argument, because, according to them, these sentences do not designate the same type of situations. It is therefore false to say, as do Frege and Church, that logically equivalent sentences have the same reference, or the same semantic value. As Barwise and Perry note, this principle, agreed by everyone who uses the slingshot argument, presupposes rejection of the very idea that sentences might designate situations.[30]

The difficulty is real, and is the same difficulty we found in Frege and the intensionalist conception of propositions: how to ensure that differences in meaning in these theories are more discriminant than differences in reference? Do Barwise and Perry avoid this difficulty by their recourse to a 'semantics of situations'? Without going into the details of a complex theory, it can be suggested that they do not. Contrary to the conception of the proposition as ordered *n*-uple of objects outlined above (§ 1.3.1), Barwise and Perry maintain that types of

situations have an internal structure: situations are objects that contract relationships between themselves: 'the sleigh *in* the snow', 'the paper *on* the desk'.
Although, like supporters of the intensionalist theory, they insist on identifying
situations with non-linguistic objects, the way in which they describe them
remains very dependent on the linguistic structure of the sentences of the
language. What, for example, distinguishes two sentences having the same truth
value such as '$7 + 5 = 12$' and '$15 - 3 = 12$'? They designate different types of
situations, but why? Because the expressions that compose them are distinct, and
differently arranged. The same would apply to situations described by sentences
such as 'My cat is on the mat' and 'Tibbles is on the mat', in the case when Tibbles
was my cat. In other words, are situations not constructions projected from the
linguistic structure of sentences?[31] In this case, is there not a more important
relationship between the meaning of sentences and their structure than this type
of theory allows?

1.4 Sentences and propositions

1.4.1 Sentences and statements

If the assimilation of propositions to intensional entities or facts is rejected, what
else can we do but assimilate them to the sentences of a language? But this
solution comes up against well-known difficulties. A sentence, that is to say a
collection of written or spoken signs, is a particular conjunction of symbols, that is
to say a physical entity. How can a physical object be true or false? What is true or
false must really be something like the meaning of a sentence, or what the
sentence says, and not the physical medium that articulates it. It is therefore
appropriate here to resort to a distinction between *type* of sentence and *token* of a
sentence. For example, the two inscriptions

> There is no happy love
> There is no happy love

are *tokens* of the same *type* of sentence, that is to say of particular concrete
occurrences of the same class of expressions.[32] If these are types of sentences that
are truth-bearers, here too we must give them precise criteria of identity: when are
two tokens of sentences tokens of the same type? In some cases, the identity of the
inscription is enough, in others something like an identity of meaning is required
(for example, the above two tokens can sometimes be voiced with a serious
intonation, sometimes with an ironic intonation). But assume that this problem
can be solved. A number of philosophers (and Strawson, in particular)[33] have
maintained that it was absurd to treat sentences as truth-bearers, because a
sentence (type or token) can be true in one situation, false in another. For
example, the above sentence can be false when I see Romeo kiss Juliet, true when I
see the end of the story. These philosophers emphasise the fact that it is use (3) of

propositions, such as what a sentence *says* in a given context, the way in which it is used in order to say something, which makes it possible to account for other uses, and in particular their use as truth-bearers. They then choose to call what is customarily designated as a proposition a *statement*. But this assimilation comes up against at least three objections.

First, it cannot be seen why the fact that a sentence can change its truth value should prevent a sentence from being a truth-bearer. An object can actually change its properties without ceasing to be the same object: a door can be painted red one year, blue the next, without ceasing to be the same door.[34]

Secondly, if, for example, one insists on saying that the following three sentences enable the same statement to be made

> I am hot (said by me)
> J'ai chaud (said by me)
> He is hot (said by you about me)

one does not really see what difference there is between this use of the term 'statement', and the use of the term proposition, to designate the contents of what is said.

The third objection, put forward by Geach,[35] is based on what he calls 'the Frege point'. A statement is both the content of an assertion and the act of asserting itself; but, as Frege emphasises, it is not the same thing simply to 'consider' a thought or a propositional content and to state that content: a thought can sometimes be stated, sometimes not stated. As Geach notes, if this distinction is not made, the meaning of useful arguments is missed, the *modus ponens*, for example

> If p, then q
> But p,
> Therefore q

in which the propositional letters 'p' and 'q' appear twice respectively, but with a different role: first, not stated, then stated. The first occurrence of 'q' must actually be able to be true or false, but it is not stated, or utilised to make a statement. The Fregean solution, which consists of prefixing assertions with the Fregean assertion sign '$\vdash$', is much preferable

> $\vdash$ If p, then q
> $\vdash p$
> Therefore $\vdash q$

I will leave on one side here the problem posed by the fact that Strawson not only accepts that statements are truth-bearers but also that certain statements cannot be either true or false.

In any case, statements do not appear in a better position to fulfil the various uses of the notion of proposition than sentences or 'propositions' as entities distinct from sentences.

1.4.2 Quinean doubts

Quine is the contemporary philosopher who has most constantly and most systematically criticised the use of the notion of 'Proposition' in the philosophy of logic and in the philosophy of language in order to designate abstract entities independent of sentences. It is he who has brought the strongest nominalist doubts to bear against the ontological inflation that the use of intensional entities seemed to him to introduce. As I suggested above, the ontological problem of propositions is not of the choice between the types of entities that one would like to introduce 'into our ontology', by virtue of (justified) nominalist or realist preferences. Despite certain manners of introducing the question, Quine's main objection is not based on such nominalist preferences, or on a principle of ontological economy. It is based on one of his fundamental ontological maxims: 'No entity without identity'.[37] In other words: do not admit into your ontology entities whose individuation conditions you are unable to ensure. From this point of view, the difficulties that have been referred to here apropos the various conceptions of propositions fully justify Quine's doubts: whether propositions as Fregean thoughts, as intensions, as facts or as statements were involved, the problem of knowing how two Propositions could be identical was found every time in each of these theories. From this point of view, Propositions really are, as Quine maintains, 'creatures of darkness'. This is another way of saying that it is difficult to support one single notion of proposition, satisfying all the more or less pre-theoretic uses of the notion.

But Quine's arguments go further: they throw doubt on the notion of Proposition by challenging the use of the very notion of meaning. The spearhead of these arguments is the famous 'indeterminacy of translation' thesis, intended to show that the notion of meaning is *necessarily* indeterminate, and that consequently the hope of constructing a coherent notion of proposition based on the notion of meaning is vain.

1.4.3 The indeterminacy of translation

The argument of the indeterminacy of translation has many forms and versions and has engendered abundant literature; the presentation which follows is necessarily oversimplified.[38] In its general form, the thesis of the indeterminacy of translation is the thesis whereby:

> Given a translation manual M for a language L in accordance with the behavioural data about speakers of L, it is always possible to construct another translation manual M', in accordance with the same behavioural data but incompatible with M.

In other words, there is no single scheme of translation for a given sentence of L in relation to given observable (behavioural) empirical data. Quine offers two main arguments in favour of this thesis.

Best known is the one called 'the argument from below'.[39] This concerns the position of 'radical translation', where it is assumed that a translator, confronted with sentences by natives and observable behaviour, tries to establish a translation manual for their language. Faced with an isolated sentence by a native – 'gavagai' when a rabbit is present – different 'analytical hypotheses' suggest themselves to him, in a case where he would have good reason to think that 'gavagai' translates as 'rabbit': the observable data do not make it possible to choose between hypotheses whereby 'gavagai' means 'rabbitness here' or 'temporal parts of rabbit co-present' or 'there is a rabbit', and so on, which differ fundamentally in the way in which the reference to the objects can be carved out. This example has given rise to a great deal of discussion, but Quine confesses that he did not intend to prove anything by it. The second and more important argument is 'the argument from above'.

This proceeds from two premises. The first is the principle of empiricism, in a form that Quine states is borrowed from Peirce:

> The meaning of a sentence consists of the difference that its truth would make to possible experience.

The second is the principle that Quine says he has borrowed from Duhem, whereby the empirical meaning of a sentence is never determinable in isolation, but only in relation to a collection of sentences, a theory, even science in its entirety. According to this 'holistic' thesis, there is no reason to think that something would exist such as *the* difference that the truth of a sentence would make in relation to possible experience. Only our theory of nature in its entirety is confronted with experience. It follows that there is no such thing as *the* meaning of an isolated sentence.

Taken together, the two premises lead to the indeterminacy of translation: Peirce + Duhem = indeterminacy (according to an illuminating formula by Føllesdal, 1975). As there is no possible way, because of the epistemological holism acknowledged by Quine, of saying how such and such a sentence expresses such and such a belief, and therefore has such and such a meaning, it can be concluded that its meaning is indeterminate. It follows that the notion of Proposition, understood in the sense of the meaning of a sentence, or of the identity of the meanings of two sentences, does not rest on any objective basis. Meaning, translation, synonymity and Propositions are notions that cannot be defined individually without recourse to others, and which are indeterminate.[40]

I will not examine the validity of these arguments (cf., however, Chapters 11 and 12 below, on Quine's holism). Here, I will deal solely with two questions: (1) What substitutes does Quine suggest to replace propositions? (2) Is a generalised scepticism in respect of the notion of 'proposition' as meaning of sentences valid?

1.4.4 Sentences and schematic letters

What are truth-bearers for Quine? There are two steps to his solution. The first consists of refusing to assimilate 'propositional letters' and the symbols of elementary logic to any entities whatsoever, and to guarantee them a status of ontological neutrality. This is his conception of *schematic letters*. The '*p*' and '*q*', etc. of the propositional calculus are not sentences but *schemas, diagrams or dummies* so that all the sentences that can be substituted for them are true.[41] One consequence of this conception is that it is not possible to *quantify* on the propositional letters, by writing expressions like, for example

$$(\forall p)\ (p \text{ is true})$$

This conception is closely linked to the Quinean theory of the objects of quantification, which must receive precise individuation conditions (cf. Chapter 4), as well as to his criterion of ontological commitment. In particular, the fact that it is not possible to quantify on the schematic letters, while this can be done on individual variables, provides a criterion of distinction between propositional calculus and predicate calculus. Lastly, this conception connects up with the Quinean theory of logical truth as *truth under all substitutions* (cf. Chapter 10).

The second stage consists of acknowledging that it is actually sentences which are the truth-bearers, since these are the entities that are substituted for the schematic letters of logic. But the adoption of sentences is not justified by the search for entities capable of being truth-bearers but by the nature of our preferred theory of truth. According to Quine (and this is also the answer I will adopt in Chapter 5 below), the best possible theory of truth is Tarski's theory. If it is not admitted that sentences are truth-bearers, then biconditionals of the form

'snow is white' is true if and only if snow is white

cease to have any meaning.[42]

How then to avoid the objections raised above (§ 1.4.1) in respect of the assimilation of sentences as truth- and falsity-bearers? To account for the fact that the same sentence can change its truth value, Quine has recourse to a distinction between *occasional sentences*, which are true in relation to a certain occasion and to given stimuli, and *eternal* or standing sentences, which are true for all time and all place.[43] For example, 'it is raining' is an occasional sentence, and it can be assumed that 'It is raining at Concarneau on 12 July 1985' is an eternal sentence. But outside of mathematics, are there sentences that are really eternal, that is to say, the truth conditions of which are not able to vary with a contextual element? Whatever the answer, Quine's strategy is clear: it is only possible to talk about truth values to the extent that one is in a position not to cease to relativise them to contexts but to remove the possibility that these relativisations be undefined.

1.4.5 Do we need propositions?

One can admit that propositions as meanings of sentences do not have well-defined conditions of identity, and still reject the general scepticism that this conclusion can induce in respect of the utility of the notion. Propositions are really abstractions and in each of the theories we have touched on, they are essentially abstractions from the syntactic and semantic structure of sentences. That is why, in the majority of theories (probably with the exception of those of propositions as 'possible worlds' or as '*n*-uple objects'), propositions as meanings of sentences appear as entities projected from the syntactical structure or as 'defrocked' sentences, if one can put it this way.[44] But do these legitimate suspicions in respect of entities with ill-defined contours justify calling a total halt to the use of the notion of 'proposition'? Does the fact that an entity is engendered by abstraction imply that this entity is no more than a fiction? One guideline is obtained by abstraction from a property that parallel lines possess. Does this mean that it is illegitimate to employ this notion, and that it is more dangerous to speak of synonymity by abstraction from the meanings of two sentences? Likewise, entities that have imprecise individuation conditions can have their uses: where to start or where to end a symphony? on the score? at the moment of its execution? and when are two executions of the same score executions of the same symphony?[45] Most theoreticians of propositions as entities emphasise the fact that their use of the notion is a construction, a theoretical tool intended to serve as *analysans* for the notion of meaning, but without representing all the aspects of that notion. From this point of view, the use of the notion of proposition (or that of 'possible world', 'fact' or 'situation') is without theoretical danger. On the contrary, the price paid for a radical rejection of propositions as meanings, like Quine's, is considerable: when two people say something, must we refuse to talk about the contents of what they are saying or to admit that they could be saying or believing the same thing? If propositions are only terms that are convenient to designate what is true or false, what is believed, understood or said, the notion has a theoretical interest which is not negligible, in the absence of a finer differentiation of what was believed, understood or said. For example, we really need the notion of proposition to distinguish the fact of *knowing that a sentence is true, and the fact of knowing what that sentence expresses*. Thus I am able to know that the sentence '$E = MC^2$' is true, without understanding it or without knowing what proposition it expresses.

But in all these uses, employing the notion of 'proposition' does nothing but state a problem, and does not make it possible to solve it. And when, going beyond the heuristic role, propositions are assimilated to certain entities, their usefulness for solving the problems of a theory of meaning is not proven and does not answer important questions: what is the relationship between the syntactic structure of sentences and their meaning? what are the objects of propositional attitudes?[46] We will find these problems again on more than one occasion in this book. None of this makes the notion of proposition illegitimate or useless. This only diminishes its theoretical capacity to solve the problems that the philosophy of logic and language confront.

——— 2 ———
THE MEANING OF PROPOSITIONAL CONNECTIVES

2.1 The problems of the meaning of connectives

What is the meaning of the usual connectives ('and', 'or', 'not', 'if and only if') of the logic of propositions? This question conceals several others.

1. First, the question of the *formal* meaning of the connectives '&', '∨', '–', '→', '≡': is this meaning better defined by the *semantic rules* or by the *syntactic rules* that govern the connectives in the standard propositional calculus? This overlaps with the question of knowing how the category of what are called the *logical constants* should be defined in a logical system. The connectives are the logical constants of propositional logic (in contrast to the 'propositional variables' 'p', 'q', etc.). All in all, this is the question of knowing how to define the realm of what is logic, because it is according to the way the class of these constants is determined that the range of the domain of logic is demarcated (cf. Chapter 11).

2. The second question is of the *informal* meaning of the connectives of propositional logic, that is to say the relationship between their meanings within the calculus and their meanings outside the abstract framework defined by logic. This problem also raises that of the nature of logic: are the rules of logic exclusively defined by their formal meanings, and therefore, in a certain sense, by virtue of the conventions that govern these meanings, or can they only be understood and defined in relation to an extra-logical meaning, determined by their uses in the customary practice of natural reasoning? This question can in its turn be interpreted in two ways, dependent on the approach adopted to natural reasoning.

2a. Natural reasoning is primarily the reasoning that we carry out with the words and sentences of a natural language. The question then is: what is the meaning of the logical connectives in natural language, and within customary reasonings in natural language? In other words, what are the linguistic counterparts, or the intuitive interpretations of the logical connectives? Can the two meanings be said to coincide, and the logical connectives to be the adequate translation of the logical connectives and particles of ordinary language? This raises the general problem of the relationship between logical language and natural language.

2b. It can be said that natural reasoning is primarily the result of the exercise of a psychological or cognitive ability of the speakers of a language, or of subjects who reason. The question then is that of the *psychological* meaning of the logical connectives, that is to say of the relationship between their formal meaning and the psychological operations of the speakers. This poses the general problem of the links that exist or might exist, between the linguistic meanings and psychological meanings on the one hand, and between these latter and the formal meanings on the other; in other words, the general links between logic, psychology and natural reasoning. A psychological analysis of the rules governing the uses of connectives in common reasoning, associated with the idea that these uses are the reflection of thought processes, leads naturally to the thesis whereby the very *rules* of logic, if they derive from their use in general reasoning, are themselves psychological rules, or laws of human psychology. This is one version of the psychologistic thesis in the philosophy of logic.

This chapter does not aspire in itself alone to provide an answer to such important problems (I will come back to them in Chapters 11–13), but I would like to show how they arise through discussion of various theories of the meaning of connectives, each of which suggests a certain interpretation of the relationship between the intuitive meaning of the connectives and their formal meaning. This is why it is necessary first to recall what this consists of.

2.2 The connectives formally defined

By '*formal* meaning' of connectives, I will understand the various ways inside the formal system of propositional logic in which a role is assigned to, and an interpretation made of, the signs '&', '$\vee$', '$-$', '$\rightarrow$', '$\equiv$'. This meaning is usually defined in two distinct ways, *semantic* and *syntactic*.

2.2.1 Semantic definition

Let us begin with the semantic definition. Once it has been specified that these connectives serve to form sentences (or, if preferred, propositions) from other sentences in determinate ways (for example '$-$' is a unary operator, '&', '$\vee$', ', '$\equiv$' are binary operators), that is to say given the *syntax* of the propositional language, the most usual response consists of saying that these connectives are truth functions: the meaning of complex sentences formed from these connectives is a function of the truth values assigned to the propositional letters ('p', 'q', 'r', etc.) that appear in these sentences. One thus says that the meaning of the connectives is *truth functional*. The characterisation of the connectives is then *semantic*: the sentences receive truth values, and have a meaning as a function of the truth values (meanings) of the expressions that compose them. One then says that the *truth conditions* of the sentences of the language have been given. The most usual way of giving the semantics of the connectives of the propositional calculus consists of providing their usual truth tables. These are the characteristic matrices that give the truth functional meaning of the connectives. A semantics can take the form of a *truth theory* for the logical language considered (cf. Chapters 4 and 5). A truth theory for the usual connectives takes the following characteristic clauses:

(I) '$-A$' is true if and only if A is false (*negation*).
(II) 'A & B' is true if and only if A is true and B is true (*conjunction*).
(III) '$A \vee B$' is true if and only if A is true or B is true (*disjunction*).
(IV) '$A \rightarrow B$' is true if and only if A is false or B is true (*conditional*).
(V) '$A \equiv B$' is true if and only if A is true and B is true or if A is false and B is false (*biconditional*).

Each of these clauses is tantamount to stating the typical line of the truth table corresponding to each connective, that is to say it makes it possible to re-create the other lines of each corresponding truth table. For example, for '$\vee$':

A	B	$A \vee B$
T	T	T
T	F	T
F	T	T
F	F	F

2.2.2 Syntactic definition

There is another way of characterising the meaning of the connectives, the syntactic way. But the meaning of 'syntactic' in question is not the same as the one referred to above, which concerns the *rules of formation* of the language considered. That only indicates what are the *well-formed formulas* (*wff*) of the propositional language, by means of clauses of the type

If 'A' is a wff, and 'B' is a wff, then '$A \rightarrow B$' is a wff (for the conditional).

In its second meaning, 'syntactic' is applied not to the rules of formation of a system, but to the rules of deduction or to the axioms that make it possible to derive theorems in the system. The syntax/semantic distinction (or the distinction between *proof theory* and *model theory*) is then related to the type of *deductive apparatus* envisaged. From this point of view the notion of logical *consequence* can be defined in a semantic way or in a syntactic way. In the semantic sense, one says that a conclusion C is the semantic consequence (or can be deduced or inferred) from premises A and B if and only if premises A and B being true, the conclusion is also true – or if A and B are true, C cannot be false, or again if all the 'models' of the premises (all the interpretations that make A and B true) are also the models of the conclusion C (are interpretations that make C true). This is the *valid consequence* relation, which is usually written as:

'A, B ⊨ C'

The characteristic of the semantic approach is that it is uses the concepts of truth, validity, satisfiability (truth of a formula under one interpretation, or existence of one model) and model, and characterises logical consequence by means of these concepts.

In the syntactic sense, the concept of logical consequence is defined by means of a *system of axioms* and *rules of deduction* from which the theorems of the system are derived. These are not valid statements, or tautologies, but propositions derived from primitive propositions or axioms by substitution or by use of the rules of inference. For example, the following system of axioms can be given for the propositional calculus (taken from Lukasiewicz):

$(A1) \ (A \rightarrow B) \rightarrow (B \rightarrow C) \rightarrow (A \rightarrow C)$
$(A2) \ (A \rightarrow (-A \rightarrow B))$
$(A3) \ (-A \rightarrow A) \rightarrow A$

from which, if the rule of inference of the *modus ponens (from if A then B, and B to infer B)* is used, all the theorems of proposition logic can be derived.[1]

The corresponding concept of deduction is the relationship that exists between a collection of sentences taken as premises, and a conclusion, so that the conclusion is derived from the premises via the axioms and the rules of inference. It is written

'Γ ⊢ C'

(where 'Γ' designates the collection of premises A, B, etc. and 'C' the conclusion).

In this sense a sentence A is a logical consequence (in the syntactical sense or proof-theoretical sense) of a collection of sentences Γ if and only if A can be derived from Γ through the axioms and the rules of inference.

However, the axiomatic presentation is not the only one. Instead of axioms, which are sometimes numerous and cumbersome, the deductive apparatus can be reduced to a small number of *rules of inference* or *rules of natural deduction*. Such a system tells us what sentences we can regard as true, given certain hypotheses. One indicates that a certain hypothesis is cleared away by putting it between square brackets (by 'discharging' it). Every rule introduces or eliminates a symbol and is consequently called a rule of *introduction* or a rule of *elimination*. The connectives can thus be defined by the corresponding rules (where Greek letters represent the various formulas of the propositional calculus):

(&-introduction)	(&-elimination)	
$\dfrac{\phi \quad \psi}{\phi \ \& \ \psi}$	$\dfrac{\phi \ \& \ \psi}{\phi}$	$\dfrac{\phi \ \& \ \psi}{\psi}$

($\vee$-introduction)

$$\frac{\phi}{\phi \vee \psi} \qquad \frac{\psi}{\phi \vee \psi}$$

($\vee$-elimination)

$$[\phi] \quad [\psi]$$

$$\begin{array}{ccc} \vdots & & \vdots \\ \frac{\phi \vee \psi \quad \theta \quad \theta}{\theta} \end{array}$$

($\rightarrow$-introduction)

$$[\phi]$$

$$\vdots$$

$$\psi$$

$$\overline{\phi \rightarrow \psi}$$

($\rightarrow$-elimination in *modus ponens*)

$$\frac{\phi \rightarrow \psi \quad \phi}{\psi}$$

($-$ introduction or
reductio ad absurdum)

$$[\phi]$$

$$\vdots$$

$$\frac{F}{-\phi}$$

(absurdity)

$$\frac{F}{\phi}$$

(double negation)

$$\frac{--\phi}{\phi}$$

(where 'F' is some contradictory proposition, like '$\phi \, \& - \phi$'

We will not deal with the rules for the biconditional '$\equiv$'.

The characteristic of a system of natural deduction is that it does not call (at least not directly, cf. § 10.6) on semantic concepts of validity, tautology or satisfiability, but on concepts of theoremhood, rule of deduction or derivation.

If for example, we abide by the introduction and elimination rules for '&', these rules are strictly equivalent to the corresponding clause of a theory of truth of type (I)–(V). In fact, to say that one proposition implies another is equivalent to saying that the first cannot be true without the second being true. Consequently, the introduction rule for conjunction is another way of saying:

'$p \, \& \, q$' is true if p is true and q is true.

Likewise the elimination rule is equivalent to saying:

'$p \, \& \, q$' is true only if p is true and q is true.

The same correspondence between theory of truth and rules of natural deduction is observed with the introduction rule for disjunction. But things are less simple with the elimination rule of '∨'. A disjunction 'p∨q' *does not imply one or the other of its members*. A system of natural deduction therefore adopts the more complex rule above, that can again be expressed as follows:

> If *p* and certain other hypotheses imply *r*
> And if *q*, joined to these other hypotheses, implies *r*
> Then *p∨q* and these other hypotheses imply *r*

But then the rule in question is no longer equivalent to the corresponding rule (III) of a theory of truth. But there are ways of reducing these differences, if the rules of natural deduction are reformulated.[2]

Despite these differences, it can be said that the formal meanings of the connectives (and the corresponding concepts of validity of the arguments composed of sentences formed from connectives) are related to the semantic or to the syntactic approach. Is there one approach that would take precedence over the other? In the ordinary practice of the logician, no. Once a formal system has been defined, the two parallel concepts of logical consequence – the semantic concept and the syntactic concept – for this system are defined, and their relationships established. They are, in the logic of propositions, extensionally equivalent, that is to say the tautologies or valid expressions that are determined by one are precisely the theorems that the other determines, and conversely. These proofs are ensured by the various completeness theorems.[3] But the question of knowing what is *de jure* the primary approach is another question that involves the way in which the notion of logical constant in general, and consequently logic itself, is defined. I will come back to this problem in Chapter 11. Here the problem that concerns us will be to know if a definition of the formal meaning of the connectives, whether it be syntactic or semantic, is in itself enough to define these same connectives, or if extra-systematic notions must be brought in.

2.3 Connectives defined by inferential role

2.3.1 Zop, tonk and flop

Can the meaning of propositional connectives solely consist of truth tables (or the clauses of a theory of truth) or of the corresponding deduction rules? In other words is it limited to the *inferential roles* that they play in deductions, or to their function within inferences? Here our intuitions can lead in two directions. On the one hand it is clear, if one refers to clauses (I)–(V) below of a theory of truth, that understanding them calls for understanding the meaning of the connectives of the language, 'and', 'or' (inclusive), 'not', etc., apart from the fact that these meanings are interdefinable, as in (IV), which presupposes understanding of (III). But on the other hand, it is equally clear that these clauses can also be said to define *every* connective which has the semantic properties under consideration. From this point of view, it is not even necessary to know what the connectives in question mean, *before their introduction as logical symbols*. For example, instead of (II), it would be just as good to have

(IIa) '*A zop B*' is true if and only if *A* is true *zop B* is true

The same argument might be made apropos the rules of natural deduction or axioms: a propositional connective is any statement that is 'implicitly' or 'contextually defined' by the rules or the axioms of the propositional calculus.

   In a famous article, Prior (1960) attempted to give a counter-example to this thesis. He only considered the syntactic definition of connectives, and invited us to define a new connective, *tonk*, obeying the following two rules of deduction:

tonk-introduction	*tonk-elimination*
$\dfrac{A}{A \ tonk \ B}$	$\dfrac{A \ tonk \ B}{B}$

If these rules are used, it is easy to show that any sentence *B* can always be inferred from any sentence *A*, in the following manner:

1. *A* (premise or hypothesis).
2. *A tonk B* (by *tonk-introduction* applied to 1.)
3. *B* (by *tonk-elimination* applied to 2.)

and more generally, given the above two rules, any two propositions are always logically equivalent (the equivalence is the mutual implication of two propositions); consequently if $A \vdash B$ (by the above reasoning) and if $B \vdash A$ (by the converse reasoning), then $A \equiv B$). For example,

My grandmother goes in for cycling $\equiv 2 + 2 = 4$

by this reasoning.
   In still other words, anything can be deduced from anything (and particularly if '$-A$' is substituted for '*B*', '$-A$' can be deduced from '*A*'). A system containing the rules for '*tonk*' would thus be contradictory. Note here that '*tonk*' is different from '*zop*' above in that '*zop*' is an arbitrary name for the conjunction, while '*tonk*' is a *new* connective. Prior concludes two things from this. First of all, he concludes that the meaning of propositional connectives cannot lie in their definition in terms of rules of inferences (or in terms of axioms, or in terms of their truth conditions, because incoherent axioms or truth tables can be constructed in the same way), and consequently that 'an expression must have some independently determined meaning before we can discover whether the inferences involving it are valid or invalid'. It follows that we must *first* determine the meaning of the connectives, *then* determine if the inferences that contain them are valid, and that there must necessarily be more in the fact of knowing what is the meaning of a connective such as 'and' than being capable of performing certain inferences. The

second conclusion that Prior draws from his argument is just as significant: it concerns the notion of *analyticity*, or 'analytically valid inference'. According to the conception that Prior attacks, an analytically valid inference is an inference that is solely true by virtue of the meaning of the logical constants that appear in it. This is the conventionalist conception of the rules of logic, that of Carnap, according to which these rules are linguistic conventions introduced by stipulation, and which can be changed *ad libitum* (cf. § 11.2 and § 12.3.1 below). But in this sense of 'analytically valid', any sentence can be validly inferred from another by one of the rules of '*contonktion*'. As Prior says, this promises to exclude *falsche Spitzfindigkeit* from logic for ever. For Prior, the notion of analytically valid inference is therefore based on a confusion: one cannot hope to introduce the meaning of connectives by *convention*.

Does Prior's argument have these consequences? For this, it would have to be acknowledged that it is possible to introduce connectives as '*tonk*'. But is it? As Belnap[4] notes, '*tonk*' is not defined in a vacuum but from a certain notion of *deducibility* or inference. For example, Prior can draw his conclusion (3) because he assumes that inference is a transitive relationship (i.e. if A can be inferred from Γ, and if B can be inferred from A, then B can be inferred from Γ). The characteristic of '*tonk*' is that it is a contradictory or incoherent connective since it makes it possible for absolutely any theorem to be derived. But can there be any concept whatsoever of deduction, and consequently of logic, if the system that results is contradictory and inconsistent? The rules for *tonk* cannot be hammered out, even by convention, because they are defective in this sense.

The problem raised by Prior is not peculiar solely to the *syntactic* concept of logical reference. As the above case of 'zop' shows, absolutely any connective of the natural language that had the truth table of '&', might be said 'to have the same meaning', even if its meaning diverged from the ordinary meaning of 'and' in the ordinary language. This would be particularly the case with the following connective '*flop*':

'$(A$ flop $B)$ and the number π is irrational'

which, since the sentence 'π is an irrational number' is always or necessarily true (if it is acknowledged that arithmetical statements are such), would have the same truth table as '&'. Would we have to say that '*flop*' and '&' *mean the same thing*? Wittgenstein, in the *Tractatus* (4.465), maintained that the truth table of a connective was essential to determining its meaning: this table cannot be changed without changing the *meaning* of the connective. But it is not apparent what the irrationality of π (or any necessarily true proposition) has to do with the meaning of '&'. However this difficulty can be removed by making an important distinction between the *characterisation* and the *definition* of a connective. A rule of inference or a truth table can characterise the meaning of a connective (on condition that these rules are not contradictory, like those of '*tonk*'), without for all that defining the meaning of that connective, that is to say giving the meaning to someone who did not know it in advance. The moral is that syntactic or semantic 'definitions' of connectives are only possible for someone who already had an intuitive idea of what the connectives in question meant. A person who did not have the logical concepts of conjunction, disjunction or of material conditional, for example, would not be able to *understand* these terms from syntactical or semantic 'definitions' of the corresponding terms. That is why it is preferable to say that these are *characterisations* and not definitions. However, these characterisations must have an essential link with the usual meaning of the connective as we understand it, without which they would be incorrect. We can even maintain that if we attribute the above connective *'flop'* to a creature, we also have every reason to reduce this connective to '&' and 'and', by virtue of the equivalence of the truth tables, and Wittgenstein's idea can thus be embraced. In any case, characterisation alone is not enough.

2.3.2 Formalisation and reflexive equilibrium

Even if Prior's argument does not have the significance he claims, it can be justified: logical systems and their rules do not fall from the sky, and their construction is motivated by the desire to account for inferences that we judge *intuitively* to be valid. Here (and one swallow does not make a summer), the philosophy of logic can draw inspiration from moral philosophy. I would like to suggest a conception of formalisation in logic close to the conception that Rawls gives of what he calls the 'reflexive equilibrium' in moral theory.[5] According to Rawls, in constructing a theory of justice (or a moral theory in general) one starts from intuitive ideas of justice for each and everyone (and particularly of 'justice as fairness') to move towards a coherent conception based on the 'principles of justice' and the theory of the 'original position'. Setting out from this provisional conception, depending on whether our intuitive judgements diverge from the theory obtained, one is induced to modify this initial theory. The best theory of justice is the one that corresponds to this *reflexive* equilibrium of judgements once it has been revised. In logic one starts from certain intuitions on the validity of the arguments and the meaning of the constants, and tries to give the formal canons of this intuitive validity. One can be induced to modify them, or to invent others, on the basis of our intuitive disagreements, within certain limits. As I will maintain in Chapter 12, this does not mean, for all that, that one is authorised to 'change logic', that is to say to carry out radical revisions because, just as the theory of justice remains based on the principles and the 'original position', logic can remain based on the same principles. Considered independently of their intuitive interpretation, the propositional logical constants are actually defined solely by their inferential role. But in some way they bear the mark of the intuitive origins of the concern for formalisation (I will try to separate out the meaning of all this more completely in Chapter 13).

2.4 The meaning of connectives in natural language

2.4.1 Logicians' and linguists' connectives

If the foregoing remarks are correct, why is there so little correspondence between the meaning of the connectives in logic and their meaning in natural language? There are abundant examples and they are generally such as to inspire students approaching elementary logic with the feeling that it is a totally artificial and arbitrary language which bears strictly no relationship to natural language. A number of differences begin at the syntactic level. For example, the grammatical transformation called the 'conjunction reduction' authorises the equivalence between

(1a) John has flu and Paul has flu

and

(1b) John and Paul have flu

which are given the same representation in propositional logic:

(2) p & q

But propositional logic cannot use a conjunction to represent a sentence such as

(3a) Charles and Diana make an attractive couple

which cannot be equivalent to

(3b) Charles makes an attractive couple and Diana makes an attractive couple.

Conversely, certain syntactic properties, such as the commutativity of '&' cannot be transposed to 'and'. Whereas 'p & q' is equivalent to 'q and p',

(4a) They married and had many children

is not equivalent to

(4b) They had many children and married

because of the temporal meaning of 'and'.

One could also mention the fact that in the natural language, unlike in logic, there is no uniform way of denying an expression, or again the ambiguity of 'or' between an inclusive meaning and an exclusive meaning. The case of the conditional 'if. . . then' is the most debated: a number of its uses are not truth functional (cf. the following section).[6] The differences do not only stem from the syntax and semantics of the connectives in the natural language, but from their pragmatic uses, or their uses in speech and conversation. For example, the particles 'but', 'because' or 'even', which logic textbooks treat as purely rhetorical effects, or choose to ignore, have very different meanings from those of truth functions when used in conversation.[7] There are many examples of this type, but I do not intend to list them here.

What sort of attitude should be adopted in view of this obvious disparity between the logical uses and the linguistic uses of connectives? There are at least three possible approaches. First, one can acknowledge that this disparity is a fact, and conclude from it that the meaning of the connectives of ordinary language has to be determined by means of another system of logical rules. The 'non-standard' uses of connectives have corresponding non-standard systems of logic, like the theory of counterfactual conditionals, developed from the semantics of modalities,[8] or 'relevance logic' (§ 12.7). In this case, the formalisms can be nearer to or further from those of standard propositional logic to varying degrees. The degree of distance in relation to the usual logical idea of deduction also varies: it is greater, for example, in 'relevance logic' than in the theory of counterfactual conditionals. The second solution is even more radical: it consists of acknowledging that the meaning of connectives in language is not and cannot be determined by something like a 'logic', and that the notion of deduction itself has to be totally revised if one wants to account for natural reasoning. Here again the degree of divergence can vary: some attempts draw their inspiration from the classical logical concept, by redefining inference, and suggest various versions of 'natural logic' applied to usual reasoning (I will look at two of these versions in the following section), others suggest systems of 'laws of discourse' or 'argumentative laws', which no longer bear any but a remote resemblance to the logical laws (and are no longer *logical* laws).[9] The third approach is the most conservative of all: it consists of maintaining that the *meaning* of the connectives in natural language is actually determined by the truth conditions provided by truth functional logic, although their pragmatic *uses* are not. The divergences in meaning between the connectives of the logician and those of the linguist then stem from pragmatic features without affecting their semantics. It is a version of that third approach that I want to defend, using the case of the conditional 'if. . . then' as an illustration.

2.4.2 'If' and '→', or saved by the implicatures

Does the meaning of '→' in ordinary propositional logic cover that of 'if' in natural language (keeping to English)? Since Philo of Megara[10], defenders of the truth-functional meaning of the conditional (or 'material conditional') have maintained that this connective has the following truth table:

	A	B	$A \rightarrow B$
1.	T	T	T
2.	T	F	F
3.	F	T	T
4.	F	F	T

The kernel of the meaning of the Philonian 'if' is, as its inventor noted, the fact that '$p \rightarrow q$' is equivalent to '$-(p \& -q)$', that is to say to the falsity of the assertion of the antecedent and of the negation of the consequent. If one agrees in general to consider lines (1) and (2) as non-problematic, this is not the case with (3) and (4). For example, (3) and (4) are violated by counterfactual conditionals such as

(5) If Marilyn Monroe had lived to sixty, she would have been a grandmother

which would all become entirely true, if the 'if' had its truth-functional meaning, since all the conditionals of this type have a false antecedent, whatever the truth value of the consequent.

Many other uses of 'if' do not seem to be truth conditional. For example, it is probable that the following conditionals:

(6) If you go on singing '*La donna e mobile . . .*' I will strangle you
(7) If butter is heated in the oven, it melts

have a more causal than a truth-functional meaning, and that if the notion of cause cannot be represented by extensional notions[11] neither can 'if' in these sentences. Lastly, one of the most frequent meanings of 'if' is as an expression serving to indicate an *inference* relationship between the antecedent and the consequent, and only corresponds to line (1) of the Philonian truth table. 'If' then has the meaning of 'therefore', or 'consequently':

(8) If today is Thursday, then tomorrow will be Friday
(9) If X is a part of Y, and if Y is a part of Z, then X is a part of Z

In each of cases (5)–(9), the meaning of the conditional sentences seems determined, not by the Philonian reading, but by the existence of a certain *relationship* between the antecedent and the consequent which is the basis of their connection and allows the corresponding sentence to be stated. It is then natural to assume that each type of conditional will have a corresponding specific collection of rules of inference, or a special 'logic'. (5) would then emerge from the logic of counterfactual conditionals, (6) and (7) of a 'causal logic'. But does a 'logic of the days of the week' have to be evoked for (8) or a 'logic of wholes and parts' for (9)? In other words, does the class of logical constants have to be expanded according to differences of meaning which, in each case, take account of the relationship between antecedent and consequent? A great deal of work in 'philosophical logic' rests on a positive answer to this question, without going so far as acknowledging that there is a logic specific to sentences like (8). Relevance logic is precisely an attempt to represent the idea that there is *some sort* of relationship between antecedent and consequent, which is the basis of their connection. This again is the idea that underlies Lewis's notion of 'strict implication' (cf. § 12.7 and 7.1 respectively).

However that may be, the conflict between these views and the theory of the truth-functional meaning of the conditional is quite clear; according to the former, the *conventional* meaning of 'if' is of a certain *well-grounded connection* between antecedent and consequent; according to the latter, this conventional meaning is reduced to the truth table of the Philonian conditional. But supporters and opponents of the truth-functional meaning both agree on the existence of such a connection or relation in uses of 'if'. The question that divides them is that of knowing whether the connection in question forms part of the *conventional* or linguistic meaning of the connective, or whether this connection is not rather a feature of the *use* of the Philonian conditional in speech and conversation.

This is the thesis that Grice defended, employing his theory of *conversational implicatures*.[12] Without entering into a description of this theory, it can be said to be based on a fundamental distinction between what a sentence *says* and what it *conversationally implicates*. What the sentence says is a function of its conventional and literal meaning in the language, whereas what it implicates or conveys is a function of the context, the speaker's intentions, and of certain general 'conversational maxims' which govern the rational use of speech and communication. To simplify, in the context of the present discussion, these can be reduced to two:

(I) *Maxim of quality*: only say what you believe to be true and justified.
(II) *Maxim of quantity*: be as informative as possible, and avoid being less informative than necessary.

These principles apply, provided that there is a minimum of rational co-operation between speakers.

According to Grice, if these principles are correct, then the truth-functional meaning of 'if' is indeed the conventional meaning. If the maxim of quality is applied, then a conditional can only be stated in three possible cases: (1) when it is only known that the antecedent is false; (2) when it is known that the consequent is true; and (3) when, although it is not known if the antecedent is false or if the consequent is true, there is sufficient reason to think that the conjunction of the antecedent and the negation of the consequent is false. But if now the truth of the maxim of quantity is also required, cases (1) and (2) must also be excluded: the statement that it is false that p or the statement that it is true that q are *more informative* respectively than the statement that it is false that p is true and that q is false, in the sense where (1) and (2) imply (3), but are not implied by (3). Consequently, if (I) and (II) are applied, only the truth-functional meaning (3) of 'if' can have anything to do with the matter.[13] The other uses of the conditional can actually be valid but they arise from particular implicatures which the speakers produce and which the hearers infer from what is said, when they conclude that one or other of the conversational maxims is violated. These other uses are therefore engendered by a calculation on the part of the speakers on the intentions of communication, *from the literal meaning of 'if' and from the maxims*.

According to Strawson (1986), from the fact that only meaning (3) is authorised by the conversational maxims it does not follow that the thesis that the conventional meaning of 'if' lies in the expression of a connection between antecedent and consequent (the thesis he calls 'consequentialist') is false: because the circumstances in which I have good reasons for stating (3) are exactly those in which I have good reason for thinking that there is a well-grounded ('ground consequent') relation between p and q. But if Strawson is right, how would this show that the conventional meaning of 'if' is not its truth-functional meaning? The argument can be turned round against him. If, when we state 'if p then q', we are stating *eo ipso* the existence of a well-founded relation between p and q, we are still expressing this relationship by saying that it is not true that p is true and q is false, how can anything other than the truth-functional reading count as the expression of the meaning of the connective?

It obviously cannot be concluded from this that Grice's 'minimalist' strategy, which consists of reducing the number of semantic principles to the minimum, and accounting for the differences in meaning by means of pragmatic principles, is generally correct. There are good reasons for thinking that it is both more elegant and more explicative (by virtue of the principle whereby one explains best with a reduced number of explicative principles than if one multiples them *praeter necessitatem*). Grice's analysis, however, encounters difficulties, and it is far from being the only available analysis of conditionals.[14]

2.5 The connectives defined by their 'conceptual roles'

2.5.1 Logic and psychology: the order of priorities

The foregoing reasoning leads to the following conclusions. Discussion of '*tonk*' led to the idea that the meaning of the connectives in logic could not be determined solely by their inferential roles, as provided by the rules of natural deduction or a theory of truth, and that it was therefore important to define this meaning according to the intuitive meanings of the connectives of natural language. But the discussion of 'if . . . then' also shows that the meaning of the connectives in natural language cannot be determined independently of their logical truth-functional meaning. There is a sense of circularity about all this: if logic needs language and language needs logic, have we not solved the difficult question of their relationships a little too easily? In fact, I would be more tempted to see these conclusions as an illustration of the Rawlsian 'reflexive equilibrium' which I suggested, in § 2.3.2, regulated the formalisation enterprise. At present I would like to try to produce a counter-proof by considering theories that explain the meaning of the connectives by the role that they occupy in natural reasoning, in so far as this reasoning is the expression of psychological or cognitive faculties. Numerous theories of this type exist, beginning with those of Piagetian developmental psychology (cf. § 13.3.2). A feature of all these theories is that they try to reformulate the rules of usual logic so that they better reflect the psychological processes at work in ordinary reasoning. The 'logic' – when it is acknowledged that a 'logic' is really involved – obtained is then often described as 'natural logic' because it has more 'naturalness' or less artificiality than standard logic. The extent of their involvement with the psychologist thesis, whereby there is a 'mental logic' (§ 13.3), varies: some of these theories assume that the rules of logic are themselves the laws of the psychology of subjects who are capable of reasoning; others acknowledge that the link between the rules formulated as substitutes for the usual logical rules and the psychological and cognitive structures is looser, and does not prejudge the 'psychological reality' of these rules. The two theories that I want to examine now belong to this second category. They both seek to reverse the order of explanation between logic, linguistic meaning and psychological role in reasoning that is ordinarily accepted (and which I have accepted here myself). In fact, according to the conception of the meaning of logical connectives that I have suggested here, this meaning is determined according to the following order of explanation:

> Contribution to truth conditions.
> Relevant logical implications.
> Linguistic meanings.
> Psychological role in reasoning.[15]

Each line determines the next.

According to this conception, the *semantics* of the logical constants (represented in a theory of truth) makes it possible to explain their *deductive syntax* (represented by natural deduction rules). The first two make it possible to explain the conventional meaning of the connectives in natural language. The three explain in turn the psychological role of the connectives in the reasoning, in other words the thought processes at work in the reasoning. By 'explanation' here, I do not mean a *causal* explanation, and I am not, for example, saying that the truth conditions causally determine the implications, meanings and psychological roles, because they have a sort of 'psychological reality'. The explanation concerns the nature of the principles that have to be invoked in order to describe the meaning of the connectives in natural language. In what follows, the theories that will be discussed reverse this order of explanation:

> Psychological role in reasoning.
> Linguistic meanings.
> Relevant logical implications.
> (or) Contributions to truth conditions.

But here it is less clear that the explanation is not causal. It invokes a psychological role by way of causal determinant of the other roles, that is to say it explains the logical distinctions by the way we think. The theory examined in § 2.5.2 tends to place the contributions to truth conditions in third place and the relevant logical implications in fourth. The theory examined in § 2.5.3 reverses this order. Both place psychological roles at the head, and are versions of what are called 'conceptual role semantics', based on a 'functionalist' theory of the mind according to which the meanings of words derive from the concepts that these words express, the contents of these concepts being principally determined by the roles that these concepts play in the thought or (functional) psychology of the subjects.[16]

2.5.2 Mental models and propositional reasoning

Johnson-Laird (1983) has proposed a theory of 'natural' propositional reasoning which makes it the result of the manipulation of certain 'mental models'. Johnson-Laird's concept of 'model' is inspired by the logicians' semantic concept but differs from it in that the mental models are not abstract constructions but the mental constructions of the subject who is reasoning. Although he proposes to model his rules of propositional reasoning on psychological processes, Johnson-Laird does not subscribe to the psychologistic doctrine of a 'mental logic', according to which the logical rules would in some way be inscribed in the mind (§ 13.3): the mental models are representations of psychological representations, the nature of which is left indeterminate and open to empirical investigation.[17] But I will leave his arguments to the side here (however, cf. Chapter 13).

   Like Grice, Johnson-Laird notes that natural propositional reasoning does not take account of the informative content of the premises and the conclusion of an argument, and in particular of the fact that a number of the conclusions of usual logic are trivial, and therefore transgress the maxim of quantity. For example, although the inference 'A, therefore A or B' is valid in propositional logic, we practically never make it in daily life, because the conclusion is less informative than the premise. Although inferences like

> Logic is boring
> *therefore* logic is boring or deconstruction theory is

are valid, their informative content is very low, and their occurrence in natural reasoning is improbable. In the same way, in logic, all the tautologies of the propositional calculus (all tautologies are logically equivalent) can be inferred from a tautology, but no one would dream of doing so; and as the class of tautologies is infinite, such a deductive task would be beyond our finite capacities (cf. § 13.5). What can be inferred in logic is not necessarily what is inferred in the natural exercise of reasoning. Therefore, if one wants logic to be able to be applied to 'natural' inferences, it seems that the usual rules of logic need to be changed in terms of the quantity of information provided by the inferences. A procedure devised by Bar-Hillel and Carnap makes it possible to define a measure of the semantic information conveyed by a sentence, on the principle that a sentence contains all the more information the more circumstances it excludes: the 'probability of a proposition' p is first defined as the sum of the probabilities of cases in which p is true (that is to say the lines of its truth table where it is true); the informativity of p is then inversely proportional to its probability (the more a proposition is probable, the less it is informative): Inf $(p) = 1 - \text{Prob } (p)$. For example, the informative) content of the proposition p is:

Inf $(p) = 1 - 0.5 = 0.5$

since the probability of p is equal to the number of cases when p can be true, that is to say, out of the two cases $(T$ or $F)$, 1/2, that is to say Prob $(p) = 0.5$. The informative content of p is thus greater than that of $p \lor q$, since Prob $(p \lor q)$ $= 3/4 = 0.75$ and Inf $(p \lor q) = 1 - 0.75 = 0.25$. This explains that it is uninformative to infer p or q from p.[18]

According to Johnson-Laird, a deduction procedure can then be provided, according to the principle whereby no conclusion should contain less information than the premises. Take, for example, the task of drawing an 'informative' conclusion from given premises. The premises are:

If p or q, then r

p

The procedure to follow is then as follows:

1. Look for the premise with most semantic information. Here, this is p, the second premise.
2. If the premise chosen figures in the first premise, substitute the value 'true' for its occurrence in the second premise if it is positive; substitute the value 'false' for it if the occurrence is negative. Otherwise, return to 1. Here the result (for the first premise) is:

If *true* or q, then r

3. Use the semantics of the connective immediately governing the substituted value to simplify the premise, and continue the process of simplification to its conclusion. If the final result is 'true', then the premises are consistent and no 'interesting' conclusion can be drawn. If the result is 'false', then the premises are contradictory. Finally, if the final result is a proposition, this is the conclusion sought. Applied to our example stage (3) gives:

If *true* then r (because a disjunction one member of which is true is reduced to its other member)

and the conclusion sought is r (because the true antecedent of a conditional can be dropped).

Johnson-Laird emphasises the fact that such a procedure does not bring into play the rules of natural deduction but the construction of 'mental models' of the premises. But it is not apparent in what way the notion of 'model' here differs from that of the usual logical semantics: a model is an interpretation of a propositional letter which makes it true. And the procedure suggested is exactly parallel to the semantic procedures derived from truth tables, like those given by

Quine, for example (Quine, 1950). Steps (2) and (3) directly invoke an analysis of the logical form of the premises, and the usual semantics (truth functional) of the connectives. Other well-known methods of decision for the propositional calculus invoke Beth's 'semantic tableaux', and consist of seeking a counter-example of the conclusion in order to test the validity of an inference, for example: the inference is valid if there is no such counter-example, that is to say if, after application of the rules governing the connectives, it is found that the premises are incompatible with the negation of the conclusion.[19] But when Johnson-Laird tells us that (natural) 'reasoning is not a matter of finding logical forms of the premises and of applying the rules of inference in order to derive the conclusion', but a matter of 'interpretation of the premises as mental models . . . and seeking counter-examples of the conclusion by trying to construct possible models of the premises', the procedure that he is describing is very similar to that of Beth's trees or semantic tableaux, and the concept of valid consequence that he employs is indeed the usual semantic concept.[20] The semantics of the connectives remain fixed for the logical form of the sentences and by their truth-functional truth conditions. In fact Johnson-Laird's analyses show (if one stands by the propositional reasoning) that the meaning of the connectives is not defined by their conceptual role, but by the semantic rules. That is because these semantic rules are more 'natural' than the syntactic rules of deduction which their use makes indispensable in the representation of natural reasoning. In this sense, there is a coincidence between 'formal' rules and 'natural rules'. But this does not imply that it is the natural rules (the construction of mental models) that fix the meaning of the logical constants. Nor does it show, contrary to what Johnson-Laird maintains, 'that it is possible to have valid reasoning without logic', because it is actually by virtue of the semantic rules of a theory of the truth of the form of (I)–(V) of § 2.2 that the propositional connectives receive their meaning, and that the inferences in which they figure are judged valid.

2.5.3 Harman on logical constants

While Johnson-Laird formulates rules for 'natural' propositional reasoning inspired by the semantic rules, Harman (1986a, 1986b) formulates rules inspired by the syntactic rules of deduction. According to him, the meanings of the logical constants are fixed by their conceptual roles in natural reasoning, but these roles themselves are not determined by the relevant logical implications. The difficulty arises from the fact that connectives that are logically equivalent or make the same contributions to the truth conditions of the sentences in which they figure, can have different meanings. Thus (to go back to an example already used in Chapter 1) 'p and q' and 'not ((not$p$) or (not$q$)), *although logically equivalent*, do not have the same meaning: their 'conceptual roles' in the psychology of an individual are not identical, since one can be affirmed without affirming the other. Like Johnson-Laird, Harman admits that the rules called 'rules of natural deduction' of the type of elimination rules and introduction rules of the connectives do not coincide with the role that these play in natural reasoning. Likewise the truth tables or the truth conditions of a theory of truth are not sufficient to ensure their meaning. The remedy consists, according to Harman, in defining *other* rules of 'natural' deduction by starting from a different concept of implication. This concept is not that of logical implication. It must correspond to the principles that govern natural reasoning, such as the following:

(a) *Logical implication principle*: the fact that the propositions which we acknow-
    ledge logically imply that p can be a reason for us to accept p.
(b) *Logical inconsistency principle*: logical inconsistencies must be avoided.
(c) *Logical closure principle*: our beliefs must 'be closed under logical implication',
    that is to say that if the propositions that we believe to be true imply others that
    we already do not believe, we must either actually acknowledge these latter or
    in fact revise our initial beliefs.
(d) *Clutter avoidance principle*: avoid cluttering your mind with trivialities.[21]

As will be noted, these principles, which are reminiscent of Grice's 'conversational maxims', are both logical principles *and* psychological principles: they are, if
this can be said, logical principles applied to psychology, or logical principles that
are equivalent *modulo* the constraints of natural reasoning, or those of what could
be called a logic of *beliefs* (cf. Chapter 13 below). In short, these are not principles of
the *validity* of reasoning but principles of the *acceptance* of reasoning. Logic can
only give us the first, and that is why Harman considers that it is not pertinent for
reasoning.

The pertinent notion of implication is that of *immediate implication*. According to
Harman, an immediate implication is an implication that is immediately obvious
to the person who perceives it. This is a psychological notion. Harman therefore
redefines the logical constants with this notion. For example, conjunction (C) and
disjunction (D) are given the following rules:

(conjunction) $C(p, q)$ immediately imply p
                 $C(p, q)$ immediately imply q
                 (p, q) immediately imply $C(p, q)$

(disjunction) p immediately implies $D(p, q)$
                 q immediately implies $D(p, q)$
                 $(p, \theta,$ implies $r)$ and $(q, \theta,$ implies $r)$ immediately
                     imply $D(p, q), \theta$ implies $r)$

Contrary to appearances, these rules are not equivalent to the introduction and
elimination rules of a corresponding system of natural deduction. In fact,
according to the rule of immediate implication for conjunction, for example, the
proposition

'not ((not p) or (not q))'

does not immediately imply

> 'p and q'

because it does not immediately imply p, not immediately q, and not immediately (p and q). The converse immediate implication is not valid, and consequently these two propositions are not 'immediately' equivalent.

Negation will be redefined in the same way. To the rule of natural deduction whereby anything can be inferred (*ex falso sequitur quodlibet*) from A and from −A, Harman prefers:

> (*negation*): not A is immediately inconsistent with A and is immediately implied by any collection of propositions that is immediately inconsistent with A.

Here again the rule is not equivalent to the rule of logical implication for negation because a logical contradiction cannot be an 'immediate' contradiction: often we do not immediately perceive the (logically) contradictory character of some of our beliefs (if God, who is logically omniscient, can, we can not). Harman does not give a rule for the conditional.

This theory calls for several comments. First, as a psychological notion, the notion of immediate implication remains ill-defined. By what criteria can an implication be immediately recognised? By the criteria of the measure of the degree of information, like those formulated in the preceding paragraph? But then one comes up against the problem that affects all theories of information: the information conveyed by a proposition is not absolute, but relative: it depends on other information that one has at one's command, and on 'general knowledge'. There is no reason to suppose that the same would not apply in a psychological theory of information for natural reasoning (the same comment obviously applies to Johnson-Laird's theory). One can ask oneself if Harman's ingenious attempt is not based on a confusion between (1) establishing the truth conditions of the sentences of a language, or the rules of deduction that govern them, and (2) giving a theory of the understanding of these sentences.

These are two distinct things, as I will also maintain in Chapter 6, even if they are closely linked. In the case of the connectives, it is one thing to give their meaning in terms of a theory of truth; it is another to say how they play certain psychological roles, or how they are understood by a real or ideal subject. Nevertheless, the two are not independent: a theory of truth enables us to explain what contribution the meaning of the connectives makes to the sentences in which they figure, that is to say to fix their meaning; it is on the basis of these meanings that the connectives then play a role in reasoning. In other words, 'conceptual role' is second, in the order of explanation, to semantic role, and not the reverse. That is why the order of dependence Harman proposes has to be reversed, as suggested in the previous paragraph (cf. also Chapters 11 and 12).

Finally, Harman's argument is based on the observation that a theory of truth would give an identical meaning to logically equivalent sentences like '(p and q)' and 'not ((not p) or (not q))', although their meaning is different. This, it will be noted, is the same difficulty as the one examined in the previous chapter (§ 1.2.3). But it is wrong to say that a theory of truth cannot represent this difference of meaning. In fact, a theory of truth assigns distinct clauses to these two sentences. For one, the truth condition is:

> 'p and q' is true if and only if p is true and q is true.

For the other, the truth condition is:

> 'not ((not p) or (not q))' is true if and only if it is not true that p is not true or that q is not true.

These are really distinct clauses, and this authorises us to say that a theory of truth is really in a position to embrace this difference of meaning and that in this sense it is not trivial. This suggests that Harman's notion of 'immediate implication' is not the primitive notion but that of the truth condition is. When does one recognise that an implication is 'immediate'? When one is in a position to recognise the *truth condition* of the sentences involved. It is therefore not the concept of immediate implication that explains the validity of the inferences, but the reverse. If this order of dependence is rejected, all means of really distinguishing between the *impression* (or the intuition, or the sentiment) that an inference is valid and its validity effective is lost. The first is a matter of psychology, the second is the logician's business, and to confuse them is to fall into a form of psychologism (moreover, one of Frege's arguments against psychologism, cf. §13.2, will have been recognised in this distinction). Here again (contrary to what Frege said) this does not imply that logic has *nothing* to do with psychology, because if what has come before is correct, the psychological theory of the understanding of propositional inferences rests on the logical theory of their truth conditions, and the concept of understanding an argument cannot be analysed independently of those of truth and validity: to recognise that an implication is immediate or psychologically 'natural' is to recognise that it is *valid*.[22]

I will conclude, therefore, that neither Johnson-Laird nor Harman succeed in showing that the meaning of the propositional connectives is solely and exclusively determined by their conceptual roles. The truth conditions play a much more important role in this determination of meaning than they accord them.

——— 3 ———

SUBJECT AND PREDICATE

3.1 The problem of the logical form of general sentences

In this chapter and the next, I will deal with the central part of contemporary logic, the theory of quantification. Here, I will analyse the logical and philosophical reasons that can be put forward for preferring the modern theory of quantification to the traditional theory of general inferences, and the notion of quantification will be examined *in statu nascendi*, as it were.

The logic of truth functions, as set out in the previous chapter, is based on a theory of the truth conditions of sentences, as has been seen. But these truth conditions cannot be described without at the same time describing the structure of the sentences, that is to say their *logical form*. Without determining the types of primitive elements that make up the parts of the sentences, it is not possible to establish the contributions that these elements make to their truth conditions. In other words, in propositional logic, semantics is based on syntax. The same is true of the theory of quantification, where the logical form of sentences must be such that it must make explicit the elements that systematically contribute to the truth or falsity of sentences. But logical form is not *grammatical form*: the elements of logical syntax are not necessarily the same as those of the syntax of the natural languages. Frege, the founder of the modern logic of quantification, has explicitly stated these two ideas, of the link between logical form and the truth conditions, and of the distinction between logical form and grammatical form.[1] Frege strongly emphasised the difference between his analysis of quantification and that of traditional logic. But it would be wrong to say that logical form in traditional logic is identified purely and simply with grammatical form. Nonetheless it remains true that logical form in it is always *more or less close* to grammatical form. The medieval theory of 'suppositions', for example, can be presented as an analysis of the truth conditions of general sentences, intended to establish the conditions of validity of inferences, based on the suppositions of terms. But it is doubtful whether this is a theory of truth conditions in the modern sense. *A fortiori* for medieval logicians, there was not an explicit connection between logical form or syntax and truth conditions.[2]

The contrast between the attitudes of traditional and modern ('post-Fregean') logicians from this point of view are often presented as originating in the two different conceptions of logic and its relationship to language: the 'constructionist' conception and the 'naturalist' conception. According to the 'constructionist' conception, the aim of logic is to formalise deductive inferences, and natural languages and the traditional grammatical categories are unsuited to this task. The syntax of natural languages therefore has to be reformed and an artificial language suited to the analysis of deductive reasoning constructed. According to the naturalist conception too, the aim of logic is to provide a theory of deductive reasoning. But this theory is not 'formal' in the same sense as that favoured by constructionism. Natural languages implicitly contain a logical syntax, which can be useful for the purposes of the logician and which for that reason does not need to be reformed, but at the very most systematised.[3] This way of presenting the constructionism/naturalism conflict is probably no more accurate, historically speaking, than the pompous way that Frege is sometimes presented as the author of a Galilean revolution in logic. What is more this conflict is itself probably largely a question of degree: some authors stress the constructionist aspect of their doctrines more strongly than others, others the naturalist aspect, and the two can coexist.[4] In what follows, I will leave this sort of historical evaluation to one side, and set out to criticise the views of one author, Sommers, who has presented the constructionism/naturalism conflict as a sort of Titanic struggle, and who seeks to defend the naturalist programme by reinstating the traditional analysis of propositions in terms of subjects and predicates.[5] I will try to show that not only are the conflicts between modern and traditional logic not in the precise area that Sommers thinks, but also that he has not given good reasons for preferring traditional to post-Fregean analysis, in the version that he recommends.

3.2 Subject and predicate in traditional logic

3.2.1 Aristotle before and after the fall

In traditional logic (Aristotelian and medieval), the 'logical form' of propositions is the *subject-predicate* form. To say that this is the general form of propositions means that this is the form taken by the simple propositions, of which complex propositions are composed. A simple proposition, in its role as *logos apophantikos*, that is to say in so far as it is capable of truth or falsity, is for Aristotle a proposition that says something about something. The thing about which something is said is the *subject*, and the thing that is said is the *predicate*. The predication relation is expressed in Aristotle by the expressions '*B* belongs to *A*' or '*B* is said of *A*'.[6] Subject and predicate are the *terms* of the propositions, which can only contain these two categories of terms. The terms have a quality (they can be affirmed or denied) and a quantity (they can be universal or particular). Syllogistics studies the possible combinations of propositions and the valid inferences to which they give rise. It is a well-known fact that it has no place, within the combination of types of terms, for singular propositions, that is to say for propositions that predicate a certain attribute of an individual, or have as their grammatical subject a proper name or an expression purported to denote an individual and as predicate any verb or any name whatsoever, such as 'Socrates is mortal'. Syllogistics is principally concerned with *general* terms. However, this does not mean that Aristotle did not know the difference between singular propositions and general propositions, such as 'All men are mortal' or 'Some man is mortal'. On the contrary, in a famous passage in *Peri Hermeneias*, he notes an essential difference between the logical behaviour of singular terms such as 'Socrates' and quantified expressions such as 'Some man': whereas by prefixing the latter with the sign of negation, contrary propositions, such as 'Some man is not mortal', can be obtained, it is impossible to do the same with singular propositions, because a singular term cannot be negated. If a predicate term such as 'man' can be negated in such a way as to obtain a negative term like 'non-man', this has not the meaning of denying a singular term like 'Socrates' in such a way as to obtain a negative singular term like 'non-Socrates'. Proper names and singular terms in general denote substances (primary) or individuals, and as Aristotle says, substances 'have no contraries'.

Aristotle therefore recognised what in contemporary terminology is called 'the asymmetry of the subject and predicate with respect to negation'. But according to Geach, instead of integrating this fact in his doctrine of terms, he abandoned it:

> He lost the Platonic insight that any predicative proposition splits up into two logically heterogeneous parts; instead , he treats predication as an attachment of one term (*horos*) to another term, whereas the *rhema* was regarded as essentially predicative, 'always a sign of what is said of something else', it is impossible in the new doctrine for any term to be essentially predicative; on the contrary, any term that occurs in a proposition predicatively may be made into the subject-term of another predication. I shall call this 'Aristotle's thesis of interchangeability'; his adoption of it marks a transition from the original name and predicable theory to a *two-term* theory. Aristotle's going over to the two-term theory was a disaster, comparable only to the Fall of Adam.[9]

In syllogistics, in fact, for a term occupying the role of predicate in a categorical premise to be able to occupy the role of the 'middle term' in another premise, it is essential that this term should be able to figure as subject in this other premise, in other words that the logical terms of a proposition should be able to exchange their roles. Thus no term is either definitively subject or definitively predicate, and in the 'logical syntax' of syllogistics there is only one category of expressions, terms that can be modified by expressions of quality (affirmation or negation) and of quantity (quantifiers). Of course, from the semantical point of view, the terms can be dependent on such and such 'categories' in the Aristotelian sense of that notion. It is in this sense that the expressions of generality ('all' and 'some') can be called 'syncategorematic', since they are indifferent to the distinctions of categories. But the logical form that Aristotle needed is confined to the existence of two terms.[10]

3.2.2 The 'wild quantity' of singular propositions

If traditional logic treats the link between subject and predicate as symmetric, how does it account for singular propositions such as 'Socrates is mortal'? There are few suggestions in Aristotle himself, but his work does contain syllogisms of the type:

> Pittacos is good
> Pittacos is wise
> therefore Some wise man is a good man.

Remember that for a syllogism to be valid, at least one premise has to be universal. In order to justify the above syllogism, it must be noted that 'Pittacos is P' means that 'Every Pittacos is P', and that 'Pittacos is R', means that 'Some Pittacos is R'. An *implicit quantity* is therefore being assigned to the premises, and by transforming the syllogism in this way, it becomes valid:

> Every Pittacos is good
> Some Pittacos is wise
> therefore Some wise man is a good man.

(Reversing the quantity of the premises would be equally suitable.)[11]

But the most explicit analysis of singular propositions as *quantified* propositions has been given by Leibniz. For him, every proposition of the form 'Socrates is mortal' has always to be reducible to the expression of a quantity:

> 'Some (every) Socrates is mortal.'[12]

Singular propositions are implicit general propositions, indifferently quantified, and interpreted, according to the case, as particular propositions. This is what Sommers calls 'the doctrine of the indifferent or wild quantity'.[13]

It is interesting to see what the logical behaviour of singular propositions is in relation to negation in this analysis. The negation of 'Socrates is mortal' is not

(1) Socrates is not mortal

but

(1a) Some Socrates is not mortal

or

(1b) No Socrates is mortal

depending on whether 'Socrates is mortal' is interpreted as 'Some Socrates is mortal' or as 'Every Socrates is mortal' respectively, that is to say as *contrary negation* and *contradictory negation* of (1a) and (1b) respectively. But as these two sentences are equivalent by virtue of the doctrine of the wild quantity, (1a) and (1b) are also equivalent, and the distinction between contrary negation and contradictory negation vanishes in the case of singular propositions. In other words, in traditional logic everything actually proceeds as if the specific logical form of singular propositions were recognised, but nevertheless treated as if derived in relation to that of general propositions since it is explained by the logical form of these latter. The reverse happens in modern logic.

3.3 Subject and predicate in modern logic

3.3.1 The Fregean atomicity postulate

In post-Fregean modern logic, the analysis of the logical form of singular propositions is understood as derived from singular propositions of subject-predicate form such as 'Socrates is mortal'. I will only give the broad outlines of Frege's famous analysis here.[14]

In such sentences, Frege analyses the subject as the expression of a *argument-place*, and the predicate as the expression of a *function*. One begins by *emptying* the place occupied by the singular term 'Socrates' in order to obtain the predicate that is the expression of the function

'( ) is mortal'

which, according to contemporary analysis, can be treated as the attachment of a free variable to a predicate letter

x is mortal

The expression then becomes true or false if a proper name or a constant is substituted for this variable:

a is mortal

or if one links the variable by means of a quantifier, conceived by Frege as a second-degree function taking the first-degree function '( ) is mortal' as argument:

$(\exists x)$ (x is mortal)
$(\forall x)$ (x is mortal).[15]

An acknowledged advantage of this analysis over traditional logic is that it makes it possible to take account of sentences where two or more quantifiers figure (multiple quantification), such as 'Everyone envies someone'. The procedure of analysis, as reconstructed by Dummett, is as follows:

1. Start with a singular sentence with a proper name as subject and remove this proper name. This gives the predicate.
2. Combine the predicate with a sign of generality. This gives a sentence.
3. Start again by removing another proper name from the sentence. This gives another predicate.
4. Combine this new predicate with another sign of generality. This gives a general sentence with multiple quantification.

Here is an example:

(1) Diana envies Sarah (a singular atomic sentence).

(2) Diana envies y (one-place predicate).

(3) $(\exists y)$ (Diana envies y) (sentence with one quantifier).

(4) $(\exists y)$ (x envies y) (two-place predicate).

(5) $(\forall x)(\exists y)(x$ envies $y)$ (sentence with two quantifiers).[16]

The fundamental principle of modern quantification analysis is therefore that there is on the one hand a difference of *type* or of category between subject and predicate, a difference that is shown in primitive propositions with elementary structure, and the other propositions, on the other hand. In other words, for modern logic, a subject-predicate proposition is a proposition that has the basic structure of a singular sentence like

> $Fa.$

According to Sommers a proposition like this can be called an 'atomic proposition', and the basic principle of Fregean and post-Fregean logic is that *there are atomic propositions*. Let us call this the *Fregean atomicity postulate (FAP)*.

Now what justifies the FAP? The principal argument that modern logicians give to justify the difference of syntaxic category between subject and predicate is precisely the Aristotelian argument of *categories*, taken up by Geach and Strawson, of the asymmetry of the subject and predicate in relation to negation: while the predicates can be negated, the subjects cannot. If it is meaningful to negate a predicate, it is meaningless to negate a subject *in an atomic proposition*, that is to say a proposition where a proper name or a singular term occupies the logical role of subject. The notion of a negative subject is a nonsense.[17]

It can be said that this particularity originates in a specific feature of modern logic compared with traditional logic: in modern logic negation is an operator that is attached to the whole of the proposition, while in traditional logic the negation can be attached to the predicate, in such a way as to produce the contrary predicate. In modern logic there is no distinction between contrary negation and contradictory negation. The negation of

> Fa

is

> $-Fa.$

But there is no more sense in interpreting this in the sense of

> $(-a)F$

than in the sense of

> $(-F)a.$[18]

3.3.2 Ramsey's objection

Ramsey (1925) has maintained that the Fregean distinction (or, in this case, the Russellian) between subject and predicate is unjustified. If one accepts the idea, present in Frege – that in a sentence of the form *S is P* (atomic), the subject is *what the predication bears on*, and the predicate *what is predicated* of the subject – why not rather adopt the inverse interpretation whereby the predicate is what the proposition bears on, and the subject is what is attributed to the predicate? How can one choose between the two readings (for a sentence and its negation respectively):

(A) Socrates (is wise)	(B) Socrates (is not wise)
(A') (Socrates is) wise	(B') (Socrates is not) wise

where it is respectively the wisdom (the non-wisdom) that is attributed to Socrates and the Socrateity (the non-Socrateity) that is attributed to wisdom? Why should it be 'more natural' to chose the first interpretation than the second?[19] The usual argument given by Fregeans (Geach, Strawson, Dummett) consists of pointing out again that the proper name 'Socrates' cannot be negated, and that in the event non-Socrateity is a nonsense.[20] But here Sommers points out that this reply is not pertinent for the couple of contradictory propositions (A')–(B') because, in the hypothesis concerned, these sentences bear not on Socrates, like (A) and (B), but on wisdom, and in the one case says solely that Socrates possesses it, and in the other, that he does not possess it.[21]

However, the Fregean still has an answer to this. From his point of view, it is perfectly possible to decompose a proposition in two different ways. The relevant distinction here is the one suggested by Dummett, when he distinguishes the *analysis* of a thought from its *decomposition*. The analysis of a thought is the process that makes it possible to arrive at the ultimate *constituents* of the thought, that is to say to determine how the meaning of the parts determines the meaning of the whole. This process can be compared to the process of chemical analysis molecule by molecule (a metaphor that Frege himself uses). Decomposition is the process whereby, for one purpose or another, various sentences endowed with different structures are singled out in the sentence concerned. It establishes the *components* related to the purpose under consideration (to account for certain inferential connections of the sentence, for example). The fact that 'Socrates is wise' could be decomposed into various components, as Ramsey and later Sommers note, does not imply that the analysis of that sentence is not unique and does not reveal two final constituents, the subject and the predicate. The components are solely related to the way in which we *grasp* the meaning of the sentence. The constituents are what permit us to determine its true structure. According to this, when (A') is interpreted as saying that wisdom is a characteristic of Socrates, what is attributed to Socrates is not wisdom but the property (property of property, or second degree property) of *being a characteristic of Socrates*. There is nothing to stop us decomposing the thought expressed by (A) as (A'). But (A') keeps the same analysis, in subject and predicate.[22]

3.4 Aristotle and Leibniz avenged on Frege?

3.4.1 Sommers's neo-naturalist programme

In his book, *The Logic of Natural Language* (1982) Sommers defends a version of the naturalist programme in logic: logic must model its syntax on the syntax of natural languages, and logical analysis must reveal the implicit logical form of the natural languages. It follows that modern post-Fregean logic, which prescribes the constructionist attitude, that is to say the abandonment of the grammatical form in favour of artificial languages based on the theory of quantification, must be rejected. A return to traditional logic therefore becomes necessary. Sommers is not the only author to adopt the naturalist thesis, and the adoption of this thesis does not always imply the rejection of Fregean logic. For example, the linguistic school of 'generative semantics', represented by authors such as Lakoff and McCawley, who seek to explain the relationship between syntax and semantics by projecting the structure of the sentences of a natural language on to their (notably quantificational) 'logical forms' so as to reveal the 'natural logic' of these languages, can also be said to be presenting a version of naturalism.[23] Sommers's naturalism is more radical. It claims to break definitively with modern Fregean logic and restore the traditional analysis of logical syntax, as outlined in § 2 above. To achieve this programme, Sommers proceeds in two stages.

First, he reinstates the Aristotelian doctrine of the two terms, adopts the traditional analysis of the logic of general sentences, that of the 'wild quantity' of singular propositions according to Leibniz, and consequently claims to reject the FAP.

Secondly, on these bases, he formulates a logic of terms distinct from traditional and scholastic Aristotelian logic, but which incorporates its main elements, and from there seeks to show that most of the analyses that are regarded as the jewels in the crown of modern logic (those of pronominal reference, anaphora, identity and existence) are at once equalled and surpassed by those of a comprehensive logic of terms.

In what follows, I will only be concerned with the first part of this counter-revolutionary programme. The whole of Sommers's argument rests on the initial hypothesis (developed in § 1 and 2 above) that contemporary logic presupposes FAP, whereas traditional logic (in Sommers's version) does not presuppose it. But is this argument correct?

3.4.2 Can the atomicity postulate be dispensed with?

The first objection that can be made to Sommers is that the doctrine of the 'wild quantity' of singular propositions that he borrows from Leibniz gives us no reason to stop seeing a justified distinction between general propositions and singular propositions. In modern logic, it is the distinction between the logical form of the two types of propositions that makes it possible to account for the invalidity of inferences like

(A) Every man is vain or wise
        therefore Every man is vain or every man is wise

in relation to the validity of inferences like

(B) Socrates is vain or wise
        therefore Socrates is vain or Socrates is wise.

But the theory of the neutral quantity also allows us to make inferences of type (B) valid:

(B′) Some Socrates is vain or wise
        therefore Some Socrates is vain or some Socrates is wise.[24]

It is this type of argument that allows Sommers to say that traditional logic is not less good than modern logic. Nevertheless it will be noticed that he has had to choose the specific quantity in (B′) rather than the general quantity, which seems a little *ad hoc*. But this equal degree of success on the part of the two analyses does not show that one is better than the other, nor that there is a real distinction between the way that each analysis suggests treating the asymmetry between singular propositions and general propositions. All that this shows is that the atomicity postulate can apparently be dispensed with, since traditional logic rejects FAP and modern logic accepts it. But if this latter statement is false, so too is the former. But it is false.

It is not accurate on the one hand (and Sommers himself acknowledges this, p. 61) to say that *all* modern logic allows FAP. It is possible to formulate the logic of quantifiers and dispense with the variables of quantification, either by using algebraic logic, or by resorting to a form of combinatory logic, or both. In these extensionally equivalent versions of the theory of quantification, the bound variables disappear in favour of other terms that play the same role, and consequently the logic is no longer formulated on the basis of a syntax founded on atomic propositions.[25] So why does Sommers think that his version of a logic without FAP is the only correct one?

On the other hand it is not true that the Fregean presentation of the truth conditions of atomic sentences (the one given in §2.2.2 above) is the only one possible. In quantification theory as Tarski has formulated it (cf. §4.1), the primitive notion is not of a proper name or constant that is substituted in a predicate expression in the empty place of that expression in order to produce a true or false atomic proposition. It is of an open *sentence* (or *proposition*) *satisfied* by an *object* or by a sequence of objects. In other words, Tarski, instead of invoking *expressions* of a language capable, once they are substituted in the appropriate places, of making sentences true or false, invokes the objects themselves which satisfy the open sentences, or which apply to the predicates. This procedure does not presuppose FAP.

However, this last objection is not convincing. Sommers could justifiably reply that the difference between *'substituting a proper name in an expression of a concept'* (Frege) and *'assigning an object to an open sentence'* (Tarski) is minimal, because in each case the truth conditions of the sentence concerned will be explained by the idea whereby a certain *object of quantification* is that to which a predicate *applies*. In other words, if there are no Fregean proper names in the Tarskian version, this syntactic difference fades away at the level of the semantics which remain the same, and in this sense FAP is maintained in the two versions.[26] Nevertheless, does Sommers's theory of general sentences resort to a different *semantics*? Sommers also explains the truth conditions of particular sentences by invoking the idea of an object something of which is true, by means of this sort of clause.

(Q) 'Something is *P*' is true if and only if something which is *P* is thereby said to be *P*.[27]

According to this analysis, the quantifier 'Something' is referential in a 'primitive' way, that is to say in a way that cannot be explained in other terms. Consequently, Sommers, like modern logical analysis, actually does invoke the idea of *singular reference* to explain the truth of quantified sentences and thereby acknowledges a version of FAP. It could obviously be said here that the fact that 'Some' is referential does not in itself show that traditional logical analysis acknowledges the concept of *singular* reference, because it is precisely one of the basic differences between this traditional analysis and modern analysis that quantifiers like 'some' are not referential *in the same sense as proper names are*. According to Sommers, the difference between modern logical analysis and his own is that the former determines the reference of the subject independently of that of the predicate, while the latter determines it through the predicate (whence the mention above of 'which is *P*'). But Sommers himself acknowledges here that clause (Q) explains the truth of the quantified sentence by the reference that is made to something that is *P*, that is to say to one or several *objects*, taken individually, to which '*P*' applies.[28] The FAP is therefore actually presupposed. But it is only presupposed in its semantic version, the one which, as we have seen, Frege and Tarski hold in common. Sommers thinks that by modifying the logical syntax and bringing it back to the traditional logical form, he has abandoned the FAP. He has not abandoned it, because the FAP is the thesis whereby, in an atomic proposition, the weight of the reference bears on the subject of the proposition.[29] Must we conclude from this that traditional logic is secretly Fregean, since it acknowledges the FAP? Yes, to the extent to which traditional logic recognised with Aristotle (before the fall) that the subject of a singular proposition was the reference-bearer. But this idea has actually been lost or at least relegated to second place, as Geach says, with the adoption of the doctrine of the two terms.

I will therefore conclude that Sommers's argument for abandoning the FAP, because it is not presupposed by traditional logic, is invalid. An analysis of the truth conditions of general sentences must, in one way or another, rest on this principle, whether it is inspired by modern or traditional logic. This does not imply that we might not have other reasons for rejecting the FAP (such as those provided by the advocates of algebraic logic). But those Sommers gives are not sufficient.[30]

3.4.3 Naturalism and constructionism reconciled

All this has some interesting consequences, which concern the conflict between naturalism and constructionism, and more generally, the relationship between logic, language and psychology. The first derives from the observation just made that *in one sense* post-Fregean logic makes use of the ideas of traditional logic. The 'revolutionary' aspect of modern logic suffers thereby. It is not an innovation.[31] This should be good rather than bad news for everyone who, like Sommers, wants to reinstate traditional analyses in logic.

The second consequence is that the contrast between naturalism and constructionism is much less clear-cut than it appears. If we construct our logic *against* natural language, as Frege recommended, we must reject the usual grammar and the naturalist attitude. But the fact that notions like those of singular reference are incorporated both in a 'constructionist' logic and a 'naturalist' logic shows that logic is not a pure creation in relation to ordinary language, and defined totally independently of it. Frege said this himself. On the one hand, 'one can no more draw logic from language than one can learn one's mother tongue from the mouth of a child'. On the other hand, logic needs language in order to define its syntactic or semantic categories. Obviously this does not mean that it has to draw *all* its structures from ordinary language. Constructionism and naturalism are extreme attitudes that no logician has perhaps really adopted to the exclusion of either.[32]

The third consequence concerns the alleged link between the naturalism/constructionism conflict and the psychologism/anti-psychologism conflict. Sommers sees a virtue of his analyses in the fact that, contrary to Frege, who rejected any relationship between logic and psychology, his 'naturalist' approach to logic can 'claim a psychological veracity which Frege had abjured'.[33] His argument seems to be as follows: (1) a logic based on a 'natural syntax' can claim a psychological plausibility; (2) a logic based on an 'ideal' syntax cannot claim this; (3) consequently, an ideal syntax has no psychological plausibility. But it does not follow, from the fact that one assigns to logic the construction of an ideal syntax detached from natural syntax and from psychology, that the structures of this ideal syntax have no psychological plausibility. Sommers, through his criticism of Fregean syntax, is aiming at the thesis inspired by Chomsky, whereby the grammatical transformations that govern the 'deep structure' of the sentences of a natural language have a 'psychological reality'. According to Sommers, logic is one part of the 'cognitive psychology'. But how is it more so in its naturalist version than in its constructionist version? Premise (2) of Sommers's argument has to be rejected: an ideal logical syntax can have a psychological veracity (for example, if the formulas of a 'language of thought' had a syntactic structure close to that of logical syntax).[34] I have already defended (§ 2.5) and will defend again (Chapter 13) the idea that the falseness of the psychologist thesis did not imply that logic was not relevant for psychology. This relevance is no more inscribed in the logical structures of the modern theory of quantification than it is in that of traditional logic.

—— 4 ——

VARIETIES OF QUANTIFICATION

4.1 The place of the theory of quantification

4.1.1 Its historical place

The theory of quantification occupies a central place within modern logic. In this system, which is very different from those that logicians had previously at their disposal, Frege and Russell, its main inventors, showed that the largest part of classical mathematics could be represented. After the failure of logicism, quantification theory remained the system (or the family of systems) within which the problem of the foundations of mathematics was posed. From the historical point of view, however, the importance of quantification theory has not been immediately perceived. It is not true, for instance, to say, with Dummett,[1] that one can find in Frege's work *all* the basic notions of what we call today quantification theory. As Van Heijenoort pointed out, Frege and Russell subscribed to the thesis of 'logic as a language', which implies, among other things, that metasystematic considerations are excluded from logic: there is no language within which one can talk about logic, since logic *is* the (ideal) language which expresses the whole universe.[2] Contrariwise, our present understanding of quantificational logic depends very much upon its metatheoretical properties (see Chapter 10). Moreover Frege and Russell did not care very much about the distinction between first-order logic (with quantification over individuals) and second-order logic (with quantification over properties of individuals) or higher-order logic.[3] Because of their conception of a *Logica Magna* as a universal language, Frege and Russell did not care either about the distinction between a syntactical and a semantical approach to logical systems, as it has been understood since Tarski. Although they provided analyses about the meaning of their logical symbols, their doctrines about meaning and reference are not systematically articulated within a *theory* of truth conceived as a set of axioms. As many commentators have remarked, they have a tendency to consider that semantical questions (in the general sense of doctrines about the meaning and use of signs) have to be settled after syntactical ones. This point of view is not surprising, given Frege and Russell's search after an ideal language, built according to the criteria of an ideal syntax.[4] Finally, because they give little room to metatheoretical considerations, Frege and Russell ignore the difference between syntax and semantics from the point of view of the distinction between proof-theory and model theory. The fact that they give an exclusively axiomatic treatment of logic implies that they privilege the syntactical or proof-theoretical concept of derivability or of deduction. For Frege, axioms are not hypotheses or assumptions that one could withdraw at will, but immutable and necessary truths.[5] This is another consequence of the point of view according to which logic is a language and not a calculus, and of the divorce which existed at that time between the set-theoretical approach, represented by Schröder's school (to which belonged Peirce, Löwenheim and Skolem) and the axiomatic approach of Frege, Peano and Russell.[6]

Quantification theory came to be isolated as a special part of logic during the 1920s when certain results were obtained. Löwenheim and Skolem, starting from the 'semantical' point of view, according to which the main notions in logic are those of truth, validity and satisfiability of formulas within certain 'domains', proved the theorem that bears their name, and which can be formulated in the following way:

> Every formula of first order quantification theory, if it is satisfiable (has a model), is satisfiable in a denumerable domain (has a denumerable model).[7]
> (see below § 11.1.3)

Hilbert and his school, starting from the proof-theoretical point of view, tried to determine whether arithmetic, or any theory that can express it, is consistent. Dealing with this problem, they formulated the question whether, for any formula of quantification theory, this formula is decidable, i.e. can be established as a theorem or not (the so-called 'Entscheidungsproblem' or 'decision problem'). Hilbert's programme was considered as unrealisable when Gödel produced in 1931 his famous proof of the incompleteness of a system (the system of *Principia Mathematica*) in which elementary arithmetic can be formalised: one cannot, within such a system, prove the consistency of arithmetic. These famous 'metamathematical' results were not only, as it often said, negative. In 1930 Gödel had proved the completeness of (first-order) quantification theory, a property that allows us to relate proof theory to model theory. As early as 1929, Jacques Herbrand, who worked within the Hilbertian framework, had given a result ('Herbrand's theorem') which has important affinities with the Löwenheim–Skolem theorem and with Gödel's completeness theorem, and which Bernays called the 'central result' of quantification theory.[8]

During the 1930s, then, the specificity of quantification theory within logic was better understood. Because of its remarkable formal properties, it began to emerge as the central system of logic, and as the basic tool for the logician. I shall come back later (Chapter 11) to the question whether and why this centrality and the purported identification of 'logic' with quantification are justified.

4.1.2 Its conceptual place

Quantification theory equally owes its central place to its conceptual structure, to the nature and range of its main concepts. From this point of view, Frege was perfectly aware of the importance of the revisions that his own system implied for logic and philosophy. The very existence of this system showed that Kant's assertion that logic had been a completed science since Aristotle was, to a large extent, false. It also allowed him to question the validity of a number of philosophical theses, in particular about the notions of existence, of numbers, about the nature of concepts, and about the general relationship between logic and philosophy. In this sense, Dummett is right to insist that Frege introduced a kind of Copernican revolution in philosophy, by putting the philosophy of language and logic in the place of a primary philosophy, and that the discovery of the modern concept of quantification has been the main instrument of this change of perspective.[9] Just as the logician is justified in considering this theory as central in view of its expressive powers and of its formal properties, the philosopher is equally justified in considering it as central for the enterprise of a 'philosophical logic' or of a 'philosophical grammar', and for the philosophy of language in general. Through the study of quantification theory, a number of philosophical notions can be studied, such as the notions of reference, of existence, of identity, of predication, or of truth. As I remarked above (in the Introduction), elementary predicate logic has more obvious philosophical implications than other logical theories, and it signals itself, as Quine says, 'by its extraordinary combination of deepness and simplicity, of elegance and utility',[10] or, as Strawson says, the richness of its fundamental notions for the analysis of the conceptual structures of natural thoughts and judgements.[11] This richness, however, does not imply that quantification theory suffices for every philosophical purpose. It may also well be that the importance of the questions of philosophical grammar has been exaggerated within contemporary philosophy. Moreover is quantification theory so 'simple'? Is the very idea of quantification so simple? I would like to show here that the structures of modern quantification theory are not such that there is only one single possible notion of quantification in logic, and that there is, rather, a variety of interpretations of what quantification is, especially when one comes to its implications for the semantics of natural languages and for ontology. In other words these implications may be less simple than is often suggested.

4.2 Syntax and semantics of classical quantification

4.2.1 Tarskian definitions of truth for a quantificational language

Just as the semantics of a propositional language can be established by giving the truth conditions of its sentences under the form of a truth definition, a truth definition can be given for a quantificational language, by following the paradigm of Tarski's truth definition for formal languages.[12] This will allow us to introduce some concepts that will be discussed further in the following chapter. I shall here be exceedingly sketchy and shall pass over many details which should be given to present fully the workings of such a definition. (For fuller accounts the reader is referred to the items quoted in the bibliography.)

In the first place, the syntax of the language (let us call it 'Q') must be specified. Let us suppose that Q is made up of the following expressions:

(I) Variables: x_1, x_2.
(II) Predicates: Fx_1, $Rx_1 x_2$.
(III) Quantifiers: $\forall$, $\exists$.
(IV) Connectives: $-$, &.

(The expressions 'Fx_1' and '$Rx_1 x_2$' are formed out of predicate symbols ('F', 'R') and variables ('x_1', 'x_2'). We shall treat them as 'open sentences', that is sentences where variables are free or unbound by a quantifier, by contrast with closed sentences, such as '$(\exists x_1) Fx_1$', where all the occurrences of variables are bound.)

Now we want to establish the truth conditions of the sentences of Q formed out of these expressions. For this we need a language other than the language Q, a *metalanguage* with respect to which Q is the *object language*. The metalanguage (let us call it 'ML') will enable us to refer to the expressions of Q. We do this by overlining these expressions. For instance

$$\overline{Fx_1}, \; \overline{(\exists x_1) Fx_1}$$

are names of the respective expression and sentence of Q. The prospect is to define truth (or 'true') for Q, or to give a 'truth definition'. As we shall see in the next chapter, Tarski imposes on such a truth definition the following 'material adequacy condition':

(T) s is true (in Q) if and only if p

(where s is a place-holder for a name of a sentence of Q, and p is either the named sentence or a translation of it in ML; we shall also abbreviate 'if and only if' by 'iff'). We have seen in § 2.2 how the truth conditions are established according to this mould in the propositional case. Here we need to define the truth of quantified sentences. For this we cannot directly speak in terms of truth, since expressions like 'Fx_1' are not, like sentences such as 'p & q', made up of sentences, nor are they true or false by virtue of the truth or falsity of their parts. We shall speak instead of individuals *satisfying* predicates, and shall set first the conditions of *satisfaction* of predicates before giving the satisfaction conditions of sentences.

In the usual terminology, it is said that quantifiers, and variables, range over *domains*, possibly infinite, of individuals. Let us suppose that in Q they range over a finite, and very small domain of three individuals: Paul, George and Ringo. To explain how these individuals can satisfy a predicate Fx_1 meaning 'used to be a Beatle', we need to suppose that they can be chosen from various possible ways of listing them, or lists. There will be 3^3, i.e. 27 such possible lists of three individuals, from those where the same individual occupies the three places like:

(1) Paul, Paul, Paul;   (2) George, George, George;   (3) Ringo, Ringo, Ringo

to those where only two individuals are present such as:

> (4) Paul, Paul, Ringo;   (5) Paul, Ringo, Paul;   (6) Ringo, Paul, Paul;
> etc.

and to those where there are various combinations of non-repeated items:

> (8) George, Paul, Ringo;   (9) Ringo, George, Paul;   (10) Paul, George,
> Ringo; etc.

The lists are distinct from one another through the possible order and identity of the items. A list is said to satisfy a predicate if the item chosen in the list has the property expressed by the predicate. To choose the individuals, we stipulate that the subscript of each variable indicates which item is to be picked up in the list, and we must specify in which list the individual is to be picked up. For instance

> List 9 $(\overline{x_2})$

says that George is the individual in question. So we shall say in general when a given individual from a given list satisfies the predicate, thus:

> (i) List n satisfies $\overline{Fx_1}$ iff List $\overline{n(x_1)}$ used to be a Beatle

and similarly for the two-place predicate $\overline{Rx_1 x_2}$ (meaning, say, 'played guitar with')

> (ii) List n satisfies $\overline{Rx_1 x_2}$ iff List $\overline{n(x_1)}$ played guitar with List $\overline{n(x_2)}$

For instance, List 8 and List 10 satisfy $\overline{Rx_1 x_2}$, but List 6 and List 9 do not (George played guitar with Paul, and Paul played guitar with George, but Ringo, a drummer, did not play guitar with either of them).

One defines also satisfaction conditions (which therefore are *not* truth conditions) for sentences with propositional connectives:

> (iii) List n satisfies $\overline{-A}$ iff List n does not satisfy $\overline{A}$.
> (iv) List n satisfies $\overline{A \& B}$ iff List n satisfies $\overline{A}$ and List n satisfies $\overline{B}$.

Things are more complex for the satisfaction of quantified sentences. The condition for existential sentences is the following:

> (v) List n satisfies $\overline{(\exists x_i)\phi x_i}$ iff some List n' differing from List n at, at most, the ith place satisfies $\overline{\phi x_i}$

(where the is and ϕs mean that we consider any subscript and predicate).

For such a condition to hold, it is sufficient that some list has in its ith place an individual satisfying the predicate. For instance if we have a sentence '$(\exists x_1)(Fx_1)$', and if we suppose that Ringo never joined the Beatles, then List 8, but not List 9, satisfies the *predicate*; but this does not prevent us from saying that all the lists other than List 8 satisfy the *sentence*, since its enough for this that at least one list satisfies the predicate. The reason why we say that List n' differs from List n at *at most* the ith place place is that we want to allow that List n satisfies the predicate.

Now the condition for universally quantified sentences is:

(vi) List n satisfies $\overline{(\forall x_i)\phi x_i}$ iff every List n' differing from List n at at most the ith place satisfies $\overline{\phi x_i}$.

The lists are such that every item appears in each place in the list; so a given list satisfies the sentence when every relevant list satisfies the predicate in the sentence.

To define satisfaction for Q in full generality, we would need to use variables ranging over sentences and predicates of Q. Let us say that 'θ' is such a variable for any sentence or predicate of Q. *Truth* is then defined in terms of satisfaction, as the satisfaction of a sentence by every list:

θ is true (in Q) iff every list satisfies (in Q) θ

and a sentence θ is false if no list satisfies it. The apparatus of lists, however, is only a convenient shorthand for introducing Tarski's style of truth definitions, and Q is a very simple language. A real Tarskian definition of truth for a standard quantificational language will deal with predicates with larger, possibly infinite, domains. For this, Tarski introduced other items than lists, *sequences*, which are infinite lists, and a more complex apparatus, which I shall not provide here. It is nevertheless possible to introduce Tarski's basic ideas without the apparatus of lists, sequences and indexed variables, by using the notion of an *assignment* of an individual to a variable.[13]

We shall suppose this time that we have a language Q' with a vocabulary of variables ('x', 'y', etc.), of names ('a', 'b', etc.), of predicate-letters ('F', 'G', etc.), of connectives ('&', '$\vee$', '$\rightarrow$' and '$-$') and of quantifiers ('$\forall$' and '$\exists$'). We shall designate by the letters 'ϕ' or 'ψ' either open or closed sentences.

Now to assign an individual to a variable is to treat it temporarily as a name of the individual, which we note:

x/α (the assignment of the individual α to the variable x).

As above, we shall overline the terms of the object language to which we refer and shall say that the denotation of a name a is α (a denotes α for whatever assignment of individuals to variables). The denotation of a variable x under an assignment s will be $s[x]$. We shall say that an assignment x/α satisfies a predicate (or open sentence) Fx if and only if $F(x/\alpha)[x]$, that is if Fa.

A sentence without variables can be considered as true if there is no assignment, or if it is satisfied, so to say, by the *null assignment* $\varnothing$ (so $\varnothing$ satisfies Pa iff Pa). To deal with sentences such as $(\exists x)Fx$ we shall need to suppose that the null assignment can be extended. $s(x/\alpha)$ will be the assignment which results from extending s in order to assign α to x; and we say that $(\exists x)Fx$ is true iff $s(x/\alpha)$ satisfies Fx. Given that both variables and names can be treated as terms t_i, one can thus analyse the satisfaction conditions of the expressions of Q':

(1) s satisfies $\overline{P(t_1, \ldots, t_n)}$ iff $P(s[t_1], \ldots, s[t_n])$

(2) s satisfies $\overline{-\psi}$ iff s does not satisfy $\overline{\psi}$

(3) s satisfies $\overline{\phi \,\&\, \psi}$ iff s satisfies $\overline{\phi}$ and s satisfies $\overline{\psi}$

(4) s satisfies $\overline{\phi \vee \psi}$ iff s satisfies $\overline{\phi}$ or s satisfies ψ

(5) s satisfies $\overline{\phi \rightarrow \psi}$ iff if s satisfies $\overline{\phi}$ then s satisfies $\overline{\psi}$

(6) s satisfies $\overline{(\exists x)\phi}$ iff there exists an α $s(x/\alpha)$ satisfies $\overline{\phi}$

(7) s satisfies $\overline{(\forall x)\phi}$ iff for all α $s(x/\alpha)$ satisfies $\overline{\phi}$

We can then move to closed sentences, and say that they are true under the following condition:

$$\overline{\phi} \text{ is true iff } \varnothing \text{ satisfies } \overline{\phi}$$

Truth is then defined ('recursively' and 'inductively', by the order of complexity of expressions and in correspondence with their structure) as a limiting case of satisfaction. Here talk of progressively extended assignments of individuals to variables has the same effect as the talk of lists above, without using Tarskian sequences.[14]

Thus we can prove that for any sentence ϕ,

$$\overline{\phi} \text{ is true iff } \phi$$

(where, as above, '$\overline{\phi}$' is to be replaced by a metalinguistic designation of a sentence of the object-language – a 'structural descriptive name' in Tarski's terminology – and 'ϕ' is a translation of that sentence in the metalanguage), i.e. our definition of truth obeys Tarski's material adequacy condition. The definition of satisfaction, and the definition of truth in terms of satisfaction are not *explicit*, but *implicit* definitions, that is they belong to what is called a 'theory' of truth: the notions of truth and satisfaction cannot be eliminated, but are, rather, presupposed. The implicit definition, however, can be converted into an explicit one, using certain formal techniques (we shall come back to this distinction between a theory and a definition of truth in Chapters 5 and 6). Such a theory of truth is a set of axioms from which, by substitution, can be derived all the true sentences of the object language.

In the theory of truth just outlined, sentences are true or false without consideration of the possible situations in which they might be true or false, and the predicates are supposed to have a fixed meaning, without consideration of the domains of individuals that satisfy them. This is why the theory of truth in this form is called *absolute*. A theory of truth can be given relative to certain situations, or to *models*. The theory is then said to be *relative*, because truth thus becomes relative to certain assignments of meanings to predicates and to names. This kind of definition is also due to Tarski, and is suited for the semantical definition of logical consequences (§ 3.2):

$\Gamma \models A$ iff for every model $\mathbb{M}$ if all the members of Γ are true-in-$\mathbb{M}$ then A is true-in-$\mathbb{M}$

Formally, a model $\mathbb{M} = (D, \_)$ is a domain D of individuals and an assignment which assigns to each distinguished name a some member $\underset{\cdot}{a}$ of D, and to each n-place predicate P a set of n-tuples of members of D. Using the above terminology, we can define satisfaction relative to a model:

(i) s satisfies $\overline{P(t_1, \ldots, t_n)}$ in $\mathbb{M}$ iff $P(s[t_1], \ldots, s[t_n])$ in $\mathbb{M}$.

(ii) s satisfies $\overline{-\psi}$ in $\mathbb{M}$ iff s does not satisfy $\bar{\psi}$ in $\mathbb{M}$.

(iii) s satisfies $\overline{\phi \,\&\, \psi}$ in $\mathbb{M}$ iff s satisfies $\bar{\phi}$ in $\mathbb{M}$ and s satisfies $\bar{\psi}$ in $\mathbb{M}$.

(iv) s satisfies $\overline{\phi \vee \psi}$ in $\mathbb{M}$ iff s satisfies $\bar{\phi}$ in $\mathbb{M}$ or s satisfies $\bar{\psi}$ in $\mathbb{M}$.

(v) s satisfies $\overline{\phi \rightarrow \psi}$ in $\mathbb{M}$ iff s satisfies $\bar{\phi}$ in $\mathbb{M}$, then s satisfies $\bar{\psi}$ in $\mathbb{M}$.

(vi) s satisfies $\overline{(\exists x)\psi}$ in $\mathbb{M}$ iff there is a member α of D such that $s(x/\alpha)$ satisfies $\bar{\psi}$ in $\mathbb{M}$.

(vii) s satisfies $\overline{(\exists x)\psi}$ in $\mathbb{M}$ iff every member α of D is such that $s(x/\alpha)$ satisfies $\bar{\psi}$ in $\mathbb{M}$.

A sentence $\bar{\phi}$ is true in $\mathbb{M}$ iff in $\mathbb{M}$ $\varnothing$ satisfies $\bar{\phi}$.

A relative, or model-theoretical theory of truth is typically used to provide the semantics of modal languages in terms of 'possible worlds' (see above, § 1.2, and below Chapters 6 and 7). We shall come back several times to the significance of the distinction between an absolute and a relative truth theory.[15]

4.2.2 Natural deduction rules for a quantificational language

Just as the deductive apparatus of standard propositional logic can be presented either proof theoretically or semantically, the same can be done for quantificational logic. Thus we can give the following natural deduction (introduction and elimination) rules for quantifiers (in the style of § 2.2.2 above):[16]

(I) $\forall$-introduction

$$\frac{\phi \, a/x}{(\forall x)\phi}$$

(II) $\forall$-elimination

$$\frac{(\forall x)\phi}{\phi(\tau/x)}$$

(provided, in (I), that a does not occur in ϕ, or in any of the assumptions on which $\phi(a/x)$ depends; in other terms the variable x must not be bound by any quantifier with a in its scope, e.g. from $(\exists x)Pa, x$ one should not infer $(\forall x)(\exists x)Px, x$, but $(\forall y)$ $(\exists x)Py, x)$

(III) ∃-introduction

$$\frac{\phi(\tau/x)}{(\exists x)\,\phi}$$

(IV) ∃-elimination

$$[\phi(a/x)]$$
$$\vdots$$
$$\frac{(\exists x)\phi \quad \theta}{\theta}$$

(provided, in (IV) that *a* does not occur in ϕ or in θ, or in any of the assumptions used in the derivation of θ from $\phi(a/x)$ – except $\phi(a/x)$ itself).

The rule (I) is usually called the role of *universal generalisation*, (II) the rule of *universal instantiation*, (III) the rule of *existential generalisation* and (IV) the rule of *existential instantiation*. All these rules can be used to construct proofs in standard quantificational logic. Let us call the system consisting of the quantificational language presented above, together with its semantical evaluation rules and its deductive apparatus (either under the form of a truth theory or under the form of natural deduction rules), *the classical theory of quantification*. This is the system that we shall use to evaluate most of the claims that we are going to discuss.

4.3 Quantification and ontology

4.3.1 The objectual theory of quantification

4.3.1.1 Existence, reference and identity

Two important features of the semantics of the quantificational language presented above are the following. (a) The variables of quantification only appear in places that are susceptible to being occupied by *names* of the language. As we have seen, one can consider the assignments of individuals to variables as a manner of considering these as temporary names of objects. (b) Quantified sentences are true by virtue of the existence of *objects* that satisfy the corresponding open sentences and predicates, since lists are made up of objects, and assignments are assignments of objects or individuals. Thus the sentence '$(\exists x)Fx$' is true if and only if a certain *object* is F.

This, however, is true only of a particular version of quantification theory. (a) holds only if quantification is restricted to quantification into nominal position, and if one refuses to put predicates in the position of variables of quantification. Second-order logic frees us from this restriction. It allows the formation of sentences such as '$(\exists F)(x)Fx$'. (b) holds only if one adopts the *absolute* version, in which the satisfaction of an open sentence or of a predicate by lists of objects or by assignments is not relative to models or to possible worlds. In relative truth theories, in principle nothing prevents us from speaking of the satisfaction, and therefore of the truth of sentences which are about *non-existent* or non-actual objects. Moreover, (b) does not hold if the truth conditions of quantified sentences are not interpreted in terms of the existence of objects for which the variables stand, but in terms of the truth of singular sentences (of atomic sentences, in the sense of Chapter 3). In this case, a sentence '$(\exists x)Fx$' is not true if there is an object x which is F, but if there is *a substitutional instance* of 'F . . .' which is true. Under this interpretation, the truth conditions of '$(\exists x)Fx$' do not depend upon the existence of the object denoted by x, but upon the truth of the corresponding singular sentence 'Fa'. This interpretation of the quantifier is called *substitutional*, by opposition to (b) which is called the *objectual* interpretation.

Are these alternative legitimate *interpretations* of quantification, which one might choose at will, or is there only one correct reading? The view according to which quantification theory *must* rest upon principles (a) and (b), and according to which quantification is to be interpreted objectually and not substitutionally, has been forcefully defended by Quine. I shall therefore call it 'Quine's thesis',[17] and shall examine its credentials.

According to Quine's thesis, the notions of nominal reference, of existence, of predication, of truth and of identity are so closely tied to one another and to the notion of objectual quantification, that it is impossible to analyse any one of them without using the others.[18]

Let us begin with the notion of reference. Within a language, reference must be provided by proper names, that is expressions that can designate one object and only one. Now a proper name is precisely an expression that must be such that it can occur in the position of a *variable of quantification*. It follows that predicates are not names, and cannot occur in variable positions. They do not designate objects, but they are *true of* certain objects. This is in conformity with the categorical distinction between subject and predicate and with the Fregean Atomicity Postulate of Chapter 3 above: subject and predicate cannot exchange their logical roles. To think otherwise would lead us, according to Quine, to treat predicates as names of attributes or of intensional entities, the conditions of identity of which are obscure, or to subscribe to a form of platonism of properties. Quine suggests that we had better renounce second-order logic, since it leads us to accept the existence of properties in the range of values of quantificational variables.

The notion of existence is represented by the existential quantifier '$(\exists x)$' and by no other sign of our logical language. The only entities that exist are those that occur in the range of values of the variables of quantification. This is Quine's famous *criterion of ontological commitment*: '*To be is to be the value of a variable*'. Quine's criterion is not only a criterion of existence, which tells us what kind of entities exist according to a given theory, or what sort of entities are presupposed by a theory. It is also a criterion of ontological admissibility, which tells us which *attributions* of existence are permitted: only attributions to entities that can figure in the position of variables of quantification. Given Quine's ontological prefer-ences, these entities had better be individual, non-abstract entities.[19] The fact that the criterion is relative to a given background theory signifies that one cannot determine the ontological commitments independently of the translation of this theory into a certain 'canonical' language, which will reveal the nature of the entities occupying the position of variables. Therefore the quantifier 'there exists' or similar natural language expressions purporting to impute existence do not express existence; only the ' ∃' of the logical language has this expressive power, once we have 'regimented' our natural language within canonical notation. It is difficult to find an explanation of the notion of existence simpler that Quine's. According to him, finding another one would be 'unreasonable'. Quine considers that existence (or being) is a univocal notion. This is why the meaning of the quantifier '∃' is not affected by the distinctions of categories of objects that could fall within the range of values of variables of quantification and the criterion of ontological commitment can count rabbits, as well as numbers and quarks among the entities admitted by a given theory, provided that the names of these objects occupy variable positions. One can find other, supplementary justifications for such attributions of existence, but these will not have different meanings nor will they provide different explanations of the notion of existence.[20]

Finally, objectual quantification is closely tied to the notion of identity. Only entities that we can identify are susceptible of being within the range of variables of quantification. This is the upshot of Quine's second criterion of ontological admissibility: 'No entity without identity'.[21] We have seen in Chapter 1 one of the consequences of this principle for Quine, the suspicion set on Propositions as entities: since Propositions do not have precise identity conditions we can ascertain their existence. Now one of the properties of identity is substitutivity: two expressions can occur on both sides of an identity sign '=' if and only if they are substitutable *salva veritate* (see Chapter 9). Failure in the substitution *salva veritate* of one name for another means a failure of reference, and a failure of quantification: if a co-referential term in a sentence '*Fx*' cannot be substituted, this means that this term has no reference (and conversely), and that one cannot draw inferences by existential generalisation and existential instantiation. In other words, for Quine, a non-denoting term cannot be a quantified term.[22]

4.3.1.2 Existence and descriptions

Quantification, reference, existence and identity can be seen to be even more on a par if one adopts, like Quine, the view that all singular terms in a language can be eliminated in favour of the notation of quantifiers, variables and identity, through their Russellian paraphrases according to the theory of descriptions (which I shall not attempt to present fully here, since my purpose is not to discuss Russell's view *per se*, but only Quine's exploitation of it).[23] Russell proposed to define contextually every definite description of the form 'The so-and-so' by replacing it, in every context in which it occurs, by an expression containing only quantifiers, variables and the identity sign. Thus a sentence like:

(1) The man who shot Liberty Valance was brave

is to be read, according to Russell's theory, as:

(1a) There was one man, and only one, who shot Liberty Valance, and he was brave

In Russell's symbolism, a description of the form 'the F' is to be represented by '$(\imath x)Fx$'. (1a) can be represented as:

(1b) $B(\imath x)MSLVx$

(by treating 'man who shot Liberty Valance' as an unstructured predicate) and the full symbolic paraphrase corresponding to (1a) will be:

(1c) $(\exists x)((\forall y)(MSLVx \equiv x = y) \,\&\, Bx)$

In such a 'contextual definition' the description 'the $MSLV$' has been replaced by an existential quantifier which tells us that three conditions are satisfied: that the individual who shot Liberty Valance exists, and that there was a unique such individual (which is expressed by the notation involving identity), and that this individual was brave.

Another important feature of Russell's theory is that it allows the occurrence of non-denoting descriptions. For instance, suppose that Liberty Valance was not shot, but died of an heart attack. Then we must allow two different readings for the sentence that is the negation of (1):

(1') The man who shot Liberty Valance was not brave

which might mean either:

(1") It is not the case that there was a man who shot Liberty Valance and who was brave

or

(1''') There was a man who shot Liberty Valance and this man was not brave

and, on our supposition that there was no such individual, (1") is true, whereas (1''') is false. The first reading is said to involve a *narrow* scope for the description 'the $MSLV$' while the second reading involves a *wide* scope for this description (or, in Russell's own terminology, respectively a *secondary* and a *primary* occurrence of the description). The formal representations, in full Russellian paraphrase, display the contrast:

(1"a) $-(\exists x)(\forall y)(MSLV\,y \equiv y = x) \,\&\, Bx)$

(1'''a) $(\exists x)(\forall y)(MSLV\,y \equiv y = x) \,\&\, -Bx)$

Now Russell was especially interested in sentences expressing assertions of existence, and in particular in negative existential sentences of the form 'The so-and-so does not exist'. Russell introduces the special symbol 'E!' for asserting existence (which accordingly is *not* a predicate). Thus a sentence of the form 'The so-and-so-exists' is to be represented as:

$$(2) \quad E!(\imath x)Fx = df\ (\exists x)(\forall y)(Fy \equiv x = y)$$

and its negation will be:

$$(2') \quad -E!(\imath x)Fx = df-(\exists x)(\forall y)(Fy \equiv x = y)$$

It is to be noticed here that for such existential sentences, the scope of the description does not matter.

According to Quine, such paraphrases are always available for singular terms, including for proper names such as 'Socrates' or 'Pegasus' (whether or not they have denotations) which can be replaced, in sentences in which they occur, by such phrases as 'The x which socratises' or 'the x which pegasises', and then by expressions containing only quantifiers and variables.[24] From this, Quine concludes that singular terms can always be eliminated, so that the onus of reference in a language shifts from names to quantifiers and variables. Given that the reference of variables can be compared to the reference of pronouns in a natural language, reference comes out to be essentially pronominal. And given Quine's criterion of ontological commitment, the weight of existential commitments is carried by variables and pronouns. So the eliminability of singular terms through their Russellian paraphrases is on a par with Quine's thesis. Reference, quantification, existence and identity appear all the more inseparable.[25]

The fact that these notions are inseparable allows us, according to Quine, to treat objectual quantification as the very essence of quantification. Quine's thesis, however, can be true only if one can show that these notions are not separable. But this can be doubted in several ways. Some writers, most notably Strawson, have criticised Russell's theory of descriptions and the thesis of the eliminability of singular terms that Quine derives from it.[26] Others have proposed logics in which the usual quantifier rules of existential elimination and of universal instantiation are not valid. Such logics are called 'free logics' since they free us from the usual existence assumptions of classical quantification theory and offer a different treatment of existence from Russell's, allowing, in particular, terms such as 'Pegasus' to have denotations.[27] Another strategy, already mentioned in § 3.4.1. above and considered by Quine himself, consists in 'explaining away' the variables of quantification by replacing them by predicate operators in a 'combinatory logic'. I shall not follow here these various ways of disentangling the notions that Quine takes as intrinsically connected, and I shall concentrate myself only upon the so-called rivalry between the objectual and the substitutional reading of quantifiers. In particular I shall try to suggest that quantification into nominal position is compatible with a substitutional interpretation, since quantification into predicate position is not only possible, but also compatible with the substitutional interpretation of quantifiers.

4.3.2 Substitutional quantification

4.3.2.1 Frege and Tarski

In §3.4.2 we have already encountered the contrast between two ways of explaining the truth conditions of atomic sentences: Frege's way, and Tarski's. For Tarski, as we have seen in §4.2, the truth conditions of quantified sentences are to be explained through the conditions of satisfaction of the *predicates*, or of the open sentences, which figure in them. And when he defines truth for closed sentences, Tarski assimilates them to predicates, by assigning to them, as well as to predicates, conditions of satisfaction. This feature of Tarski's account is manifest from the clauses of a truth theory for propositional constants, such as (iii)–(iv) and (2)–(5) above (§4.2.1). Lists (or sequences, or assignments, according to the version adopted) of objects are said to satisfy these sentences, although it would seem to be more natural to provide them with classical clauses such as (I)–(IV) of §2.2.1. In other words, with such clauses as (iii)–(iv) or (2)–(5), the truth-conditional role of propositional constants seems to be a particular case of the role played by an expression that is satisfied by objects: non-quantified sentences and closed sentences are true if they are satisfied by all the lists (sequences) of objects, and false if they are satisfied by none. Truth is thus defined through satisfaction for predicate logic as well as for propositional logic. Thus the role of predicates for forming sentences appears to be, on this Tarskian account, more fundamental than the role of connectives, and the sentences seem to lose their central role as units of meaning. This seems unnatural, given that although a sentence is true or false, a predicate is not true or false, but true or false *of* an object.[28]

In a Fregean account, on the contrary, the notion of a predicate being true of an object is derived from the notion of the truth of a sentence: a predicate is true of, or applies to an object if there is a true atomic sentence resulting from the substitution of a name of an object in the place occupied by a variable in a predicate.[29] In this case, we must suppose that there is a sufficient stock of *names* for the appropriate substitutions in our language. On the Fregean approach, therefore, it is not necessary to use the notion of satisfaction to explain the notion of truth: truth conditions are directly explained in terms of the latter notion. Sentences, instead of predicates, are now taken as the primary vehicles of truth and meaning, according to Frege's famous 'context principle': only in the context of a sentence do the words have any meaning.[30]

Now if one accepts this way of characterising the contrast between a Tarskian and a Fregean account of the semantics of quantified sentences, one should be struck by the analogy between the latter and the substitutional conception of quantification, whereas the former seems to be closer to the objectual conception. Nevertheless the Fregean account is not identical with the substitutional account, and it shares with the Tarskian account more similarities than differences.[31] In the first place, Frege, like Tarski, accepts the atomicity postulate, and the idea that quantification always occurs in a nominal position. Second, although he explains truth in terms of the role of sentences, Frege still does not explain their truth in terms of the existence of objects denoted by their parts. For instance, a clause in a Fregean theory of truth such as

'($\exists x$) Fx' is true iff something is F

relies upon the usual, objectual, notion of existence, just as for Tarski (or for Quine): the 'something' in question is supposed to refer to one or to several definite existing objects. It is implicit, on Frege's account, that the names that can be substitutional instances of quantified sentences are necessarily *denoting*, or non-empty, names. For instance, in a perfect language or *Begriffsschrift*, a sentence such as 'Cerberus is a dog' cannot be a substitutional instance of 'x is a dog'.[32] In other words, whereas there is a semantical contrast between a Fregean and a Tarskian account, there is no ontological contrast, and both can be taken as possible interpretations of the objectual interpretation of quantification and of the Atomicity Postulate. Until now, then, using the notion of substitution to analyse the semantics of quantified sentences cannot threaten Quine's thesis.

4.3.2.2 Substitutional quantification *ab omni neavo vindicata*

The theory of substitutional quantification has been principally developed by writers such as Ruth Marcus in order to validate certain semantical interpretations of modal logic.[33] The basic idea consists, as in Frege, in interpreting existential sentences such as '($\exists x$)Fx' as meaning 'a substitutional instance of "Fx" is true', and universal sentences such as '($\forall x$)Fx' as meaning 'all the substitutional instances of "Fx" are true'. But unlike what goes on in Frege, nothing, under the substitutional interpretation, prevents us from considering the class of the objects that can be substituted for the variables as the class of singular terms or as the class of expressions susceptible of occurring in nominal position, and nothing obliges us to consider those *substituenda* as names of *existing* or real objects. For instance 'Pegasus is a winged horse' is a respectable substitutional instance for the sentence '($\exists x$) x is a winged horse' which can be taken as true. Non-existing objects or possible objects could be the reference of the substituted names.[34] This does not mean that a substitutional account commits us to such entities, but that our ontological commitments to various entities is left open. It follows that the link between reference and quantification, and the link between quantification and existence are broken. The reasoning that leads us to these notions seems to be the reverse of the reasoning that led Quine to give a privilege to the notion of objectual quantification. Whereas Quine started from the idea that the attributions of being or existence to fictitious or non-existing entities is a nonsense that our canonical grammar must avoid, a substitutional account seems to admit that such talk is acceptable. The dispute between the upholders of the respective interpretations would thus arise from a divergence between alternative ontologies, and not from logic as such. But this way of presenting the conflict between the two theories is fallacious, since the opposition does not come from two different conceptions of being or existence, but from two conceptions of quantification: what the supporter of the substitutional account says is that quantification is not a linguistic construction that would allow us to assert the existence of whatever entity, but which commits us only to postulate *names* belonging to the appropriate substitutional classes. In so far as it commits us only to linguistic entities, the substitutional conception is nominalistic in spirit: strictly speaking the only entities that are said to exist are names and expressions.[35] It follows that this conception goes against Quine's criterion of ontological commitment: bound variables are not bearers of existence more than predicates can be such bearers. Thus the problem is not: what is there, and how must we, according to our ontology, interpret quantification? The problem is, rather: what is quantification, and how can we, according to its structure, interpret ontological assertions? From this point of view, the problem is posed in the same way on either account, although the answers are different.

Quine has objected that the substitutional account encounters the following serious difficulty: all the objects in the domain considered as the range of values of a variable need not have a name. We must suppose that all the objects are susceptible of having a name, but in an infinite universe it is not necessarily the case.[36] It follows, in particular, that the familiar equivalences of standard predicate logic between a universal quantifier and the conjunction of its instances:

$$(\forall x)Fx \equiv Fa \,\&\, Fb \,\&\, Fc \,\&\, \ldots \, Fn$$

and between an existential quantifier and the disjunction of its instances:

$$(\exists x)Fx \equiv Fa \vee Fb \vee Fc \vee \ldots \, Fn$$

cannot hold in the same way in the substitutional account. For in a theory with an infinite domain, a universal (existential) quantification will be equivalent to an infinite conjunction (disjunction), whereas these quantifications will be equivalent to only finite conjunctions or disjunctions for a theory with a finite domain, and this will be the case if the stock of names is supposed to be finite. As Quine remarks, when the universe of objects is infinitely rich, the substitutional reading of the quantifiers is not coextensive to the objectual reading, for an existential quantification could be false when read substitutionally but true when read objectually, if there are appropriate objects that nevertheless do not have names. And a universal quantification could be false when read objectually, but true when read substitutionally, if there are no objects that nevertheless do not have names. Thus the substitutional reading seems to alter the very structures of objectual quantification, and cannot be a coextensive alternative to it. This objection, however, can be met, as Kripke has claimed: if one considers the stock of names of a language L for which a concept of substitutional quantification is defined in advance, and if this class of names is extended through specific procedures, nothing prevents us from giving an adequate semantics for L, since objects that could be, so to say, anonymous, are not taken into account.

It has been suggested above that the substitutional account violates the requirement (a) (§ 4.3.1) of reference and quantification into name position. But this restriction can be removed: one can give a substitutional interpretation for which only names are admitted within the substitution class. It can even be specified in advance that all the names have a reference. In this case, the distinction between the objectual and the substitutional interpretation does not affect the form of the truth theory for the quantificational language under consideration. In other terms, *a Tarskian truth theory can be given for one or the other interpretation.* One cannot say, then, as some writers did, that the very form required by a *T*-theory forces upon us the objectual interpretation rather than the substitutional interpretation. This has been shown in particular by Kripke (1976).[37]

These remarks, however, do not solve the problem raised by the admission of non-denoting names in the substitutional framework. Kripke shows that in this case too it is possible to give a *T*-theory. A denotation is there assigned to names through a relation of 'pseudo-denotation' which can be defined without assuming that all the names have a denotation (they may have a denotation or not).[38] Moreover Kripke is able to answer another Quinean objection: in the cases where substitutional quantification receives a coherent semantical account, this account can be established only by adopting *in the metalanguage* an objectual interpretation, according to which quantifiers range over linguistic objects. To answer this objection, one stipulates that the metalanguage quantifiers receive also a substitutional reading. In other words, a substitutional quantifier is not an objectual quantifier upon expressions, although we must presuppose the existence of expressions to account for substitutional quantification. In a *T*-theory for a language *L* with substitutional quantifiers, we can formulate such axioms as

$(\exists x)Fx$ is true iff Fa/x for any name a of L

(where 'Fx/a' is the result of the substitution of a name for the variable x). No use is made here of the Tarskian apparatus of lists or sequences, and truth is defined, as in Frege, directly from the atomic sentences. It can be doubted, however, whether an ontological commitment to linguistic entities is avoidable, but at least such a commitment is, compared to the commitments of the objectual reading, minimal.

A number of other virtues of the substitutional reading have been advanced: its capacity, already mentioned, for dealing with intensional or opaque contexts, its capacity for dealing with the natural language quantifiers, which are not necessarily referential, and its capacity for dealing with quantifiers in mathematics. I shall not examine these points.[39] My sole purpose has been to defend the *coherence* of substitutional quantification, as a genuine alternative to objectual quantification, although this does not imply that there is a genuine rivalry between the two readings. It follows that the requirements (a) and (b) of Quine's thesis are by no means imposed on us, since they can be dissociated: although the variables of quantification appear in nominal position, they may not be referential.

4.3.3 Predicate quantification and second-order logic

Quine's thesis implies that quantifying over predicates is not allowed. To allow such quantifications would involve, according to Quine, treating predicates as names of attributes (as the supposed intensions of predicates) or of sets (as the extensions of predicates). For in such ordinary quantifications as '$(\exists x)(x$ walks$)$', '$(\forall x)(x$ walks$)$', the open sentence after the quantifier shows 'x' in a position where a name could stand (here names of walkers), but these quantifications do not mean that names walk. It follows, according to Quine, that if one puts the predicate letter 'F' into a quantifier, as in '$(\exists F)($Aristotle $F)$', one has to treat predicate positions as names positions, and therefore one has to treat predicates as names of certain entities.[40] Now Quine's objection to predicate quantification may be interpreted in two ways: either predicate quantification is objectionable because it commits us to the entities (sets or attributes) named by the predicates, or it is objectionable because predicates are confused with names. Quine has indeed reservations against attributes as entities (although has no such reservations against sets or classes), but this is not his point here: his point is that *because* predicates are not names, predicates cannot be put into variable positions. But one can agree with Quine that predicates are not names of anything without agreeing with him that the very essence of quantification is to be a quantification into name position. In the first place, we can have other reasons for distinguishing names from predicates which are independent of our understanding of the concept of quantification. For instance, such arguments as Geach's and Strawson's about the asymmetry of subjects and predicates (see Chapter 3) can be considered as sufficient to establish the distinction between names (subjects) and predicates, although such arguments do not involve the notion of quantification. Contrary to what Quine says, we are not obliged to consider that our only way of understanding the notion of a name is to notice that a name is an expression that is accessible to quantification.[41]

Another reason for rejecting Quine's argument is the following. If we accept predicate quantification, we accept such second-order sentences as:

> (3) $(\exists F)\ Fa$

as meaning: 'There is something F which is possessed by the individual a'. The predicate 'F', although it occurs as a variable of quantification, still functions as a predicate in the other part of the sentence, and thus does not lose its usual logical role. Is there any good reason to object to sentences such as (3) on the grounds that one cannot infer such sentences from sentences of the form 'Fa'? But, as Strawson notes, 'Socrates does something' (or 'Socrates is something') is just as good and *just as direct* a generalisation from 'Socrates swims' (or 'Socrates is brave') as 'Someone swims' (or 'Someone is brave'). Now is it presupposed in (3) that the predicate 'F' functions as a name in its first occurrence?[42] No such presupposition is made, since as George Boolos has pointed out, putting a predicate in a variable position is to treat this predicate as having a *range* containing the objects (extensions) which can be had by predicates in predicate positions, but it does not imply that one treats the predicate variables as *names* of the objects:

> '(∃F)' in (3) does not have to be taken as saying that some of the entities of the sort named by predicates are thus and so; it can be taken to say that some of entities (extensions) had by predicates contain thus and such. So some variables eligible for quantification might well belong in predicate positions and not in name positions.[43]

So there does not seem to be anything objectionable *per se* with predicate quantification, in so far as it does not lead us to confuse predicates with names and is perfectly meaningful.

There is, however, a more general and different kind of objection: by quantifying over predicates as in (3), we are led to accept a different concept of quantification – second-order rather than first-order quantification – but it can be doubted that second-order logic is really 'logic', and therefore that second-order quantification is really 'quantification'. Second-order logic is distinct from first-order logic, notably because it lacks some of its important metatheoretical properties: in particular the completeness theorem, the Löwenheim–Skolem theorem and the compactness theorem fail for second-order logic.[44] I shall not deal here (but in Chapters 11 and 12 below) with the question of whether first-order logic is the 'right' logic. But there is no reason to suspect that second-order logic rests upon a different *semantics* than first-order logic. A *T*-theory can be given for a second-order language, and the usual model-theoretic notions of validity, of consequence and of truth under an interpretation. Although Quine sees second-order logic as 'set theory in sheep's clothing', and suggested that it hides 'vast and staggering' ontological commitments and confusions,[45] many writers have argued that once a domain for the first-order variables is fixed, one can understand clearly such locutions as 'all properties' or 'all subsets'.[46] Much more should be said to justify second-order logic as such, but it seems that quantification over predicates is an admissible variety of quantification.

4.4 Quantifiers and natural languages

Quantification theory owes its place not only to the role it has played, since Frege, in the task of formalising mathematical statements and inferences, but also to its capacity to express a lot of natural language inferences. Many natural sentences and inferences that cannot be accounted for by traditional logic can be dealt with easily with modern quantification theory. Examples of these are, notoriously, inferences involving relations ('A horse is an animal, therefore the head of a horse is the head of an animal') and sentences involving multiple quantification ('Somebody envies everybody', see § 3.3.1 above). This does not mean that one cannot, within traditional pre-Fregean logic, account for the logical form of such sentences. Sommers, for instance, holds that when traditional logic is recast into its own theory (see Chapter 3), its expressive resources are not as poor as they were claimed to be by writers such as Geach and Dummett.[47] Nevertheless, modern quantification theory has played a paradigmatic role for the analysis of natural language sentences. But the question is: what kind of 'analysis'? One way or another, philosophers like Frege and Russell believed that one could give a unique and perspicuous 'logical form' for any natural language sentence. Philosophers like Quine, on the contrary, do not hold that their canonical notation allows us to capture faithfully the meaning of natural language quantified sentences, but that the 'regimentation' of those sentences is but a 'paraphrase' that does not amount to any 'analysis' or 'translation' of such sentences (this, of course, squares well with Quine's own doubts about translation or synonymy). For Quine, the aim of a paraphrase is to dispel the ambiguities of natural language, and not to give a relevant linguistic analysis: there is no such thing as *the* logical form of a natural language sentence.[48] Some linguists, however, believe that quantification theory can be used as the source of fruitful empirical hypotheses about the syntax and semantics of natural language (I shall not mention here work about pragmatics). Thus writers in the 'generative semantics' school have proposed to relate the surface structures of natural language sentences directly to their quantified logical forms.[49] the programmes of semantics for natural language of the 1970s, such as Davidson's or Montague's, rest on similar hypotheses (see Chapter 6).

One encounters, however, a lot of well-known difficulties when one tries to use the standard quantification form as a source of semantical insights for natural languages. In many instances, natural language quantifiers do not seem to be the counterparts of the logician's quantifiers '$\forall$' and '$\exists$'. For instance, the same logical representation with '$\forall$', i.e.

(4) $(\forall x)(x$ is a doctor and x will tell you that Blurp is a good medicine)

can be used to represent a variety of natural language quantifiers:

(4a) All doctors will tell you that Blurp is a good medicine
(4b) Every doctor will tell you that Blurp is a good medicine
(4c) Any doctor will tell you that Blurp is a good medicine
(4d) Each doctor will tell you that Blurp is a good medicine

Vendler (1967) has shown that these sentences do not have the same meaning. For instance (4c) refers to an hypothetical situation (if you consult a doctor) and can be true even if a number of doctors never give any opinion about Blurp. But the other sentences will be false unless every doctor gives this advice about Blurp. Quine proposes to account for the difference between 'any' and 'every' in canonical notation by distinguishing the different scopes of the quantifier. Thus

(5) The shy girl does not kiss any boy
(6) The shy girl does not kiss every boy

have respectively a wide and a narrow scope for 'any' and 'every' (compare with (1') above), and can be represented as:

(5') $(\forall x)(x$ is a boy $\rightarrow -$the shy girl kisses $x)$
(6') $-(\forall x)(x$ is a boy $\rightarrow$ the shy girl kisses $x)^{50}$

but it is not certain that all uses of 'any' and 'every' can be paraphrased by using such distinctions of scope. Some uses of 'all' presuppose a reference to a group of individuals, whereas in other uses it refers to each of the members of a set. Only in the latter case, is an inference by universal instantiation possible. For instance the following inference, where 'all' has a group reading, is invalid:

(7) Maurice Heine has compiled a catalogue of all of D. A. F. de Sade's works. *The Prosperities of Vice* is one of D. A. F. de Sade's works. Therefore Maurice Heine has compiled a catalogue of *The Prosperities of Vice*[51]

Part of the difficulty encountered when one tries to transpose the properties of the standard quantifiers to natural language quantifiers comes from the fact that modern logic (and especially Frege's logic) typically supposes that all the variables in a quantificational formula range over the same domain of individuals, that is are *unrestricted*, whereas natural language quantifiers are typically supposed to range over a specific domain of individuals, or are *restricted*. For instance when I say that 'Everybody likes eating snails', my quantifier does not range over humanity at large or over people across the Channel, but on a specific domain – my French compatriots, my Parisian friends, and so on.[52] In general, the specificity of a domain can be represented within an unrestricted reading of quantifiers by incorporating a specific predicate into the predicates that the quantifier applies to, such as in

(8) $(\forall x)(x$ is French $\rightarrow x$ likes eating snails)

But then the two quantifiers are not treated in the same way, since a universal quantification such as (8) takes an *if* conjunct to restrict the variable of a universal quantifier to a specific domain, whereas an existential quantification takes an *and*-conjunct to restrict the variable as for 'Some French like eating snails':

(8') $(\exists x)(x$ is French & x likes eating snails

Many, often subtle (see, for instance, § 11.3.2 below) strategies can be used to deal with *prima facie* refractory natural language quantifiers while staying within the confines of standard predicate logic. Many natural language quantifiers, however, do not lend themselves to such treatments. A famous example is the so-called 'Geach–Kaplan sentence':[53]

(9) Some critics admire only one another

which is supposed to mean that there is a collection of critics, each of whose members admires no one not in the collection, and none of whose members admires himself. A translation into first-order predicate logic like:

(9') $(\exists x)(\exists y)((x$ is a critic) & $(y$ is a critic & $(x \neq y)$ & $(\forall z)$ $(x$ admires $z \equiv "z = y)$ & $(y$ admires $z \equiv z = x))$

is inadequate, since this translation supposes that there are only two such critics, although there can be a larger group of them. So it has has been suggested that (9) should receive a second-order formulation:

(9'') $(\exists X)((\exists y)Xy$ & $(\forall x)(\forall y)((Xx$ & $Axy) \rightarrow (x \neq y$ & $Xy)))$

(where 'Axy' means 'x admires y' and 'X' designates the set, or the collection of critics, or the property of being a critic). As we saw, a disputed question is whether we can avoid here an ontological commitment to classes or collections. Quine claims that we cannot. Boolos, however, has claimed that we should understand such sentences as (9) as involving 'plural' quantifiers of the form 'There are Fs such that . . . they . . .', or 'For every A there is a B', so that (9) should read:

(9''') There are some critics such that any one of them admires another critic only if the latter is one of them distinct from the former

According to Boolos, such second-order reformulations do not commit us to sets or classes.[54]

Other 'plurality quantifiers' are *most*, *very few*, *many*. Sentences of the form:

(10) Most A are B

are, *prima facie*, similar to sentences with universal or existential quantifiers. But if we suppose that in the mould of '$\exists$' or '$\forall$' there is a sentential connective, (10) can be represented neither as '(Most $x)(Ax$ & $Bx)$' (since most A might be B without it being true that most things are both A and B) nor as '(Most $x)(Ax \rightarrow Bx)$' (since anything is if A then B, given than almost everything in the universe is not an A).[55] David Wiggins has proposed that such quantifiers as 'most' (or 'many') in sentences of the form (10) should be understood as two-place or 'binary' quantifiers binding two open sentences: 'Most x (Ax, Bx)'.[56] Thus appropriate clauses of a T-theory could be given thus:

(10') For any sequence σ, σ satisfies $\overline{(\text{most } x_i)(A, B)}$ if and only if, for most z such that $\sigma(i/z)$ satisfies $\bar{A}$, $\sigma(i/z)$ satisfies $\bar{B}$

(where '$\sigma(i/z)$' is the sequence got from σ by substituting whatever is in the ith place of the sequence with the object z.

One could expand the list of non-standard quantifiers, and it is at least an open problem whether they can be dealt with by using first-order resources. Three strategies have been adopted by writers on these topics. The first one, which can be called minimalist, has just been mentioned: it consists in attempting to force the refractory quantifications into the mould of first-order logic, in order to preserve the simplicity of logical grammar. But the results are moot: in some cases it can be done, in other cases not. The second strategy can be called pluralist or pragmatist. It consists in admitting as many logical formalisms as necessary, in accordance with the variety of the phenomena. One can thus have gains in expressive power, but losses in explicative power and unity. The third strategy consists in adopting at once the richest possible language to save the unity of logical theory.

Recent work in the semantics of natural language has illustrated various versions of these three strategies. Davidson's programme (see Chapter 6) is a version of the first. Many linguists and logicians adopt the second. For instance, McCawley believes that there are no real boundary lines between logic and the semantics of natural language because he holds that:

> the units that one does 'the logic of' [are] the elements of meaning and thus [are] in the province of linguistics as much as of logic. Logic is an empirical enterprise at least to the extent that investigation of natural language provides evidence about what elements of meaning there are and what their combinatory possibilities are.[57]

It follows, according to McCawley, that one may count among the elements of 'logical form' *all* the structural elements that contribute to the meanings of sentences: each one of them has a right to be included among the 'logical constants'. This methodology is perfectly acceptable for linguistic theory (in so far as it does not interfere with such requirements as simplicity), but it encounters obvious limits when our concern is the nature of *logic*, since it would assimilate logical form with grammatical form (see § 11.3 below).

The third strategy has been illustrated, for instance, by Montague's work.[58] Montague proposes a grammar and a semantics for English, the logical representation of which requires a higher-order logic, and a hierarchy of logical types, including individuals, properties of individuals, properties of properties of individuals, and so on. This system is very complex and I shall just mention some of the properties of its treatment of quantifiers. Montague interprets quantifiers as kinds of singular terms. A predication such as 'John is wise' expresses the membership of wisdom in the class of John's properties. Quantifiers are put on a par with proper names like 'John'. Thus a quantifier such as 'Every man' denotes the collection of properties that are true of every man, and is the intersection of the collections of properties assigned to John, Paul, George, and so on. 'Some man' denotes the collection of properties true of at least one man, and is the union of the collections formed out of John, Paul, George, etc. This account faces difficulties, because the parallelism between quantifiers and singular terms has obvious limits. One is that the negation of a quantified sentence such as 'Every man came' cannot be 'Not every man came', whereas 'John did not come' is the negation of 'John came'. Another is that 'John loves Mary' introduces no problem of scope, whereas 'A man loves every woman' does.

Which strategy is the best? I shall not attempt to answer this question here. The problem of giving a correct semantic account of natural language quantifiers gives rise to a subtle dialectic.[59] On the one hand, it is claimed that natural languages are more complex and unsystematic than any logician can dream of their being. On the other hand, the complexity of the logical structures invented by logicians and linguists can make us doubt that natural languages can be *as* complex as the logical structures that are supposed to represent their syntax and their semantics, and it might be that any apparent complexity can be reduced, through one analysis or another, to an underlying unity, so that, in the end, the early hopes of the founders of modern logic to find *the* underlying structures are not doomed to failure, although – as it is suggested for instance by Sommers (Chapter 3) – these structures might not look like those of standard post-Fregean quantification theory.

The only proper conclusion that can be drawn from these sketchy remarks seems to me to be the following. In logic and in linguistics, there is not one, but many concepts of quantification, and there are at least several meaningful interpretations of this notion. I have claimed, against Quine, that the classical objectual concept of quantification is not the only coherent concept of quantification available in logic. This is even truer in the field of the semantics of natural language. So it is more appropriate to talk of the varieties of quantification rather than of a single concept that would express the very essence of quantification. But the semantics of natural language is one thing, and logic is another thing, and there are obvious limits to this pluralism, which I shall examine in Chapter 11.

── PART 2 ──
Truth and meaning

THEORIES OF TRUTH

5.1 The problem of a theory of truth

The notion of truth is at the centre of logic. Our intuitive concept of inference calls directly on the idea of truth: an inference from premises A, B, ..., T to a conclusion C is said to be valid if and only if, if A, B, ..., T are true C is too. As has been said, a valid inference 'preserves' the truth of the premises in the conclusion. The notion of validity is thus defined by means of that of truth, and therefore the latter is primitive in relation to the former. But in a formal system, as has been seen (§ 2.2.2), the notion of truth only arises in the *semantic* definition of the notion of logical consequence. This latter relationship can also be *syntactically* defined: a set of premises A, B, . . ., Γ will entail, in the syntactic sense, inside a certain system of axioms or inference rules S, a conclusion C if and only if C can be derived from A, B , . . ., Γ, by means of the axioms of S or the inference rules of S. What is primitive in this syntactic definition is the notion of deducibility, and not that of truth. The question that can then be asked is: which notion is the more primitive, that of valid consequence in the semantic sense or that of deduction in the syntactic sense? Does the notion of truth take precedence over that of deduction or vice versa? We have already met this question apropos the meaning of propositional logical constants, and our answer in that case tended to favour a semantic conception of the meaning of the constants. I will come back to the definition of the notion of inference and the question of knowing if this idea should receive a primarily semantic or a primarily syntactic characterisation in Chapters 11 and 12. Here I will assume that the semantic characterisation comes first and that the notion to be clarified is that of truth. Our main question in this chapter is this: what is the meaning of this notion of truth and what is a theory of truth, that is to say a semantics, for a logical language?

To state this question more precisely, in the way that it arises for philosophy of logic, one can ask what the relationship is between two senses of the expression 'theory of truth'. In one sense, a theory of truth is a *philosophical* theory of the meaning of this notion: it is a theory that gives a philosophical definition of what it is to be true, for a given sentence (or for any other entity that could be given the predicate 'is true'). In providing such a theory, there is no way of escaping approaching the manner in which the problem of truth is traditionally posed in philosophy. Following Wiggins (1981), such a theory of truth can be called 'substantial'. A substantial theory of truth is a philosophical or metaphysical theory that gives the *meaning* of the word 'true' and seeks to *define* the notion of truth. A distinction is generally made between such a theory and an analysis of the *criteria* of truth.[1] A substantial theory must also tell us what entities are 'truth-bearers'. In what follows I will contrast such theories with theories that, although they still give an analysis of the concept of truth, are based on a version of what is called the *equivalence thesis*: *p* is true if and only if *p*. These theories can be called 'modest' truth theories. I will examine the two principal ones: the 'redundancy' theory, whereby saying that *p* is true is saying nothing more than asserting *p*; and Tarski's 'semantic' truth theory. Tarski's 'truth theory' is both a modest theory and a theory (in the logical sense of a set of axioms) of the *interpretation* of syntactically specified signs of a logical language, in other words, a semantics. The interesting question then is: what is substantial about a 'substantial' truth theory in relation to a modest theory? I would like to maintain that if, in fact, a modest theory, and the semantic theory in particular, is less substantial than a philosophical theory of truth, a semantic theory is for all that not a superficial or a trivial theory of truth.

5.2 Correspondence and coherence

5.2.1 Correspondence

I will give two examples of 'substantial' theories of truth, the correspondence theory of truth and the coherence theory of truth. These are far from being the only possible theories. Others, for example, are the pragmatic theory in James's sense (truth defined by its effects, or by utility); and the verificationist theory (truth as assertability). This latter will be mentioned in the next chapter. There are several versions of the correspondence theory and the coherence theory in philosophy, and it is not my purpose to examine them; here, I will limit myself solely to indicating the general form that they can take, with the aim of then comparing them with modest theories of truth.

As Austin (1950) has said, a theory of truth rests on a collection of platitudes. The first platitude is that a judgement (or a belief or a proposition, etc. – for the moment we do not have to decide which entities are true and which false) is true if there is something *by virtue of which* it is true, or if there is something which *corresponds* to it. Another platitude is that if *p* is true, then it is a *fact* that *p*, or *p* is a fact. These platitudes are innocuous. They tell us nothing about the definition of 'true'. For these common intuitions to be stated in a correspondence theory of truth, the proper correspondence relationship has to be defined, and clear individuation conditions of entities as 'facts' given.

What would be a substantial correspondence theory of truth? The most characteristic contemporary expression of a theory of this type is the doctrine of 'logical atomism' maintained by Wittgenstein and Russell in the 1920s.[2] Simplifying the thesis of the *Tractatus* to the extreme, it can be said that Wittgenstein there maintains that propositions are complexes, truth-functionally composed from elementary or atomic propositions, themselves formed of arrangements of names. The structure of the atomic propositions reflects that of the world: to atomic propositions correspond facts, themselves arranged in states of affairs, which are themselves formed of arrangements of objects. The names directly designate objects and, because the elementary propositions are made up of names that exhibit the same arrangement as the arrangement of the objects in the elementary states of affairs, this isomorphism makes it possible to say that the atomic propositions 'represent' states of affairs. (An important point of the *Tractatus* is that the correspondence only applies to elementary propositions and not to complex propositions.)[3] In the Russellian version of the doctrine, the logical atoms or the simple entities are sense data and the propositions derive their meaning from these primitive data. The difficulties with these theories are well known: what are the criteria of identity of the elementary facts? Are they independent of each other as Wittgenstein maintains? Is it possible to speak of negative facts in the case of negative propositions? What is the precise definition of the relationship of structural isomorphism between propositions and facts?

But the difficulties of the correspondence theory of truth are not peculiar to the doctrines of logical atomism. As was seen in § 2.3.2, any theory that identifies a true proposition to a fact, or seeks to define truth as correspondence between judgements (propositions, beliefs, etc.) and facts or circumstances, encounters the problem of the individuation of facts, and seems to come up against the Fregean 'slingshot' argument, in one or other of its versions. At least this is the meaning of Davidson's utilisation of the Fregean argument (§ 1.3.2). However, there are ways of avoiding the slingshot difficulties and making the notion of fact or state of affairs respectable. I will not go into the complexities of this sort of theory.[4] Whatever the validity of the Fregean argument, it is a good illustration of the general problem of a theory of facts: how to specify a notion of fact which is at the same time neither trivial ('It is a fact that Naples is north of Red Bluff') nor obviously false (in such a manner that totally irrelevant facts, such as the fact that London is the capital of Great Britain, would 'verify' statements such as 'Naples is north of Red Bluff'). In other words, as Davidson notes, we can actually reject the slingshot argument, by rejecting one or other of the principles on which it is based. And it is possible to imagine constructing the facts acceptably without seeing our ontology break down. But

> From the point of view of the theory of truth, however, all such constructions seem doomed by the following difficulty. Suppose, to leave the frying-pan of extensionality for the fires of intention, we distinguish facts as finely as statements. Of course, not every statement has its fact; only the true ones do. But then, unless we find another way to pick out facts, we cannot hope to explain truth by appeal to them. (Davidson, 1984, p. 43)

What is common to the various theories of truth as correspondence to facts is their ontological character. But it is also possible, like Austin (1950), to give a formulation of the correspondence theory of truth independently of such an ontology of 'facts'. Instead of defining an isomorphism relationship between language and the world, Austin explains the correspondence relationship as a purely conventional relationship between words and things. According to him, two sorts of conventions come into play: (a) 'descriptive' conventions, which link words to types of situations; and (b) 'demonstrative' conventions, which link words to specific situations. For example, if someone states the sentence: 'I am eating' at time t, the descriptive conventions link these words to situations in which someone is eating, and the demonstrative conventions link the words to the state of the person at t. The sentence 'I am eating' is true if and only if the specific situation linked to the words by the demonstrative convention is of the type of the situation linked to the words by the descriptive convention. The fact that the correspondence relationship is conventional means that the correlations between the words and the world are arbitrary: any situation can be correlated to any words. No form of structural isomorphism is required. A current objection to Austin's theory is that only indexical sentences show the two types of conventions: the demonstrative conventions do not play a role in 'eternal' sentences such as 'Brutus assassinated Caesar' or 'Reagan kissed Gorbachev on 27 April 1986' which only designate a single type of situation. A more important objection is that, according to Austin's theory, when we say that a statement p is true, we are saying that the relevant conventions are satisfied; but these conditions are not identified with what is asserted when p is said to be true. In other words, when we say that p is true, we are talking about the meaning of words, or we are saying that the speaker has stated these words correctly. But that is not what we are doing when we say that a statement is true.[5]

5.2.2 Truth as coherence

A theory of truth as coherence maintains that truth must be defined as a certain type of relationship between judgements (beliefs, propositions, etc.). A judgement or a proposition is true if and only if it forms part of a coherent set of judgements or propositions. But in the same way as the correspondence theory of truth comes up against the problem of the definition of the relationship 'corresponds to', a coherence theory of truth comes up against the problem of the definition of the relationship 'is coherent with'. Right from the start, it will be observed that the theory does not identify truth with coherence: the notion of a *true* set of propositions does not have a meaning, although that of a true proposition as a member of a set does. As such, the theory gives both a definition of truth and a criterion of truth. The minimal coherence relationship is, it seems, that of consistency, or non-contradiction: two propositions that mutually contradict each other cannot be in a coherence relationship. Another minimal requirement is that the coherent set be sufficiently comprehensive, or sufficiently large. The traditional objection is that a system of false propositions can be coherent. More precisely, the objection is as follows:[6] suppose that we have a coherent and comprehensive set S of propositions describing a certain historical period. Then we can maintain or increase the coherence of S and make it comprehensive by adding to S a certain proposition E, which is found to be false. $(S + E)$ can thus be enlarged by falsehoods and can also permit the introduction of divergent subsystems. In other words, nothing in the definition of coherence makes it possible to say that there is only one single and unique coherent set of beliefs. And if there is more than one single system, what could be said about a plurality of systems? If each of them is complete, how can it be acknowledged that all the parts of these different descriptions of the world are true? If the descriptions are different, they enter into competition, and what they are competing for is the truth. Either coherence truth presupposes the definition of truth as correspondence or else it is more valuable to define coherence.[7] To answer this type of objection, the coherentist must state the coherence relationship precisely: it is not possible to add to the system propositions that would not have certain characteristics, that would in some way permit the entry of new propositions into the system to be controlled. But how can these characteristics be defined? Here, the answers belong to epistemology and metaphysics. One of them is Peirce's pragmatist theory, whereby truth is the coherence of a belief with an ideal set constituting the ultimate scientific truth. Because of this latter claim, the pragmatist theory is therefore also a correspondentist theory, since truth is correspondence to the ideal limit of scientific research. This conception should not be confused with what is usually called the pragmatist definition of truth by usefulness, formulated by James, although this latter is also a coherentist theory, for which the criterion of coherence is utility. But I am leaving these theories on one side here.[8]

There is no lack of attempts in contemporary epistemology to formulate a precise definition of the coherentist theories of truth and knowledge. And the list of possible substantial theories is far from closed when one has mentioned the correspondentist theory and the coherentist theory. Perhaps a correct conception is a combination of the two: we demand of our theories that they be coherent and at the same time that they correspond to the facts.[9] It is not the particular developments of these diverse conceptions of truth that interest us here, but only the question of knowing whether, independently of their intrinsic difficulties, such theories of truth as correspondence or as coherence merit development.

5.3 Transparency and redundancy

5.3.1 Transparency

The main difficulty with the correspondence theory of truth is that any attempt at elucidation of *p is true* by means of *p corresponds to the facts* seems circular. It is hard to go beyond the truism 'if *p* is true, then it is a fact that *p*'. The coherence theory of truth seems to promise more, but it appears hard to justify our intuitions concerning coherence without resorting again to the idea of truth as correspondence to the facts, and thereby without even falling back into the difficulties of the latter. When we try to give a substantial definition of truth, do we succeed in going beyond what Dummett calls the 'equivalence thesis': *p is true if and only if p?* It is true that Paris is the capital of France if and only if Paris is the capital of France. It is true that $7 + 5 = 12$ if and only if $7 + 5 = 12$, and so on. In other words, to say that it is true that *p* simply comes back to saying that *p*. Let us say, following Blackburn, that the equivalence between *p* and *it is true that p* illustrates the 'transparency' property of the predicate 'is true': 'It is as though you can always look through "it is true that" to identify the content which is judged, inquired after, and so on, if the reference to truth were not there.' As Blackburn emphasises, the transparency of 'is true' poses a problem that recalls the 'paradox of analysis'.[10] Either we give an *analysans* or a synonym of 'it is true that', but this synonym is trivial and empty, such as when we say that 'it is true that *p*' means 'it is a fact that *p*'. Or else this *analysans* is substantial, has an effective content, but in this case the content of 'it is true that *p*' will diverge from that of '*p*'. In this second case, 'it is true that *p*' no longer has the same meaning as '*p*', and the property of transparency is lost.

The dilemma seems to show that it is impossible to give a substantial definition of the notion of truth without losing the notion of transparency, and consequently that there is nothing more in the idea of truth than transparency. This is what Frege maintained, by an argument which, following Blackburn, can be paraphrased as follows.[11]

Let us suppose that, in a substantial truth theory, there is always a difference of content between '*p*' and 'it is true that *p*'. Let the judgement that there is such a difference of content be called '*q*'. A different judgement, that it is true that *q*, can then be formulated; let us call this latter *r*. A hierarchy of distinct judgements is then obtained, each of which confirms that its predecessor is true. But how can these judgements really be distinct? Let us suppose that our substantial definition of truth is correspondence. From the judgement that *p*, one passes on to the judgement that *p* corresponds (C) to a fact (F): *pCF*. The judgement *pCF* itself is true: it corresponds to another fact (F∗). We therefore have: *pCFCF∗*. *pCFCF∗* in its turn is true and leads on to the judgement *pCFCF∗CF∗∗*, and so on.

To give the argument in another way, let us suppose that truth is analysed by means of any definition ϕ (correspondence, coherence, pragmatist, etc.). One then has the two series (where '*T*' is the operator 'it is true that'):

$$p \ Tp \ TTp \ TTTp \ldots$$
$$p \ \phi p \ \phi\phi p \ \phi\phi\phi p \ldots$$

The Fregean argument is then as follows:

(I) In the first series, each member has the same content as every other (property of transparency);

(II) if ϕ is a definition, or an analysis of truth, then ϕ must have the property of transparency;

(III) either ϕ has a specific and independent content, or ϕ is a trivial simple synonym of T;

(IV) in the second case, ϕ cannot be a definition of truth;

 (V) in the first case, ϕ does not have the property of transparency, and by (II) is not a definition of truth;

(VI) therefore truth cannot be defined.

5.3.2 Redundancy

Two sorts of conclusions can be drawn from the Fregean argument: either that truth cannot be defined and consequently that it is a primitive notion, the content of which cannot be made explicit by means of other notions; or else that transparency itself *is* the definition of truth and that there is not a more elaborate one to be sought. Frege himself seems to oscillate between the two positions.[12] But other authors have explicitly adopted the second, which is known as the 'redundancy' theory of truth. The redundancy theory of truth is a strong version of the equivalence thesis (or to be more precise, it exploits the equivalence thesis by transforming it into a *definition* of truth: there is nothing more in 'it is true that p' than the affirmation or the assertion of p). The notion of truth itself is an empty notion, without content, that is to say redundant. 'It is true that p' *means that p*, and 'it is false that p' means *not-p*. This thesis has been defended most explicitly by Ramsey and Wittgenstein. As Ramsey says: 'There is no separate problem of truth, but merely a linguistic muddle.' And as Wittgenstein says: 'What does it mean that a proposition "is true"? "p" is true = p. (This is the answer)'.[13]

The principal attraction of the redundancy theory of truth is that it does away *de facto* not only with the problem of the search for a more substantial definition of truth, but also, it seems, the problem of the nature of the truth-bearers. It does not much matter in the equivalence between p is 'it is true that p' if p is a judgement, a belief, a Proposition or a sentence. The theory seems to allow us to remain neutral in this ontological debate, although, in general, the redundancy theory of truth is conceived as dealing with propositions, as the contents of what people say or believe, in the innocuous sense mentioned in § 1.4.5. It permits us to remain neutral at another level. To say that 'kangaroos leap' is true, is doing nothing but asserting that kangaroos leap, and to say that '$2 + 2 = 4$' is true is doing nothing more that stating that $2 + 2 = 4$, and so on. But the reasons that we have for affirming these statements, or the criteria whereby we recognise them as true, are distinct: each statement has, in some way, its own manner of being true. Nevertheless, truth is what they have in common. Is it possible to say precisely what is common to all true sentences, that is to say to all the reasons that we have for affirming any truth at all? This appears illusory, and that is why the scholastic philosophers called true a 'transcendental' term which transcends the categorical predications. To give the predicate 'true' its neutral and redundant meaning is perhaps the best way of accounting for this fact. Given any sentence prefixed by 'it is true that' – and therefore mentioned or quoted in order to be considered – the redundancy theory of truth and the equivalence thesis, *p is true if and only if p* allow us to 'disquote' that sentence, in such a way as to say what has to be judged or asserted in order to confirm its truth. This simple 'disquotation' procedure is possible without the need to seek what is common to true statements.[14] The redundancy theory of truth therefore deserves the epithet *modest* theory of truth compared with any substantial theory.

However attractive it may be, the redundancy theory of truth runs into difficulties.

A first difficulty is that the equivalence between *p* and *it is true that p* seems to disappear in contexts such as

(1) What Aristotle says is true

where we make explicit reference to the content of Aristotle's sayings. Ramsey suggests that we simply reformulate (1) by means of

(2) For all *p*, if Aristotle asserts that *p*, then *p*.[15]

But in this case, is not a quantification on sentences or on Propositions being introduced, contrary to the ontological agnosticism the theory advocates? The redundancy theorist (Prior, 1971, for example) wants to ignore the distinction between object-language and metalanguage (contrary to Tarski's semantic theory as will be seen): according to him, 'it is true that scientists are often absent-minded' applies to the scientists and not to the sentence 'scientists are often absent-minded'. But one cannot account in this way for the numerous contexts in which 'it is true that' plays the role of a metalinguistic predicate, and ceases thereby to be redundant. However, it is clearly the case in the usual clauses of a theory of truth for the propositional connectives (§ 2.2), or when one wants to distinguish the principle of the excluded middle ($p \vee -p$) from the principle of bivalence (*for every p, p is true or false*).

Let us suppose that Ramsey's reformulation (2) is correct. The problem, apart from the reference to specific entities such as sentences or propositions, is that if we understand (2) in this way

(3) For all the propositions *p*, if *X* asserts that *p*, then *p* is true

then, whether the quantifier 'for all' is understood objectively, as a quantifier upon objects, or substitutionally, as a quantifier upon expressions, the reference to *is true* which appears to the right of (3) has not disappeared: 'is true' has not been eliminated, contrary to the redundant analysis sought.

Several solutions to this problem have been given. One of the most ingenious comes from Prior and has been adopted by various authors (notably D. Grover and C. J. F. Williams), and is called the 'prosentential theory of truth'.[16] The difficulty Ramsey encountered with (2) is that no linguistic expressions exist which can represent sentences in the same way as anaphorically employed pronouns represent nouns. Such expressions, prosentences, are then invented.

Prosentences are to sentences what pronouns are to nouns. A pronoun can be used anaphorically, as in 'Pedro has a donkey, and he beats *it*'. Prosentences resemble pronouns in that they occupy the places that pronouns can occupy. According to the prosentential theory, (3) must be reformulated

(3) For all propositions, if X states that thatt, then thatt

where 'thatt' is a prosentence that can be used anaphorically in place of any sentence. 'Is true' is thus eliminated in (3), in accordance with the redundancy theory of truth, and (3) is just as compatible with the objectual interpretation and a substitutional interpretation of the quantifier 'for all'. However, the manoeuvre appears too *ad hoc* to be satisfactory.[17]

Another objection to the redundancy theory of truth originates in the existence of truth value gaps. If, as Frege, for example thought, certain sentences that contain singular terms without reference, such as 'Pegasus flies' or 'The king of Poldavia sneezes', are neither true nor false, then the statement that *it is true that p* will be false, and in this case *it is true that p* cannot be equivalent to *p*.[18]

But even if we reject the idea that certain statements can be neither true nor false, the redundancy theory of truth cannot give the full meaning of the word 'true'. Dummett maintains that this theory is incompatible with the customary truth-conditional analyses of propositional connectives.[19] Let us suppose that '*p* is true' has the meaning of '*p* is assertable' in accordance with the theory. If we actually have the equivalence

(4) *p* is true and *q* is true if and only if *p* can be asserted and *q* can be asserted

we do not generally have the equivalence

(5) *p* is false iff not *p*

because, unlike a logical language, ordinary language does not have only one way of expressing negation (there is not just one rule which tells us when one sentence is the negation of another, for example: 'Someone has left'/'No-one has left'). We cannot call on a principle like (5) to explain the notion of negation, since we are already using the notion of negation there in order to explain the meaning of the word 'false'.

According to Dummett, the same difficulty affects our explanation of the meaning of 'or' by the equivalence

(6) '$p \lor q$' is true if and only if one is in a position to assert p and one is in a position to assert q

because we often assert $p \lor q$ in cases when we are not in a position to assert either one or the other. For example, if the teacher told the pupil 'Aristotle Onassis is a philosopher or Aristotle of Stagira is a philosopher', the pupil could assert the disjunction without being in a position to assert any one of its members. From this Dummett not only concludes that the redundancy theory of truth is incompatible with the analysis of the meaning of sentences in terms of truth conditions, but also that this analysis is incapable of explaining the meaning of sentences because, according to him, what the preceding difficulties show is that, in order to establish the truth conditions of a sentence, we must already know its meaning.[20]

The general difficulty with theories like the redundancy account of truth is that they describe only the external conditions of our use of the word 'true'. As Dummett says, we must also say what purpose the concept 'true' itself serves. From this point of view, truth is internal to judgement, in the sense when to accept a judgement is to *aim* for truth. Dummett compares true and false with winning and losing a game. But to describe a game solely by its result, by saying that it has been won or lost, is to miss the essential point, which is that the game is played in order to be won. In the same way, judgements are made in order to attain truth.[21] Carrying on the game metaphor, in this case, we are also in a redundancy situation: to play and to play to win are equivalent, or to play and to play correctly are redundant activities. But the fact that there is redundancy here, as in the case of truth, does not mean that we do not have a conception of what winning is, or a conception of what being true is for a judgement. The redundancy theory of truth is right in that, since truth is success in making a judgement, to make a judgement and to describe it as true are equivalent. But it can no more be concluded from this that the word 'true' is empty or devoid of content than it can be concluded from the fact that to play and to play to win are redundant, that there is no possible description of what it is to win a game.[22] In other words, if it is true that an analysis of the concept of truth that excluded the property of transparency would be inadequate, this does not imply that transparency is the only possible explanation of the concept of truth, as the redundancy theory of truth states. A distinction must therefore be made between transparency and redundancy, which is but one interpretation of it. A more satisfactory theory in this respect would be one that would take account of *both* the transparency of truth and of our intuitions regarding a more substantial theory, while still remaining a modest theory of truth. The semantic theory of truth permits precisely this.

5.4 The semantic theory of truth

5.4.1 Convention T

The previous paragraph concluded that, although the equivalence thesis (*p is true if and only if p*) was not sufficient to define truth, no adequate definition of truth could dispense with the equivalence thesis (and therefore with the 'transparency' of truth that it illustrated). Now when Tarski suggests what he calls the 'semantic' conception of truth, he takes this same equivalence thesis as the basis on which to formulate his 'material adequacy condition' for any definition of truth.

But the expressions 'theory of truth' or 'definition of truth' are ambiguous here and can have two meanings.

In the first place, the 'semantic theory of truth' sometimes designates a philosophical theory, purporting to be rival to the correspondence theory of truth or the redundancy theory of truth, for example, which Tarski suggested in his famous articles 'The Concept of Truth in Formal Languages' and 'The Semantic Conception of Truth'.[23] The second title probably suggests that the semantic conception might be one philosophic conception of truth amongst others. But Tarski denies that he wanted to propose any philosophical theory of truth. On the contrary, he maintains that the 'definition' that he proposes is neutral in relation to any substantial theory that we might have:

> The semantic definition of truth implies nothing regarding the conditions under which a sentence like . . .
>
> *Snow is white*
>
> can be asserted. It implies only that, whenever we assert or reject this sentence, we must be ready to assert or reject the correlated sentence . . .
>
> *The sentence 'snow is white' is true*
>
> Thus we may accept the semantic conception of truth without giving up any epistemological attitude we may have had: we may remain naive realists, critical realists or idealists, empiricists or metaphysicians – whatever we were before. The semantic conception of truth is completely neutral toward all these issues.[24]

I will come back in the next paragraph to the question of knowing whether the conception that Tarski proposes actually is neutral. But it is clear that if this conception is a theory of truth, it belongs to the category of modest theories, like the redundancy theory of truth.

In the second sense, a theory of truth is a semantic definition of truth for a language L, of the type presented in §2.2.1 and §4.1.2 for a propositional language and a classical quantificational language respectively. In order to distinguish this meaning from the previous one, I will in future refer to a 'T-theory' or to a 'theory of truth for L', when it is a question of designating a set of truth-conditions for the sentences of a given language L. Now it is clear that when Tarski talks about his 'semantic conception of truth' he is not talking about a philosophical definition of truth, or even, as is the case for the redundancy theory of truth, of an analysis of the meaning of the predicate 'is true' in a natural language, but of the way in which truth can be characterised *in relation to a formal language L*. In other words, according to Tarski, the properties of a theory of truth can only be evaluated in the framework of a T-theory.

A T-theory, or a definition of truth for L, must first and foremost be '*materially adequate*'. This means that the semantic predicate 'is true' which it characterises must 'retain the actual meaning of this old notion'. The material adequacy condition is what Tarski calls 'Convention T', that is to say the condition whereby the theory must have as its consequences all the instances of the following schema:

(T) S is true if and only if p

where S is a sentence or a description of a sentence and p a translation of that sentence (see below).

(T) is none other than the equivalence thesis, and in view of Tarski's statement quoted above, Convention T seems indistinguishable from a formulation of the redundancy theory of truth. But this impression is deceptive. In the first place, unlike supporters of the latter, Tarski emphasises the fact that (T) is in no way a definition of 'true'. It is only a condition of such a definition for a language L, which excludes definitions of truth that are not implied by schema (T). In the second place, a T-theory is relative to the *sentences* of a language L. Tarski explicitly acknowledges that truth is a predicate of these sentences and consequently is more ontologically committed *vis-à-vis* the truth-bearers than the redundancy theory.

The material adequacy condition is not enough. A T-theory must in addition be 'formally correct', that is to say bear on a language of which the syntactic structure is already specified. This is the case with the logical languages like the one for the first-order predicate calculus or the language for the calculus of classes analysed in the 1936 article. This is the first reason why Tarski thinks that a T-theory cannot be applied to a natural language: natural languages have an unspecified syntactic structure which allows ambiguity and vagueness. A T-theory in relation to a language L, of which it is the theory, is a *metalanguage* for L, which is its *object-language*. Without this distinction between metalanguage and object-language, a T-theory has no grounds for being, any more than does the semantic conception of which it is the expression. This in particular is the reason why Tarski thinks that a T-theory cannot be applied to a natural language, but only to an artificial or formal language. Natural languages do not respect the metalanguage/object-language distinction, and that is why, according to Tarski, they give rise to semantic paradoxes, such as that of the Liar, by allowing the statement of sentences like

'I am lying'

or

'The sentence written on line 34 of page 106 is false'.

The natural languages are in this sense 'semantically closed'; a formal language must be 'semantically open', that is to say it must refer to a distinct metalanguage of semantic terms like 'refer', 'designate' or 'is true'. This is the principle of the Tarskian solution of the Liar Paradox (cf. § 5.5 below).

Consequently, in the schema (T), 'S' designates a sentence in the object-language, and p is a sentence in the metalanguage of the theory, which gives an appropriate translation of S in the metalanguage. 'S' is therefore a *name* in a sentence in L, and is *quoted* or *mentioned* in (T), and not *used*. In case we are tempted to forget this fact, Tarski reminds us that 'S' can be replaced by what he calls a *structural noun* which *spells* the noun 'S' by means of signs of concatenation, such as for example

(7) S⌢n⌢o⌢w⌢i⌢s⌢w⌢h⌢i⌢t⌢e is true if and only if snow is white

This is another reason why (T) cannot be transformed into a definition of truth, according to which we might generalise (T) in the way in which Ramsey (cf. (2) above) generalises the property of the transparency of truth in

(8) $(\forall p)$('p' is true in L iff p).

In fact (8) would imply that one is quantifying within the quoted context (that is to say a non-extensional context (cf. § 6.2.2). 'S' functions as a proper name, with the result, to adopt an example of Quine's, that

Snow is white

is no more part of

'Snow is white'

than 'rat' is part of 'Socrates'.[25]

5.4.2 What a theory of truth does not tell us

Let us now come back to the T-theory for a classical quantificational language presented in the previous chapter (§ 4.2.1). This theory defines truth for the language Q, of which the syntactic structure is specified. Each of the theorems of the theory is an instance of schema (T), and all the sentences actually formed from the predicate calculus can be derived from the clauses of the theory. These latter determine recursively the truth conditions of the sentences of Q from features of their structure. Tarski's construction, which starts off from the predicates and their conditions of satisfaction by lists (sequences) of objects, defines truth by satisfaction by all the lists (sequences) (and falsity by satisfaction by no list (sequence)). The question is to know what the term 'definition' means here. The Tarskian construction has generally given rise to three sorts of interpretation.

The first interpretation tends towards the meaning of the statement by Tarski quoted above, whereby a semantic theory of truth is neutral in relation to any philosophical analysis of the concept of truth that we might have. I will call it the 'neutralist' or 'deflationary' interpretation. According to this interpretation, the Convention T is compatible with *any* substantial truth theory. For example, if we maintain that truth is correspondence with the facts, nothing prevents us from replacing any instance of (T) by

(T) 'S' corresponds to the facts iff p

or, if we maintain that truth is the warranted assertion or the assertibility of a sentence, by

(T) '*S*' is assertible in a warranted way iff *p*

or according to any other 'metaphysical' conception of truth. The fact that the conception proposed by Tarski is neutral in this sense explains the positivists' enthusiasm for it: it becomes possible to talk about truth or falsity without subscribing to any metaphysic of truth. This is the interpretation notably of Carnap, Ayer and Quine.[26]

According to a second interpretation, also favoured by positivist authors, the Tarskian 'definition' of truth is not really neutral, but used to serve a 'scientific vision of the world' according to which through their languages all the sciences can be reduced to physics and to the physicalist language of the unity of science. In this sense, what Tarski gave was a definition of truth in the sense of a *physicalist reduction* of this concept. This interpretation is obviously compatible with the first, in so far as the 'language of science' must exclude any metaphysical presupposition.

In his articles, Tarski himself seems to oscillate between the two interpretations. On the one hand, he declares that his theory is netural; and on the other, he suggests that it makes it possible to establish a scientific semantics, in which the concept of truth and the other semantic concepts, such as reference and designation, can through his definition be reduced to the status of respectable scientific concepts, in accord with the physicalist ideal of the positivists.

Lastly, according to a third interpretation, notably favoured by Popper,[27] Tarski's theory of truth is not neutral in relation to any substantial conception, but constitutes a version of the correspondence theory of truth, by giving such a theory a precise meaning. I will start by analysing the first two interpretations, in order to examine the third in the following paragraph.

Let us start with what militates in favour of the neutralist interpretation. The first thing to bear in mind is that the definition in question is related to a specific language *L*. Not only is the definition always relative to any *L*, but again *there is no formal definition of truth*, that is to say one that is valid for any language. This is one of the fundamental results Tarski gave in 1930: for a given object-language, it is not possible to formulate a theory of truth that satisfies Tarski's adequacy conditions within this object-language, and more generally no theory of truth for a language can be given within this same language. In other words, we must always have a hierarchy of object-languages and metalanguages that is infinite, and consequently prohibits any universal definition of truth.[28]

In the second place, the Tarskian definition of truth is not a definition of the meaning or of the intension of the predicate 'is true', but a definition of its *extension*. It is ascertained that this definition is extensionally correct, that is to say that the *T*-sentences of the theory enable all the true sentences in the language *L* under consideration to be expressed. If two *T*-theories imply the same *T*-sentences, then they are coextensive, and describe the same truth predicate. As already noted in the previous paragraph, the *T*-sentences are of no help to us in contexts where we use the word 'true' to designate the contents of statements, as in 'Everything Aristotle says is true' or 'What you said yesterday was true'. As Davidson notes:

> *T*-sentences do not . . . show how to live without a truth predicate; but taken together, they do tell what it would be like to have one. For since there is a *T*-sentence corresponding to each sentence of the language for which truth is in question, the totality of *T*-sentences exactly fixes the extension, among the sentences, of any predicate that plays the role of the words 'is true'. From this it is clear that although *T*-sentences do not define truth, they can be used to define truth predicatehood: any predicate is a truth predicate that makes all *T*-sentences true.[29]

In other words, a characterisation of truth for a language *L* can be considered as simply specifying the extension of the truth predicate, which explains how the truth value of any sentence in *L* depends on the semantic properties of its parts, and provides the foundations of a logical analysis of truth and of logical consequence for *L*. A *T*-theory in this sense does not provide any explanation of truth. This accords well with the deflationary or neutralist conception.

None the less, is it not possible to say that the Tarskian definition is a definition in a stronger sense, that is to say in the sense of an *elimination* of the predicate 'is true'? In a *T*-theory, like the one presented in § 4.2.1, the *T*-sentences allow us to eliminate every occurrence of the notion of truth to the right of the biconditionals, in favour of the notion of satisfaction. In this sense, Tarski can claim to have defined the notion of truth by means of a more primitive notion, and thereby to have effected a form of conceptual reduction, of the type the positivist philosophers sought in the 1930s. In an important passage in his article 'The Establishment of a Scientific Semantics', he declares that if a definition of semantic concepts like that of truth could not be given 'it would be difficult to bring this method into harmony with the postulates of the unity of science and of physicalism (since the concepts of semantics would be neither logical nor physical concepts)'.[30] It must be acknowledged that this is an isolated statement, and insufficient to attribute explicit physicalist motivations to Tarski. But at least one contemporary philosopher, Hartry Field, has taken it seriously and has tried to find out how the Tarskian definition could achieve this reductionist programme.[31]

Rather than go back again to the example of *T*-theory for the language of the predicate calculus used so far, let us consider an even simpler language, which we will call *L*, of which the syntax is composed of two nouns, *a* and *b*, and two predicates, *P* and *P'*. The only axioms we need in a theory of truth for *L* are respectively

(A) two axioms specifying the reference of *a* and *b* in *L*:
   (I) *a* in *L* denotes Marilyn Monroe
   (II) *b* in *L* denotes Margaret Thatcher;

(B) two axioms specifying the conditions of satisfaction of the predicates
   P and P' in L:
   (I) an object satisfies P in L iff it is sexy,
   (II) an object satisfies P' in L iff it is permed;
(C) one 'compositional' axiom specifying the truth conditions of every
   sentence composed from the primitive vocabulary of L: a sentence
   coupling a noun n with a predicate P is true iff the object denoted by
   the noun n satisfies the predicate P.

The language L is a finite language; in fact it only allows four sentences to be formed; the T-theory for L enables us to establish their truth conditions.

If, like Field, we taken the reductionist intention of Tarski's definition seriously, we will say that the axioms of the T-theory for L constitute *partial definitions* of semantic concepts of truth, reference and satisfaction; their *complete* definitions will be given by the set of these partial definitions.[32] But how can the axioms of L be considered as definitions of the semantic concepts in question? The only definitions are the following:

(D) for any noun n in L, and for any object o, n denotes o in L iff: n is a and o is Marilyn Monroe, or n is b and o is Margaret Thatcher;
(S) for any predicate P in L, and for any object o, o satisfies P iff: n is P and o is sexy, or n is P' and o is permed;
(V) for any sentence s of L, s is true in L iff: s is Pa, and Marilyn Monroe is sexy, s is $P'a$ and Marilyn Monroe is permed; s is Pb and Margaret Thatcher is sexy, s is $P'b$ and Margaret Thatcher is permed.

(D), (S) and (V) are in fact definitions, for L, of the semantic notions of denotation (or reference), satisfaction and truth, since no mention is made, on the right-hand side of the biconditionals, of these semantic notions. In a more complex language, like Q in the previous chapter, reference and satisfaction are not defined, as here, by finite enumerations, since it is assumed that there can be an infinity of objects in the sequences that satisfy the open sentences of Q. In this case, the definition of truth is recursive.

But, according to Field, these definitions cannot be true reductive definitions of semantic concepts. All that Tarski shows is that truth can be reduced to satisfaction, and satisfaction to the notion of primitive denotation, that is to say semantic notions can be reduced to *other semantic notions*. But this is not a *bona fide* physicalist definition. The T-theory for L is extensionally correct. But extensional correctness is not everything. A true reduction must be able to tell us how semantic facts, like the fact that a name designates a certain object, or that a certain sentence has certain truth conditions, depend on facts concerning their users and their environment. By this, Field does not only mean that a *semantic* theory is not a *pragmatic* theory for a language. He means that the notion of primitive denotation, which the T-theory invokes, must itself be physicalistically reduced, in the same way as the concept of valency in chemistry was defined in atomist terms. It is just as absurb to claim authentically to define truth by satisfaction as it is to want to define the chemical valency of a body by means of 'definitions' of the type of:

> ($\forall E$)($\forall n$) (E has the valency n iff E is potassium and n is $+1$ or . . ., or E is sulphur and n is -2).[33]

How, according to Field, could the appropriate reductions of semantic concepts be effected? By defining the notion of reference in a *causal* way; that is to say by establishing the link of cause and effect that could exist between the physical facts and the semantic facts of reference or denotation.[34]

To advance a reductionist ideal of this type is not the same thing as achieving it, and Field gives no more than indications on this score. But even if he showed exactly how to reduce reference in the way in which chemical valency can be reduced, his argument would not be acceptable. A first reason is that in some way Field makes a category mistake: when we use the notion of reference, in relation to a natural language, we do so to explain the content of what someone says, that is to say to rationalise his behaviour. In this sense, unlike the chemical valency of a body, reference is not a causal notion. To explain a human behaviour is relative to our explanatory interests: why did X do this or say that? When we ask these sorts of questions, we are not expecting an answer in causal and physical terms, or at least in terms of physical causes.[35]

A second reason is that if, as Field maintains, Tarski had wanted actually to reduce semantic concepts to physicalistically acceptable concepts, then he would not even have reduced reference to primitive denotation. Field's objection is that if, for example, we have two distinct languages in which a same predicate R applies respectively to round objects and to red objects, the clauses of a T-theory which would ascribe these differences would not explain why these differences arose. But the same objection can be addressed to Tarski, in the case where there were two distinct languages for which the connective '$\lor$' meant respectively 'and' and 'or'. The clauses (T) which ascribed the respective truth conditions of the sentences containing this connective, would no more explain the difference.[36] The reason is that Tarski's type of definition of truth supposes the meaning of the logical constants, such as '$\&$', '$\lor$' or '$\to$', to be fixed in advance. Tarski explicitly maintains that a list of these constants can only be given because there is no objective foundation for the distinction between logical and non-logical constants.[37] Consequently, all that can be said is that Tarski has reduced certain semantic notions, like those of truth and reference, to other semantic notions, like those of reference of a noun to an object, satisfaction, predicate, negation of a formula, disjunction and conjunction of two formulas, and existential generalisation.

The moral is clear. Whether or not Tarski wished to establish a 'scientific semantics' by physicalist reduction of the semantic concepts, he has shown that semantics can be a logical discipline constructed from exact concepts and methods. But he has not reduced the semantic notions to primitive physicalist notions. A T-theory in itself does not imply any particular conception, nor any explanation of the semantic relationships, truth or reference, and in this sense can only be a 'pure' and not a 'descriptive' semantics, according to Carnap's distinction.[38]

I conclude from this that the neutralist or deflationary interpretation of Tarski's theory of truth is correct. I would also like to conclude that it is the correct theory of truth. But we must take care here not to confuse two things; (a) the fact that the semantic conception of truth neither explains nor defines the concept of truth (and of reference), but only specifies the extension of the truth predicate (and the relationship of reference) for one language; and (b) the thesis according to which the semantic conception is compatible with *any* substantial conception of truth.

(a) does not imply (b). (b) would be true if, like the redundancy theory of truth, Tarski's theory aimed to give the meaning of the word 'true' and to explain every use of this term. But, as we have seen, it does not do this, any more than it is equivalent to the redundancy theory of truth. And above all (b) is false because Tarski's theory is not compatible with any substantial conception of truth. Why?

1. If we acknowledge that certain sentences can be neither true nor false (such as sentences that contain nouns without denotation), then the equivalence thesis on which Convention T rests ceases to be valid. Let us suppose that 'p' is neither true nor false in

   'p' is true iff p.

This biconditional will then be false, since the right-hand part of the biconditional will be neither true nor false.

2. According to Dummett's argument, presented above (§ 5.4.2), the equivalence thesis is incompatible with a truth-conditional analysis of the connectives, and consequently with the idea according to which a T-theory would give the meaning conditions of the connectives by giving their truth conditions. Dummett concludes from this that it is not the truth conditions of the connectives that give their meaning, but their assertion or verification conditions. He suggests substituting this latter notion for that of truth. If he is right, the Tarskian theory is not compatible with a verificationist conception of truth. I will examine this point in the next chapter.

3. It is difficult to harmonise Convention T with a theory of truth as coherence. Let us suppose that we adapt schema (T) in this way

   (CT) 'p' is true if L iff 'p' is coherent with other sentences of L.[40]

We then lose the effect of the 'disquotation' of (T), since the right-hand side of the biconditional mentions sentences of L. The coherence theory of truth supposes that truth is a relationship between sentences, and not between sentences and reality. It is this that makes the coherentist theory so different from what (T) suggests. To adopt Dummett's expression, (T) suggests that there is something *by virtue of which* 'p' is true. Dummett calls this intuition 'realist'. If there is one substantial theory to which Tarski's semantic conception seems to be *nearer* than others, it is the correspondence theory of truth.

5.4.3 What a theory of truth can tell us

According to Popper, Tarski's theory of truth is 'a *rehabilitation* and an elaboration of the classical theory that truth is correspondence to facts'.[41] But the only reason he gives is that the fact that we can talk, in a metalanguage, about the truth of sentences in an object-language shows that we have the means to express what the object-language describes, namely, according to Popper, the facts. In other words the *T* convention can be interpreted by

P corresponds to the facts iff *p*.

But, as has been seen, it is difficult for this to pass for a definition of correspondence, and even harder to provide a criterion for the individuation of facts.

It is not at this level that Tarski's theory is correspondentist. It is rather, as Davidson has suggested,[42] by virtue of the role played by the concept of satisfaction in that theory. Truth is the satisfaction of an open sentence by all the sequences of objects. But Davidson observes that sequences do not play the same role as facts, particularly because of the variables, which do not refer to particular individuals: as has been seen, one must consider satisfaction by functions from variables to sequences of objects. But the idea of a relationship between a language and reality remains at the centre of the theory.

Davidson constructs a contrast between two sorts of correspondentist theories: one invoking the notion of fact, the other invoking the satisfaction relationship. According to him, the error of the first arises from the fact that they seek to include in the entity to which a true sentence corresponds not only the objects on which the sentence bears, but also everything the sentence says about them. The result is that it becomes difficult to describe the fact that a sentence expresses without using the sentence itself, in a redundant or trivial way. When, on the contrary, the concept of satisfaction is invoked, the sentences really are being anchored in a reality, but this reality is not intended to imitate or to represent what the sentence describes. The entities, the sequences, which 'correspond' to the sentences, are arbitrarily associated with the variables. According to Davidson, Tarski's theory therefore makes it possible to reconcile two of our most fundamental intuitions about truth: 'Statements are true or false because of the words used in making them, and it is words that have interesting, detailed, conventional connections with the world.'[43]

There is no doubt that if Tarski's theory is correspondentist, it is in this sense that it is. But is this enough to justify a truly correspondentist theory? To say that the truth of 'Every marmoset likes bananas' is explained by the satisfaction of the predicates 'marmoset', 'likes' and 'banana' by the sequences of objects to which these predicates apply does not teach us a lot. By virtue of *what* is 'marmoset' applied to marmosets? We fall into the difficulty Field put forward apropos the idea of reference: a satisfactory correspondentist theory must, in one way or another, *explain* the relationships between the words and the world. To say that these are conventional relationships leaves us feeling frustrated.

That satisfaction offers us a point of anchorage between the words and the world does not mean that Tarski's theory of truth is a correspondentist theory in a stronger sense. According to Davidson, truth is 'correspondence with the way things are', but this correspondence does not imply that intermediary entities are postulated between the sentences and reality, and does not imply that there is a *confrontation* between these latter. The notion of reference, no more than that of truth, does not need to be defined, or reduced to a more primitive notion.[44] We really can agree with the idea that what is involved there is a form of realism, in the sense evoked above: there is something by virtue of which sentences are true. But if Davidson's interpretation is correct, nothing more can be asked of a realist thesis. Is this a trivial realism, similar to that expressed when we say 'it is true that p' has the meaning 'p corresponds to the facts', or is this a more substantial realism? Davidson suggests this. But in order to be able to evaluate his argument, we have to analyse a point that has not yet figured in our discussion here: the relationship between a theory of truth and a theory of meaning. As I observed above, Convention T does not allow us to account for contexts such as 'What he says is true', any more than the redundancy theory of truth does. The Tarskian theory makes truth a predicate of *sentences*. In this sense, it justifies a philosophy of logic for which the truth-bearers are entities like sentences. But it can be legitimately maintained that truth is a predicate of *propositions*, in the sense of the contents of sentences, as is illustrated by the difficulty of making the equivalence thesis compatible with metalinguistic statements such as 'What he said is true' Of course, nothing obliges us to say that these statements must be analysed with the help of a quantification on propositional entities, and analyses, such as those of the 'prosentential' theory, are attempts to avoid this implication.

If the preceding remarks are correct, although Tarski's theory of truth is, in an important sense, 'deflationary', there is more to say about truth than is implied by a deflationary or 'minimalist' theory such as the redundancy conception of truth. In particular, if the latter is best conceived as predicating truth of contents of propositions or judgements, we need an account of these contents, which cannot simply be presupposed.[45]

To answer these questions, we have to know how Tarski's type of truth theory can be a theory of *meaning*. The next chapter will be devoted to this problem.

5.5 Truth and the Liar Paradox

The adequacy of a theory of truth is not only measured by its capacity to account for the ordinary meaning of the word 'true', or by its relationship to the substantial philosophical theories. A logical theory, as Russell said apropos his theory of descriptions,[46] also owes its value to its capacity to resolve a certain number of puzzles and paradoxes. One of the principal problems that motivated Tarski's theory was, as I indicated above, the Liar Paradox. I will be able to mention only some of these difficulties.[47]

In its most classic version, the paradox concerns the sentence

    (M) (M is false)

Let us suppose that (M) is true; in that case, it is false. Let us suppose that (M) is false, in that case it is true. Consequently, if (M) is true, it is false.

Tarski's diagnosis consists of noting that (M) is a self-referential sentence, which predicates in the object-language the truth of a sentence of this object-language. All that is necessary to avoid the paradox is to prevent the formation of such self-referential sentences, by relativising truth to a language, by prohibiting the truth predicate from being defined within the object-language, and by postulating a hierarchy of object-languages and metalanguages. This strategy can only be applied within the framework of a formal language, as natural languages lead to the formation of suspect self-referential sentences.

Tarski's solution is far from being the only one possible. As has been seen, Convention T does not apply to sentences that are neither true nor false. A possible solution of the Liar is to say that (M) is neither true nor false, and to adopt a three-valued logic, in which the third truth value is the 'paradoxical' value.[48] But this solution runs into the following difficulty: one can state the sentence

    (R) (R) is not true

Let us suppose that (MR) is neither true nor false, and 'paradoxical'. It follows that the sentence above is not true. But the sentence above is (R) and therefore (R) is not true. We have stated that what we said was neither true nor false. In addition, the statement that (R) is not true involves us in saying that '(R) is not true' is true, contrary to our hypothesis. This paradox is known as the 'Strengthened Liar'.[49]

This shows that the three-valued solution is probably not as natural as it seems. But neither is Tarski's solution. It suggests that we can mark out the levels of statements which allow us to relativise the truth at these different levels, each of which have their index of truth. But, as Kripke observes, a number of the statements that we make do not attach an implicit index to the predicate 'true'. For example

    (8) Most of Nixon's statements about Watergate are false

bears, it seems, on the higher level of Nixon's statements on Watergate. But if these statements include

    (9) Everything Dean says about Watergate is false

then what Dean says will be one degree higher than what Nixon says, and what Nixon says one degree higher than what Dean says. Ordinarily, we have no means of determining the 'level' of someone's statements. The problem is even trickier when it is Dean who states (8).[49] In other words, Tarski's theory is artificial and does not account for natural uses of 'is true' in these cases. A correct approach must account for the fact that our attributions of truth are 'risky': they do not depend on the level of language of what someone said, but on what someone is found, empirically speaking, to have said.

Kripke suggests an approach that has affinities with the three-valued solution, but differs from it in that he does not suggest giving paradoxical sentences a third truth value, but suggests not giving them any truth value at all.

Kripke's basic idea is as follows. Although a sentence such as

(10) (10) is true

is not paradoxical, it has not got determined truth conditions. In general, when one asserts sentences like

(11) Most of what you say is true

which say that the sentences of a certain class C are true, the truth value of sentences of type (11) can be established if the truth values of the sentences of class C are. If some of these sentences themselves make use of the idea of truth, their truth value must be established by invoking other sentences, and so on. Lastly, if the process is completed by sentences that do not mention the concept of truth, so that the truth value of the initial statement can be established, these sentences will be called *grounded*; if not they will be called *ungrounded*. All the sentences will not have a truth value. For example, (3) is not grounded, any more than is (6) and, of course, the condemned sentence (M). In formal terms, Kripke constructs a hierarchy of languages, where at each level the truth predicate is the predicate of the level immediately below it. At the lowest level, the predicate 'is true' is totally undefined (ungrounded). At the next level, it is applied to sentences that do not contain 'is true', following the rules of a three-valued logic.[50] These evaluations go towards constituting the extension of the predicate 'is true' to the next level, and the process continues until it stops at a 'fixed point', a point at which all the sentences that belong to the extension of 'is true' already belong to it. This construction accounts for the fluctuating and risky character of attributions of truth, since the paradoxical character of a sentence can be intrinsic ('This sentence is false') or circumstantial ('The sentence quoted on p. 116, line 33 is false').[51]

The interest of Kripke's solution is that it rejects the idea of a *fixed* or *intrinsic* hierarchy of object-languages and metalanguages which the orthodox solution acknowledges. As Kripke says, each statement must find its own level. None the less, this does not mean that the idea of a hierarchy of languages is being abandoned. How can Kripke's approach account for the difficulty of the Strengthened Liar, which threatens any theory that invokes the idea of truth value gaps? 'Grounded' or 'paradoxical', says Kripke, do not belong to the hierarchy of languages but to the *metalanguage* of this hierarchy. If we say 'This sentence is false or paradoxical', we are as a result making a statement in this latter metalanguage and we escape the Strengthened Liar. But then, as Kripke says, 'the ghost of Tarski is still with us'.[52]

The discussions about the Liar reveal the conflict that exists between Tarski's semantic conception, which seems to rest on the notion of bivalence, and the theories that reject it. The next chapter is devoted to another version of this conflict.

——— 6 ———

TRUTH, MEANING AND REALISM

6.1 Theories of truth and theories of meaning

Frege maintains that to give the sense of a sentence is to give its truth conditions, and that the sense of a constituent part of a sentence determines the meaning of the latter. The first principle is usually called the *principle of truth-conditionality*, and the second *the principle of compositionality*.[1] For Frege, a theory of sense or meaning for a logical language (a *Begriffsschrift*) has the following form: its assigns a certain property, which we can call *semantic value*, to each simple component of a sentence formed according to the rules of syntax of the language, and establishes rules that determine the semantic value of complex expressions, given the semantic value of their components. For Frege, the semantic value of an expression is its reference: for names, objects; for predicates, functions; and so on. For a sentence, its reference is its truth value, the true or the false. If we disregard this latter feature, specific to the Fregean conception, we will say that the semantic value of a sentence is the property it has of being true or false, if and only if certain truth conditions are realised.[2]

If we adapt these Fregean conceptions to the ideas set out in the previous chapter, we can say that a theory of meaning for L is a theory which shows us how to derive a theorem of the form 'S is true iff p' for each sentence of L. In other words, a theory of meaning is nothing but a theory of truth, or a T-theory. In fact, T-sentences establish, in a metalanguage, the truth conditions of sentences of the object-language L, situated to the left of the biconditional sign. To give the sense of a sentence for a formal language is simply to give its truth conditions. A Tarskian theory of truth satisfies the requirements both of truth-conditionality and of compositionality, since it shows recursively how to determine the truth conditions of complex sentences from those of simple sentences, and these latter from the conditions of reference and satisfaction of their component elements.

This picture of the relationship between a theory of meaning and a theory of truth raises several questions.

(I) First and foremost, is a Tarski-type truth theory the only possible form of semantics for a language? We saw in § 4.2.1 that the absolute concept of truth used by Tarski was not the only one possible. A truth theory can relativise truth and reference to a model or a structure.[3]

(II) Then, must the concept of truth be the central concept for an analysis of meaning? In other words, does a theory of meaning necessarily take the form of a theory of *truth*? The previous chapter showed that a theory of truth did not provide any analysis of the concept of truth, even if it retained a modest or minimal concept of truth. The question here is to know if this concept is enough, and even necessary for an analysis of meaning.

(III) The preceding two questions relate to meaning in a *formal* language. But in order for them to remain fully general, it must also relate to meaning in a *natural* language. Can a theory of meaning for a natural language be a theory of truth?

As has been seen, Tarski rejected the application of his definition of truth to natural languages. The two authors who have posed questions (I) and (II) most clearly in the recent tradition of the philosophy of logic and language are Davidson and Dummett. Davidson has suggested a set of adequacy conditions in order that a theory of meaning for a natural language can take the form of a theory of truth in Tarski's sense. Dummett has maintained that this proposition rested on debatable presuppositions as to the nature of meaning and of truth. This led him to reply to (II) and (III) in the negative. For Dummett, these theses, specific to the philosophy of language, have an immediate consequence for the philosophy of logic: depending on the answer given to questions (I)–(III), a conception of logic is 'realist' – whereby the only possible logic is classical logic – or anti-'realist' – whereby the only possible logic is intuitionist logic. In other words, according to Dummett, the status of logic hangs on the status of a general theory of meaning, common to natural languages and formal languages. That is why examination of the structure and range of a general theory of meaning must concern us here. In what follows, I will allow the close dependence that Dummett suggests between logic and language: logic *is* a language, and in this capacity, we must investigate the general form that a theory of meaning must take both for logical languages and formal languages, and the possibility of applying one to the other. The whole problem is to know if a general theory of meaning can have the general structure that Davidson and Dummett give it, and if it has precisely the consequences that Dummett draws from it.

6.2 Davidsons's programme

6.2.1 Meaning elucidated by truth

The phrase 'theory of meaning', as used in the previous paragraph, is potentially ambiguous. In a general sense, a theory of meaning is a philosophical analysis of the concept of meaning, analysing this concept in terms of other concepts, or at least establishing its relationships to these concepts. In the specific sense that interests us here, a theory of meaning is a theory in the axiomatic sense of the term, that is to say a set of axioms from which it is possible to derive theorems establishing, for each sentence of a given language, its meaning of the form

(M) *s* means (in *L*) that *p*.

It seems that there are only two ways of making such a theory of meaning accurate. Either the sentence 'p' situated to the right in (M) is s itself, as in

(1) 'Héloïse loves Abélard' means that Héloïse loves Abélard

but in that case, the theory is trivial, because it only 'establishes' the meaning of the sentence in question for those who already know this meaning. Or else the sentence that takes the place of 'p' is a *translation* of s, in which case we must know on what bases this translation was carried out, that is to say either already actually know the meaning of s and p, or else know that one is the translation of the other, without knowing their meaning, as in

(2) 'Héloïse liebt Abélard' means that 'Héloïse aime Abélard'

a sentence that we know is true without knowing what either of the sentences thus translated means (in *our* language).

In either case, one is therefore led to presuppose the concept of meaning, or, which amounts to the same thing, that of identity of meaning. A change of tactics is therefore necessary, and a theory formulated that does not invoke the concept of meaning itself but a concept that can adequately play the role of this concept. Davidson suggests simply resorting to the concept of truth and replacing the form (M) by the familiar formula

'(T) s is true iff p'

where p is either s itself (in which case the theory in question is *homophonic*), or a sentence that establishes the truth conditions of s in the metalanguage. In other words, Davidson suggests applying Convention T to the sentences of a natural language and identifying a theory of meaning for a natural language with a theory of truth for that language. But how can (T) teach us anything about the *meaning* of s? Just as someone can know that (2) is true without having the slightest idea what the sentences to left and right mean, someone can know that

(3) 'Snarks are boojums' is true iff snarks are boojums

without having the slightest idea what the sentence means.

Apart from this, if the T-sentences supposed to give the meaning of the sentences of the language under consideration are true, if the biconditional 'iff' which appears in the latter is understood in the truth functional sense, it only requires the *truth* of the sentences situated to its left and right, with the result that

(4) 'Snow is white' is true iff grass is green

should 'give us the meaning' of the sentence 'snow is white'!

If it were reduced to this, Davidson's proposition would obviously be absurd. It is not purely and simply a question of substituting the concept of truth for that of meaning, but of extracting sufficient information capable of providing us with T-sentences in order to determine meaning through them.

It is not true that the *T*-sentences are trivial. To state that

(5) Something satisfies the predicate 'bald' iff that thing is bald

is saying something entirely informative about the relationship between an English word and objects. In this sense, it is extremely plausible that (5) states a satisfaction condition of the predicate 'bald', in such a way that a speaker who did not know the *meaning* of this predicate could not be said to know it.[4] The same applies to apparently trivial *T*-sentences, such as

(6) 'Snow is white' is true iff snow is white

or even such as (3). To know the sense of a sentence, is *at least* to know its truth conditions. In this sense, the Fregean principle of truth-conditionality is justified for a natural language.

On the other hand, it is true that (4) in no way establishes the 'truth conditions' of the sentence concerned. But this is only true if one confines oneself to (4) taken individually. But a *T*-theory is not only a list of sentences such as (4) or (5). A *T*-theory does more. It does not treat sentences such as 'snow is white' or 'grass is green' as unstructured, but on the contrary as composed of elements that contribute to the truth conditions, and therefore (by the hypothesis under consideration) to the meaning of the sentences. This fact cannot fail to emerge as soon as we do not consider isolated *T*-sentences, but a *set* of *T*-sentences, and the general structure of the theory. This can be shown in the following way.[5]

Let us suppose that we are dealing with a language, Hanglish, characterised by a *T*-theory, which provides *T*-sentences such as

(7) 'Armadillos curl' is true (in Hanglish) iff oil prices go up.

We want to know if Hanglish, characterised by this type of *T*–sentences is our language, English, that is to say if the *T*-theory is actually a theory of meaning for English, making it possible to *interpret* the statements of this language. How is it possible to arrive at such clauses? There are two possibilities. Either Hanglish treats *T*-sentences like (7) as unstructured, but in that case Hanglish is not our language, because we are taking into consideration the manner in which the words 'Armadillos' and 'curl' systematically contribute to the sense of the sentence 'Armadillos curl'. Or else theorem (7) systematically derives from other clauses governing the reference and satisfaction of its components. Let us suppose that these clauses are

(8) 'Armadillo' is satisfied by oil prices
(9) 'curl' is satisfied by entities that go up.

In this second case, we must become aware of the anomaly by the indirect route of other *T*-sentences. Let us suppose that in Hanglish (as in English), the predicate 'is a mammal' is satisfied by objects that are mammals. In this case, other T-sentences in the T-theory for Hanglish might be derived, such as

(10) 'Armadillos are mammals' is true iff oil prices are mammals.

Most of us do not believe that oil prices are mammals but we believe that the sentence on the left of the biconditional in (10) is true. An interpreter of English who uses the meanings of the T-sentences for Hanglish to characterise it would not fail to become aware of this fact. He would discover, for example, that most people acknowledge the truth of 'Armadillos are mammals' but doubt whether oil prices are, or behave as if they are. He would conclude that Hanglish is not our language. These empirical facts, taken together with consideration of the overall structure of the T-theory, should dismiss irrelevant T-sentences such as (10), (7) and (4).

Davidson therefore does not deny that Tarski's sort of theory of truth is not in itself a theory of meaning for a natural language. If his programme were confined to this identification of meaning and truth conditions it would lay itself open to the objections raised by numerous critics: T-theories can be constructed for a natural language (or a fragment of natural language) L, which preserve the deductive relationships between its sentences, give the correct truth conditions of these sentences, but which are nevertheless inadequate to give the meaning of the sentences of L, or do not permit us to interpret L.[6] Davidson's idea, however, is that a T-theory for a natural language must make it possible to represent a *sufficient* amount of the relationship of identity of meaning used in (S) by means of a less fine relationship of identity of truth values used in (T) for a T-theory to be able, provided the empirical constraints of interpretation are observed, not to *constitute* a theory of meaning, but to *serve* as a theory of meaning. As John McDowell says: 'The thesis should be, not that sense is what a theory of truth is a theory of, but rather that truth is what a theory of sense is a theory of'.[7]

This circuitous approach to meaning in natural languages does not therefore originate from an application of a logical semantics to a semantics for natural languages, which is at first glance completely illegitimate (for reasons which Tarski put forward). Davidson follows Quine here. Like him, he is doubtful whether the notion of meaning can be given a precise or non-circular analysis and thinks that difficulties of principle affect this notion as well as the correlative ones of translation and of propositions as meanings of sentences (cf. § 1.4). But unlike Quine, Davidson does not conclude that the notion of meaning is irremediably indeterminate. He does not deny – to answer the question we asked at the end of the last chapter – that we predicated the truth of the contents of sentences, or propositions, and not only of sentences as linguistic entities, with the result that T-sentences state a property of the sentences of the object-language *individuated* by virtue of their content. But here it is the same for theories of meaning as for theories of truth: some are substantial or, to adopt Dummett's expression, *full-blooded*, and seek their basis in a rich concept of meaning, while others are modest, minimalist, grounded in the modest concept of truth. The programme for the analysis of meaning in natural language that Davidson suggests obviously belongs to the category of modest theories.

So far, my aim has been to set out the motivations of Davidson's programme. I will now give a more synthetic presentation of the requirements which, according to him, must govern a theory of meaning for a natural language.[8]

The first and main requirement set down by Davidson is that a theory of meaning for a natural language must permit us to explain how the speakers of this language can *understand* the sentences of it. As numerous linguists have recognised, and as Chomsky in particular has emphasised, this is the aptitude that every speaker has to understand a potentially infinite set of sentences on the basis of a finite set of elements composing these sentences. This requirement is satisfied by the recursive character of a Tarskian theory of truth, which shows how the truth conditions of complex sentences are determined from a stock of primitive elements constituting their structure. Davidson suggests that a theory of the syntax of a natural language must have recourse to this model, which corresponds to the Fregean principle of compositionality. But a distinction must be made here between two sorts of *T*-theories. A *T*-theory can take the form of a set of *T*-sentences (theorems) which simply reproduce the sentences of the language in question to the left of the biconditional. Such theories simply take the form of lists (if necessary infinite). They are correct (they match each sentence with its homophonic truth conditions), but inadequate because, as in the example examined above, they reveal nothing of the structure of the sentences. *T*-theories, resting on a *finite* set of axioms giving the clauses for every primitive semantic component of the language, will, on the contrary, make it possible not only to discern the structure of the sentences, which is an essential element of their meaning and understanding, but also to show how our infinite aptitude has finite bases. A finite *T*-theory therefore accounts for the fact that a language must also be *learned* in order to be understood.

In the second place, a *T*-theory must 'give the meaning' of the sentences of the language under consideration, and must in this sense enable us to interpret this language. As seen above, *T*-sentences fulfil this function. But the preceding discussion shows that it is the overall structure of the theory, with its axioms and its theorems, and not *T*-sentences taken individually, which can give these truth conditions. The crucial point of Davidson's proposal is that the truth conditions are applied to a *holistic* structure of natural language under consideration. Meaning in a natural language is, according to Davidson, holistic: the sense of an isolated sentence cannot be determined and understood independently of the sense of the *other* sentences of the language, and consequently of the way in which the elements that compose them make a recurrent systematic contribution to the truth conditions of the sentences of the *whole* of the language. On this point too, Davidson agrees with Quine, who also defends a holistic conception of meaning (§ 1.4.3).[9] The holism of the *T*-theory and of the language it takes as its target is matched by the holism of the interpretation procedure. According to Davidson, the interpreter considers a set of sentences, and discerns their structure from recurrent elements in the set. As in the example of Hanglish, he excludes undesirable candidates by invoking both his own beliefs, which he supposes to be true, and the external conditions of the interpretation (what he knows about the behaviour of the speakers, and the causal relationships they maintain with the world). In doing this, the interpreter is making use of a principle of 'charity' or of 'maximisation of agreement' between his beliefs and those of the speakers he has the task of interpreting: he must not attribute false or absurd beliefs to the speaker of the language that he is interpreting as long as he has no other confirmations of what the speakers believe. In other words, he must not suppose to be true more beliefs of the people he is interpreting than he himself supposes to be true (cf. § 13.4.2). These empirical interpretation conditions – which I have done no more than sketch out here – form what Davidson calls a theory of *radical interpretation*. It plays an essential and indispensable role in filling in the distance that from the start exists between a theory of meaning and a theory of truth.[10]

A third requirement of a theory of meaning is that, in order to state the truth conditions of sentences, it must not resort to richer concepts than those that these sentences contain. This requirement is ensured by a homophonic T-theory or, failing this, by a T-theory, the metalanguage of which is not essentially richer than the object-language. This is the case for an absolute theory of truth, such as that presented in § 4.2.1. Davidson is doubtful whether this requirement is satisfied by T-theories invoking the concept of truth under an interpretation, or in a model, like those that invoke the notion of 'possible world' in order to analyse languages containing modal operators ('it is possible that', 'it is necessary that', cf. Chapter 7). It is on these terms that a theory of meaning can have the required modesty.[11]

A fourth and last requirement is that a theory of meaning be *empirically testable*. According to Davidson, this is satisfied if the three previous requirements are met, and if the theory can be successfully used in a radical interpretation procedure. Like Quine, Davidson supposes that a theory of meaning can only be tested if it is possible, on the basis of the behaviour of the speakers of a language, to determine which T-sentences of the corresponding T-theory they *hold true*, or to which they give their assent. Here again, it is by supposing that truth is a property towards which assertions tend, that it is possible, from the attitude of 'holding true', to determine the meaning of these assertions.

As has been seen, these requirements depend on each other, and can only function in conjunction. To understand a language (one's own or someone else's) is to be in a position to interpret it, and to be in a position to interpret it is to be capable of determining the meaning of sentences of that language, which in turn is only possible by giving their truth conditions and their structure. A theory of meaning in the Tarskian mould and obeying the prescribed empirical conditions aims, by presupposing as little as possible of the content of the concept of meaning – that is to say by systematically exploiting the link between this latter and truth – to represent what the speakers understand, that is to say the knowledge they have of their own language. In what sense is a T-theory a representation of the understanding that the speakers have of their language?

This cannot be the explicit and conscious understanding that they have of it, for obvious reasons: we cannot attribute speakers of English, for example, with an explicit knowledge of a T-theory for English, any more than they have knowledge of the technical notions used by this type of theory, such as sequence, satisfaction or theorem. In other words, understanding a language is not simply knowing a T-theory for that language, but a T-theory describes *what the speakers are understanding when they understand their language*. Consequently, if a T-theory represents the semantic competence of actual speakers, its way of doing so is much more like the way a map, which is an abstract representation or a projection, does so for an actual piece of land. And the knowledge so represented is not explicit, but tacit or implicit. Although Davidson does not make a clear statement on this point, it seems that this is the sense in which his proposal must be understood.[12]

6.2.2 Truth and extensionality

Just as a modest theory of truth aims to grasp the extension of the truth predicate without presupposing anything about the concept of truth other than the equivalence thesis expressed by Convention T, a modest theory of meaning aims to represent meaning, which is an *intensional* concept, through use of the *extensional* concept of truth. It should have become sufficiently apparent from what has gone before that at no point is the Davidsonian strategy an attempt to *reduce* meaning to truth. Nor is it based on an explicit or implicit definition of the truth predicate. Unlike Tarski, who aspires to define the predicate 'is true' in terms of more primitive semantic concepts, Davidson *presupposes* the concept of truth in his procedure for constructing a theory of meaning and interpretation. The concept of truth is regarded as already understood.[13]

Here I shall not examine all the problems that this conception can pose. But one of them is particularly important for my purpose. It concerns the antithesis that we have already met on several occasions between an extensional theory of meaning and an intensional theory, and the general distinction between extensionality and intensionality in logic.

So far we have confined ourselves to the domain of the usual first-order logic, and this is extensional. Extensionality is principally a property of linguistic or logical *contexts*, that is to say of expressions.

In a first sense, a context is extensional if it is *truth functional*, that is to say if the expressions that compose it are formed from elementary truth functions. The contexts in the usual propositional calculus are extensional because the extension of the sentences of this calculus (their truth values) is a function of the extension of the atomic sentences that compose them. In truth-functional logic, the principle of extensionality simply amounts to the *material equivalence* of the sentences: two sentences are extensionally equivalent if and only if they have the same truth value, and if it is possible to substitute sentences of the same truth value for the given sentences. In contrast, intensional contexts are not truth-functional contexts. They are, for example, contexts introduced by operators such as 'it is possible that', 'it is necessary that', or 'X believes that'. Unlike a sentence such as '$p \lor (p \to q)$', for example, 'John believes that p' is intensional, because the truth value of this sentence cannot be determined from the truth value of p.

In a second sense, a context is extensional if the truth value of the sentence forming this context remains unaltered if other expressions having the same *reference* are substituted for the expressions appearing in this context. This is the case, for example, with contexts in which we are able, *salva veritate*, to substitute one co-referential singular term for another, as in

> (11) Cicero was a Roman orator.

Two names 'Cicero' and 'Marcus Tullius' designate the same individual. Consequently, if (11) is true, then

> (12) Marcus Tullius was a Roman orator

also is. This is not, for example, the case with

> (13) Millicent believes that Cicero was a Roman orator

which can be true if

> (14) Millicent believes that Marcus Tullius was a Roman orator

because Millicent may not know that Cicero = Marcus Tullius. This last context is intensional, because the truth values of (13) and (14) do not depend solely on the extension of the names 'Cicero' and 'Marcus Tullius', that is to say on their reference. Several theorists, foremost among whom is Frege, maintain that the truth value of sentences such as 'John believes that p', or (13) and (14), also depend on the *sense* of the expressions that compose them, and identify this sense with a certain *entity* distinct from the reference, the *intension* of the name, predicate or sentence. It is in this sense that propositions are said to be the intensions of sentences (§ 1.2).

It can justifiably be maintained that the two senses of 'extensional' are identical, in other words that if a context is truth functional, it is extensional in the second sense, and that if a context is extensional in the second sense, then it is truth functional. This is what the Fregean 'slingshot' argument purports to establish (§ 1.3.2)[14]

We can then sum up these conditions in the following way:

(a) A context $f(s)$ is extensional iff $f(s)$ & s iff s' conjointly imply $f(s')$ (where s and s' are materially equivalent sentences).
(b) A context $f(a)$ is extensional iff $f(a)$ & $a = b$ conjointly imply $f(b)$.
(c) A context $f(F)$ is extensional iff $f(F)$ & all the Fs and only the Fs are G conjointly imply $f(G)$.[15]

A language generally is extensional if all its contexts are extensional. What is true of a language is equally true of a metalanguage: a theory of truth is extensional if and only if all its contexts are extensional. This is the case with Tarskian theories of truth. Consequently, when Davidson prescribes constructing a theory of meaning by making use of an extensional theory of truth, his modest strategy prescribes extracting the maximum that the *extensional* concept of truth can extract from the *intensional* concept of meaning. The fact that meaning is an intensional concept of that sort is clear from the non-equivalence of (M) and (T) above: two sentences that have the same truth conditions, such as 'Every mammal has a heart' and 'Every mammal has kidneys', do not for all that have the same meaning (cf. § 1.2.3). Natural language offers a very great variety of intensional constructions according to the preceding definitions. It can even be asked if extensional contexts are not in a minority among natural language contexts. The problems concerning the meaning of the connectives (Chapter 2) show that the truth-functional interpretation is dubious for a large number of them. But one might cite adverbial constructions (*negligently*, *intentionally*), completive constructions governed by 'that', counterfactual conditionals and so on. The notion of an extensional language, which the languages of first-order logic or set theory are, seems to be an invention peculiar to logicians. In such circumstances, what chances are there for a theory of meaning, which has recourse to an extensional metalanguage, to be able to be applied to natural languages? A current position, apart from Davidson's, among linguists, logicians and philosophers who do not conclude from this that the only possible attitude is a generalised scepticism towards any systematic attempt at description of meaning and who want to maintain the basic idea that a semantic is a theory of *truth conditions*, is as follows. The intensional character of the semantic constructions of natural language invokes a language of description that is itself intensional. The truth conditions of the sentences of a natural language must then be established in the framework of a language and a logic that are rich in intensional constructions. This is the case, for example, with the logical semantics for the modal, epistemic or temporal languages, which invoke intensional operators and truth conditions established with reference to models or possible worlds (cf. Chapter 7).[16] But in this case, the metalanguage of the semantic theories becomes essentially richer than the object-language, and invokes a relative theory of truth.[17] But this then violates the third requisite of a theory of meaning given by Davidson.

Nevertheless, a supporter of a modest conception of a semantic theory for natural languages is not bound to acknowledge the principle whereby an intensional language calls on a semantic that is itself intensional. In addition, as we have seen, an extensional semantic does not aim to *eliminate* the intensionality, but rather to *circumvent* it. Davidson's strategy prescribes the use of the least rich concepts possible in a theory of meaning. This supposes that it is possible, in effect, to buy back the gold of meaning with the bronze of truth. Logicians, since Russell in particular, have shown how it was possible to account for the truth conditions of certain expressions that have an apparent form, such as definite descriptions, by reformulating the *logical form* of these expressions. Inspired by these reformulations, Davidson has shown how certain intensional fragments of natural language could, if their logical form were redefined, be led back to an extensional treatment of the truth conditions. Adverbial constructions (or some of them) are an example of this: Davidson shows that an extensional quantification logic is sufficient to represent their truth and inference conditions.[18] Another example is constructions of propositional attitudes, which will be examined in Chapter 8.

The value of Davidson's programme as an attempt to describe meaning in natural languages therefore depends on the degree to which one is prepared to acknowledge that 'to serve as a theory of meaning is not the same thing as being one' (McDowell, 1977). In cases where the distance between the linguistic meanings and the truth conditions provided by an extensionalist theory of truth appears to be too great, it can be asked if there is not some form of 'schizophrenia' or quite simply of wishful thinking to be sought in regimenting intensional constructions in an extensional theory.[19] The success of the venture can only depend on recognition of the fact that in a natural language truth conditions do not integrally determine meaning, but that it is, on the contrary, meaning which determines truth conditions.[20] In this case, the problem of a modest theory of meaning becomes one of knowing what sort of principles must be brought to bear on the actual notion of meaning for a theory of truth in some way to reveal it. Davidson states some of them when he describes a procedure of radical interpretation. They are probably not the only ones.[21] Many other problems are raised by Davidson's programme in the semantics of natural languages: for example, how can a Tarskian type semantic account for phenomena such as those of indexicality and vagueness? As has been seen, this was one of the reasons why Tarski rejected the application of his paradigm to natural languages. Here too Davidson has suggested indirect ways that make it possible to bring these phenomena back into the Tarskian mould.[22] But I will leave these points to one side, because they concern the applicability of Davidson's programme (many linguistics find it dubious), while what concerns me here is its philosophical coherence.

6.3 Realism and anti-realism in semantics

6.3.1 The Dummettian contraposition

In § 5.4.3, I followed Davidson and maintained that even if a Tarskian theory of truth does not give any substantial definition of the concept of truth, it is none the less in accordance with the realist intuitive conception of this concept, according to which if a statement is true, there is something in the world by virtue of which it is true. It follows that if, like Davidson, it is acknowledged that a theory of meaning for a natural language must take the form of a theory of truth, this theory of meaning must incorporate this realist conception in one way or another. The problem is to know exactly how.

This is the problem that Dummett addresses. He has no doubt that a truth-conditional theory of meaning – whether it is applied to formal languages or to natural languages – is realist, *from the very fact that it uses the concept of truth as the central concept*. But in fact he argues against Davidson's programme for it, and thereby against any truth-conditional theory of meaning. A theory of meaning for a language (formal or natural) must be based on a different concept from that of truth. Adequate semantics must substitute the concept of *assertion condition* or *verification condition* for this concept. The statements of a language are not true by virtue of transcendent truth conditions in relation to the conditions in which we might be able to verify them. On the contrary, their meaning is determined by these verification conditions. It follows that a semantics based on the realist notion of truth condition is inadequate. According to Dummett, a semantics must be *anti-realist*.[23]

The originality of Dummett's argument originates in the way in which he connects three forms of realism:

(I) *Metaphysical* realism: the conception according to which there is something in the world, independent of our knowledge, that is capable of making our statements true.

(II) *Semantic* realism: the conception according to which the meaning of our statement is determined by truth conditions independently of the ways in which we can or might be able to verify them.

(III) Realism in *logic*: acceptance, as a fundamental principle of logic, of the principle of *bivalence*, that is to say of the principle according to which a sentence is true or false, in a determinate way, whatever the means that we may have of recognising it as such.

According to Dummett, these three forms of realism are so closely linked that rejection of any one of them must entail rejection of the others. Dummett's position is that they should all be rejected, and the negation of these theses adopted in every case:

(I') *Metaphysical anti-realism* or *verificationism*: our statements are not true by virtue of a reality independent of our powers of verification, and reality is relative to the knowledge that we have of it.

(II') *Semantic anti-realism*: the meaning of our statements is determined by their conditions of verification and use.

(III') *Logical anti-realism* or *revisionism*: refusal to assert the principle of bivalence, as well as the principle of the excluded middle, and revision of the laws of classical logic that this refusal entails, in favour in particular of an *intuitionist* conception of logic.

A large part of the discussion concerns the question of knowing if these characterisations are adequate, that is to say if an authentic realist must acknowledge the conjunction (I)–(III), or at least one of its members. In particular, are authors such as Aquinas, Descartes or Russell (for example), whom philosophical tradition describes as 'realists', bound to accept (I)–(III)? And are 'idealist' authors like Berkeley, Kant and Hegel bound to adopt (I')–(III')? This is questionable. Do the various forms of metaphysical realism (such as realism with respect to universals, or realism with respect to the existence of the external world) fall into this characterisation? And must scientific realism, the belief in the existence of theoretical entities in science, be included? This is questionable and Dummett himself does not think so.[24] However, he does think that acceptance of semantic realism and logical realism controls numerous philosophical theses, usually described as 'realist', such as belief in the existence of Platonic entities (numbers, for example), in the philosophy of mathematics, in the existence of the past in ontology, or in the existence of moral values in ethics. These theses of Dummett's are based on the conviction – which he attributes to Frege – that the philosophy of language and the theory of meaning form a first philosophy in relation to other domains, such as epistemology and ontology, and form its sub-foundations and final justification. All this poses the problem, very interesting in itself, of knowing if the antithesis between 'realism' and 'anti-realism', as Dummett formulates it, is pertinent in philosophy, and, if he is right, we should be able to expect a great deal from a reformulation of the realist theses such as he gives.[25] None the less, I will leave this question to one side, because I will limit discussion here to the question of the relationship between (II) and (III) and (II') and (III'), respectively. I will therefore ignore the purely epistemological and ontological aspects of Dummett's programme. Nevertheless, the link he establishes between semantic and logical realism on the one hand, and metaphysical realism on the other, constitutes an original way of posing the problem of the ontology of logic and semantics, and is therefore eminently important for us.

The synthetical presentation of Dummett's position we have just given must not tempt us to misjudge the actual nature of his argument. If he was content to contrast the anti-realist theses (I')–(III') with the realist theses (I)–(III), he would only be guilty of begging the question in favour of the former. The general form of his argument is as follows:

(A) A truth-conditional conception of semantics, like Davidson's, stumbles against what his aim actually is, that is to say to enable us to account for meanings in a language as its speakers *understand* them. In other words, if a theory of meaning *is* a theory of understanding of a language, a truth-conditional theory reveals nothing about this understanding.

(B) Understanding a language does not rest solely upon a theoretical, but also upon a *practical* knowledge. This practical knowledge, which must essentially be implicit, can only be manifested in the use that speakers of a language make of its expressions, that is to say in a set of abilities to recognise or to verify the truth conditions of the sentences that they use. Consequently, we must abandon a truth conditional semantics in favour of a semantic in terms of assertion or verification conditions.

(C) A truth-conditional conception of meaning entails acknowledging the principle of bivalence and the laws of classical logic: a conception in terms of assertion conditions, on the contrary, entails a refusal to assert this principle.

(D) Consequently, if we reject the truth-conditional conception, we also have to reject the principle of bivalence and the laws of classical logic.

In addition, Dummett argues in favour of the following theses:

(E) Metaphysical realism entails an acceptance of bivalence.

(F) Consequently, by (D), we also have to reject metaphysical realism.

As has been seen, the argument is based on semantic premises, that is to say related to the form of a theory of meaning, and it concludes, from the link between these premises and logical and ontological theses, that the theses linked to these semantic premises should be rejected, and not the reverse. It is sometimes difficult to see the argument under this linear form because it often happens that Dummett purely and simply identifies truth-conditional theory of meaning, metaphysical realism and the principle of bivalence.[26] But McGinn (1980) has given a simple and illuminating formulation of Dummett's argument, parallel to the one adopted here. Let us call 'realism', as Dummett does, the thesis according to which the principle of bivalence is universally valid. Let us, as Dummett invites us to do, identify a truth-conditional conception of meaning with a conception whereby *'meaning transcends use'*, that is to say whereby a sentence can be true or false independently of our means of *recognising* it as such, that is to say of its *use*. Dummett thus establishes the link between realism and the theory of meaning:

> (A) If realism is true, then meaning necessarily transcends use.

This corresponds to our premise (C) above. Dummett then maintains that

> (B) Meaning does not transcend use.

This corresponds to our premises (A) and (B) above. Dummett concludes by contraposition, or *modus tollens*, on (A) and (B):

> (C) Consequently, realism is false.

This corresponds to conclusions (D)–(F) of the above argument.[27] In what follows, I will examine each of the semantic premises (A)–(C) in turn, and anti-realism in logic and conclusions (D)–(F) of Dummett's argument in the ensuing paragraphs.

6.3.2 Holism and molecularism

Let us first examine premise (A), on which the weight of the argument rests. Like Davidson, Dummett maintains that a systematic theory of meaning for natural languages is possible and must explain the understanding that the speakers have of their language by giving 'a theoretical representation of a practical ability'.[28] Like Davidson, he acknowledges that such a theory must permit us to derive a set of sentences of the form 's is t iff p'. But according to Dummett, if t is the truth predicate, there are good reasons for thinking that the theory will not represent the practical ability in question. the principal reason he gives for this is inspired by considerations very close to those of § 6.2.1 above: someone can know a set of T-sentences for a language L without knowing what those sentences mean. By establishing truth conditions, the T-sentences give no means of understanding what the sentences of the object-language mean. Someone who knows that in L

'Horses are equidae' is true if horses are equidae

can know *that* this sentence is true, without knowing *what* that sentence means. He can know without having the slightest means of recognising a 'horse' when he is presented with one, and without having the remotest idea of the reason why the T-sentence is true. From this point of view, a T-theory is no more a theory of understanding of L than is a translation manual providing sentences like (3) above. It is trivial, and can at the most only represent the semantic competence of someone who *already* knew the meanings of L.[29]

But, as has been seen, this objection to Davidson is only valid for *isolated* T-sentences, while a truth-conditional theory of meaning functions on the hypothesis of a *holism* of the semantic structure. But Dummett's argument is directed precisely against this holism. Let us acknowledge, says Dummett, that a speaker's semantic competence could be represented as competence in respect of the systematic roles that the components of sentences play through the language as a whole, and that their contribution to the truth values of isolated sentences cannot be elucidated. But in that case, we no longer have any means of testing the theory, which becomes *transcendent* in relation to any empirical confirmation.[30].

It is this transcendence of meaning in relation to 'use' that Dummett rejects. According to him, it is only possible to account for the meaning of a sentence by *first* accounting for the meaning of its components, then for the way they contribute to the meaning of the whole sentence. Against Davidsonian (and Quinian) holism, Dummett is thus setting what he calls his 'atomism' (specification of a practical capacity to know the sense of an *isolated word and simple sentences*) and his 'molecularism' (specification of that capacity for *complex sentences*) in a theory of meaning. This antithesis between holism and molecularism again corresponds to the antithesis between a 'modest' theory of meaning and a 'full-blooded' theory. A 'modest' conception of a theory of meaning, like Davidson's, does not account for the semantic competence of a language because it does not account for the *concepts* that the speakers employ, nor their content. A 'full-blooded' conception, on the contrary, would have to explain this competence integrally, from primitive concepts to derived concepts. It would have to connect the expressions to their cognitive value for the speakers, and to their use in acts of assertion. In other words, according to Dummett, Davidson is committing a similar error to the one that a theoretist would commit if he reduced semantics to the theory of *reference* (and of truth) in the Fregean sense, while ignoring the theory of *sense*, which Frege identified with the analysis of cognitive value or understanding.[31]

6.3.3 Truth conditions and assertion conditions

It is Dummett's anti-holism that leads him directly to (B): since a truth-conditional theory of meaning does not account for semantic competence, and since only a non-holistic theory can do so, we must reject the truth-conditional conception in favour of a conception for which sense is immanent in use. What would be its general form?

Dummett's answer to this has varied. I have already mentioned (§ 5.3.2) his argument in 'Truth' (1959), according to which a redundancy theory of truth is incompatible with a truth-conditional theory of meaning. In this article, Dummett adopts the redundancy theory of truth which, as has been seen, he interprets in the sense of equivalence between '*p* is true' and '*p is assertable*'. He therefore purely and simply rejects the concept of truth conditions, and sets out to formulate an analysis of logical constants in terms of their assertion conditions (cf. §6.4 below).[32] Later (Dummett, 1976), he admits that the idea of truth conditions specifies *one part* of what a statement means; but another – the most important – part of meaning depends on the use of the statement, given its truth conditions. What Davidson calls a theory of truth corresponds to what Dummett calls a 'theory of reference'. He has to add a 'theory of sense', that is to say a specification, for each type of particular sentence, of its assertion conditions.[33] He explicitly borrows this latter idea from the intuitionist philosophy of mathematics: in the same way as for an intuitionist, an object only exists (a statement is only true) if there is a way of *actually deciding* its reality (its truth) or having a proof of its existence (its truth); so, in semantics, a statement only has a meaning if it is possible to specify its verification conditions in addition to its truth conditions. In other words, Dummett does not totally reject the concept of 'truth conditions'; but he substitutes *knowledge of truth conditions* for it.

Dummett requires two things from knowledge of the truth conditions of a sentence: (a) that they be manifest in use, that is to say that there be an observable difference between the behaviour of someone who knows the meaning of a sentence and someone who does not know it; and, in order for this, (b) that they consist of the exercise of a capacity to recognise them when they are realised. Dummett takes (a) as equivalent to the Wittgensteinian thesis according to which meaning is something public, recognisable by everyone. (b) like (a) has sometimes been considered as a form of behaviourism. I will leave this point to one side.[34] In general, to have such a capacity is to have a certain disposition to engage in a certain activity which finds its expression in a behavioural manifestation of recognition of the obtaining or not of the truth conditions. Dummett considers that he is thereby doing no more than following the Wittgensteinian slogan: 'Meaning is use'.

There is a difficulty for the anti-realist in this. Many sentences of our language seem to have truth conditions that go far beyond our power of recognition: 'counterfactual' conditionals such as 'If Cleopatra's nose had been less long, the face of the world would have been changed', sentences about the past, sentences about the future, sentences implying a quantification over an infinite domain in mathematics, sentences bearing on the existence of other minds than our own, vague statements, and so on. I will call these sentences 'transcendent'. These are sentences that we cannot verify in the strict sense Dummett requires. But they none the less have a meaning, and we understand them. This fact seems to validate the conception according to which, when we understand these sentences, we are understanding the *transcendent* truth conditions.[35] A crucial problem for every semantics, as we will see notably in Chapters 7 and 9, is to know if these sentences really do have truth conditions. What reason, Dummett objects, have we to suppose that these sentences have transcendent truth conditions in respect of our powers of verification? Here Dummett turns the difficulty posed by sentences with 'transcendent' truth conditions around to his advantage: they are only apparently transcendent. In fact, it is not because we understand their *truth conditions* that we understand them, but because we understand something *other* than their truth conditions. We understand their verification conditions. There is a great temptation at this point to identify the verification conditions of transcendent sentences with the ideal verification conditions of a being with infinitely superior cognitive powers to our own. But Dummett resists this temptation: what right do we have to suppose, for example, that statements about the future or about the past, or statements bearing on numerical conjectures (Goldbach's conjecture, for example: any even number higher than 2 is the sum of two prime numbers) *do have* ideal verification conditions? Perhaps their truth value is *undecidable* and perhaps the *als ob* strategy (to distinguish actual verifiability and verifiability in principle or ideal verifiability, that is to say treating these statements *as if* they were decidable) is only an illegitimate way of saving our realist intuitions.[36] It is here that Dummett suggests identifying a truth-conditional theory of meaning with acceptance of the principle of bivalence, and of the laws of classical logic, and identifying these principles with the *realist* position. We have therefore reached step (C) of the argument. A verificationist conception of meaning, on the contrary, must refuse to assert this principle, and construct the assertion conditions of the statements on the model of intuitionist logic. It will in this sense be *anti-realist*. This completes the argument in favour of (A)–(B). We can reconstruct it in this way, following Crispin Wright:[37]

> *Premise 1 (recognition thesis)*: knowledge of the truth conditions must be a recognitional capacity: the aptitude to recognise the circumstances that do or do not achieve the truth conditions of a sentence, and consequently to be prepared to give assent or dissent to this sentence.

Premise 2 (realist thesis): the knowledge of meaning is the knowledge of truth conditions.

Premise 3 (concluded from 1 and 2): knowledge of meaning is the capacity to recognise if the truth conditions are or are not realised.

Premise 4 (transcendent sentences): the truth conditions of a considerable number of sentences transcend our recognitive capacities.

Conclusion: if 1, 3 and 4 are true, then 2 (realism) is false.

This argument has the form of a *reductio ad absurdum*: if realism is true, then it is contradicted by the existence of transcendent sentences. Therefore it is false for at least this class of sentence (Dummett does not deny that it may be true for the restricted class of 'actually decidable' sentences). Consequently, it is false.

It remains to be seen how intuitionist logic rejects bivalence and, according to Dummett, realism.

6.4 Logical anti-realism and revisionism

6.4.1 The intuitionist conception of logical constants

Intuitionist logic rejects the classical concept of truth, which rests on the realist conception according to which a statement is true or false in a determinate way whatever the means we have of recognising it as true or false. This is none other than the principle of *bivalence*:

> *(Bivalence): Every statement is true or false determinately.*

'Determinately' means that vague statements are not bivalent and are excluded from classical logic (cf. Chapter 9).

The principle of bivalence is a *semantic* principle, which must not be confused with the corresponding *syntactic* principle of the *excluded middle*:

> (Excluded middle): $A \vee -A$

which says that $A \vee -A$ is always a theorem.[38]

Intuitionism substitutes the concept of proof or assertibility for the classical concept of truth. A sentence is true if and only if there is an *effective* proof of it, that is to say acceptable by intuitionist criteria (cf. Chapter 11) warranting its assertibility. This entails rejection of, or at least refusal to assert, the classical, fundamental logical principle of bivalence and the law of the excluded middle. Intuitionism's principal objection to the law of the excluded middle is that it cannot always be true that $A \vee -A$, because we very often do not have the means of recognising that A is true, and that $-A$ is *true* (cf. § 5.3.2). Another classical principle that intuitionism rejects is the law of double negation:

> *(Double negation)*: $--A \vdash A$

In fact we can recognise that we have no means of refuting *A*, though without having the means to assert it. If the intuitionist is right, it is a fact that people who believe in miracles or supernatural phenomena should think about: the fact that for the moment we have no means of refuting the existence of the Loch Ness monster does not mean that we have the means of asserting it either.

Consequently, intuitionism suggests a revision of the classical truth conditions of the logical constants presented in § 2.2, which takes the following form of a systematic replacement of the truth conditions by assertibility conditions:

A is assertible iff we are justified in asserting *A*.

A & *B* is assertible iff we are justified in asserting *A* and justified in asserting *B*.

A ∨ *B* is assertible iff we are justified in asserting *A* or justified in asserting *B*.

A → *B* is assertible iff we have a general procedure whereby justifications for our assertions of *A* can be transformed into justifications for asserting *B*.

(I have left out the clauses for the quantifiers.)

Intuitionist *negation* can be expressed in classical terms, as meaning *A*→*F*, where '*F*' designates any atomic statement that is obviously false, such as '1 = 0'. In other words, in the intuitionist sense, '−*A*' means that we never had reason to assert *A*, or that, as the intuitionists say, *A is absurd*. The intuitionist rules of natural deduction could be formulated in the same way.[38]

In this logic, it is not possible to derive either *A* ∨ −*A*, or the law of double negation. Other classical theorems and equivalences equally cease to be valid.

Step (D) of Dummett's argument assimilates the truth-conditional theory of meaning (semantic realism), acknowledgement of the possibility of a truth transcending our verification (metaphysical realism), and adoption of the principle of bivalence (logical realism), and concludes that these three forms of realism should be rejected. The '*revisionist*' thesis, according to which the principles of classical logic must be abandoned, particularly the law of bivalence, follows directly from this. Revisionism, according to Dummett, is the natural consequence of semantic anti-realism.

6.4.2 Inference, molecularism and conservative extension

The intuitionist interpretation of the logical constants is not the only element of intuitionist logic to fit in with the verificationist conception of meaning. As has been seen, anti-holism is one of the essential components of this conception. But semantic holism, the thesis according to which a sentence or an isolated expression of a language cannot be understood outside of the context of a command of the whole language, has its correspondent thesis in logic. It brings into play the notion of *inference* in logic itself.

Probably the most characteristic feature of inference in deductive logic – which amongst other things distinguishes it from inductive inference – is that the conclusion of a deductive argument seems in some way already 'contained' in the premises. This gives rise to a well-known dilemma, which has been developed by Mill: either the conclusion is 'already' in the premises, and the argument teaches us nothing new, or the conclusion *is* new, but in that case it seems that the conclusion changes the *sense* of what is contained in the premises.[40] The appearance of triviality emerges clearly in the simple arguments of elementary logic which, even when they suppose a certain number of intermediaries, owe their evidence to the fact that the link between premises and conclusion appears trivial, particularly by the use of the rules of natural deduction, which aim precisely to establish a direct link between premises and conclusions. But what must we say when the proof proceeds via *indirect* routes? To grasp the contrast, it is enough to consider the difference between the rules of inference themselves in a system of natural deduction such as the one presented in § 2.2.2. The rule of '∨-elimination' is not in line with the rule of '&-elimination', because in the case of the former we have to invoke other premises and another inference.[41] In other words, it can happen that a conclusion *surprises* us. But in another sense, we would like to be able to say, as does Wittgenstein, that 'in logic there are no surprises'.[42]

The problem posed is as follows: when we have established a certain conclusion on the basis of certain premises, by an indirect proof, in what sense can we say that we have remained *faithful* to the initial sense that we gave the conclusion? According to Dummett, this is not a problem for a holistic conception of meaning: as the sense of a sentence is dependent on the sense of all the other sentences possible in the language, the fact that a proof is possible is itself already contained in our linguistic practice and in the inference principles that we accept.[43] This is in fact the usual attitude of logicians: once they have characterised the notion of inference in syntactic and semantic terms, they prove, by completeness theorems, that the two ideas are equivalent, first by showing that any tautology is a theorem of their system, then that any theorem is a tautology. According to the usual conception there is no other 'justification' of deduction than that.[44] This usual conception is holistic, because it supposes that our logical practice is in some way self-justified: our primitive inference rules justify our deductions, and we invoke the primitive inference rules to prove their completeness. This attitude does not satisfy Dummett. The holist has no means of answering the question of our faithfulness to the sense that we give to the sentences of our language. For him, the question of knowing if a logical system is complete, that is to say preserves truth, has no precise meaning. In a molecular conception, on the contrary, the question arises of knowing if new uses of the sentences, which emerge when a language is extended in a certain way, fit in with the meanings primitively assigned to these sentences. It must in particular be asked if the introduction of a new inference rule will modify the meanings of existing sentences of the language.

Here Dummett uses the notion of *conservative extension* of a theory, which he borrows from proof theory.[45] In general, a theory T' is a conservative extension of a theory T if and only if all the theorems of T' which contain only the constants of T

are already theorems of T.[46] Suppose that we are dealing with a very simple theory, consisting solely of relationships of deducibility on atomic sentences. Suppose that we add the usual logical constants to the language of this theory, defined by means of the usual rules of natural deduction, and permitting the formation of complex sentences. The new theory is a conservative extension of the first if and only if any theorem of the first is a theorem of the second. The molecularist doctrine in logic is the doctrine according to which any addition of logical constants to a language that does not contain them must be a conservative extension of the initial language. But this requisite is also valid for semantic molecularism: the meaning of complex sentences must be a conservative extension of the meaning of simple sentences. This means that the meaning of a complex sentence must always depend on the meaning of its component sentences, and that the meaning of a sentence must never depend on the meaning of more complex sentences. When Dummett requires that the inference rules that we use in logical deductions always be faithful to the content of the sentences that figure in the deductions that use these rules, he is demanding that our inferential practice always be a conservative extension of our previous practice. An example of a logical connective that does *not* introduce a conservative extension in the initial language is 'tonk' according to Prior (§ 2.3.1): 'tonk', as has been seen, is a connective that leads to the assertion $\vdash A \rightarrow B$. But this theorem is not a theorem that can be obtained from the initial classical propositional language. That is why a language with 'tonk' is not conservative in relation to that language, as Belnap notes (1962). The requirement that the logical constants introduced be of a conservative nature is therefore tantamount to saying that we must not be able to prove *new* theorems from the *old* notation by the introduction of constants. In other words, 'tonk' is not faithful to our conception of deducibility, since the latter implied that incoherences such as $A \vdash B$ were not produced. On the contrary, if the requirement of conservative extension is satisfied, according to Dummett, a real justification of deduction is given, which the holistic conception did not provide.[47]

It can be seen how semantic molecularism is linked to the intuitionist rejection of the law of the excluded middle. To authorise the use of this law in deductions to prove any conclusion is to acknowledge that the meaning of this conclusion might be proved via a deduction having as premise a sentence of greater logical complexity, because it is acknowledging that the conclusion might be true independently of our actual means of recognising it as such, and this is acknowledging that its meaning has to be established with the help of the meanings of the language as a whole.[48] (I will come back to these points in Chapter 12).

6.5 Realism and bivalence

The strength of Dummett's argument rests on the way in which he shows how semantic realism, logical realism and metaphysical realism are linked by the intermediary of the holistic conception of language, and how a molecularist theory leads to the anti-realist rejection of these three theories. Dummett often writes in fact as if each of the following theses taken individually were constitutive of realism in general (as a conception common to the three forms):

(a) the truth-conditional conception of meaning;
(b) the adoption of the principle of bivalence;
(c) the admission of verification-transcendent truths;
(d) the holistic conception of language.

But these theses are not equivalent, because it can be shown that they do not imply each other.

In the first place, (a) does not imply (b), by virtue of a well-tried logical fact: truth can be exactly defined as Tarski defines it for a language, the logical constants of which receive an intuitionist definition.

In fact, that the propositional connectives, as defined in § 6.4.1, have a different meaning from the classical connectives does not prevent a *reinterpretation* of the latter by means of the former, as follows:

1. − (classical) is identical to ¬ (intuitionist)
2. & (classical) is identified with ● (intuitionist)
3. $p \vee q$ (classical) is identified with $-(-p \,\&\, -q)$ (intuitionist)
4. $p \rightarrow q$ (classical) is identified with $-(p \,\&\, -q)$ (intuitionist)

With this interpretation all the theorems of classical propositional calculus become theorems of intuitionist logic. How is this possible, since it has been seen that the intuitionist rejects classical theorems like the law of the excluded middle or the law of double negation? Because he is not rejecting the theorems but the *sense* that we classically give them. In particular, although the intuitionist rejects $p \vee -p$, he does not reject its double negation: $- -(p \vee -p)$; and although he rejects $- -p \vdash p$, he does not reject the converse of this law. Hence the importance of the distinction between the *logical law* (or theorem) of the excluded middle, and its corresponding *semantic* concept, the principle of bivalence. The intuitionist does not reject the first, but the second, or only rejects the first *interpretation in the classical sense*. According to the reinterpretation (1)–(4), intuitionist logic, which has the same theorems as classical logic, is extensionally equivalent to it. What differs is the *sense* accorded to the constants, and the idea of truth, interpreted as assertability or demonstrability. In other words, the intuitionist is stating the same thing as the supporter of classical logic, but he is not talking about the same thing. This does not stop a Tarskian *T*-theory from being able to establish exactly the same extension (the same *T*-sentences) for the predicate 'is true' as for the predicate 'is assertable'. This, as can be seen, confirms the universality of Convention *T*.[49]

It follows that Dummett cannot identify, as he often does, a truth-conditional theory of meaning adopting the Tarskian schema, with adherence to bivalence. This also weakens his argument in favour of logical revisionism, when he identifies the truth-conditional conception with acceptance of classical logic. Dummett is obviously aware of this fact. That is why he is more true to his intentions when he maintains that realism is not identified with the adoption of bivalence, but with acceptance of the latter in conjunction with a truth-conditional theory of meaning.[50]

In the second place, does (b) imply (c)? Yes, according to Dummett, because acknowledging that transcendent sentences in relation to our powers of verification have determinate truth conditions is acknowledging, at least for those sentences, that their truth is transcendent. What the realist who adopts (c) is saying is that a statement can be true or false even if we do not have the means to verify it. But, as Crispin Wright comments, to acknowledge bivalence in this sense does not imply that one is postulating the existence of transcendent truths in relation to our verification, unless one does not acknowledge that 'p is not verifiable' entails 'it is possible that not p'. In other words not to have a guarantee that p is not tantamount to asserting that not p. Both realist and anti-realist can acknowledge this.[51]

Conversely, does (c) imply (b)? If we acknowledge the identification that Dummett makes of the truth-functional conception of meaning (a) with recognition of the possibility of transcendent truths (c), it seems clear that the realist in sense (a) and (c) will acknowledge that it is possible to *understand* (in the sense of knowing the truth conditions) transcendent statements. But this does not entail acknowledging bivalence for these statements. Since the principle of bivalence asserts that every statement is true or false in a *determinate way*, it ceases to be valid, for example, for *vague* statements, such as 'John is bald'. But does this not prevent the champion of a truth-conditional conception of meaning and understanding saying that someone who understands this sentence understands something such as

'John is bald' is true iff John is bald

No. We can say 'no' to that, whether or not we have the means of saying in what circumstances an individual is or is not bald.[52] In other words, we can both acknowledge that to understand a vague sentence is to understand what state of affairs would be realised if it was true or not realised if it was false (that is to say the truth-conditional conception) *and* that the distinction between the states of affairs is itself vague (this in substance is the solution that I will defend apropos vagueness in Chapter 11). This is only repeating the point put forward above, that a *T*-theory can be provided for an intuitionist language.

Finally, is Dummett right to identify (a), (b) and (c) with (d), the holistic conception? If my presentation of his argument is correct, the weight of the latter rests on criticism of the truth-conditional conception (§ 6.3.2–3), which in turn rests on his criticism of holism. There is a risk of circularity here. For Dummett's argument to be interesting, it is necessary for holism to be a presupposition *independent* of the other realistic theses that he attacks, which implies them without them implying it. If the realist theses (a), (b) and (c) are themselves independent, which the foregoing tends to show, the true divergence between the realist and the anti-realist must turn on the question of holism.

The problem is that Dummett rarely dissociates his criticism of holism from his criticism of the truth-conditional conception of meaning. In particular, it is because, as we have seen, he maintains that the understanding of a sentence must depend on the understanding of its parts, which must be obvious and consist of a recognitional capacity, that Dummett denies Davidson's conception. But if anti-holism is identified with rejection of this conception, it cannot easily constitute an *argument* against the latter.[53]

The principal reason why Dummett rejects the truth-functional conception of meaning is, as has been seen, that it does not answer the requirement that a theory of meaning be a theory of *understanding*. According to Dummett, Davidson's 'modest' theory, by identifying sense with truth conditions, at best, only permits us to represent one part of semantic competence. A 'full-blooded' theory must represent complete competence, and tell us not only what concepts someone who acquires a language acquires, but also establish the content of these concepts. It is here that molecularism comes in. It may be thought that a theory of truth does not succeed in this and that holism purely and simply dodges this problem. But it is precisely to make good this lack that Davidson resorts to a theory of interpretation. To be able to evaluate the respective merits of realism and anti-realism on this point, it would be necessary to know if a truth-conditional conception of semantics is as incapable as Dummett says of representing comprehension of a language. This is a question I cannot examine here.[54]

All this shows, not that Dummett's criticisms of what he regards as variants of realism are inoperative (I have not maintained that they are), but that perhaps the antithesis between realism and anti-realism is not as clear-cut as he says. It is possible to be a realist on some points, without being one on others. This in no way detracts from the interest of the antithesis itself, which will reappear in various forms in the following chapters.

—— PART 3 ——

Limits of extensionality

MODALITIES, POSSIBLES AND ESSENCES

7.1 Modal logic as an extension of classical logic

The logic discussed here so far has principally been bivalent and extensional classical logic. But is this the only possible logic? Two motivations can cause us to modify this logic, and two sorts of changes can be envisaged as a result. One rests on a rejection of fundamental laws of classical logic, such as the principle of bivalence. This is the case with intuitionist logic. The revision that the intuitionist logician suggests is radical, because it challenges the very notions of truth and meaning on which classical logic is based. The other motivation is less radical. It starts from the statement that classical logic does not make it possible to account for a certain number of ordinary inferences that we none the less judge to be intuitively valid. The appropriate strategy then does not so much consist of revising classical logic but of *extending* it, and of extending the classical notion of validity, so that it also applies to these inferences.

These inferences include all those containing non-extensional, or intensional, contexts, that is to say for which it is not in general true that the truth conditions and references of complex sentences depend on the truth conditions and references of the sentences that compose them (§ 6.2.2). The existence of these contexts can lead us to abandon the idea that the sentences concerned do actually have conditions of truth or falsity. This is not the position generally adopted by logicians, who are not prepared to surrender the idea of truth conditions easily. The most common solution consists of saying that these truth conditions are determined not only by the reference of the expressions, but also by their sense. The rules that govern these truth conditions will therefore be those of an intensional logic. But the problem then arises of knowing what the rules of this logic are and whether they do not diverge so much from the classical rules that the use of the classical ideas ceases to be valid. This, it seems, is the case with the logic of modalities.

But the wish to account for a larger number of valid inferences is not the only consideration that can motivate the extension of classical logic. Specific reasons motivate the study of modalities in logic. In the first place, there are a certain number of propositions in logic that we not only want to be able to say are true, but also that they are *necessarily* true. This is the case with tautologies or the valid expressions of a calculus. The notion of necessity undeniably has a metalinguistic character: we use it to designate the nature of these propositions, and we can want to construct rules for its use. Secondly, there are concepts in classical logic that seem to call for the use of this notion. This is the case with the notion of implication. Philosophers and logicians since antiquity have come up against what are called the 'paradoxes of material implication':

$$p \to (q \to p)$$
$$- p \to (p \to q)$$
$$(p \to q) \lor (q \to p)$$

The third proposition, for example, says that if one takes two sentences at random ('Thatcher is prime minister' and 'Heseltine is prime minister'), the first will imply the second, or else the second will imply the first.

One of the origins of the development of contemporary modal logic, according to C. I. Lewis, is an attempt to formulate a *modal* concept of implication prohibiting these paradoxes, 'strict' implication, defined by means of the notion of necessity:

     p *necessarily implies* q (or: if p is true then q *cannot* be false).[1]

Nevertheless, there are as many reasons for introducing modalities into logic as there are reasons for not introducing them. The modal notions, those of necessity and possibility, are notoriously obscure, and it can be asked if modal logic was not 'conceived in sin', as Quine said. Philosophers traditionally question the legitimacy of modal ideas: are there such things as possible objects, necessary facts or necessary properties of objects in the world? A version of this problem in the philosophy of logic consists of asking if the introduction of these notions into logic does not threaten the coherence of logic itself. From this point of view, the contemporary development of modal logics has proved the movement on the move. If the Aristotelian modal syllogistic is left aside,[2] it can be said that there have been three traditions in modal logic since the beginning of the twentieth century. The first, essentially born with Lewis, is the syntactic tradition. It deals with necessity and possibility as certain operators on sentences, and analyses the various systems engendered by the combination of these operators. The second is the algebraic tradition, initiated by Lukasiewicz, who essentially conceives modal logic as a three-valued logic, where a third value, the possible, is added to the two classical truth values.[3] The third and most recent is the semantic tradition, based on the theory of models and initiated in the 1940s by Carnap, Kanger, Hintikka and Kripke.[4] It is this tradition that has produced the real contemporary efflorescence of modal logics. This is the one that will principally concern us here. The purely logical problem is of knowing if modal calculi can receive a real *semantics*. But this is also a philosophical problem in so far as it involves giving certain *interpretations* of modal notions.

Alongside the modal logics is a whole variety of related intensional logics that are based on the analogy between modal operators and other operators: these are (for example) epistemic logics, temporal logics, causal logics, deontic logics.[5] At the logical level, the problems they raise are often similar to those raised by the modal logics. The philosophical problems vary with each of the notions concerned, and form one of the most fertile fields of investigation for formal 'philosophical logic'. However, I will not consider them here, and will restrict myself to the modalities called 'classical' or 'alethic'.

7.2 Semantics for propositional modal logic

The syntax of a model propositional calculus consists of adding to the classical propositional operators, the two operators 'it is possible that' and 'it is necessary that', which are operators on sentences (comparable in this sense with classical negation) which can be written respectively:

$\Diamond p$' (it is possible that p)
$\Box p$' (it is necessary that p).

They are inter-definable thus:

$$\Diamond p \equiv -\Box -p$$
$$\Box p \equiv -\Diamond -p$$

A striking analogy is noticeable from this point of view between the modal operators and the usual quantifiers '$\exists$' and '$\forall$'. Lewis established that there was not one but a variety of modal calculi, according to the theses or axioms acknowledged. One of the weakest systems, T, is obtained from the axioms

$T_1 \Box p \rightarrow p$
$T_2 (p \rightarrow q) \rightarrow (\Box p \rightarrow \Box q)$

and from the *rule of necessitation*

(RN) If A is a theorem ($\vdash A$), then $\Box A$ is a theorem ($\vdash \Box A$).

Stronger systems come from the addition of axioms where the modalities are 'reiterated'. In particular, S_4 comes from T to which is added:

$\Box p \rightarrow \Box \Box p$

S_5 comes from the addition to S_4 of:

$\Diamond p \rightarrow \Box \Diamond p$

The system known as 'Brouwer's' (B) comes from T and

$p \rightarrow \Box \Diamond p$

The order of dependence of these systems (which are far from being the only possible ones) can be represented thus:[6]

The problem is to know how these modal notions can be interpreted. There are two sorts of questions from this point of view. The first concerns the meaning of the notions of possibility and necessity. Possibility can be understood in an epistemic sense. '$\Diamond p$' then means that one *can know that p*, or that *there is nothing contradictory about conceiving or imagining that p*. It can be understood in a '*metaphysical*' sense. '$\Diamond p$' then means that *there is a possible state of affairs (a way in which the world might be)* such that *p* is true. Parallel to this, necessity can be understood in two senses. The operators '$\Diamond$' and '$\Box$' are compatible with either interpretation. On the other hand, the choice of one or the other depends on the philosophical justification that is given to the modal concepts. The principal question then is knowing if there are necessary or contingent possible facts in things and, above all, if these notions themselves have a sense. A second type of question concerns the purely semantic evaluation conditions of modal state-ments, that is to say their truth conditions. The problem arises because modal contexts are not extensional. If we try to evaluate a statement such as '$\Diamond p$' in this way, we can certainly fill in the first line of its truth table:

$$\begin{array}{c|c} p & \Diamond p \\ \hline T & T \\ F & ? \end{array}$$

but how can we fill in the second? That *p* is false does not make it possible to say that *p could have been* true. Customarily, if we say that *p* is false contingently, then *p* can be true. But if *p is not only false, but necessarily false* (contradictory, for example) then it could not have been true. If we are fatalists, every true proposition will be necessarily true, and every false proposition necessarily false. But every interpretation of modalities is not necessarily fatalist (with all due deference to supporters of the famous 'Master' argument).[7] As is seen, this second type of semantic question is not independent of the first: to evaluate the truth conditions of modal sentences, is also, it seems, to make a decision on the actual nature of the modal facts involved in these evaluations. Do these facts reside in the actual nature of the reality designated by the modal sentences or in the nature of our *assertions* on the world? In other words, are necessity and possibility metaphysical notions, inscribed in the nature of things, or are they metalinguistic notions that relate to the character of always being true, or demonstrable, which we grant to our statements?

The privilege of propositional modal logic is that it allows us to maintain the two interpretations, without forcing us to acknowledge the first. This is the sense in which Quine says that it only gets over a 'first grade of modal involvement'. If the modal operators apply to propositional variables, we can consider them, in the Fregean way (§ 1.2), as operators on intensional entities, Propositions that are the meaning of sentences. We can also take them as *names of statements*, that is to say as predicates of notational forms. Thus 'It is necessary that *p*' has the form

$$\Box \; 'p'$$

where *p* is a quotation of the sentence *p* itself (and does not designate the Proposition expressed by that sentence). In a second interpretation (a 'second grade of modal involvement'), modality is a sentence operator:

$$\Box(p)$$

These contexts are non-extensional, in the sense of § 6.2.2. But this interpretation of modality does not concern things. To use the medieval distinction back in fashion today, it is not modality in respect of things (*de re*), but modality in respect of statements (*de dicto*).[8]

But even if we abide by these interpretations, they do not provide an interpretation of the propositional modal calculus in the *semantic* sense. The classic semantics today is essentially Kripke's (1963), which is based on model theory. As in Tarskian semantics, the truth conditions of modal sentences are evaluated in it. But the theories of truth obtained are not absolute theories but *relative* theories (§ 4.2.1), that is to say theories of truth *within certain structures*. The strategy consists of postulating these structures from a certain intuitive analysis of the modal notions themselves. The striking analogy, observed above, between model operators and quantifiers serves as a guide. In the same way as truth, in a relative theory of truth for an extensional language, is evaluated by reference to a certain *domain* of objects in a model, modal sentences will be evaluated by reference to models. As before, a model is a certain evaluation function which assigns truth values to propositional letters. But specification of certain entities, the 'possible worlds' will be added to it, by supposing that every modal sentence can be legitimately paraphrased as involving a quantification on these worlds. Thus

     'It is possible that p'

will be paraphrased in the metalanguage as

     'There is a possible world m in which p is true'

and

     'It is necessary that p'

will be paraphrased by

     'In all the possible worlds p is true'.

The analogy noted between the quantifiers and the modal operators then takes on its full meaning in this 'Leibnizian' formulation.[9]

A possible world is a *complete* set of ways in which the world could have been. This means that *every* modal sentence is assigned a truth value relative to a world (there are not truth value 'gaps'). It is therefore supposed that the notion of possibility is determined, and that it is possible to say for every sentence, if it is true or false in a possible world.

A *model* (called 'Kripke's') for propositional modal logic will then be set $U = <M,I>$ of two elements comprising (a) a (nonempty) set M of all possible worlds, with an element m^* designated as the 'actual (or real) world', and (b) a function I of evaluation of M to the truth values T and F. The clauses of such a semantics then have the same form (except for the specification of the model) as those of a relative theory of the type described in § 4.2.1:

(I) A propositional letter A is true in a world m in a model U iff I assigns to A the value T in m.

(II) $-A$ is true in a world m (in U) iff A is false in m (in U).

(III) $A \vee B$ is true in m (in U) iff A is true in m (in U) or B is true in m (in U) (and so on for the connectives '&' and '$\rightarrow$'). The important definitions are:

(IV) $\Diamond A$ is true in m (in U) iff there is a world u in in M so that A is true in u (in U).

(V) $\Box A$ is true in m (in U) iff, for all the possible worlds u in M, A is true in u (in U).

The notion of validity remains the classical one: an argument of modal propositional logic is valid if there is no model in which its premises would be true but its conclusion false.

But the semantics corresponding to clauses (I)–(V) is only *one* possible way of understanding the notion of possibility. In particular, it supposes that if A is possible in one world, then A is equally possible in *another* world; i.e. that if $\Diamond A$, then $\Diamond \Diamond A$. But we are not obliged to acknowledge this thesis, any more than we are obliged to acknowledge its converse, $\Diamond \Diamond A \rightarrow \Diamond A$. The relation whereby one world is possible in relation to another is called *accessibility* ('R'). The model U supposes that every world is accessible from another world, which can itself be accessible from the former. This thesis can be rejected and a weaker thesis be acknowledged. The accessibility relation permits us to represent Lewis's different systems exactly:

(T) R is reflexive (if for every m, mRm);

(B) R is symmetric and reflexive (for every m, and every m', if mRm', then $m'Rm$);

(S_4) R is transitive and reflexive (for every m, m', m'', if mRm', and $m'Rm''$, then mRm'');

(S_5) R is reflexive, symmetric and transitive (if R is an equivalence relation).

7.3 The 'reality' of possible worlds

'Possible worlds' semantics therefore offers a very clear representation in an extensional set-theoretic metalanguage of the truth conditions of intensional modal sentences. But the effect of this construction has been the opposite of what might have been expected: instead of quelling discussions on the interpretation of modalities, it has on the contrary engendered a vast literature on the nature of the possible worlds and their existence. If we take the modal semantic literally, it seems that we would have to acknowledge that the possible worlds exist, since (according to Quine's criteria of ontological commitment) they are entities on which we quantify. But there are three possible forms of realism with respect to these worlds.

The first can be called an extreme realism. The principal contemporary representative of this position is David Lewis.[10] According to him, possible worlds are not heuristic metaphors or the artefacts of our semantics. There are other worlds than our own, just as real as it, although most of them are inaccessible to our knowledge. These worlds resemble ours, although they are not identical to it, and they cannot be reduced to other more primitive entities.

The second position can be called a moderate realism: the possible worlds are possible states of the real world, ways in which things could have been or alternative histories of *our* world. But only the actual or real world exists. This position, which is defended by R. Stalnaker for example,[11] is sometimes called *actualism*, in contrast to extreme realism, which is a 'possibilism'.

The third position is a reductionist realism: the possible worlds exist but they can be reduced to more primitive entities. Thus certain authors identify them with maximal sets of propositions, understood as descriptions consisting of possible histories of the world.[12] This analysis is the opposite of the one described in §1.2.2, which on the contrary consists of defining propositions by means of possible worlds.

Each of these positions rests on highly metaphysical premises, which actually recall the traditional discussions on the nature of possibles.[13] But are they, for all that, *analyses* of the notion of possibility? No. The notion of possible world does not *define* the notion of possibility, since it actually invokes this notion. At the most it is a paraphrase, and raises none of the traditional difficulties that result from the justification of the modal concepts. For example, one of these difficulties concerns the analysis of dispositions and dispositional terms. One of these terms, for example, 'soluble' can be paraphrased by means of a counterfactual conditional statement:

> *x* is soluble = if *x* were plunged in water, it would dissolve.

But, as a classic discussion by Goodman has shown, the truth conditions of counterfactual conditionals are no clearer than those of sentences containing the dispositional terms that they are supposed to analyse.[14] In the same way, it is possible to try to 'analyse' the counterfactual conditionals by means of the notion of possible world. But what can a formulation such as

> If there is a possible world in which *x* is plunged in water, then *x* dissolves in this world

add to the previous one? The problem of establishing conditions of relevance (or, as Goodman says, of 'cotenability') of the antecedent in relation to the consequent arises in the same way in both cases: we must specify what worlds are relevant.[15]

This does not mean that the notion of possible world is trivial. On the contrary, as has been seen, it is a useful tool to construct the semantics of modalities, that is to say in order to formulate the problems that such an analysis encounters. But it does not *resolve* them. The worlds in themselves are only sets of assignations of truth values to propositional letters. It is in this sense that we can say that propositions are sets of possible worlds. We can ask (§ 1.2.1) if such sets can be defined, that is to say if they have strict conditions of identity, and if they can define the intensional propositional notion. But this does not imply that the worlds are problematic entities. As Stalnaker observes,[16] a world is a formal or functional concept, and it is presupposed by the use of our semantical framework for modal logic, just as the notion of *individual* is presupposed by the semantics of our usual extensional logic for predicates. An individual there is not a certain sort of thing, but a certain role that things of this type can fill, that of a subject of predication. The semantics of quantification theory no more involves accepting a certain metaphysical analysis of what individuals are, than the semantics of modalities involves adopting one conception or another of the nature of possible worlds. The problematic 'ontological commitments' of modal logic hold elsewhere.

7.4 Quantified modal logic according to Quine

According to Quine, modal logic becomes really problematic when it is quantified, that is to say when the possibility and necessity operators no longer modify only statements, but predicates of individuals, which leads us to acknowledge essentialism, that is to say the doctrine according to which objects have necessary properties. A 'third grade' of modal involvement is thus crossed.

The famous argument that Quine uses to this effect is an adaptation of Frege's 'slingshot' (§ 1.3.2).[17] According to Quine, this argument shows that if a context is extensional, it is 'referentially transparent', that is to say that the singular terms which figure in it can be substituted *salva veritate* (this corresponds to condition (b) for extensionality in § 6.2.2). Take the following sentences:

(1) The number of planets is 9
(2) Necessarily 9 is larger than 7.

If necessity is taken here as bearing on the statement that the operator 'necessarily' modifies, that is to say on its *de dicto* sense, it is not possible to infer from (1) and (2) by substitution:

(3) Necessarily the number of planets is larger than 7

since the context by definition is non-extensional. But the contentious interpretation is the one that no longer takes the *de re* modality as bearing on the statement, but on the number 9 itself. According to Quine, no longer is it only the rule of substitutivity that ceases to apply, but the usual rules of quantification, such as inference by existential generalisation which one should have been able to do from (2), if 9 was the object attributed with the necessary property of being larger than 7:

(4) (∃x) (x is necessarily larger than 7)

But what, asks Quine, is this object x which is said to be necessarily larger than 7? If it is 9, then it is incompatible with the falsity of (3). If it is the number of planets, then it is incompatible with the truth of (2). (4) leads us to attribute a necessary property to an unspecified object, designated by a variable of quantification. In other words, *de re* quantification within a modal context, like (4), leads us to maintain that *an object can have necessary properties independently of the way in which it is described*. This is the thesis that Quine calls *essentialism*. It is, according to him, absurd: an object only has necessary properties in relation to the way it is described. By a certain description, if I am a cyclist, then I necessarily have two legs; by another description, if I am a mathematician, then I am necessarily rational. But if I am both a cyclist and a mathematician, it does not make sense to say that I have one of the properties essentially and the other contingently.[18] The only legitimate modalities are *de dicto*. Either we agree to quantify into contexts of modality – but then we must accept essentialism – or we reject these quantifications – but then modal logic is limited, as Quine recommends, solely to a calculus of statements.

There are two answers to the problem Quine raises (if we acknowledge its legitimacy, that is to say if, like him, we are going to regard essentialism as a problematic doctrine). The first, inspired by Frege, consists of acknowledging that the variables of quantification which figure within the scope of a modal operator do not have objective referents, but designate something like individual concepts of these referents. Carnap, for example, has recommended this solution.[19] It must then be acknowledged that quantified modal logic bears on objects that are distinct from those of usual extensional logic, and possible domains of objects and concepts must be introduced. The quantification and reference rules specific to these entities therefore have to be specified. As these are intensional, this solution cannot satisfy Quine, since his objection is precisely directed against the idea that there should be such entities. The second answer is inspired by Russell and resorts to one feature of the theory of descriptions (cf. § 4.3.1.1), ignored by Quine in his treatment of the 'number of planets' example. A description such as the 'number of planets' can have a *narrow* scope, in which case it designates every object that satisfies the description. But it can have a *wide* scope, in which case it designates the number that in fact happens to be the number of planets, that is to say 9. If we make this distinction, then (3) is false if 'the number of planets' is a narrow-scope description. But (3) is true if it is a wide-scope description. In this latter interpretation, the description is just as referential as the proper name '9' in (1). But this solution can no more satisfy Quine than did the first. The theory of descriptions shows us how to paraphrase a description of the form '$(\imath x)\phi x$' by means of quantifiers and signs of identity. Once the description is paraphrased, (3) would still contain a *de re* quantification in the scope of a modal operator:

> (3′) There is one and only one x which is the number of planets and this x is necessarily larger than 7.[20]

But this is just the sort of quantification that Quine finds problematic.

7.5 Semantics for quantified modal logic

None the less, some of the doubts that Quine aroused are dissipated when the classical semantics for quantified modal logic is considered. In the same way as for the propositional modal semantic, one gives oneself a set of possible worlds M and an accessibility relation which satisfies the various formal constraints of each system. Each world is assigned a domain of objects, individuals and properties. But here a problem arises that did not arise in the propositional case: are the domains of objects assigned to each world identical to those in the actual world, or are they different? If they are coextensive with those of the actual world, one has a form of 'actualism' according to which any entity present in the actual world cannot be absent from a possible world. This makes the following two formulae, known as 'Barcan's formulae', true:

$$(BF1)\Diamond(\exists x)\ Fx \rightarrow (\exists x)\Diamond Fx$$
$$(BF2)(\forall x)\Box Fx \rightarrow \Box(\forall x)\ Fx$$

(in other words, respectively: if an individual is F in one world, then there is an individual such that there is a possible world in which that individual is F; and if all individuals are F in all the possible worlds, then in every possible world all individuals are F).[21]

But we can also remove this option of coextensive domains, and acknowledge either that there are certain individuals in other possible worlds than the actual world who are different from those of this world, or that there are worlds in which there is no individual of the actual world. We will then meet the problem of empty names or names without denotation. What truth value should be assigned to sentences containing names designating objects which are only possible, such as 'Pegasus' or 'Baba Yaga'? Do we, like Frege, acknowledge that these sentences do not have truth value? Or do we utilise a Russellian paraphrase strategy and treat these names as abbreviated definite descriptions? (§ 4.3.1.1). Kripke's semantics (1963) adopts the convention that all atomic sentences of the form 'Fx' (where 'x' is a free variable), have a truth value, even in worlds where the objects assigned to the variable do not belong to the domains of these worlds. But *quantificational* variables, in Kripke's semantic, are world bound, and are only capable of designating entities belonging to the domain specific to each world. In this semantics, Barcan's formulae cease to be valid. For example, the sentence '$\Diamond(\exists x)$ (x is a winged horse)' is true, but '$(\exists x)\Diamond(x$ is a winged horse)' is false, because there is no *actual* object that is a winged horse in an accessible possible world (if Pegasus is in a world, it is not ours).

In this semantics it is possible to add individual constants (which Kripke, 1963, does not do). But it is then necessary to suppose that these constants designate the same individuals in all possible worlds. I will discuss this point later (§ 6).

A semantics for a quantificational language then takes the form of a 'model structure' corresponding to these assignations, which is a natural extension of the propositional semantics presented in § 2 above. The details of the clauses which have just been informally presented can be delegated to a footnote. The Kripkean version of this semantic is far from being the only possible one.[22]

This semantics gives us clear evaluation rules for quantified modal formulae. As before, validity remains in accordance with classical concepts. This answers Quine's doubts which concerned the actual possibility of proving a semantics of this type. But it may be thought that we are finding the same problems, simply transposed to the level of the metalanguage. First and foremost, in Kripke's version (but, as has been seen, not in the version that Barcan's formulae legitimise), we have to acknowledge the existence of possible individuals and properties. But these entities are at least as problematical as the worlds themselves. Because how are we going to identify them? To take Quine's famous example, what distinguishes that possible fat man in the doorway from that other possible fat man in the doorway?[23] Then, and whether or not we acknowledge possible objects distinct from objects of the actual world, how will we identify the individuals of one possible world from another? How does one know, for example, that Adam, no sinner in one possible world, is the same Adam as Adam the sinner in another world? Contemporary literature calls this the problem 'of transworld identification'. According to Quine, it can only be solved by essentialism: in order to identify an individual of one possible world with another, we have to postulate the essential properties that one individual has in all the worlds.[24] We therefore come back to the essentialism which, according to Quine, we have never left from the moment when we acknowledged *de re* quantification in modal contexts.

7.6 Reference without modality

Quine's objection to quantified modal logic amounts to this: it is impossible to assign clear *reference* (and therefore truth) conditions to modal sentences, without associating these conditions with questionable modal notions, such as of those of essences and possibles. There is nothing surprising about this according to Quine, since it amounts to stating the triviality that truth and reference conditions in a *modal* context must invoke *modal* notions. There are two possible answers to Quine on this point. The first consists of biting the bullet, as it were, and acknowledging that the reference conditions depend on modal notions, which one then tries to justify in the best possible way. The second answer consists of rejecting the triviality in question. We are in no way bound to acknowledge that the specification of the reference conditions in modal contexts *must* invoke these notions themselves. This answer seems to me far preferable to the first.

Let us begin by considering the first answer. The problems Quine raises arise from the particularly strong condition that he imposes on every reference and every quantification, that is to say what I called 'Quine's thesis' in § 4.3.1: no quantification or reference without entity, no entity without identity, and no identity without discernibility. In other words, Quine imposes the Leibnizian condition of the *indiscernibility of identicals* on every possible object of quantification (cf. § 9.3):

$$(Ind\ Id)(\forall x)(\forall y)((x=y)\rightarrow(\phi x\equiv\phi y)).$$

The difficulties with the notions of possibility and essence arise precisely from the fact that it seems impossible to satisfy that condition for the objects of reference in relation to possible worlds, except by acknowledging that the properties ϕ of the above schema are necessary or essential properties, which we are equally hard-pressed to specify. In the actual world, we have criteria of identity of objects (for example, material, spatial, temporal continuity). But what are we going to base ourselves on in the possible worlds? A good illustration of this fact is provided by a paradox, first formulated by Chisholm. Let us suppose that there were (in the actual world) a table, T, composed of a piece of wood H. We can acknowledge that this table, if it had been composed (in a possible world m_1) from a piece of wood H_1, very slightly different from H (for example, about a cubic millimetre different) would have been the same table T. If it had been composed (in a world m_2) of a piece H_2, about two cubic millimetres different from H, it would still have been the same table T, and so on. By the same 'increasing' reasoning, T could have been composed (in a world m_n) of a piece H_n totally distinct and not coextensive with H, and would thus, it seems, be another table. This is a form of sorites paradox, of a type that will be discussed in Chapter 10 below. As Quine says apropos this paradox: 'You can change anything into anything, by easy transitions across any series whatsoever of connected possible worlds.'[25] But similar changes are not possible with material particulars, or with objects which we suppose change in time. The reason is that possible worlds are not based on any strict condition of identity, while our conditions of material and temporal individuation must at least be based on certain considerations of continuity or displacement, distortion or chemical change.

   This does not discourage the champions of possible worlds. Most of them acknowledge that the conditions of transworld identity of individuals are not as firm as those of ordinary spatio-temporal objects. These criteria are vaguer, but it does not follow that there are no criteria. Thus David Lewis has formulated a version of modal semantics, in which the relationship between the individuals in the worlds is not a strict relationship of identity, but a relationship of *comparative similarity*.[26] The possible individuals in different worlds from ours (which are just as real as our world, under the terms of Lewis's realism) are *counterparts* to a greater or lesser extent of the individuals of our world. The accessibility relation between worlds is therefore based on a relation of similarity, which is a gradual notion like that of counterpart. In this case, the variables of quantification are assigned objects that must bear *more* resemblance to those that exist in the actual world than to those that exist in other worlds. From the point of view of this interpretation of modalities, a counterfactual conditional such as

   If I had lived in the Middle Ages I would have been a monk

is true if in a possible world sufficiently similar to our own, one of my counterparts is (a counterpart of) a monk in the Middle Ages. Lewis thus makes the transworld identification of individuals depend on quantitative criteria capable of varying in degree. There is then a natural solution to Chisholm's paradox, if we specify a threshold beyond which the comparative degree of similarity between the wooden table of this world and the table composed of different pieces of wood in other worlds ceases to apply. But the paradox is also implicit in any semantics based on such degrees of similarity which prohibit talk about the absolute essence of a thing, and only authorise *degrees* of essences, in relation to the comparisons.[27]

Other theories refuse to adopt such qualitative criteria in order to fix the transworld identity of objects. They suppose that there is an irreducible original essence attached to each object that cannot be given by a list of the properties of the individual and continues to exist across the worlds. This individual essence is a *this*, or a sort of Scotistic 'haecceity', and the theories concerned are called *haecceitist*.[28]

One of the charms of the semantics of possible worlds is probably that it has revived a form of metaphysical speculation in contemporary philosophy, which the dominant tradition in the philosophy of logic, born of logical positivism, had tended to dismiss. But do we need to invoke this type of doctrine in order to answer Quine's problem on essentialism?

It seems to me that we do not. The error common to Quine and the doctrines of transworld identification like Lewis's is to have supposed that in order to clarify the reference conditions to objects in relation to possible worlds, we have to specify the modal properties that these objects must have. This leads to the adoption of essence as a criterion for reference, for better or for worse, according to the diagnosis made. But it can be shown that reference does not require essence, or at least not the type of essence that Quine or those he criticises invoke.

There are two sorts of essential properties: *strong* essential properties, which are supposed to be necessary and sufficient individuation conditions of an object; and *weak* or *trivial* essential properties, which provide no individuation conditions. Examples of strong essential properties would be: *to be composed of a certain matter* (for a material object), *to be conscious* (for a person), *to have a certain origin* (for an organism). The burden of proof that these properties actually are essential properties and that talking about such properties has a sense, rests on the essentialist, and the type of proof that he might be able to give is not obvious. Examples of weak or trivial essential properties would be: *to be red or not red, to be identical to oneself*, or *to be white if one is white*. There is some paradox in talking about essential properties in this sense because none of these properties *individuates* the least object. Defending essentialism at this price is not defending essentialism. But several authors (Ruth Marcus in particular) have maintained that if modal logic was essentialist, it could only be so in this *weak* or trivial sense, and consequently inoffensive.[29]

But this argument is only of interest if it is completed by another. To say that there are essences but that they are trivial, is to acknowledge that we do not need essences to identify the reference objects of modal logic from one world to another. We do not need essences from the moment when we introduce singular terms into our semantics, which have the property of designating their objects *independently of properties or descriptions which we can associate with these objects*. Such terms will be referential by definition, that is to say they will be able to suit all the substitutions *salva veritate* of co-referential terms. These will be *genuine* singular terms. The other category of terms will be that of non-referential or descriptive singular terms, which only designate objects through associated properties.

A genuine singular term is precisely a term suitable for *de re* quantification in a modal context, that is to say a term that designates a possible object, or an object that has necessary properties *independent of the way in which this object is described*, if this object has necessary properties. But that corresponds exactly to Quine's definition of the essentialism which he imputed to modal logic (cf. § 4 above). We seem to be going round in a circle: Quine challenges *de re* quantification in a modal context because of the essentialist involvement that it implies, and we want to justify essentialism by this *de re* quantification! But, as Føllesdal has maintained, there is nothing circular about it.[30] The essentialism concerned does not lie in the *existence* of essential properties of objects, whether or not they are trivial, but only in the fact that our singular terms are referentially transparent. It postulates no essential property, any more than it specifies what these properties can be, contrary to what Quine seems to suppose, and contrary to what is supposed by authors who specify essences in order to identify individuals across worlds. This 'essentialism' only lies in the fact that genuine singular terms are stipulated to designate the same individuals in all possible worlds.

It is very clear that what Quine is attacking in his criticism of modal logic is this distinction between two sorts of singular terms. Quine, on the contrary, maintains that there is only one type of singular term: definite descriptions, to which all the other terms can be reduced, by the Russellian procedure. Essentialism is only a by-product of the distinction between the two sorts of terms and is not the true nub of the discussion. *De re* quantification is possible not because individuals are said to have essences, but because the reference of genuine singular terms is constant. As Føllesdal says:

> The notion of a genuine singular term is not fundamentally a modal notion. It is not a notion that requires appeal to necessity or essentialism for its definition or clarification. That genuine singular terms refer to the same object 'in all possible worlds', to use modal jargon, is not definitory of such terms. It merely follows from the fact that these terms are referring expressions.[31]

A genuine singular term closely corresponds to what Kripke calls a 'rigid designator'.[32] These are designators whose reference is constant across all possible worlds. But Kripke's version of the notion is ambiguous and over-determined. It corresponds to at least three notions:

(a) the notion of a term which is stipulated '*de jure*' to designate the same individual in all possible worlds;

(b) the notion of a definite, *wide-scope* description, in contrast to defined *narrow-scope* descriptions in the sense of § 4 above;

(c) the notion of a term designating an individual by virtue of essential properties ('*de facto*' rigidity).

In sense (a), Kripke is saying that a term is a rigid designator if it designates the same individual in a modal context as it designates in the actual world, and in all other worlds. Thus in

> (5) Nixon could have had an Irangate under his mandate

'Nixon' is a rigid designator, because it designates Nixon himself, and not another individual, in the possible world evoked.

In sense (b), the definite description 'the number of planets' (§ 4) is a rigid designator when it has a wide scope, that is to say designates the actual number of planets, that is to say 9. When it has a narrow scope, and designates the number, whatever it is, which is the number of the planets, it is not a rigid designator.

In sense (c), 'the square root of 4' is a rigid designator because it designates an object which is *necessarily* 2.[33]

Only rigid designators in senses (a) and (b) correspond to the genuine referential terms we are talking about here. Sense (c) invokes an essence of the object concerned in order to ensure rigidity. But we have in fact precisely defined these terms as terms that ensure reference without modal properties.

Perhaps the best means of defining genuine singular terms is to compare them, as most authors do, with proper names in natural language. Proper names are supposed to be means of designating objects independently of the properties, essential or not, that these objects possess. It is in this sense that Kripke makes the proper names of natural language rigid designators.[34] But this question, so copiously discussed, does not concern us in this chapter. It concerns the theory of reference, that is to say the study of the relationship between linguistic expressions and their objects, and not the logical semantics which is all that concerns us here (§ 8.2).

In fact, there are many ways of understanding and analysing the notion of direct reference in a natural language, and I will come back to these problems in the next chapter. Following authors like Føllesdal,[35] I have maintained no more than this: the only essentialism to which modal logic constrains us is weak essentialism (which is only essentialism in the Pickwickian sense) which corresponds to the idea that reference can be made to objects independently of their properties, essential or not, by terms that play the role of genuine referential terms. These terms are referential by definition. This corresponds to the logician's practice. In possible worlds semantics, the functions that identify the objects from one possible world to another are given, just as the individuals of an extensional semantics are given right at the start. The way in which we identify individuals, in knowledge, does not concern the logician, who 'quite simply assumes that this identification has been achieved and accepts the abstract result'.[36] The fact that the reference of the terms which designate these individuals is fixed is simply a transcription of this fact.

One of the motivations of the logicians who have constructed modal logics was undeniably philosophical. Modalities (not only alethic modalities) are obscure and controversial notions, which one could have hoped to clarify by studying the deductive properties of inference where the terms that express them figure. Although I have not shown it here, modal logic is very useful in this respect.[37] It is equally a fertile field for logical, particularly metalogical, investigation.[38] But it can also give rise to a hope, and correlatively, a fear. The hope would be born amongst philosophers who think that there are modal properties in the world, necessary facts and essential properties, that modal logic *justifies* this belief, and that it is in some way possible to derive essences or possibilities from our formulation of sentences and modal inferences. The fear, on the contrary, would be that modal logic leads us to adopt such doctrines despite ourselves. But neither hope nor fear is justified. We can utilise the semantic models of modal logic without taking a stand on the nature of essences or possibles, and the philosophical problems posed by these ideas remain the same as they were before. No essentialist rabbit pops out of the hat of logic, unless we have already put it there. From this point of view, this logic is much less 'interesting' than certain philosophers think. But it also thereby acquires the status of a completely legitimate extension of classical logic.

—— 8 ——

REFERENCE AND PROPOSITIONAL ATTITUDES

8.1 'Frege's problem'

At the beginning of *Über Sinn und Bedeutung*, Frege raises the problem that led him to make his famous distinction between sense and reference. Two sentences $a = a$ and $a = b$ are obviously different in that the first is trivial and known as *a priori*, while the second is informative and *a posteriori*. How is this possible? Because if $a = b$ predicates the relation of identity between the referent of 'a' and the referent of 'b', and if $a = a$ states the relation of identity between the referent of 'a' and the referent of 'a', then if $a = b$ is true, this sentence predicates the same relation between the same pair of objects as $a = a$. The two sentences therefore have the same truth and reference conditions. But they do not have the same informative content, or, as Frege says, the same 'cognitive value'. The cognitive value of a sentence is therefore distinct from its truth value. The first is the sense of the sentence; the second its reference. The senses of the two sentences differ because the senses of their parts differ: the names 'a' and 'b' do not have the same sense.

   Frege presents his problem as relating to the notion of identity: is it a relation between objects or between signs of objects? But it can be formulated without explicitly resorting to statements of identity. For example, 'The author of *Les Pieds Nickelés* drew *Bibi Fricotin*' and 'The author of *Bibi Fricotin* drew *Bibi Fricotin*' do not have the same cognitive value, but they do have the same truth value and the same reference. It is more accurate to say that the problem relates to the *substitutivity salva veritate* of co-referential singular terms in certain contexts (although it is true that *substitutivity* supposes the relation of identity between the references of the intersubstitutable names (cf. § 9.3)).[1] In what contexts? Precisely in contexts formed by sentences that someone can *recognise* the truth of without recognising the truth of another sentence with the same truth (reference) conditions. The problem is simply that from

   (1) $a = b$ has a cognitive value

and from

   (2) $a = a$

it cannot be inferred that

   (3) $a = a$ has a cognitive value.

But the same problem would arise if one were dealing with any intensional

161

context in which '*a*' and '*b*' are two co-referential terms and '*F*' any predicate (which may or may not be the identity) such as

(4) X thinks that Fa
(5) $a = b$
(6) X thinks that Fb

and more generally in any context that is 'indirect' or 'oblique' or is a 'propositional attitude' context of the form 'X says that p', 'X believes that p', and so on. Frege's problem generally arises because it is possible that (4) is true and that (6) is false. Note that the same problem would still arise if the substitution did not relate to singular terms like '*a*' or '*b*', but to predicates:

(7) X thinks that every F is a G
(8) every G is an H and every H is a G ('G' and 'H' are coextensive)
(9) X thinks that every F is an H.

Frege concludes from this that the semantic contribution of sentences completing contexts such as '— has a cognitive value' or 'X thinks that —' cannot be limited to their reference or their truth value. It is also necessary to postulate that they have a *sense*, and that their component parts also have a sense (by virtue of the principle of compositionality: § 6.1). As has been seen (§ 1.2.1), this sense according to Frege is an objective and eternal 'thought', corresponding to the sentence's cognitive value and intended to explain what a speaker understands when he understands the sentence in question. The Fregean argument therefore consists of concluding, from the fact that certain terms are not substitutable *salva veritate* in contexts which are indirect or of propositional attitudes, that the sentences completing these contexts or 'embedded' in them[2] have a sense, and that *if* they have a sense in these contexts, they must also have a sense outside them. The argument in itself does not tell us if the sense of a sentence 'p' outside of such a context is the same sense that this sentence has in this context. But Frege adds that, while a sentence in an extensional context designates its truth value (the True or the False) and expresses its sense, the same sentence in an indirect context or in an attitude context designates the sense it has in an ordinary extensional sentence (its 'ordinary' sense), and expresses *another* sense (its indirect or 'oblique' sense), specific to this indirect context. Thus the sentence 'Hesperus is a planet' has an ordinary sense and reference, like the words that compose it. In an indirect context such as 'John believes that Hesperus is a planet', the same sentence has its ordinary sense as reference, and its oblique sense as its sense.

What is the sense of an expression, outside of the fact that it concerns a certain entity associated with the expression, and designated by it in a non-extensional context? Frege also identifies it with its role: the sense is the 'mode of presentation' of the expression and what determines the reference or the truth conditions. It is hard to know what Frege really means by this.[4] For the moment I will call any theory Fregean if it claims that *every extensional sentence expresses a thought (or Proposition) that is a certain entity determining its reference or truth value, constituting the cognitive content of the sentence, and designated by the sentence in a context of propositional attitude (and likewise for every expression figuring in a sentence).*

In what follows, I will confine myself to an examination of *singular* (or 'atomic' in the sense of § 3.3.1) sentences, that is to say sentences where the subject is a singular term designating an individual of the form '*Fa*'. It will be stated that this type of sentence expresses 'Fregean' thoughts or Propositions if and only if they meet the above definition.

The Fregean theory of Propositions is opposed to another theory that can be maintained concerning the informative content and truth conditions of singular sentences. This other theory is simply that in a singular sentence '*F*', the semantic contribution of the name '*a*' is confined to its *reference*, that is to say to the introduction of the object *a* itself. John Stuart Mill supported this sort of conception when he said that the sense of a proper name was reduced to its 'denotation', or to the object it designated.[5] Mill's theory is typically the theory of reference of proper names in a Tarskian logical semantics (§ 4.2.1) for predicate calculus, where a simple list of names and their denotations is enough to account for their semantic contribution. In the previous chapter I maintained that such a theory was also sufficient for a logical semantics of modalities (§ 7.6). But knowing what reference the terms of an ideal logical language should have and what their reference in a natural language is are two different questions. The first concerns what can be called 'pure' semantics, the second 'applied' semantics.[6] Frege considered that expressions had to have a sense in the logical language *and* in natural language, and in this sense the logic that he formulated was an *intensional* logic. The question that concerns us here is related to both the sense and the reference of expressions in logical semantics and in the semantics of natural languages.

A Millian theory of reference in singular sentences cannot be only a theory of the truth conditions of these sentences. These truth conditions can be identified with Propositions, not understood as the senses of sentences, as Frege understood them, but as certain entities in the world, in the sense of 'proposition' examined in § 1.3. In this case, a singular sentence '*Fa*' expresses a singular Proposition composed of two objects, the individual *a* itself and the property *F*, that is to say of the ordered pair <*a,F*>. As has been seen, Russell at one time supported this theory.[7] That is why in what follows any theory according to which *a singular sentence expresses a singular Proposition, which is a certain entity existing in the world, composed of objects and properties designated by its component expressions*, will be called 'Russellian theory', and this type of Proposition will be called a 'Russellian Proposition'. According to a Russellian theory, the cognitive value of a singular sentence is reduced to the Russellian Proposition which it expresses, and the semantic contribution of a name '*a*' is not the sense or 'mode of presentation' of the object *a*, but that object itself.

The Russellian theory appeared completely incredible to Frege. How can a sentence such as 'Mont Blanc is the highest mountain in Europe' be true by virtue of the fact that it expresses a singular Proposition composed of Mont Blanc itself, with its snows and its rocky slopes? How can the mountain itself, as Russell maintained, be a *component* of the Proposition?[8] It was to avoid this conclusion that Frege suggested his own conception of Propositions. In the event, Frege's problem and the contexts of propositional attitudes seem to create an insurmountable obstacle to any Millian theory of reference and any Russellian theory of propositions. But as we saw in Chapter 1, the Fregean conception of Propositions is not self-evident either. Are there such entities and what are they? Would it not be better to leave out Propositions and say that there are only sentences?

In Chapter 1, I examined the difficulties with these theories. Here, our problem is to know if one or other of them can furnish a plausible analysis of the attributions of propositional attitudes, and if the notion of 'proposition' can adequately characterise the content of the propositional attitudes themselves. Like most authors who have dealt with these questions, I will suppose that belief is a paradigmatic propositional attitude. I will examine three sorts of theories of the logical form of attributions of belief: (a) theories that hold that sentences of the form '*X* believes that *p*' represent a relationship between a subject and a *sentence* of a language; (b) theories that claim that they represent a relationship between a subject and a *Fregean Proposition*; and (c) theories stating that they represent a relationship between a subject and a *Russellian Proposition*. Each of these theories encounters immediate objections, but can be modified accordingly. The whole problem is of knowing if the modifications meet the initial difficulties.

8.2 Three theories of the logical form of propositional attitudes

8.2.1 The quotational theory

In the first place, the logical form of attributions of the form '*X*' believes that *p*' can be analysed in a similar way to the logical form of sentences of the form *X* says '*p*', where '*p*' is a *quotation* or a *mention* of a sentence stated by *X*, and reported by the speaker. Thus the logical form of a sentence such as

> (10) Rodolphe believes that Paris is the capital of philosophy

> is

> (10a) Rodolphe believes 'Paris is the capital of philosophy'.

The problem is that Rodolphe can (in his naïveté) believe the content expressed by the sentence embedded in (10) without stating the corresponding sentence. Carnap, who proposes this analysis, suggests that (10) should rather be rendered as

> (10b) Rodolphe is disposed to assent to 'Paris is the capital of philosophy'

or to every sentence that is synonymous or translated into another language.[9]

But even if we accept this analysis of belief, we encounter a difficulty that has been brought out by Church. Translated into German (10) is

(10c) Rodolphe glaubt dass Paris ist die Hauptstadt der Philosophie.

But if the object of Rodolophe's belief is the sentence 'Paris is the capital of philosophy', the translation of (10) should not be (10c) but rather

(10d) Rodolphe glaubt 'Paris is the capital of philosophy'.

But a German who did not know English would not understand what Rodolphe believes. He might perhaps infer from the fact that Rodolphe is asserting this sentence that he believes that it is true. But he would have no means of determining thereby the content of the sentence. If (10d) reproduces the meaning of (10a), then (10a) cannot be a correct translation of (10). Church concludes from this that beliefs cannot be relations to sentences but must be relations to meanings of sentences, that is to say to Propositions, which he construes as intensional entities.[10]

8.2.2 The Fregean theory

This suggests that a Fregean theory is more appropriate. As has been seen, according to such a theory, a singular sentence '*Fa*', embedded in a context of propositional attitude '*X* believes that *Fa*', designates the Fregean Proposition that this sentence would express in an extensional context, and expresses the corresponding indirect Fregean Proposition. According to this theory, therefore, the truth conditions of a sentence like (10) must be evaluated on two levels:

(a) first, at the level of the ordinary sense and reference of the non-embedded sentence;
(b) then, at the level of the indirect sense and reference of the embedded sentence.

But the determination of (b) depends on that of (a). If in fact the ordinary sense and reference of the non-embedded sentence are not known, it will not be possible to say what its oblique sense and reference are. However, a Fregean theory encounters difficulties at both of these levels.

At the first level, the question is one of knowing whether singular sentences express Fregean Propositions. This is essentially the heavily debated question of knowing whether all singular terms designate their bearer through the intermediary of a sense or mode of presentation. In definite descriptions such as 'the merry widow' or 'Rameau's nephew' (§ 4.3.1.1), there seems to be no doubt about this, since a description *is* a term designating an individual through a property of that individual. The problem arises with proper names where the grammatical form does not contain any predicate of their bearer. According to the Fregean theory, however, they can only designate an individual via a mode of presentation. Frege does not say what this mode of presentation consists of, but suggests that it can at least be represented by means of a description. For example, 'the teacher of Alexander' can be a mode of presentation of the name 'Aristotle'.[11] All we need to suppose here is that the mode of presentation in some way *gives the meaning* of the name, or that an expression representing it is *synonymous* with the name itself, so that everything that is true of the individual designated by the description must be able to apply to the individual designated by the proper name. But there are several counter-examples to this Fregean theory, taken both as a theory of the use (pragmatic) of names by speakers in given contexts, and as a semantic theory.[12] Staying solely on the semantic level, Kripke has provided the following ('modal') argument relating to the reference of proper names in modal contexts. Let us suppose – in accordance with the Fregean theory – that a name 'Aristotle' has the same sense as a description 'the teacher of Alexander'. In that case, a statement such as

> (11) Aristotle is the teacher of Alexander

would necessarily have to be true, either analytically or *a priori*, and a counterfactual statement such as

> (12) Aristotle could have not been the teacher of Alexander

would necessarily have to be false. But (12) can be true: it can be true about Aristotle himself, that he would have been able never to have met Alexander, nor to have taught him, however that may be. (12) is in fact a 'metaphysical' truth about Aristotle. It follows, according to Kripke, that (11) is not necessarily true, and therefore that 'Aristotle' does not mean 'the teacher of Alexander'. Kripke invites us to make a distinction between the modal status of a sentence such as (12) (the fact that it is 'metaphysically' necessary or possible) and its *epistemic* status (that is to say, the fact that we are able to know it as true, or imagine it as true). From the modal point of view, a proper name can only designate its bearer, because it is a metaphysical truth that Aristotle *is* Aristotle as an individual (an individual is unable not to be identical with himself). But from the *epistemic* point of view, a proper name can be equivalent to a description, if we acknowledge that the latter *fixes the reference* of the name, though without *giving its meaning*. For example, I can call Aristotle 'the sage of Stagira', without giving the sense of 'Aristotle', because another individual can instantiate the description. On the other hand, I cannot fail to designate Aristotle when I use the name 'Aristotle'. According to Kripke, because the Fregean confuses fixing the reference of a name with giving its meaning, he is led to identify the sense of a name with a mode of presentation.[13] As I pointed out in § 7.6, this argument can appear unconvincing, in so far as it invokes our 'metaphysical intuitions' as to the essence of the individual Aristotle. But if we separate off these metaphysical intuitions and only keep the *semantic* thesis put forward by Kripke, according to which 'Aristotle' is a 'rigid designator' that designates Aristotle 'in all possible worlds' independently of how Aristotle is described, then this semantic thesis is actually tantamount to the Millian thesis according to which the sole function of names is to introduce their referent. If this thesis is correct for modal contexts, considered to be intensional, why should it not be so for ordinary extensional contexts? In any case, for these contexts, it is not obvious that a name, or even a description, designates its bearer through a 'mode of presentation' and therefore that there are, in this sense, Fregean Propositions.

But even if we are not convinced by the argument that singular sentences express Fregean Propositions outside contexts of propositional attitudes, how could we refuse to say that these sentences express such Propositions when they are embedded in these contexts? Here, the Fregean argument seems inescapable. Let us suppose that a detective, Javert, believes that a certain man, Jean Valjean, is meaner than another, Monsieur Madeleine. Unknown to him, the two men are only one. We can therefore apparently report his belief in this way:

> (13) Javert believes that Jean Valjean is meaner than Monsieur Madeleine (true)

but not in this way:

> (14) Javert believes that Jean Valjean is meaner than Jean Valjean (false).

In the first place, by supposing that (13) is true, but (14) false, the Fregean is supposing that (13) and (14) express two determinate Propositions. But these two sentences do not express the same Proposition, because the two sentences embedded in (13) and (14) do not express the same Proposition. The intuitive criterion of this difference is that Javert can assert the first embedded sentence but deny the second (cf. § 1.2.1). The semantic explanation of this difference is that (13) and (14) each designates the ordinary sense of the corresponding non-embedded sentences, and have as sense the oblique or indirect sense created by their occurrence in the context governed by 'believes that'. Likewise, the names that figure in these sentences designate their ordinary sense and have as sense an oblique sense. The Fregean solution is to say that the names in the embedded sentences in (13) and (14) are singular terms that do not designate objects, but modes of presentation of objects. Let us suppose that 'MP_J' is any mode of presentation of Jean Valjean for Javert, and that 'MP_M' is any mode of presentation that Javert has of Monsieur Madeleine (these can be descriptions such as 'the man who has the property ϕ' or other determinants). In this case we must represent the contents of the beliefs above in this way:

> (13a) Javert believes that the individual determined by MP_J is meaner than the individual determined by MP_M (true)
> (14a) Javert believes that the individual determined by MP_J is meaner than the individual determined by MP_J (false).

The names cannot be substituted *salva veritate*, because they designate distinct modes of presentation. But this solution cannot be correct. Because the following argument is valid:

> (A) Jean Valjean is a renegade
>   Javert thinks that Jean Valjean is a renegade
>   *therefore* Javert is thinking something true

while the following argument is invalid:

> (B) Jean Valjean is a renegade
>   Javert thinks that the individual determined by MP_J is a renegade
>   *therefore* Javert is thinking something true.

This second argument cannot be valid because Javert can believe what is reported in the second premise without his belief relating *to* Jean Valjean. The problem comes from the fact that, according to the Fregean solution, a singular sentence (embedded or not) is not related to the *object* designated by the name which is the subject of it, but to a concept, or a qualitative mode of presentation of this object. But the same mode of presentation can define two distinct objects. Javert can represent to himself a man who *is* Jean Valjean under a mode MP_J, but also another similar but distinct man who is not Jean Valjean.[14] It follows that (13a) does not correctly represent Javert's belief, and that, contrary to the initial hypothesis, neither (13) nor (14) expresses determinate Fregean Propositions. For them to be effectively determinate, the modes of presentation postulated would have had to be able actually to determine the references of the names, which they do not.

We can present the difficulty with the Fregean theory in a different way, using the traditional distinction, brought back into fashion by Quine and others, between two sorts of modes of attribution of beliefs, one *de dicto*, the other *de re* (and parallel to the one that was valid for modalities, cf. § 7.4). We can represent Javert's belief attributed by (13) as relating to the propositional content expressed by the embedded sentence:

> (13b) Javert believes that [Jean Valjean is meaner that Monsieur Madeleine]

or as relating to the individual that *we* identify as Jean Valjean:

> (13c) Javert believes of Jean Valjean that he is meaner than Monsieur Madeleine

Quine calls the first style of attribution (13b) *de dicto* or 'notional' because it only involves the person who is attributing the belief in postulating objects belonging to the subject's doxastic or notional universe. He calls the second style of attribution (13c) *de re*, because it exports the object of belief outside of the context governed by 'believes that', and involves the person who is attributing the belief in identifying the object of belief independently of the subject's 'notional' content. Let us acknowledge with the Fregean that the name 'Jean Valjean' has a mode of presentation both *in* the embedded sentence governed by 'believes that' (in the *de dicto* attribution) and *outside* the embedded sentence (in the *de re* attribution). The problem stated above is that the mode of presentation of the object of the person who is attributing the belief may not to coincide with the mode of presentation of the subject of the belief. For example, if I, the attributor, associate the description 'the most dangerous criminal' with Jean Valjean, and if Javert associates the description 'the man I am going to imprison' with him, how can attribution (13b) or attribution (13c) account for the content of Javert's belief if he states that these descriptions do not define the same object? The whole difficulty arises from the fact that the Fregean makes the hypothesis that sentences such as (13) and (14) express determinate Propositions. If he were content to say that these sentences were vague, and that their semantic content was capable of varying according to which way one looked at it – from the point of view of the attributor or of the subject of the belief – these variations would present no problem for him. But he means to maintain that the reference and the sense of these sentences, therefore their truth conditions, are determinate and he is hard-pressed to say how.[15]

8.2.3 The Russellian theories

I talked above about *the* Russellian theory of Singular Propositions, but there are in fact two of them, which we can call the 'naïve' theory and the 'sophisticated' theory respectively.[16] The one described above is the naïve theory. According to this, singular sentences express singular Propositions directly, introducing their referent and attributing a property to it. Kripke's arguments mentioned above in favour of the Millian theory of reference can be utilised in support of Russellian singular Propositions in ordinary contexts. The whole problem is to know if the attributions of beliefs can be treated as relations to this type of singular Propositions.

According to the naïve Russellian theory every singular sentence expresses a singular Proposition, including in non-extensional contexts. If Kripke is right, this is true of modal contexts too. But it would also have to be true of attiude contexts. It is there that the most obvious difficulty appears because, according to this theory, sentences (13) and (14) above would have to express the same Russellian Proposition, and state a relationships between Javert and the same singular Proposition, which we can represent in the following way:

(15) Believes (Javert, <Jean Valjean, Monsieur Madeleine, is meaner than>)

where the nouns 'Jean Valjean' and 'Monsieur Madeleine' designate the men themselves and the predicate 'is meaner than' a real relation between these men. But in this case, we are forced to attribute to Javert a belief relating to a relation between the man and himself, because of the identity of denotation of the two names:

(16) Believes (Javert, <Jean Valjean, Jean Valjean, is meaner than>)

that is to say, the contradictory belief expressed by (14) above. This absurd result seems to be a consequence of the Russellian hypothesis, itself apparently absurd, whereby names, in attitude contexts, designate the actual object that is their bearer, which is a component of the Propositions. Russell was obviously aware of this difficulty; it was one of those that led him to suggest his theory of descriptions (cf. § 4.3.1.2). The resulting theory is the one that I have called 'sophisticated'.

In the framework of this theory, the problem of the reference of names in attitude contexts is solved by supposing that every ordinary proper name (and every description) can be paraphrased according to Russell's procedure. (13) and (14) become (maintaining the conventions of § 4.3.2.1):

> (13d) Javert believes that the x who Jean Valjeanises is meaner than the x who Monsieur Madeleinises
> (14d) Javert believes that the x who Jean Valjeanises is meaner than the x who Jean Valjeanises.

The sophisticated Russellian theory thus resembles the Fregean theory, since the descriptions defined seem to take the place of modes of presentation. But it is not equivalent to the latter. Russell, unlike Frege, does not suppose that names in contexts of attitudes are distinct syntactical unities. In fact, he suggests that the *logical form* of names be modified and that they be analysed 'contextually' according to the canonic paraphrase of the theory of descriptions. The ambiguities in *de dicto* or *de re* interpretations noted above become ambiguities in the *scope* (or the 'occurrences') of the descriptions equivalent to the nouns.[17] The *de dicto* reading of (13d) is:

> (13e) Javert believes that there is a single x who Jean Valjeanises and that there is a single y who Monsieur Madeleinises and that x is meaner than y

and the *de re* reading is:

> (13f) There is a single x who Jean Valjeanises and there is a single y who Monsieur Madeleinises and Javert believes that x is meaner than y.

But in this case, on the one hand, Russell has to abandon the naïve theory and the thesis according to which singular sentences express singular Propositions: if the former express Propositions, the latter are exclusively composed of general properties (what Russell calls 'propositional functions') which are said to be instantiated by *one* individual, but the individual himself does not form part of the Proposition. As Russell suggests that proper names are equivalent to descriptions in intensional contexts as well as in extensional contexts, singular Propositions can at best only be theoretical ideal entities that are never expressed in usual speech. Russell only maintains this thesis in one case: when the singular term (principally a demonstrative such as 'this') puts a subject in touch with an object of direct knowledge or of *acquaintance*, so that if the object is in this relationship with the subject, it cannot fail to exist and to form part of its content of belief. We will see what can be made of this suggestion further on.[18] On the other hand, Russell has to abandon the theory according to which singular sentences in attitude contexts have to express determinate Propositions, since ambiguities of scope can affect all the occurrences of descriptions. The sophisticated Russellian theory therefore actually confronts the same difficulties as the Fregan theory. These are the difficulties of identifying the objects of beliefs: the sentences reporting them might be able to have clear truth conditions if it were possible to identify these objects and from that say that these sentences express determinate Propositions. But this is just what it seems cannot be said.

According to Quine, these difficulties are only one particular case of the impossibility of *quantifying* into intensional and modal contexts and into contexts of attitudes.[19] According to him, the problem is that if we can give a meaning to a *de dicto* quantification inside a context of attitude such as

(17a) Javert believes that $(\exists x)(x$ is a dangerous criminal)

we cannot give a clear meaning to a *de re* quantification outside of the context such as

(17b) $(\exists x)$(Javert believes that x is a dangerous criminal)

because, on one hand, the belief reported by (17a) does not imply that there is such a renegade and, on the other hand, how can we identify this x (as, according to Quine, use of quantification prescribes)? From this point of view, when the sophisticated Russellian theory suggests that we eliminate singular terms in favour of expressions containing quantifiers, it is not abolishing this problem of quantification in opaque contexts. These difficulties reappear when one wants to distinguish the *de dicto* and *de re* attributions of beliefs expressed by singular sentences, as above, like

(18a) Javert believes that Jean Valjean is a renegade
(18b) Javert believes of Jean Valjean that he is a renegade

because either context (18a) is 'opaque' and one does not know what mode of presentation corresponds to the name, or else it is, like (18b), 'referential' (by definition, since the name is outside the scope of the verb 'believes that'), but in that case Javert can be attributed both with the belief reported by (18b) and the contradictory belief:

(18c) Javert believes of Jean Valjean that he is not a renegade

in the case where Javert confuses Jean Valjean with another man. Quine maintains that this difficulty underlies every quantification in a non-extensional context. According to him, the same difficulty is reproduced if we suppose that the embedded Propositions are composed of intensional objects and intensional attributes. In this case, (18c) has the form

(18d) Javert believes z (z is a renegade) of Jean Valjean where 'z(z . . .)' indicates that an abstraction has been carried out on a property attributed to an object. One then comes back to the problem: how can intensional objects be identified?[20]

This *de dicto/de re* ambiguity of the attributions of belief reflects the difficulties themselves of theories which infer that distinct *types* of Propositions correspond to these attributions. The Fregean theory supposes that Fregean Propositions correspond to *de dicto* attributions, and the Russellian theory supposes that Russellian Propositions correspond to *de re* attributions. But we saw that none of the arguments in favour of the existence of either of these types of Propositions was acceptable. None the less perhaps it is possible to try and modify these theories in order to make them acceptable? In what follows I will consider three possible modifications of the three theories – quotational, Russellian and Fregean.

8.3 The paratactic analysis of indirect speech

The Fregean analysis of propositional attitude contexts (but also the modified Russellian theory) is counter-intuitive when it suggests that a sentence used in indirect speech or figuring in the scope of an attitude verb ceases to have the meaning that it has in an ordinary extensional context. How is it possible that the words

(19) The Earth moves

can, when they are reported, for example in this way:

(20) Galileo says that the Earth moves

have a *different* meaning in this context from the one they had in (19)?

In acknowledging the Fregean theory, we lose what Davidson calls 'semantic innocence', which decrees that words keep their usual meaning in these contexts.[21] Of course, the failure of the substitution of co-referential terms is the principal motivation for abandoning this innocence. But this innocence is not always unjustified. There are attitude contexts in which substitution is permissible, for example those where verbs of perception are completed by what are called 'naked infinitives' such as:

(21) John saw Maggie leave.

If Maggie is the prime minister, it follows that

(22) John saw the prime minister leave.

But is is possible to deny that these contexts are really contexts of attitudes because as soon as a clause with 'that' is reintroduced, the substitution is no longer permissible:

(23) John saw that Maggie had left

does not imply

(24) John saw that the prime minister had left.[22]

Notwithstanding, we can try and regain our semantic innocence while still explaining the failures of substitutivity. This is what Davidson suggested, in providing a modification of the quotational theory.

As has been seen, this theory comes up against Church's translation argument (§ 8.2.1). Following Quine, Davidson notes that, when we report a sentence in indirect speech, we are stating in our language a sentence that we hope is similar in meaning to a sentence stated by the person whose potential or real sayings we are reporting.[23] In other words, a correct analysis of (20) would take the form of

(20a) Galileo stated a sentence that coming from his mouth meant what 'the Earth moves' means from mine.

This line of analysis maintains the idea that propositional attitudes (here, 'to say that') are relations to sentences of a language, and not abstract entities like Propositions. But the whole problem consists of avoiding the difficulty posed by the notion of identity or similarity of meaning that they raise and which Church's objection makes explicit.

Davidson then suggests that we construct every sentence reporting something someone else has said in indirect speech as stating a specific relation between someone else's statement and our own. For this, we have to modify the *logical form* of the sentences reporting the statements so that they make explicit reference to such statements. Davidson's very ingenious solution consists of dividing every sentence of the form of (20) in two in the following way

(20b) Galileo said that. The Earth moves.

Here, the first sentence designates, by means of the demonstrative 'that', a certain utterance, the content of which is reported by the second sentence. (Here Davidson is playing on the sense of the term 'that', which can either introduce a completive 'that' clause or be a demonstrative.)[24] But, according to Davidson, this content is not reported in the way in which a sentence completed by 'that' would report it: I am only stating that a certain event took place, which is an utterance by Galileo, and that *my* utterance is in a certain relationship *vis-à-vis* Galileo's utterance, which Davidson calls 'samesaying', which only implies a similarity between what I say and what Galileo said. The complete logical form of (20) is:

(20c) ($\exists x$)(the utterance x of Galileo and my utterance make us 'same-sayers').

If this 'paratactic' analysis (since it treats the embedded sentence as a non-embedded paratax) is correct, it follows that the logical form of sentences in indirect speech is not that of sentences *embedded* in 'that' clauses. The first sentences ('Galileo said that') has the function of designating an utterance by means of a singular term (the demonstrative 'that'). The second sentence ('The Earth moves') is independent of the first and reports the content of what Galileo said in the language of the attributor. But it does not *quote* Galileo's actual words (probably 'E pur si muove'). Church's objection is thus avoided. As this sentence is independent of the first, there is no reason to predict that the singular terms change their sense or reference in it. However, they are not substitutable because their substitution *could* change the reference of the demonstrative 'that', designating the statement similar to Galileo's. But, contrary to the Fregean hypothesis, it does not follow that *every* substitution would change the truth value of the sentence. In this sense, there is no reason to predict that the designated sentence is non-extensional. One sees what benefit Davidson can derive for his extensionalist programme in semantics (§ 6.2) from this analysis, since paratactic analysis avoids having to postulate intensions or Propositions in the semantic analysis of indirect speech.

The immediate objection that can be made to this theory is that, with the relation of 'samesaying', it presupposes the similarity of meaning between my utterance and the utterance of the subject whose saying I am reporting. But it seems that it is just the nature of this relation that is in question. However, this objection does not threaten the theory, in so far as it is a theory of the logical form of indirect speech and not an *analysis* of the relation in question.[25] Davidson's idea is that there must be some sort of a relation of similarity of this type *if* indirect speech is possible. On the other hand, three problems do directly threaten this theory.

The first is that if it is possible to be able to determine what reference is made in (20) to a statement by Galileo, it is much less clear with sentences where one verb of attitude is (by supposition) embedded in another, as in

(25) Copernicus said that Galileo said that the Earth moves

because the Davidsonian paraphrase

(25a) Copernicus said that. Galileo said that. The Earth moves

implies that the first demonstrative is referring to an utterance itself referring to the last utterance. But the second demonstrative is not necessarily referring to an utterance alluded to by Copernicus, but by the attributor (me). How can we ensure that the initial demonstrative refers to the final utterance? The difficulty would be even worse with three successive reports of contents.[26]

The second problem is that if Davidson's proposal seems correct for reports of attitudes *vis-à-vis sentences* like 'to say that', it is not so easy to generalise to attitudes such as beliefs which are not necessarily relations to *utterances*. It seems that it is possible to believe something without ever asserting a sentence corresponding to what is believed, and an analysis like (10b) above, in terms of dispositions to assert sentences, encounters well-known difficulties.[27]

The third problem is the most pressing. Even if it is acknowledged that the relation of 'samesaying' or of similarity of content is the one that governs our reports of other people's beliefs, is it possible to report what someone else has said without knowing the content of his *thought*? Is it sufficient to suppose that there is a relation of similarity between two *utterances* in order to account for what has been said? No, because if Galileo says (literally) 'E pur si muove', meaning thereby (for example, in order to escape from Church's criticism) that the Celestial Sphere moves, if (20) has the form (20b) what he *said* could have been correctly reported, but would the content of his thought have been reported? It seems that something like Galileo's meaning intentions need to be invoked and in any case some determination of the content of what Galileo *thinks*. This problem is not specific to Davidson's theory but to every theory that makes reports of beliefs and attitudes relations to utterances or to sentences.[28]

8.4 The neo-Russellian theory

It does happen that a good (I am not saying the best) means of defending a philosophical theory is to postulate that this theory *must* be true, however contrary it is to our intuitions, and to the apparently decisive objections that can be made to it. This is the strategy Nathan Salmon adopted in defence of the naïve Russellian theory of singular Propositions.[29] Taking the naïve theory literally, Salmon maintains that the following two sentences:

(26) Zorro is a masked avenger
(27) Diego de la Vega is a masked avenger

express the same Russellian Proposition, connecting one single individual, Diego de la Vega, with the property of being a masked avenger, because the truth conditions of these sentences are simply their conditions of reference. There is nothing surprising about this if one accepts the Millian theory of names. What is surprising is to maintain, as Salmon does, that

(26a) Sergeant Garcia believes that Zorro is a masked avenger

and

(27a) Sergeant Garcia believes that Diego is a masked avenger

are both simultaneously true because these sentences express the same Russellian Proposition. Salmon maintains not only that Sergeant Garcia is not irrational (he has not got contradictory beliefs) but also that it is false to say

(28) Garcia does not realise that Zorro is Diego de la Vega.

Our immediate reaction is that we do indeed see *one* sense in which (26a) and (27a) can be true simultaneously, and (28) false. This sense is the *de re* sense of attribution which enables us to say, for example:

(27b) Of Diego, Garcia believes that he is a masked avenger

in the case when Diego is the man whom , in *our* language, we identify with Zorro (because we know the story). Salmon does not deny this. He admits, for example, that Garcia's behaviour towards Diego is not the same as his behaviour towards Zorro. He maintains in fact that the *de re* sense is the sense which correctly expresses the situation, but that, beyond the singular Proposition with which Garcia is in a relation, it is necessary to specify the mode of presentation in which this Proposition is presented each time. According to Salmon the correct form of attributions (26a) and (27a) is:

> (29) There is a certain mode of presentation of Zorro (under which Zorro appears as a bandit) so that, under this mode of presentation, Garcia believes of Zorro that he is a masked avenger
>
> (30) there is a mode of presentation of Zorro (under which Zorro appears as a sympathetic squire), so that under this mode of presentation, Garcia believes of Zorro that he is not a masked avenger.

These two attitudes are relations to the *same* Proposition (Zorro is a masked avenger), but in two different modes of presentation. Let 'p' be a Russellian Proposition, 'MP' a mode of presentation, and 'BEL' the relation of belief. In this case 'X believes that p' is analysed in:

$$(\exists MP)(X \text{ grasps } p \text{ under } MP \ \& \ BEL \ (X, p, MP)).$$

In other words a belief is a three-place relation between a subject, a Proposition and a mode of presentation.[30]

Are we not back to a form of Fregean solution? No, according to Salmon, because, contrary to the Fregean thesis, modes of presentation are not semantic *components* of Propositions designated by names. Semantically, they do not form part of the attributions of attitudes, but are *pragmatically* implied by them, in the sense where Grice's 'implicatures' (§ 2.4.2) no longer form part of the semantic content of the sentences. A mode of presentation is such an implicature.[31] Whatever one might think about this resort to pragmatic implicatures here, Salmon's neo-Russellian solution comes up against the same problem as the naïve Russellian solution: if Garcia gives his assent to the Proposition that Zorro is a masked avenger, and if he denies the Proposition that Diego is a masked avenger (since these two Propositions are identical), he must be saying that Zorro is and is not a masked avenger. (28) is therefore false. In both cases, Garcia believes the same thing but he is wrong about the mode of presentation. Salmon is telling us there that Garcia is not contradicting himself: he is simply making an error of identification. But the problem is that the two modes of presentation are contradictory: they determine distinct individuals and they determine distinct judgements. But if two modes of presentation can determine distinct judgements, does this not show that they form part of the semantic content of the Propositions maintained, which are thus distinct, as the Fregean asserts? In this case, one does not really see what distinguishes the neo-Russellian theory from the Fregean theory.

8.5 The neo-Fregean theory

As has been seen, what distinguishes the classical Fregean theory of the nature of Propositions from the naïve Russellian theory is that the former treats these Propositions as having a *general* content. What figures in the content of the Proposition is not the individual who is the object of an attitude but an individual concept or an identifying property. The same hypothesis governs the sophisticated Russellian theory which replaces expressions denoting individuals by general descriptive expressions containing quantifiers. A (naïve) Russellian Proposition, on the other hand, is genuinely singular in the sense that it is the individual himself who is a component of the Proposition. Consequently, the Fregean has a tendency to favour *de dicto* attributions of beliefs while the Russellian tends to favour *de re* attributions. The contrast between the two theories only exists because it is supposed that the first introduces the *sense* of nouns into the content of Propositions, while the second objects to this. But this contrast disappears if the Fregean acknowledges that there are certain senses that are not general but have the function of determining a *singular* individual. What would such senses be? They would be senses such that the subject who grasps them has an *essential* relation with an object existing in the world, so that if he grasps this object in a mode of presentation, this mode of presentation *must* be *about* this object. Let us follow Gareth Evans and John McDowell and call such senses *de re* senses.[32] It is typically senses of this type to which the Fregean can resort when accepting Salmon's interpretations (29) and (30) above. A *de re* sense is such that *the subject who grasps it must be, vis-à-vis the object that this sense determines, in a certain appropriate relation with this object.*

   What is this relation? It can be presumed that it is an epistemic relation through which the subject can directly grasp the object. This can be perception, memory or any form of direct contact with the object. It is here that the Russellian conception mentioned above (§ 8.2.3) – according to which a subject supports a genuine singular Proposition when it is in a relation of *acquaintance* or direct knowledge *vis-à-vis* an object – can come in. Russell contrasts this direct knowledge with knowledge 'by description', which he supposes to be general.[33] But it can be maintained that a description of an object, in so far as it brings in a *causal* relation between the object and the subject's thought, can be *de re* in the desired sense. From this point of view, the appropriate relation can come about through indirect knowledge, implying inferences, the evidence of someone else, and so on, provided that it is possible to *trace* the path leading from the object to the subject who thinks it. If such a relation exists, the names of attitude contexts can be genuine or purely referential names in the sense of § 7.6. What Gareth Evans calls 'Russellian thoughts' are thoughts that are the content of this type of singular Proposition, that is to say thoughts the content of which cannot be specified without reference to the objects on which they bear. A *de re* sense would thus occur in every case where a thought content is not completely conceptualised, that is to say where the mode of presentation of the object involves the essential reference to the object itself. Typical *de re* or Russellian thoughts seem to be thoughts where the reference is ensured by demonstratives or personal pronouns, such as 'I am ill' or 'This is red Bordeaux'. When we report them, we are not simply referring to a description of the object but to the object itself: 'He believes that he is ill', 'He thinks that this is red Bordeaux'. The problems of the reference of demonstrative singular terms are complex, and I will not examine them here. But in the case of each reference, the appropriate relation to an object is intended to avoid the difficulty of the Fregean theory which we pointed out above (§ 3.2 *in fine*): when someone has a single mode of presentation for two distinct objects (for example Hesperus and Phosphorus, or Jean Valjean and Monsieur Madeleine), his correct reference to the two objects cannot be ensured by description but by the causal relation that he has with these objects.[34]

Wherever it is possible to specify the appropriate relation between the thought and its 'real' objects, we can accept a sort of compromise between the Russellian position and the orthodox Fregean position, and say that there are *de re* beliefs, attributed by means of sentences, the semantic contents of which contain *de re* senses. But in this case, it is no longer simply the notion of a semantic content of sentences that is being evoked. The notion of sense ceases to be a purely semantic notion and becomes a *psychological* notion or, in any case, a notion that invokes a subject's state of mind in an essential way.

Beyond all the problems that the correct specification of such a relation poses, there is one that remains particularly striking. This is the problem posed by the occurrence of empty names or names without denotation in attitudes contexts and by negative existential sentences such as:

> (31) Peter believes that Father Christmas brings him toys
> (32) Father Christmas does not exist.

How, in these contexts, is it possible to avoid saying that the names designate non-existent objects, with which the subject cannot actually have the type of relation with a *res* postulated by the neo-Fregean theory (or the neo-Russellian theory which would be a version of it)? Is it not possible that the content here is *general*, as the theory of definite descriptions prescribes (§ 4.3.1.2)? In this case, existence, as Frege and Russell maintain, is a property of property, or a property of objects as *described* in a certain way.[35] Or is it necessary to go back to a Meinong type of theory postulating non-existent objects, and treat existence as a *predicate* of these objects, and not as a presupposition of our semantics of singular terms? These problems are considerable, and they form a very full chapter of contemporary philosophy of logic and theory of reference.[36] However, I am not going to deal with them here.

We are therefore not forced to adopt one or other branch of the alternative: are Propositions Fregean or are they Russellian? In the first case, one would say that the content of *every* thought is general or universal, that is to say does not require the object of the thought to be mentioned for it to be thought. In the second case, one would say that the content of every thought is singular and requires the presence of the *res* on which the thought bears. The position I would be tempted to adopt is a weak version of the second thesis or a weak version of the first: certain thoughts (Propositions) are singular, but others are general.[37] But in itself (in so far as it expresses a thought) a singular Proposition is neither singular nor general. This means that neither the logical form nor the truth conditions of the sentences that express it determine its content. It is this point that I will try to explain in the remainder of this chapter.

8.6 Semantic content and psychological content

Frege's problem, as presented in § 8.1 above, concerns the *semantics* and *logical form* of the attributions of propositional attitudes. Frege was anxious to disting-uish this problem from problems concerning the psychological nature of the thoughts and representations of individuals. But the 'neo-Fregean' theory that we have ended up with *refers* to the psychology of individuals, since the *de re* senses are certain representations in the subjects' mind. This is thus a long way from Fregean thoughts, but equally far from the singular Propositions of the naïve Russellian theory, which are objective complexes of objects and properties of the world. If the neo-Fregean theory outlined above is correct, Propositions are rather psychological entities, as Russell maintained at another period in his philo-sophical career. The contemporary philosophy of reference would thus have retrodden the path Russell followed.[38] Likewise, I suggested (§ 8.3, *in fine*) that Davidson's modified quotational theory had to resort to a specification of the thought content in order to account for the semantic content. But if we do not forget that our problem here has also been that of the nature of propositions in logic (can they be identified with the content of propositional attitudes?), is this not reintroducing into logic the psychologism which Frege wanted to banish from logic for ever?

   Yes and no. The problem posed by the semantics of sentences reporting propositional attitudes cannot be *purely* semantic problems, by virtue of the very nature of these attributions. When we report someone else's thought in indirect speech, or by means of a clause governed by 'believe that' (or any other verb of attitude), we are making a certain *representation*, or a certain linguistic description of something that we can suppose concerns another mental or psychological *representation*. We are describing these psychological contents with words. The function of the sentences reporting these psychological contents is, on the one hand, to attribute certain states (beliefs, desires, and so on) to creatures and, on the other hand, to specify the content of these states, essentially with a view to explaining the behaviour of these creatures. We then project the content of our *own* representations, expressed through *our* words, on to the content of the representations that we suppose exist with other creatures. This process is so common that we have no hesitation in employing it for creatures who do not apparently have language, like animals or children. We are then doing something very similar, but in a rough form, to what a scientist does when he postulates theoretical entities (in this case, words and their sense) on certain observable data (behaviour) or certain non-observable or inferred entities (thoughts). Propositional attitude reports are thus semantic representations of psychological contents, that is to say representations of representations.[39]

Consequently, when we pose the question: 'Do sentences reporting the contents of attitudes have truth conditions?', we are asking: can these representations of representations be adequate?

These questions are extremely difficult because we must reply at every level. First of all we have to say how certain representations can be representations of things in the world: if we hold that beliefs are certain representations, how do they represent their object? Then, if we suppose, as the quotational theory requires, that beliefs are relations to sentences, we have to say how these sentences represent things in the world. And finally we have to say how the sentences that we use in order to represent these beliefs actually represent them. A reply at each of these levels is very complex, and supposes such a degree of philosophical elaboration, that it can be asked how the problems posed here, apparently so local and so innocently 'analytical', can be solved without venturing into the terrain of metaphysics and epistemology. But this will cause people to turn tail if they might have believed that these apparently purely logical and linguistic problems could *only* receive answers that were themselves 'logical' and 'linguistic'.

The question, 'Do sentences reporting propositional attitudes have truth conditions?' is therefore not *solely* a semantic question. When we ask it, we cannot escape asking what sort of relations join sentences to the world and what relations join semantic descriptions of mental contents to these mental contents. I am not able to attempt to answer these questions here, but neither can I avoid a short incursion into the sector where the philosophy of language and logic meet the philosophy of mind. I would only like to indicate four forms of possible answer that can be found in contempory works.

1. The first consists of saying that sentences reporting propositional attitudes do not have truth conditions because they do not describe anything. That position is taken up by Quine for whom there are no mental entities or mental representations but only physically observable behaviour and dispositions to behaviour. It is possible to take the intensionality of sentences reporting attitudes as a criterion of the intensionality that Brentano takes as the criterion of the irreducibility of the mental, but only to the extent, according to Quine, that a science of intension is void: the very incoherence of the intensional idiom confirms the absence of the mental that it is supposed to describe. To accept the use of intensional idioms is to accept the idea that there might have been relations of translation and synonymity between the reported sentences, relations which Quine judges impossible. Propositional attitudes can have a practical utility, even be indispensable, but they cannot form part of the language of science which only permits quantification on physical objects.[40]

2. According to the second conception, sentences reporting propositional attitudes have truth conditions, but these truth conditions have a dual aspect. One concerns the *semantic content* of the sentences, which reports the contents of attitudes. The other concerns the *psychological content* of the attitudes as particular mental representations. The semantic content is determined by the truth and reference conditions of the sentences of the language used to report the contents of attitudes. The psychological content is determined by a psychological theory of individuals' mental states.[41] At the semantic level there are various ways of representing the content, depending on whether the truth and reference properties of the sentences are relativised to the 'possible worlds' in the framework of an intensional semantics, or whether these properties are construed in an extensional framework.[42] At the psychological level, thought contents can also be individuated in various ways, according to the psychological theory favoured. For example, they can be treated as symbolic representations written down in a 'language of thought', and subject to individuation criteria in terms of their 'functional' role in an information-processing system.[43] According to this theory of the 'bifurcation' of content, the two contributions to the determination of the content are distinct, and there is no hope of determining one from the other. That is why the semantic content (the truth and reference of sentences), in Frege's problem, does not coincide with cognitive content. Identifying Fregean sense with a psychological notion, this is the way in which the supporter of the theory of dual content explains why there can be contradictory determinations when the two levels are confused. Javert or Sergeant Garcia are not irrational: they have a distinct (psychological) relation to the same semantically determinate Proposition (respectively that Jean Valjean is a renegade, and that Zorro is a masked avenger), but the psychological content cannot exhaust the semantic content and vice versa. It will be noted that this theory is compatible both with a conception whereby semantics is autonomous with respect of psychology, and with a conception whereby it must be complemented by psychology, without necessarily being reduced to it.[44]

3. The third theory is the neo-Fregean or neo-Russellian theory mentioned in § 8.5 above: propositional attitude sentences have determinate truth conditions and semantics, but this semantics must invoke psychology. Fregean sense, in the final analysis, is a psychological notion which can only be fully explained by an analysis of specific representational contents. Ultimately semantics is reduced to psychology. This is just one of many versions of this theory.[45]

4. The fourth theory rests on an idea close to the idea that guides Davidson's theory examined above: when we report the contents of someone else's thought with words, we do not aim for perfect accuracy of these accounts. What we do aim for is a certain *similarity* between the semantic content of our sentences and the contents of the thought which we attribute to individuals. In this sense,

propositional attitude sentences do not really have *determinate* truth conditions, because they do not aim at grasping the identity of psychological contents, but only at producing representations that are more or less similar to these supposed contents. This explains why the semantic contents are not always faithful to what people have 'in mind': the descriptions of thoughts that we provide are only approximations.[46]

Each of these theories, taking into account the difficulties we have examined, has its attractions and, as I have indicated, they are not totally incompatible with each other. A complete discussion of each of them would take us much further afield than the remarks on the logic and semantics of attitude sentences to which this chapter is limited. But it seems to me that the fourth, the theory of similarity, is the most plausible when it comes to accounting for our common practice of attributing thoughts to someone else, and the one that best accounts for the facts analysed by the others. If what we are aiming for is a similarity in the attribution of contents, it explains why, according to Quine, it is not possible to have an objectual quantification in linguistic attitude contexts, that is to say strict criteria of identity of the entities on which we are quantifying, and consequently no strict criteria of identity of the Propositions (Russellian or Fregean) which would be designated in these contexts. By virtue of this same fact, there are not Propositions that are totally Fregean or totally Russellian, if this is taken to mean that their content would be exhausted by their truth conditions or their conditions of meaning. In certain cases, we report a thought in a way to suggest Russellian truth conditions for it (this is particularly the case when we make *de re* reports). In other cases, we report a thought in a way to suggest Fregean truth conditions for it (with *de dicto* reports). But thoughts, beliefs, Propositions are not *in themselves de re* or *de dicto*. This depends on the perspective we adopt to report them.[47] This also accounts for the duality between semantic content and psychological content that the theory of the dual aspect puts forward: if accounts of contents of attitudes are representations of representations, why should we expect these representations to be faithful in every point? When, for example, words are used to describe the content of another representation, pictorial for example, the description is not perfect because words do not necessarily say what a picture says. Likewise when we represent thoughts with words. Lastly, the theory of similarity accounts for the appropriate relation between semantics and psychology. A certain system of representation (mental) is perhaps only possible if another system of representation (verbal) is present. But why should we expect these systems to coincide on every point? Words do not only have a meaning by virtue of their relations to our mental states, but also by virtue of their relations to the world and our practices. Perhaps it is possible to arrive at a complete determination of meaning by examining these interactions. But in so far as these latter have not been completely specified, if they can be, we are in the situation that Wittgenstein was describing when he said: 'If God had looked into our minds, He would not have been able to see *there* whom we were speaking of.'[48]

── 9 ──

IDENTITY

9.1 The formal principles of identity

The theory of first-order quantification can be enlarged with the (two-place or relation) predicate '=' of identity if the following two (schemas of) axioms are added to its axioms or rules:

> (I) $x = x$ [reflexivity]
> (II) $(x = y \ \& \ \phi x) \rightarrow \phi y$ [indiscernibility of identicals]

The quantification theory (or quantification theory with identity) thus obtained is complete (every theorem or every valid formula where '=' figures is provable in this system).[1] In that case, identity is a primitive notion, or a logical constant, which cannot be defined. On the other hand, if we allow a quantification on properties in a second-order predicate calculus, we can define identity from the following two principles:

> (III) $(\forall x)(\forall y)((x = y) \rightarrow (\forall \phi)(\phi x \equiv \phi y))$ [ind.id.]

that is to say, (II), with quantification on the properties 'ϕ':

> (IV) $(\forall x)(\forall y)((\forall \phi)(\phi x = \phi y) \rightarrow (x = y))$ [id.ind.]

or the *principle of identity of indiscernibles*. (III) is often called 'Leibniz's law', and the same name is also sometimes used for the combination of these two principles, that is to say:

> (V) $(\forall x)(\forall y)((x = y) \equiv (\forall \phi)(\phi x = \phi y))$ [Leibniz's law].

From these two principles (or from (V) alone) all the properties characteristic of the relation of identity can be deduced, that is to say:

> (VI) $(\forall x)(x = x)$ [reflexivity]
> (VII) $(\forall x)(\forall y)((x = y) \rightarrow (y = x))$ [symmetry]
> (VIII) $(\forall x)(\forall y)(\forall z)(((x = y) \ \& \ (y = z)) \rightarrow (x = z))$ [transitivity]

The same principles, without quantification on properties, can be derived from (I) and (II) in the theory of first-order quantification. In what follows, I will ignore the distinction between first and second order and take principles (III)–(VIII), or their first-order versions, as forming the formal theory of identity.

To these can be added another, which is also sometimes called 'Leibniz's law'. This is the principle of the *substitutivity of identicals*, which we have already encountered on numerous occasions (§ 1.3.2, 4.3.1.1, 6.2.2, 7.4, Chapter 8). The Leibnizian formulation of this principle is: *eadem sunt quorum unum potest substitui alteri salva veritate*, 'terms of which one can be substituted for the other without affecting the truth [of the propositions in which they figure] are identical'.[2]

Do these principles of the formal theory or logic of identity *define* the notion of identity, and can this notion be defined at all, or is it, as Frege thought, primitive and indefinable?[3] In particular, what is the relationship between this formal theory and the specific identity statements of the form '$a = b$' that we are led to make in usual practice? The most frequent reaction to the statement of these principles is that they may be able to define the formal properties of the relation of identity, but they do not permit us to justify specific assertions of identity, that is to say to answer the questions that concern the *identification* and *individuation* of specific entities which we say are identical. What, in this sense, is the relationship between a general theory of identity and a theory of the individuation of the things or substances of the world? Such a theory undoubtedly belongs to ontology or metaphysics, and it does not come within my brief to formulate one. The distinction between a metaphysic and an ontology of individuation and a formal theory of identity is very similar to the distinction between 'substantial' theories of truth and neutral or trivial theories that we encountered in Chapter 5. The question that concerns the philosophy of logic is therefore the following: do the *logical* properties of identity condition a metaphysical theory of individuation? I would like to show that this question can be answered positively, without maintaining that logic obliges us to adopt a specific ontology and that, in the case of identity as in the case of truth, a 'non-substantial' formal theory can condition 'substantial' theories.

I will first run over a certain number of objections that have been raised to the formal principles of the theory of identity, before considering what seems to lie at the root of these objections.

9.2 The reflexivity of identity

Each one of the principles (I)–(VIII) of the formal theory of identity appears obvious at first glance. But in every case, this obviousness has been judged problematic, either because it was considered that these principles were *too* obvious – that is to say trivial – or because they were considered *not sufficiently* so.

First of all, what is more obvious than principle (I) or (VI) of the reflexivity of identity? It seems to state that everything is identical with itself, or that everything has the property of being-identical-with-itself. But how can this property really be a property? A property in the usual sense is such that at least two objects can possess it, while being-identical-with-itself is by definition a property that can only be possessed by *one single* object, the object for which this property is actually predicated. The same problem can be formulated in another way: if it is stated of two things a and b that they are identical ('$a = b$'), how can such an assertion be made without asserting of *one single* thing that it is identical with itself, that is to say that '$a = a$'? In order words, if *being-identical-with-itself* is a property of objects, it is a strange property, because it cannot be put on the same plane as other properties, such as *being red* or *being a good oarsman*. And if a statement of identity always asserts this relation of identity of a thing with itself, how can one ever say that two things are identical? This is what Wittgenstein pointed out: 'To say of two things that they are identical is nonsense, and to say of *one* thing that it is identical with itself is to say nothing at all.'[4] Is it possible to say that identity is a relation between objects? It was this sort of difficulty that caused Frege to maintain in his *Begriffsschrift* (1879) that identity could not be a relation between *objects*, but was only a relation between *names* or signs. If, in fact, '$a = b$' stated a relation between objects, how could this statement be distinguished from '$a = a$' which was trivial? Therefore, at this period, Frege concluded that it was not things, but names that one was asserting were identical.[5] But Frege abandoned this conception in *Über Sinn und Bedeutung* (1892) because, he tells us, if identity were only a relation between arbitrary signs, statements of identity would not give us any objective information, any 'cognitive value', about the things themselves, which they obviously do. We have seen what Frege's solution was (§ 8.1): it consists of distinguishing the sense and the reference of statements of identity, in such a way that the latter relate to things, in so far as they have a reference, and to what signs express, in so far as they have a sense. This avoids both the difficulties of the theory that would reduce identity statements to assertions on things (which would therefore reduce all identity to the trivial assertion '$a = a$') and the difficulties of the theory that would reduce these statements to assertions on signs.[6] As we saw in the previous chapter, 'Frege's problem' affects every theory that would reduce Propositions expressed by sentences to Russellian Propositions, formed solely of objects and their properties. According to such a theory, '$a = a$' and '$a = b$' would express the same Proposition. I will therefore not repeat the arguments against this conception, and will take the Fregean solution as the correct one, subject to the amendments stated in § 8.5. Moreover, Frege recognised the distinction between the predicate, or the relation of identity, and other predicates of objects: the 'is' of predication must be distinguished from the 'is' of identity. The first states the relation between an object and a concept (or a function), while the second only states a relation between objects. This does not preclude our talking about identity as a 'property', on condition that we do not forget that this property only states a relation between *objects*.[7] Consequently, according to the Fregean solution, $(\forall x)(x = x)$ actually states a property (trivial) of every object, but statements of identity of the form '$a = b$' are not reduced to the statement of that property, and therefore this triviality is not communicated to the content of these statements.

9.3 'Leibniz's laws'

As was seen above, the four principles, (III), (IV), (V) and the principle of the substitutivity of identity, have been given the name of 'Leibniz's law'. In order to avoid ambiguities, I will call them respectively *the principle of the indiscernibility of identicals, the principle of the identity of indiscernibles, and the principle of substitutivity*, and I will reserve the name 'Leibniz's law' solely for (III), the principle of the indiscernibility of identicals.

(III), the principle of the indiscernibility of identicals, states that if two objects are identical, then they are indiscernible, that is to say have all their properties in common. This principle has barely been challenged. How, if *a* is *b* might there be something that is true of object *a* without being true of object *b*? Of course, the principle ceases to be valid in non-extensional contexts, as we have seen. But for all that, is this a counter-example to the principle of indiscernibility of identicals? If we acknowledge the Fregean principle according to which the real reference and the apparent reference of the expressions diverge in these contexts, we have no reason to expect that this principle will continue to be valid.

The indiscernibility of identicals only states a necessary condition for the identity of two objects. Its converse (IV), the identity of indiscernibles, states a sufficient condition: if two objects have all their properties in common, then they are identical. This is the principle that has been challenged. Leibniz calls it the *principle of indiscernibles*: there cannot be two distinct individuals who are indiscernible or there cannot be two individuals who are distinct *solo numero*, only numerically. In fact, Leibniz requires that indiscernible entities have only their *qualitative* properties in common. This excludes spatio-temporal properties or relations, or all those properties, like number, that are 'extrinsic' or external. This doctrine is itself closely linked to the Leibnizian theory of substance, relations, number, space and time.[8] But it is possible to try and discuss it without recourse to these highly controversial Leibnizian doctrines.

A first objection frequently raised to the principle of the identity of indiscernibles is that it is trivial or circular. As has been observed, notably by Ayer, in (IV), if no restriction is placed on the type of predicate that can be substituted for 'ϕ', and if 'ϕ' is the property of *being-identical-with-itself* that an object *a* maintains with itself, then there will be at least one predicate that will not be included in any set of predicates applying to something other than *a*: the predicate of being-identical-with-itself. Consequently, if *a* is distinct from *b*, (IV) is trivial.[9] It is generally concluded from this that the principle of the identity of indiscernibles presupposes a definition of the identity of two objects, instead of providing such a definition, in other words that it is circular. To put it another way, as long as it has not been said *what* properties, other than identity itself, must count as common to two objects in order to constitute their identity, the commonness in question will not be defined and should rather be considered as a *consequence* of identity than as a *basis* of it. This suggests that the sole principle that can be resorted to is the identity of indiscernibles. But this does not exclude the possibility that (IV) can, in the absence of a basis of identity, constitute a criterion of *difference*, or of refutation of specific identities, because if it happened that we had identified two objects that we then discovered did not have all their properties in common, this might constitute a good reason for distinguishing them.[10]

Let us now suppose that we are able to limit the properties 'ϕ' in (IV) to properties that do not invoke objects *a* and *b* themselves or their supposed identity, and that we are looking for positive principles of the commonness of these properties. In this case, the objection is that the principle of indiscernibility of identicals might actually be false and if it can be, how might it be an obvious *formal* or *logical* principle? Let us suppose, for example, that the universe contains two exactly similar spheres, so that all the properties and all the relations of one are the properties and relations of the other. Is such a universe impossible? Apparently not. But the indiscernibility of identicals denies its existence.[11] Here, it is difficult not to introduce the doctrines on which Leibniz and his Newtonian adversaries differed. Because if these spheres had all their properties in common except their numerical or spatial relations, then either these relations would be internal to these spheres, as Leibniz maintained, and in that case the spheres would not be distinct, or else these relations would be external to the spheres, as Clarke maintained, and they would be distinct. But in either case, a position would have to be taken on the principles of the spatial and temporal individuation of objects, and we would no longer only be dealing with a formal theory of identity but with a material theory of their individuation. In other words, indiscernibility can only define identity if certain metaphysical hypotheses are added to it (for Leibniz, God and the principle of sufficient reason).[12]

It is generally concluded from these difficulties with the principle of the identity of indiscernibles that (III) and (IV) taken together, that is to say (V) cannot *define* the notion of identity, or form a criterion to decide the truth of specific statements of identity, but that it constitutes a regulative principle, making it possible at least to refute counter-examples to assertions of specific identities.[13]

The same seems to apply to the last of the Leibnizian principles stated above, the principle of substitutivity *salva veritate*. This must not be confused with (III) or (V). It does not relate to objects and their properties, but to expressions, their reference, and the truth value of the sentences in which they figure. None the less, the relations between the principle of substitutivity and the principle of indiscernibility is very close. If it is acknowledged that non-extensional contexts are exceptions to the principle of substitutivity, then there can be cases in which indiscernibility does not imply substitutivity.[14] But is the converse implication valid? If two names of objects are substitutable *salva veritate in a true statement of identity*, can what is true of one object fail to be true of the other, and can they fail to be identical? In this sense, the principle of substitutivity implies both the principles of indiscernibility of identicals and of the identity of indiscernibles, that is to say (V). But, like these latter, the principle of substitutivity cannot be taken as a definition of identity, but only, as Frege says, as 'a principle which expresses the relation of identity'.[15]

The reason why we cannot take one or other or the combination of principles (III)–(VIII) of the formal theory of identity as definitions of identity seems to result from the fact, pointed out above apropos reflexivity, that these principles are trivial or circular in so far as we have not stated what *justifications* we have for asserting such and such a specific identity. It is in this sense that to say of two objects that they are identical does not convey any 'cognitive value'. In other words, if we want to be able to give statements of identity a sense, we have to say what specific *criteria* permit us to state identities. This suggests that statements of identity are incomplete as long as these criteria have not been specified. It was this consideration that led to the idea that identity could not be an *absolute* relation between objects, but a relation *relative* to a certain mode of identification.

Contemporary philosophers who have pondered over the problem of identity have generally drawn two sorts of consequences from the fact that the formal principles of identity do not allow specific identities to be defined or justified. Some have supposed that every assertion of identity has to be based on specific criteria of individuation of the types of entity considered. In this sense, every entity would be based on a more fundamental relation which would guarantee it: for example, spatio-temporal continuity for material bodies, physical continuity or continuity of memory for people. In this way, identity would only be a consequence of these various principles of individuation. Other philosophers accept this relativity of the criteria of individuation, but still do not renounce giving a general and formal definition of identity. They maintain that identity must be defined as a relative notion.

9.4 Absolute identity and relative identity

The theory of identity considered so far supposes that one can ask if two objects a and b are identical *simpliciter*, or absolutely. But does this correspond to the way we customarily use statements of identity? Apparently not. It seems that statements of the form $a = b$ or $x = y$ are only found in logic. Ordinary statements of identity are more statements of the type: 'Is this *table* identical to that one?' or 'Is this *man* the same as that one?' The question: 'Is a identical to b?' only has a sense if we relativise this identity to a certain concept, or property, in relation to which we are stating the identity concerned. This thesis according to which the real form of statements of identity is always

> a is the same F as b

where 'F' is a 'sortal' predicate indicating what *sort* of object a and b are, is the thesis of *relative* identity or the thesis of the *relativity* of identity. It has been defended by Geach in particular:

> 'I am arguing for the thesis that identity is relative. When one says '*x* is identical with *y*', this, I hold, is an incomplete expression; it is short for '*x* is the same *A* as *y*', where *A* represents some count noun, understood from the context of utterance – or else, it is just a vague expression of a half-formed thought.'

Geach criticises Frege who, in his analysis of numerical statements, correctly saw that an assertion on a number is related to a concept – is an assertion on a concept under which as many objects fall – for not having maintained an identical thesis in respect of identity. On the contrary, Frege upheld the thesis according to which identity is an *absolute* notion 'which is given to us in such a specific way that it is inconceivable that it could have varied forms'.[17]

According to the thesis of the relativity of identity, a statement of identity is therefore always ambiguous: there is an indefinite number of ways of identifying two objects *a* and *b* according to the context in which it is stated and the sortal predicates in view in each circumstance. It follows that not only does $a = b$ always mean *a is the same F as b* (which we can write as '$a =_F b$'), but again that if *a is the same F as b*, it does not follow that *a* is *the same G* or *the same H* as *b*. Two objects can coincide under one given sortal predicate (like 'man'), without coinciding under others. The familiar problems about the identity and individuation of material objects can apparently be solved in this way. For example, Dr Jeckyll is the same *man* as Mr Hyde, but not the same *person*, or not the same *character*. I can bathe twice in the same *river*, but not twice in the same *water*. The baby in this photograph is the same man as the fat mustachioed gentleman in this other photograph, but he is neither the same *child* nor the same *old man*. Theseus's boat, which is continuously repaired by replacing all the planks with others, is the same *boat* from the point of view of its design (its form) and its spatio-temporal unity, but not the same *assembly of planks*. Conversely, if the boat is dismantled and then reconstructed with the same planks several centuries later and some kilometers away, it is the same *assembly of planks* but the *spatio-temporal unity* is no longer the same.

The thesis of the relativity of identity is very plausible intuitively. But it is important to look at its consequences. Does the fact that it makes it possible in principle to have an indefinite number of responses to the question 'is *a* the same as *b*?', according to the nature of the sortal concepts employed each time, imply that there is no way of saying that the procedures of individuation or identification of objects can converge and the determined properties be congruent? The problem is that if we suppose that these procedures do not converge, then we must abandon the principle of the indiscernibility of identicals, which actually expresses this convergence of individuation procedures. But the thesis of the relativity of identity actually maintains that it is impossible that two things be indiscernible from the point of view of *all* their individuation procedures. It therefore leads to the rejection of Leibniz's law. This can be shown, following David Wiggins, in the following way.

Suppose that we expressed each of the principles of the formal theory (III)–(VIII) of *absolute* identity in terms of the theory of relative identity. For this purpose it is enough to relativise each occurrence of '=' to any sortal predicate F, so that this sign expresses the relationship of identity indexed to this predicate, or ' $=_F$'. Principles (III), (IV) and (VI) respectively become (omitting the quantification on properties ϕ, but quantifying on the sortal predicate F):

$$(III_r) \ (\forall x)(\forall y)(\exists F)((x =_F y) \to (\phi x \equiv \phi y))$$
$$(IV_r) \ (\forall x)(\forall y)(\exists F)((\phi x \equiv \phi y) \to (x =_F y))$$
$$(VI_r) \ (\forall x)(\exists F)(x =_F x)$$

It can already be seen that it is bizarre to assert that x is identical to itself relative to a sortal property F. If x is identical to itself, it seems that it is relative to all its properties, and not relative to one of them. But let us suppose that we can ignore this problem and confine ourselves to reformulating (III_r), the 'relative' version of the indiscernibility of identicals or Leibniz's law. As has been seen, the thesis of the relativity of identity (let us call it 'TRI') acknowledges that a can be the same F as b, without for all that being the same G as b, and $F = G$. In other words, according to TRI.

(1) $(a =_F b) \ \& \ (a \neq_G b) \ \& \ Ga.$

It follows that it is possible in the schema

(2) $(a =_F b) \to (\phi a \equiv \phi b)$

to accept that '$a =_G x$' be substituted for 'ϕ'. But in that case, the premise

(3) $(a =_F b) \ \& \ Ga$

contained in (1) contradicts the other conjunct. In fact, (3) implies

(4) $a =_F b.$

If we then take '$a =_G x$' as a substitutional instance of 'ϕ' in (2), we obtain

(5) $(a =_F b) \to ((a =_G a) \equiv (a =_G b)).$

But by (4) and the *modus ponens*, it is possible to detach the consequent of (5) to infer:

(6) $(a =_G a) \equiv (a =_G b).$

But by the reflexitivity of '$=_G$' (that is to say (VI_r) above), we have:

(7) $Ga \to a =_G a.$

And thus, by detachment from the second component of (3)

(8) $a =_G a.$

And by *modus ponens* on (8) and (6) we have

(9) $a =_G b$.

But (9) contradicts (1). It cannot be true that (1) and (9) are true at the same time. *TRI* is therefore contradictory, if Leibniz's law is accepted. But if this principle is abandoned, how would it still be possible to talk solely about identity? What would be the objects which would be individuated according to a relative principle of identity of indiscernibles? *Relative* objects? But can there be such an ontology of *relative* objects?[19]

Wiggins concludes from this that identity cannot be relative in the sense of *TRI*. But for all that he does not conclude from it that the intuition which underlies *TRI*, that is to say 'the sortal dependence of individuation' of objects, is false. This dependence solely expresses the necessity when any object is designated of answering the Aristotelian question: 'what is it?' that characterises the quiddity, the essence or the substance.[20] *That* Aristotelian question is eminently legitimate, but it does not necessarily lead to *TRI*.

9.5 Identity and individuation

According to Wiggins, the only means of preserving what is correct in the idea of relative identity at the same time is to acknowledge that the individuation of objects is relative to a sortal concept, but to refuse to try and specify this concept. The thesis of the sortal dependence of individuation (which Wiggins calls 'D') therefore maintains that if *a* is identical to *b*, then *a* is the same *something* as *b*. Wiggins does not deny that every assertion of specific identity must be based on some justification of the coincidence of all the properties of two given objects under a certain sortal concept, and that, in this sense, the concept of identity itself neither guarantees nor defines the accordance of properties. In each case, the coincidence of properties will be specific to the sortal concept required. But contrary to the philosophers cited above (§ 9.3 *in fine*), he does not intend to define identity itself by a form of continuity or persistence of an object in time and space. Relations, like continuity or material composition, form the foundations of identity, but the latter is not confined to these relations, or they to it. For example, the material composition of a table (the fact that it is wooden, for example) is a principle of its individuation. But it alone does not define identity.[21] According to Wiggins, identity is primitive: it cannot be defined by any congruence of properties; on the contrary, this congruence must be a consequence of the identity itself. To identify an object *a* with an object *b* is to make it a 'continuant' under a certain sortal concept *F*. Every way of establishing the congruence of the properties of *a* and the properties of *b* will be a way of establishing the identity of the two objects. The question of knowing *what* sortal concept ensures identification can remain compatible with the indiscernibility of identicals (in this sense it is in accordance with the absolute conception of identity). Thus the formal principles of identity are both the condition and the consequence of every form of specific individuation appropriate to each entity. For any species of entity, there is a 'substantial' analysis of the individuation of the members of this species, and conformity with the principle of indiscernibility is a consequence of this specific analysis. This enables us to grasp exactly in what sense the formal theory of identity is *formal* or logical. The Leibnizian principles cannot take the place of a theory of individuation, and in this sense they cannot define identity. But a definition of identity that would not accord with these principles would not be a theory of identity. It would be a theory of another relation which founds identity: spatio-temporal continuity, persistence, or the material composition of objects. In other words, a purely logical principle, like Leibniz's law, *describes* nothing about the world or specific objects. But it none the less states a norm to which every actual description of identity and individuation must conform. (We will find this idea again in Chapter 13).

9.6 Identity and necessity

Wiggins's theory of identity (as expressed by thesis D) implies that every individuation of an object must conform to the condition stated by Leibniz's law. At first glance, therefore, it does not seem to differ from Quine's thesis according to which every entity must correspond to this Leibnizian principle, since there is 'no entity without identity' (§ 1.4.2, 4.3 and 7.6). The difference is that Quine regards identity as an open relation. Consequently the thesis of the sortal dependence of individuation can be stated as follows:

(D) $a = b$ iff there exists a sortal concept f so that:
   (1) a and b belong to a kind that is the extension of f;
   (2) to say that x falls under f (that x is f) is to say what x is (in the Aristotelian sense of *tode ti*);
   (3) a is the same f as b, or a coincides with b under f according to the type of coincidence required for the members of f.

In this way, we avoid the consequence for *TRI* entailed by acknowledgement of the fact that a can be the same F as b without being the same G as b. This is because here we are making the hypothesis that if $a = b$, a is the same F as b, but cannot be the same G as b if the predicates F and G state distinct conditions of continuity. In other words (D) must be matched by a very strong condition whereby every sortal predicate ensures unique conditions of temporal continuity of the objects that come under it;

(D') $(\forall x)(\exists f)(\forall t)((x$ exists at $t) \rightarrow (fx$ in $t))$.

In other words, a sortal predicate prescribes the conditions of persistence that an object cannot not exemplify at every moment of its history, on pain of ceasing to be this object. If this principle were false, Wiggins tells us, then the history of Lot's wife who was changed into a pillar of salt, according to the Bible, would be true. But these cases of the rupture of sortal continuity can no more be counter-examples to (D′) than can the stories of pumpkins changed into stage-coaches.[22]

Wiggins's theory of identity therefore makes it possible to account both for the necessity to complete every statement of identity between two objects of an analysis by their conditions of individuation (in this case, it does justice to the idea that motivated *TRI*) and for the necessity to make these conditions of individuation conform to the formal principle of absolute identity between objects. However, Wiggins acknowledges the 'sortal dependence' of every individuation (without for all that conceding that identity is relative).[23] The consequences of the relativisation of identity are only escaped by postulating that every entity must come under a constant sortal concept. But what is such a concept if not a property that an object *must* have, that is to say an *essence*? Consequently, how can Wiggins maintain that the indiscernibility of identicals is a *formal* condition of identity without maintaining a thesis which, in the eyes of someone like Quine, is anything but 'formal', that is to say essentialism? As we saw (§ 7.4), to acknowledge essentialism is to acknowledge *de re* quantification in modal contexts. Since all quantification supposes identity, it is therefore to acknowledge that Leibniz's law can be valid in these contexts and, consequently, the *substitutivity* of co-referential expressions in these contexts that it implies. I already showed, in Chapter 7, how the Quinian objection can be answered by postulating a weak essentialism, based on the idea that objects can be designated independently of the way in which they are described. Here I would only like to give a sort of counter-proof of these arguments, by showing how Wiggins's theory of identity itself only presupposes a weak essentialism.

The Quinian 'paradox' of the 'number of planets' (§ 6.4) is not the only paradox that can be invoked against the use of quantifiers in a modal context. Ruth Marcus Barcan has shown that a conclusion, apparently at least as paradoxical, can be derived in modal logic from Leibniz's law.[24] It involves the following reasoning. Let us suppose that a and b are identical. By Leibniz's law they have all their properties in common. But one of the properties of a is that it is necessarily identical to a. But this must also be one of the properties of b. Consequently, if $a = b$, then *necessarily* $a = b$. More formally:

take a specific instance of Leibniz's law:

(10) $(a = b) \rightarrow (\forall \phi)(\phi a \equiv \phi b)$

and take the following premise:

(11) $a = b$.

Then if we acknowledge that identity with itself is a property of an object, and a *necessary* property of this object, that is to say if $\square(a = b)$ is a substitutional instance of 'ϕ' in (10), we have

(12) $\square(a = a) \rightarrow \square(a = b)$

and if the reflexivity of identity is, as has been supposed, necessary:

(13) $\Box(a = a)$

whence, by *modus ponens* on (12) and (13):

(14) $\Box(a = b)$

and finally, by $\rightarrow$-introduction on (11) and (14):

(15) $a = b \rightarrow \Box(a = b)$.

This result has been regarded as paradoxical because it would show that every statement of identity, if it were true, was *necessarily* true. Thus there would not be contingent identities. But how is this possible? How can empirical discoveries, such as the discovery that Hesperus is Phosphorus or that virus X is identical to virus Y be necessary? The derivation itself has been challenged, particularly the transition from (10) to (12): can we accept that the identity of a with a is a property of a? As we saw above (§ 3), it is possible to challenge whether this is a genuine property of a and whether Leibniz's law allows identity to be mentioned among the properties 'common' to the two identical individuals.

None of these objections shows that (15), which has been called the 'necessity of identicals', is unacceptable, if it is interpreted in a certain way. Kripke (1980) maintains that (15) is perfectly natural if the names 'a' and 'b' which figure in it are 'rigid designators' (§ 7.6), that is to say if they designate 'the same individuals in all possible worlds', or again are purely referential terms. If the virus that has the property ϕ is identical to the virus that has the property ψ, then this identity is not necessary, because 'the virus that has the propery ϕ' can designate a *different* virus from the one it does in fact designate. But if 'a' and 'b' are genuine names, and not descriptions, then identity is necessary. If it is true *of* Hesperus and *of* Phosphorus that they are identical, then if it is true of Hesperus that it is necessarily Hesperus, it must be concluded that it is true of Hesperus and of Phosphorus that they are necessarily identical. Stated in this way as a *de re* necessity, true of objects, there is nothing shocking about the necessity of 'Hesperus = Phosphorus'.[25] This necessity does not show that the *statement* (or the sentence) in question is necessary (*de dicto* reading), but only that two objects, if they are identical, cannot fail to be identical. The problem here is once again Frege's problem (§ 8.2.3). '$a = a$' and '$a = b$' have the same truth conditions, and if '$a = a$' expresses a Russellian Proposition, '$a = b$' must express the same Russellian Proposition, and the theorem of the necessity of identicals says nothing else. But this does not imply that these two sentences express the same Fregean Proposition or have the same informative content or the same sense. Kripke himself is restating this difference when he says that '$(a = b)$' can be necessary and *a posteriori* (empirically discovered) without being necessary and *a priori*.[26]

It is therefore possible in the *de re* interpretation of (15) to acknowledge that an object, *if it is identical* to another, has the necessary or essential property of *being identical to this other object*. Certainly, *being identical to Cicero* is a bizarre essential property of Cicero. It is a trivial essential property (§ 7.6). But the necessity of identicals is only a consequence of the fact that if we acknowledge that identity with itself can be one of the common properties 'ϕ' of Leibniz's law, then that law does not define identity, since the *definiendum* is included in the *definiens*. But this circularity is not vicious, from the moment that we distinguish the (metaphysical) *fact* that two individuals are identical from the (epistemological) *reasons* that we have for being able to assert this fact. The necessity of identicals only relates to the fact of identity, not to its reasons or justifications. The important point, as Wiggins emphasises, is that we can speak of essential properties in this way without hazard. An individual is necessarily identical to everything to which he is identical.[27] But does this not make a *petitio principii* in favour of essentialism? No, in so far as the essentialism concerned does not presuppose that there are *individual* essential properties, or individual essences of objects. Essentialism, according to Wiggins, can be limited to this assertion: for every object of reference, there is an essential sortal feature by virtue of which, if we distinguish this object as *this F*, it cannot fail to be *this F*. Caesar is *that man*, Lassie is *this dog*. This does not suppose the existence of a sortal predicate which would exhaust the individual essence of the individual and would constitute his *infima species*.[28] Nor does it suppose the existence of a collection of properties which would completely define the essence of an individual, what Leibniz called its 'complete notion'.[29] Wiggins's essentialism is realism in so far as it supposes that there are objects in the world independent of our mind that cannot fail to have the essential features that they have. This is a conceptualism in so far as the essential properties that we are capable of articulating depend on *our* classifications:

> The essential necessity of a trait arises at that point of unalterability where the
> *very existence of the bearer is unqualifiedly conditional* upon the trait in question.
> Here, at this point, a property is fixed by virtue of being inherent in the
> individuation of it – inherent in the very possibility of the drawing of a
> spatio-temporal boundary around it. The closer the source of the attribute to
> the singling out of the thing itself – the more it is bound up with the whole
> mode of articulating reality to discover such an object in reality – the more
> exigent, obviously, is the necessity that, *if there is to exist such a thing as the bearer*,
> it should have the feature in question. The *de re* 'must' of causal inflexibility
> here passes over at a certain threshold into an inflexibility that is conceptual
> (though only loosely speaking logical). There is no reason why this should
> make the essentialist *de re* attribute any less of a real attribute of the thing
> itself.[30]

In this sense, for Wiggins, the paradigmatic sortal concepts are comparable with 'natural kinds' terms, like 'tiger', 'aluminium' or 'apricot'. As Leibniz and Locke had already noted, and as Putnam and Kripke have pointed out again, when we use these terms, we are supposing that there is an underlying common essence, without our use resting on their association with a list of necessary and sufficient characteristics that define them. A natural kind term, like 'gold', designates the extension of a certain property, but it is this extension that determines the meaning of the term and not the associated property. These terms have a Millian reference (in the sense of § 7.1). It is *in this sense* that we can say that reference presupposes essence.[31]

Here, no more than before (§ 7.6), we are not drawing a substantial philosophic doctrine – essentialism – from our use of modal operators and from our use of Leibniz's law. Necessity designated by '□' and identity designated '=' do not define essential properties or individuation. As Wiggins says, 'logic cannot force us to adopt a particular ontology'. As we have seen, this is true of an extensional logic as well as a modal logic. But it outlines the form and the boundaries that a theory of individuation must take.

9.7 Can identity be vague?

If the foregoing is correct, though the logical theory of identity in no way defines the conditions (metaphysical, epistemological) of the individuation of things in the world, there are nevertheless logical conditions of individuation to which every specific conception of the latter must correspond. According to these conditions, identity is an absolute relation between objects, in conformity with Leibniz's law. In this sense, I see no reason to refuse to say that logic is 'transcendental', that is to say, determines the *a priori* form of our thought of objects in general. But this sense of 'transcendental' must not be confused with the Kantian sense. According to Kant, logic is formal in the sense that it concerns only the form of thought, without concerning the objects that are the 'matter' of the thought. For Kant, the distinctive feature of objects is their relationship to sensory intuition, and in this sense they are necessarily represented in forms of pure intuition of space and time. Logic for him is therefore perfectly foreign to determination of the nature of these objects. Several contemporary authors, Granger in particular, have suggested transferring the Kantian transcendental, that is to say the *a priori* conditions of the objectivity of forms of sensibility, to forms of symbolic thought. Logic, in so far as it is the expression of this symbolic thought, is transcendental. For all that, this does not imply that there is a special logic, Kantian 'transcendental' logic, which differs from formal logic by establishing 'material' or objectual conditions of the *a priori*. Logic, even if it is transcendental, does not cease to be *formal*. It does not describe a world, but prescribes the conditions of its description (cf. Chapters 12 and 13).[33] What has been said about identity, in so far as it is possible to take the latter as a logical constant, can be regarded as an illustration of this thesis. However, it can only be explicit to the extent that the sense in which the logic in this conception is formal will have been specified (I will do so in Chapter 11).

The thesis according to which identity must be an absolute relationship has been challenged for other reasons than those advanced by theoreticians of relative identity. They emphasise that the conditions of identity of many objects, events or states are *vague*. Does an artefact, such as a chair or table, have definite conditions of identity (for example, does a chair cease to be a chair if it loses one of its legs? from what moment is one a person? where does a town begin and where do its suburbs start? at what point does cohabitation become concubinage? and so on). In several cases, vagueness seems essential to certain objects, and even objects that are not vague in appearance seem to be able to be so if we apply sorites reasoning to them. Let us mentally dismember a table, molecule by molecule. At what point does it cease to be a table and no longer be anything but a pile of wood? Even arbitrary stipulations do not help us.[34] Perhaps vagueness is associated with certain physical processes, and our theories have to account for them. René Thom is suggesting something of this sort when he states:

> Catastrophe Theory allows a continuum logic where one considers the 'variable' concepts Fu, where the parameter u varies in a control space U: when u describes a path uv in U, it is possible that the concept Fu is continuously changed into a concept Gv, whose relationship with Fu will not immediately appear with Fu, because there is a threshold in normal thought, a 'taboo' separating u from v in the control space U. The CT therefore offers the possibility (extended) of transgressing the principle of identity.[35]

The point here is not that identity is related to such and such a concept, but that it might not be possible to know relatively *to what* concept it is related. Thom does not say that our language of description is vague, but that there might be true descriptions (those provided by the CT) of vague phenomena (in this case 'catastrophic' phenomena). Identity itself is vague because the objects are vague. As I will explain in Chapter 12, I have doubts about the 'extended' possibility that such and such *phenomena* might make us abandon a classical principle of logic.

Let us suppose that there are vague objects (and not only vague descriptions of objects) and that identity is vague (and not that the statements that we use to assert it are). Is this idea sound? According to an argument due to Gareth Evans (and independently to Nathan Salmon), it is not.

Let 'a' and 'b' be singular terms so that the sentence '$a = b$' has an indeterminate truth value. Let us express this indetermination by an operator '∇'. In that case, we have

(1) $\nabla(a = b)$.

(1) reports a fact in respect of b which we can express by attributing it (by abstraction) with the property '$\hat{x}[\nabla(x = a)]$'

(2) $\hat{x}[\nabla(x = a)]b$.

But we have

(3) $-\nabla(a = a)$

and consequently

(4) $-\hat{x}[\nabla(x = a)]a$.

But by Leibniz's law it is possible to derive from (2) and (4),

(5) $-(a = b)$

thus contradicting the initial hypothesis.[36]

Consequently, if identity is vague, we have to abandon Leibniz's law. Thom would probably accept this consequence (I am supposing that by the 'principle of identity' he meant this law), and therefore this does not refute his argument. But, as I have maintained in respect of relative identity, it is not certain that this is the same notion of identity that is involved when Leibniz's law is rejected. Therefore, it is not certain that it is a real violation of identity that is involved or that it can be concluded from it that *objects* of the world can be vague. Evans's argument has been challenged: if the singular terms '*a*' and '*b*' themselves are vague, the negation (3) is true, and the argument is not valid. Evans would therefore be making a *petitio principii* by supposing that these terms are genuinely referential (or rigid designators).[37] But if singular terms are vague, then a *petitio principii* is also being made in favour of the hypothesis that vagueness is not peculiar to things but to our statements. Like everything touching on vagueness, this distinction is very obscure. The next chapter relates to this idea. But it appears desirable at the very least that authors who advance hypotheses on the violation of classical logical principles consider this type of argument, before concluding in favour of this violation.

—— 10 ——

VAGUENESS

10.1 Vagueness and its species

In logic, as in mathematics and the other sciences, people seek to eliminate vagueness and construct artificial languages in which the syntax, sense and reference of expressions are clearly and precisely specified. On the other hand, a glance at the logical arguments expressed in natural language is enough to show that they are contaminated by vagueness, and that this feature often trammels their comprehension and evaluation. The natural reaction of logicians is therefore to adopt the 'constructionist' attitude (§ 3.1) that natural language must be reformed and purged of all trace of vagueness and indetermination. This is the attitude of Frege and Russell, for example: in their view, logic must eliminate vagueness at all costs. Nevertheless, the 'naturalist' logician's attitude is not necessarily far removed from the 'constructionist's' on this point. Consider, for example, a canonical syllogism expressed in ordinary language:

(A) All logicians are men
     All men are mortal
     _____

     Therefore, all logicians are mortal

The predicates ('is a man', 'is a logician') can be considered as 'vague': 'logician' is a title given on more or less strict or informed criteria; 'man' is ambiguous and can designate males, adults or members of a biological species. The domain of the quantifier 'all' can be the set of objects, the set of men, the set of logicians, or only a specified subset (for example the set of men in this room). Nevertheless, no one would dream of describing argument (A) as 'vague' or invalid. What we do is implicitly choose a fixed interpretation of these predicates, which makes them absolutely true of the individuals to whom they apply, or which relativises them with respect to an arbitrary domain of objects.[1] Even if (A) is considered a logical argument in good and due *form*, one undertakes an implicit elimination of the vagueness that the use of usual language could have introduced. This suggests a strategy for dealing with vagueness: to treat vague predicates *as if they* were precise. The questions that the constructionist asks the naturalist are: is this strategy always possible? Is the vagueness of natural language contingent or essential? This is the dilemma that seems to grip every scheme for a 'logic of vagueness': either vagueness is essential and irreducible, in which case, how is it possible to talk about establishing a *logic* of it? Or else vagueness is inessential and reducible, but in that case, how it is possible to talk about a logic of *vagueness*?

199

These are questions that we need to understand, before trying to answer them. The notion of vagueness covers several distinct notions.

In general, every sentence can be called 'vague' if the truth value 'true' or the truth value 'false' cannot be attributed to it; that is to say, it does not satisfy the *principle of bivalence*, the principle whereby a sentence is true or false, *tertium non datur* (§ 6.4.1). By extension, every expression is called 'vague' if, when it figures in a sentence, it is capable of producing an exception to bivalence for that sentence. Vagueness generally, is the failure of bivalence, or the domain where 'truth value gaps' arise.[2] But there are several varieties of vagueness from this point of view, not all of them ineliminable.

1. In this sense, all sentences of natural language would be vague if they did not have extensional truth conditions: modal sentences (Chapter 7), sentences reporting the contents of propositional attitudes (Chapter 8), and all sentences containing modal or intensional operators (time, adverbs, modes and so on) generally. But the diagnosis that these sentences are vague is only valid if they cannot be given truth conditions. However, we have seen that, in so far as a semantics can be given for intensional sentences, they do have bivalent truth conditions (the case is less clear for propositional attitudes, as has been seen).

2. Certain sentences would be vague in this sense if they contained non-denoting or empty singular terms, such as 'Pegasus' or 'the series that converges the least rapidly'. But here too vagueness is eliminable if one supposes, as does Frege, that all singular terms must denote, or if one reduces these terms to definite descriptions, as does Russell, or again if rules of presupposition are established.[3]

3. Sentences would be vague in this sense if they were dependent on a categorical incompatibility, that is to say where a predicate is not applied to an object of the category to which the predicate belongs (*a blue love, an impassioned safety pin*). As we know, the mechanism is constantly used in metaphors, zeugmas and other rhetorical or poetic uses of speech. Are metaphorical sentences true or false? It can be maintained that they have an indeterminate sense though their truth values are not indeterminate.[4]

4. Another type of vagueness can be called *contextual* or pragmatic vagueness. This results from an expression that only receives a reference, a truth value sentence, in a determinate context. This is, in fact, the case with the predicates of (A) above, or definite descriptions, like 'the Prime Minister of Britain', 'the MP for Oxford North', which can designate different individuals at different times. Here too it can be supposed that specification of the context can remove the indetermination.

5. Lastly, it is possible to talk about the vagueness of certain predicates, such as 'pearl', 'logician', 'crook', and so on, for which the question arises of knowing

whether or not they apply to their object in a determinate way. Here too vagueness seems eliminable, if one defines what a pearl, a logician or a crook are by means of more precise criteria ('X is a logician if he has proved a logical theorem').

The list is probably not complete, even if these cases must be distinguished from simple lexical ambiguity ('bank'). But what is involved in each of them is a phenomenon that it is important to distinguish from vagueness proper: a phenomenon that can be called *indetermination* or, in Frege's terms, *the incompleteness of sense*. In each of cases (1)–(4), as has been seen, vagueness is eliminable in one way or another, provided that the interpretation of the sentences that make it possible to fix their truth value is specified.

Frege generally characterises vagueness in two ways, which he often confuses. On the one hand, he requires that, in a logically perfect language, every function defined for every object. He calls this the principle of *completeness*. On the other hand, he requires that every concept whose 'boundaries' are not precisely defined be banished from logic. This can be called the principle of *precision*.[5] Frege tends to confuse these two principles, because both lead to the failure of bivalence. But each of cases (1)–(5) can be considered as a case of incompleteness of sense (or, if preferred, of indetermination), capable of being completed under a given interpretation, and not as cases of imprecision. For example, the predicate 'is a pearl' implies that it is true of every object formed in an oyster, and false of every object not issuing from an oyster. But it does not imply that it cannot be applied to an object of the same shape composed of pearliferous material, but not issuing from an oyster, any more than it only implies that it can be applied to such an object. The predicate can be completed in one way or another, by allowing or by not allowing the application of 'pearl' to artificial pearls, and so on. 'Vague' predicates of type (1) are in this sense neutral predicates in respect of a possible evaluation which makes them true or false of an object. From this point of view, it can even be maintained that it is essential to linguistic communication to be able to have such vagueness (and the other forms (1)–(5)) at its disposal, and that it is one of the conditions of the pragmatic functioning of natural languages.[6] On the other hand, compare type (5) vagueness with the following vagueness.

6. This is the vagueness of adjectives such as 'tall', 'small', 'child' 'adult', 'bald', and so on. Their case is apparently no different from (5), since their meaning and reference can also be specified. But they are not vague in the same sense, because our attempts to specify them ('someone over 6 feet is tall', 'someone with fewer than 9678 hairs is bald') are doomed to defeat, in so far as a delimitation of their domain of application would *pervert* their sense instead of completing it, as Sainsbury noted (1988). If 'tall' is solely true of people who are 6 feet or taller, then this implies that the predicate 'tall' cannot be applied to individuals of 6 feet or less, with the result that the term 'tall', unlike 'pearl', is not neutral in respect of the implications of sense that its 'precisification' could introduce. The difference is apparently that, if one knows how to specify 'pearl' in a satisfactory way, one does not know how to do the same with 'tall'.[7] That is why this vagueness will be called

vagueness proper, or *constitutive* lack of precision. Although it is not possible to reduce this type (5) vagueness to the other cases and treat these latter as equivalents, it can be said that (1)–(5) all result from the principle of incompleteness rather than from the principle of imprecision or vagueness proper.

What follows will be concerned with this last type of vagueness. It is this type, and not the incompleteness of sense, which justifies the exclusion of vagueness from logic required by Frege. In fact, there are various ways of reducing vaguenesses (1)–(5), even if all of them do not result from classical logic.[8] The question that arises apropos vagueness proper or constitutive vagueness is of knowing if it itself is reducible, that is to say if there is a form of coherence of vague predicates that would allow a 'logic' of vagueness to be envisaged or if, on the contrary, it is irreducible and essential. Frege suspects that genuine vague predicates are essentially incoherent. Having a tendency to confuse vagueness and incompleteness of sense, he extends this characterisation of incoherence to natural languages in general, probably illegitimately since, as has been seen, linguistic communication has the means of reducing indetermination. But the question still holds for constitutive vagueness. In this sense, there are two sorts of questions concerning a possible 'logic of vagueness'. The first concerns the phenomenon of the indetermination of certain predicates or of certain linguistic expressions, the application of which to objects is indeterminate. In this case, the problem is simply that a concept *can* have imprecise 'boundaries': if these boundaries are specified, vagueness disappears, or can be reduced, and in this sense is only a superficial phenomenon. The other type of question concerns the actual *absence* of precise boundaries for an expression. In this case, the difficulty is not that there are circumstances where we do not know if a predicate does or does not apply, because this fact is compatible with a very precise conception of the circumstances in which these applications are indeterminate. The difficulty is that, for *essentially* vague predicates, even the determination of these circumstances leads to *contradictory* instructions, and therefore to the idea that these predicates are incoherent.[9]

10.2 Sorites

Vague predicates (hereafter, this term will denote vagueness proper), such as 'bald', 'tall', or 'child', are those that give rise to paradoxes, well-known since antiquity by the name of sorites arguments.[10] The most famous is the Megarian sorites of the heap. To take one grain away from a heap of corn does not make it stop being a pile, likewise two grains, and so on. But at the end of the process of substraction, can a single grain form a heap? This is said to be a sorite of 'decomposition'. But it is obviously possible to envisage it from the angle of composition: after how many grains is there a heap? how many seconds of life make an adult? and so on. The characteristic of vague predicates is that they all show a certain *tolerance* of the concept expressed, or the idea of a *degree* of change in application, too weak to make the difference between a case where the predicate applies and a case where the predicate does not apply. Or more exactly, vague predicates apply, and do not cease to be stated, in order to say something about something, but in a way that seems arbitrary, from the point when a limit to their extension is indicated. Why would a plot of land that has 26 bumps be 'flat' while a piece of land with 27 would not? It is this feature which, if P is a vague predicate, might in certain circumstances lead one to assert that Pa and in other circumstances to assert that not Pa, is at the origin of sorites paradoxes. A sorites argument generally has the following form:

(S)

$$Pa_1$$
$$Pa_1 \rightarrow Pa_2$$

$$\vdots \qquad \vdots$$

$$Pa_{n-1} \rightarrow Pa_n$$

$$\overline{\phantom{Pa_{n-1} \rightarrow Pa_n}}$$

$$Pa_n$$

The tolerance of the predicate shows in the fact that each conditional of the form

$$Pa_i \rightarrow Pa_{i+1}$$

is true. The argument has the form of a classical *modus ponens* (if p then q, p; therefore q). But the paradox comes from the fact that the conclusion does not seem to be true, although the premises seem true and the conclusion is inferred from the premises by a valid rule of inference. For example, for the premise 'a_1 is small', where a measures 5 feet, the conclusion, obtained by a series of inductions on the premises, 'a_n is small' is false, if for example, a measures 10 feet.

An interesting instance of the sorite paradox is what has been called 'Wang's paradox' (cf. Dummett, 1978):

> 0 is a small number
> If n is small, then $n + 1$ is small
> Therefore every number is small.

It can be objected that this is not a paradox, because the conclusion is true in the usual sense of 'small': a natural number is smaller than an infinity of larger natural numbers. But this is a paradox in so far as it is possible to find interpretations of 'small' for which the premises are true but the conclusion false.

Let us go along with Sainsbury and call a 'sorites predicate' every predicate P that is a predicate of degree, or to which a dimension of comparison d is associated, so that:

(I) small d-differences do not affect the applicability of P
(II) large d-differences affect the application of P
(III) d-differences are cumulative: large d-differences can be attained by a series of small d-differences.[11]

The dimension of comparison is what makes someone be *more or less* bald, *more or less* tall, and so on, and which causes the applicability of the predicate to reside in the quantity of hairs or the number of feet and inches. The paradoxical character of sorites predicates results from the fact that the sense of the predicate, in a given real situation, implies that an object *a* is *P* and that *a* is not *P* at the same time. In this sense, it seems natural to say that sorite predicates are contradictory or incoherent. The philosophical problem posed by these predicates is the following: are these predicates really incoherent, and consequently incapable of receiving coherent conditions of reference, or is this incoherence only apparent and capable of being brought back to an underlying coherence? This problem must not be confused with another, though connected one: if vague predicates are incoherent, do they denote real properties of the world? In other words, is vagueness real, a feature of reality? But what is a vague property? If there are vague properties, can there be vague objects (cf. § 9.7)? Or does the incoherence of vague predicates only imply an imperfection in our understanding, faced with a reality, which, in the final analysis, has precise boundaries?[12]

The problem that will principally concern us in this chapter is that of the coherence or incoherence of vague predicates and the possibility of giving them a semantics, that is to say of establishing truth conditions for the sentences in which they figure. I will return to the metaphysical question of the reality of vagueness more briefly in § 10.5.

10.3 The incoherence of vague predicates

10.3.1 'Penumbral connections'

In order to be able to ask the question about the coherence of vague predicates, we need to have a better idea of their functioning. The fact that a sorite predicate *P* shows its incoherence by giving rise to paradoxes of the same name does not imply that *P* is incoherent to the point of prohibiting any inference from *P*. For example, if 'tall' is a sorites predicate, we can, despite the fact that by definition it allows borderline cases of application, infer '*a* is tall' from '*a* is tall and *b* is tall'. Or again, from 'tall', we can infer comparison judgements such as:

> If *a* is taller than *b*, and if *b* is tall in an imprecise way, then *a* is tall in an imprecise way.

Consequently, from the point of view of their inferential power, it does not seem that sorites predicates are distinct from non-vague predicates. What this shows is that though sorites predicates have imprecise domains of application, they are not *absurd* predicates. They have a kernel of sense that applies in borderline cases.[13] Nevertheless, is this sufficient to make us say that vague predicates are coherent? Kit Fine calls these logical relationships that vague predicates are subject to 'penumbral connections' because, although they are *bona fide* logical connections, they confuse the truth conditions of sentences containing vague predicates.[14] According to Fine, the existence of penumbral connections is what shows that a certain approach to the problem of vagueness, according to which vagueness might be eliminated by being reduced to a form of incompleteness, cannot succeed.

According to this approach, it might be possible to give a semantics for vague predicates, by attributing the sentences that contain them with truth values other than true and false, and by acknowledging that for every vague sentence, there is a certain range of ways of making it definite, by connecting determinate truth conditions to it. Suppose that we reject the principle of bivalence for these sentences, since they appear to be exceptions to it, and adopt a logic with three truth values: true (T), false (F) and a third value, indeterminate (I).[15] Let us suppose that we are dealing with a language in which only predicates are vague (and not, for example, names or quantifiers) and where the logical constants receive their usual sense. The idea is that if a vague predicate can receive a precise assignation of reference – for example, if we acknowledge the baldness of Yul Brynner, Kojak or Michel Foucault, but not that of Jean-Paul Sartre or of Clement Attlee – a corresponding sentence *Px* will have the value true or the value false. If the predicate does not have a precise reference (Frege's baldness or G. E. Moore's), *Px* will have an indeterminate value. This guarantees us classical truth conditions for every vague atomic sentence *Pa*, as long as the truth value of *Pa* is implicitly specified. Nevertheless, these conditions are subject to fluctuations, because the degree to which *Pa* can receive a determinate truth value under a given specification can be minimised or maximised. If it is minimised, the value *I* is dominant: every sentence, a subsentence of which has the value *I*, also has the value *I*. If it is maximised, the value *I* is dominated: every sentence is defined if its truth value is unchanged for every assignation of a definite value to its immediate subsentences. For example, a combination of two members, which are respectively indefinite and false, is indeterminate under the first hypothesis, but false under the second. In fact, the policy of maximisation is the one we follow naturally when we decide to take the vague predicates of ordinary language as precise, thus validating inferences such as

> Some philosophers are bald
> Every philosopher is an intellectual
> _____
> therefore Some intellectuals are bald

Although these inferences contain a (some) Sorites predicate(s). The fact that, in natural language, even vague predicates can give rise to adjectives that accentuate the vagueness, or to corresponding modifiers ('reddish', 'whitish', 'vaguely bald', and so on), seems to indicate that we are implicitly following a maximising interpretation, even if we are tempering it according to the case involved. According to the same three-valued approach, it can be seen that the law of the excluded middle does not cease to be valid for vague predicates. The statement

'Michel is bald or Michel is not bald' is always true, although each member of the disjunction is indefinite.[16] But, as Fine notes, the existence of penumbral connections makes the strategy of maximisation ineffectual. Let us suppose that a patch of colour *a* is on the borderline between pink and red. Let *Pa* be '*a* is pink', and *Ra*, '*a* is red'. Then, the combination *Pa and Ra* is false, because 'red' and 'pink' are (by hypothesis) opposites. But according to the maximisation strategy *Pa and Ra* is indefinite, because the two members of the combination are indefinite. Another penumbral connection makes *Pa* & *Pa* indefinite since they are equivalent to *Pa*, while *Pa* & *Ra* is false. The difficulty with a three-valued approach is that it does not respect the penumbral truths peculiar to vague predicates.[17] It therefore seems that the existence of penumbral connections is a major obstacle to a semantic of vague sentences.

10.3.2 The incoherence of observational predicates

Dummett has extended this diagnosis of the incoherence of vague predicates to the category of predicates of observation, or phenomenal qualities, such as the terms designating colours, sounds or tactile properties.[18] Dummett maintains that these predicates are vague by reason of a feature peculiar to all observational predicates: the non-transitive character of the relation 'is discernibly different from' applied to these predicates. 'Red', for example, is a vague predicate if it is governed by the principle according to which, if I am not able to discern the difference between the colour of *a* and the colour of *b*, I must agree to say that *b* is red if *a* is red. But this principle cannot be true of 'red' in a coherent way. Let us suppose, in fact, that we have a continuous gradation of colours on a strip of paper, going, for example, from red to blue, via violet. Each area of colour will be contiguous to an area of a different, but indiscernibly different, colour on either side (except at the extreme points of the strip). It follows that for every way of specifying the predicate 'red', there will be red areas that will not be discernibly different from areas that are not red. It will therefore not be possible to say, by simple observation, if the area is red or not red. Consequently, if 'red' is a term whose application is determined solely by observation, it is necessarily a vague term, which leads to the formulation of contradictory judgements. Frege would therefore be right to say that vague predicates (in any case, those of observation) are essentially incoherent.

Could we react to this conclusion by noting that we do actually use these predicates in ordinary language, and that on the whole, reach sufficient agreement to say that an object is red or not red? Of course, but we have no means of saying if there are any grounds for this agreement: there is nothing to prevent a coherent practice resting on ideas that are incoherent themselves.[19] Another suggestion in the same sense might rest on the very plausible idea that when we use a certain number of terms, observational or not, we are fixing their reference implicitly in respect of an exemplar or a paradigmatic case. 'Red' would mean 'red in relation to a set of exemplars of red'. This latter predicate would not be sorite, since the indiscernibility of a colour in respect of a paradigm of that colour does not mean that we have *another* paradigm of that colour at our disposal. But this suggestion fails, because 'is paradigmatically red' is either an observational term, in which case it is sorites, or else it is non-observational, which is doubtful: for example, we do not determine whether an object is red by considering the light-waves to which it is subject. Vague predicates really do seem to be incoherent. If they are essentially incoherent, it is to the extent to which they are an integral part of our use of ordinary language. To try and eliminate or reduce this incoherence by means of some sort of 'logic of vagueness' would not only be impossible but would imply a radical misunderstanding of their use in natural language: we can use them, and learn them precisely *because* they are vague. To reduce this vagueness would be not to understand their actual relevance, which results from their constitutive vagueness.[20]

Crispin Wright (1975) has maintained that the incoherence of vague predicates, and particularly of observational predicates, threatens one possible conception of the semantic competence and command of expressions of a natural language. This is the common conception that we master the sense of the expressions of our language because we master the rules governing the use of these expressions. But if certain terms of our language are constitutively incoherent, because of their 'tolerance' or their sorites character, then the rules that govern the use of these terms are themselves incoherent, and the conception of semantic competence as mastery of the rules is also incoherent – at least for vague terms.

What Dummett and Wright see as being at stake in this question is important. If vagueness is an ineliminable feature of certain sentences of natural language, then these latter do not have definite truth conditions. They therefore directly threaten the 'realist' thesis whereby every sentence has definite truth conditions, that is to say obeys the principle of bivalence (§ 6.4). If bivalence is absent for vague sentences, then realism cannot be valid for these sentences, or the vagueness of a sentence is a feature incompatible with its possession of a determinate truth value.[21]

Must we acknowledge arguments like Dummett's and Wright's and conclude not only in favour of the incoherence of vague predicates, but also of the consequences that these authors draw from it? The problem is one of knowing whether we can provide a solution to the sorites paradoxes engendered by these predicates, and which ones. Because if we can block these paradoxes, that is to say show in what conditions these arguments can be invalid, then we might be able to reveal a form of coherence of vague predicates.

10.4 The coherence of vague predicates

10.4.1 A semantics of vague terms

In the first place, is it true that condition (I) for a Sorite predicate is satisfied by the predicates so described? Is it not possible to say that small differences in the dimension *d* of comparison *affect* the applicability of predicates such as 'tall', 'small' or 'bald'? If John is almost a micromillimeter smaller than Paul, although both are borderline cases of tall men, it is slightly less true that John is tall, than it is of Paul. Even if this sort of intuition is not acknowledged, the fact remains that insignificant differences of degree of application of predicates can produce significant differences if they are cumulative. If this is the case, we have a solution to sorite paradoxes of type (S) above. In these arguments it is false to say that *all* premises of the form

$$Pa_i \rightarrow Pa_{i+1}$$

are true. At least one of the premises of this form must be false, after a certain degree of application of the predicate. For example, there is a threshold after which a questionably bald man can become an unquestionably bald man, and a threshold after which a questionably hairy man can be hirsute.

In the second place and as a corollary, we can suppose that the three-valued approach of the previous paragraph is still too close to classical semantics for non-vague predicates to provide an adequate semantics for vague predicates. The paradoxical character of the results would thus come from the application of a semantic framework unsuited to vagueness.

These remarks lead to the formulation of an appropriate 'logic of vagueness', based on the idea that it is possible to have assignable degrees of application of sorites predicates, which thereby cease to be paradoxical. Several versions of this type of logic exist. The most famous is probably Zadeh's theory of 'fuzzy sets' or 'fuzzy logic', which has had important applications in artificial intelligence[22] Another analysis, resting on similar ideas, comes from Goguen (1969). This is the one that I will give (in a simplified form) in what follows.[23]

An attempt to modify the classical semantics will therefore be made by acknowledging a semantics based on the notion of *degrees of truth*, comprised between absolute truth and absolute falsity, on a continuum comprised between 0 and 1.

An atomic sentence *Pa* will be true to a degree *n* comprised between 0 and 1. If absolutely true, it will be at degree 1. If it is absolutely false in will be at degree 0. We start from the fact that a disjunction is true in bivalent logic if one of its members is true, and a combination is false if one of its members is false, in the sense in which Quine says that the falsity of one is *recessive* and the truth *dominant*, while the reverse applies for the other. We then give the following clauses for the disjunction and the conjunction:

(I) $\text{Val}[A \lor B] = \text{Max}\{\text{Val}[A], \text{Val}[B]\}$
(II) $\overline{\text{Val}}[A \ \& \ B] = \text{Min}\{\text{Val}[A], \text{Val}[B]\}$

In bivalent logic, the value of a negation is the complement in the set $\{0,1\}$ of the degree to which the negated sentence falls below absolute truth. The clause for the negation is therefore:

(III) $\text{Val}[-A] = 1 - \text{Val}[A]$.

As in classical logic '&' and '$\vee$' are interdefinable via (I)–(III). But the corresponding clause for '$\rightarrow$' does not reflect the same interdefinability. According to the analysis in question, a material conditional must be true if the consequent is at least as true as the antecedent. But it is also possible to have values that reflect an important difference in the degree of truth of the antecedent in respect of the degree of truth of the consequent, or the converse. If the antecedent is only marginally more true than that consequent, the conditional must be only marginally less than totally true, while if the antecedent is much truer than the consequent, the conditional would have to be at a degree much below the degree of total truth. The clause for '$\rightarrow$' is therefore:

(IV) $\text{Val}[A \rightarrow B] = 1 - (\text{Val}[A] - \text{Val}[B])$ if $\text{Val}[A] > \text{Val}[B]$.
$= 1$ otherwise.

Clauses for quantifiers (which can also be treated in the framework of Zadeh's type of fuzzy logic) will be left on one side.

In a logic based on the idea of degree of truth, the validity of a formula is defined as degree 1 of that formula for every assignation of truth values to its component letters, and an argument is said to be valid if there is not an assignation of degree of truth to its sentences such that the value of the conclusion comes below the value of the premise to the weakest degree of truth. (This analysis can be compared with the analysis of the degree of information of a propositional formula according to Carnap/Bar-Hillel (cf. § 2.5.2 above).)

It can now be seen how clauses (I)–(IV) make it possible to resolve the sorites paradox (S). Each of the conditionals that form the premises of the argument has a degree of truth less than 1, because the degree of truth of the antecedent is marginally greater than the degree of truth of the consequent (since every a_i is marginally more P [bald, small, tall, etc.] than the corresponding a_{i+1}. By clause (IV), every conditional has a degree of truth less than 1. It might be concluded from this that sorites arguments, if they are formally valid, are nevertheless not sound, because all their premises are not true.[24] But in fact, according to analysis in terms of degrees of truth, neither are they valid, because *modus ponens* is not applicable. In fact, if $\text{Val}[A \rightarrow B] = 1$, then the applications of *modus ponens* are correct. But in the case of the sorites, the rule is applied in order to detach the consequents whose degree of truth moves closer and closer to 0. The rule of detachment is therefore inapplicable here. The paradox therefore does not arise merely from the presence of a sorites predicate in an S-type argument, but from the fact that it is not possible to have such a predicate in an inference, and *at the same time* to apply *modus ponens* in a valid way.[25]

This solution has the virtue of accounting for the obvious fact that sorites predicates are predicates of degree. It accounts for the corresponding paradoxes, and invalidates the arguments in a way that accords with our intuitions. According to this analysis, the idea of degree of application of a predicate is not an observational idea: two objects can be observationally indiscernible from one another, although the degree to which an observational predicate applies to the two objects is different.[26] Dummett's objection is thus eluded. Consequently, this semantics makes it possible to talk about a coherence of vague predicates, in so far as it provides truth conditions for the corresponding sentences.

10.4.2 Some light on penumbras

Despite its virtues, analysis in terms of degrees of truth can give rise to some reservations, which I will attempt to dissipate.

A first reservation can come from the fact that truth does not seem to be a question of degree. In usual language, we certainly use expressions such as 'This is truer than that', 'This is certainly not totally true'. But does it follow that 'true' itself is a vague predicate or a predicate of degree? Is it possible to say, for example, that a statement is only true to the degree 1/5? The feeling of doubt that this type of assertion arouses is similar to the doubt aroused by the analysis of Bayesian statisticians when they talk about degrees of belief.[27] In addition, linguistic data are far from establishing that we use terms like 'true' or 'false' by attributing them with a similar functioning to the functioning of 'tall' or 'bald'. For example, 'very true' is not the opposite of 'very false', while 'very tall' is the opposite of 'very small'. But there is an answer to these doubts. The fact of acknowledging degrees of truth, as in the semantics described in § 4.1, does not imply that truth is being defined as a comparative idea. For example, it is possible to set out, as Popper does, a theory of approximation to truth or probability (whatever the difficulties) without truth itself being reduced to probability at the same time.[29] Likewise, the notion of degree of truth in the above analysis can be a theoretical construction intended to account for the semantic functioning of vague predicates, just as is the notion of degree of belief in Bayesian theories of belief and confirmation, without the notion of truth itself being, ultimately and metaphysically, defined as a comparative notion.[30]

A more serious reservation can come from the argument of penumbral connections itself. According to Fine, penumbral connections show that the truth value of a complex vague formula is not always a function of the truth value of its subformulas. But the approach in terms of degrees implies this same truth functionality, and is therefore inconsistent with penumbral connections. To go back to the example above (§ 10.3). If 'is red' and 'is pink' are opposites, 'a is red and a is pink' must be totally false or contradictory. But this is not true if a is midway between the canonic red and the canonic pink, in which case each member of the combination must have the value 0.5, and the combination the value 0.5 as well (by clause (II)). However, the approach in terms of degrees makes it possible to answer this objection. According to this approach saying that 'is red' and 'is pink' are opposites is not saying that nothing can be both at the same time, but saying that nothing can be *totally* red and *totally* pink at the same time. But a thing can be red to a certain degree and pink to a certain closely related degree. There is therefore no reason to say that 'a is red' must be totally false if 'a is pink' is totally true, and the other way round.

But in an attempt to defend a similar position to Dummett's, Crispin Wright has maintained that the approach in terms of degrees does not dissipate vagueness. It simply transposes it to the level of the metalanguage in which we define our degrees of truth. According to Wright, in fact, anyone who is tempted to adopt the solution in terms of degrees and who thinks

> that he at last feels the cold wind of sanity fanning his brow would do well to be clear why we do not still have *this* principle: if b is marginally less F than a, then if the less misleading description of a is 'F', the less misleading description of b is 'F'. Yet if this principle is false, there must, in any sorites type series, be a last case of which we are prepared to say that if we *had* to describe it either as F or as not-F, the better description would be 'F'. Why, then is it usually embarrassing to be asked to identify such a case without any sense of arbitrariness? Let us say that 'a is F' has a *positive* value just in case 'F' is a less misleading description of a than 'not-F'. Then our embarrassment is exactly to identify a last object to which the application of F would receive a positive value. But then the suspicion arises that tolerance is with us still; only it is not now the *truth* of the application of F that would survive small changes but, so to speak, its positivity.

Wright objects that the introduction of a complex structure of degrees of justification of vague sentences cannot help us avoid sorites paradoxes because, in the degrees of justification we would have to distinguish the ones for which application of the predicate is 'on balance' justified. For example, if our justification rests on our memory, and if we are capable of *remembering* how to apply the vague predicate P, then differences that are too weak to be memorised cannot transform a situation for which its application is actually on balance justified into a situation that is not.[32] Wright's argument is that we can reformulate our definition (I)–(III) of a sorite predicate in this way, and continue to have paradoxes:

(I') small d-differences do not *on balance* affect the justification for applying P;

(II') large d-differences *on balance* affect the justification for applying P;

(III') d-differences are cumulative: large d-differences can be reached via a series of small d-differences.[33]

In this case, the incoherence of a vague predicate F will consist of the fact that it can be justified to say that an object a is F and not justified to say that a is F.

It is possible to agree with Wright that this transposition of the definition of a sorite predicate at the level of the justification of its applications enables the paradoxes to be reproduced. But why would the champion of an approach in terms of degrees refuse to say here that the notion of justification itself is capable of varying in degrees? If sorites arguments are invalid, by virtue of variations in the degree of truth of the premises, why would these variations in degree not induce differences in the degree of justification 'on balance' that a subject who applies them can have? Sainsbury (1988) has shown that it is possible to make degrees of justification vary in parallel with the degrees of application of a vague predicate, whatever the notion of justification acknowledged. The important point here is not that 'on balance justified' would itself be a (metalinguistic) vague predicate. It is rather that the degrees of justification of a statement containing a sorites predicate can vary with the degree of truth of that assertion.[34]

A common version of Wright's objection consists of noting, as he does, that an approach in terms of degrees simply transposes vagueness to the metalinguistic level: if a vague predicate F is applied only to a certain degree to an object a, then it can be said that *it is vague that Fa*, or that *vaguely Fa*, and the vagueness is then 'second-degree' vagueness. But this vagueness can itself be vague: it is vague that it is vague that Fa. In fact, there is no reason for knowing a priori when a vague predicate is applied vaguely or not. There can be borderline cases of borderline cases, and borderline cases of borderline cases of borderline cases, and so on. Why should the same not be true of degrees: in what cases do we recognise that a sentence is neither totally true nor totally false, and therefore, that sorites reasoning can be applied?[35] But this is a point that the approach in terms of degrees recognises and acknowledges. As Sainsbury says:

> A plausible degree theory will not hold that there is a definite point on the associated dimension of comparison at which the borderline case begins. So it will not hold that there is a definite point on the dimension at which the predicate is associated with intermediate degrees of truths: a definite extension to the cases in which the application is neither (completely) true nor (completely) false. This higher-order vagueness, representable as the vagueness of 'definitely F', should also be manifest in actual use.[36]

It follows that the approach in terms of degree does not amount to saying that vagueness might be *eliminated*, in the sense that it would always be possible to give precise conditions of application for a vague predicate. But by acknowledging that *there are* degrees of application of a vague predicate, and that the presence of these degrees accounts for the fact that the sentences in which they figure are able not to be totally true or totally false, the champion of this theory is accounting for cases in which these predicates can give rise to sorite reasoning and offer a diagnosis enabling them to be blocked. What the theory in terms of degrees denies is that the use of a vague predicate is incoherent in the sense that it would produce contradictions that sorite arguments exemplify, that is to say is arbitrary.

One generally comes up against two sorts of cases: on the one hand, those in which the object considered will be clearly recognised as a borderline case; on the other hand, those where one does not know whether one is dealing with a definite case or not. In terms of degrees, the difference is between the case where neither the application nor the non-application of the term is correct (if the degree of truth of a combination $Fa \ \& \ -A$ is of 0.5 for each member; in which case, the combination has 0.5 as its value), and between the case where one does not know if the application is entirely correct (if the degree of Fa is 0.75, for example). In the first type of case, the subject will refrain from judging that Fa. In the second case, the subject will be able to judge that Fa, but will be able to abandon his judgement if necessary in the presence of data that attenuate it. But in a general way the use of a vague predicate does not lead to arbitrariness. It is certainly arbitrary to say that an individual is a child if his existence has lasted n seconds, and that he has ceased to be a child at $n + 1$ seconds, and it is in this sense that sorite predicates are regarded as contradictory. But if the theory in terms of degrees is correct the use of vague terms like 'child' is not arbitrary in the sense that in borderline cases, for example a children's judge might be able to assert that x is and is not a child at the same time.

10.5 The 'reality' of vagueness

The approach to vagueness defended here is far from being the only one possible. In particular, it contrasts with the three-valued approach suggested above (§ 3.1) which, as has been seen, comes up against the problem of penumbral connections. It admits that the principle of bivalence ceases to be valid for a vague language; it admits that *modus ponens* cannot be applied when dealing with a sorites predicate; and it admits that when a combination $A \ \& \ -A$ contains a proposition A of a degree 0.5, this combination has the same value as A itself. This supposes a radical divergence from classical logic. But this approach does not admit that vague sentences do not have truth value. If truth values have degrees contained on a continuum between 0 and 1, the truth values of complex sentences remain a function of the truth values of simple sentences, and vague sentences are not merely given the value 'indeterminate' as in a three-valued logic.[37]

What are the consequences of this distinction between classical logic and semantics, on the one hand, and the logic and semantics of vagueness on the other? In particular, if classical logic and semantics are connected to the 'realist' thesis as Dummett maintains (§ 6.3–5), does the adoption of a logic and semantics peculiar to vague languages lead us to abandon this thesis and opt for anti-realism and for a radical revision of classical logic?

According to Dummett, the realist maintains that every statement is true or false in a *determinate way*: for every statement, there is something in reality by virtue of which it is true or false. If this something is a fact, there cannot be 'vague' facts, and every statement divides the world into only two possible states of affairs: those that make the statement true, and those that make it false.[38] If certain statements, such as 'There were an odd number of blades of grass on the lawn at Luxembourg on 29 May 1903', are unverifiable, the realist maintains that there is nevertheless a 'fact of the matter', a fact in the world, that verifies it, even if we are not in a position to establish it. For the realist, vagueness cannot be a feature of reality but only a feature of our knowledge, or the product of a limitation of our abilities. It follows that reality must always be able to be described in precise terms. The anti-realist, on the contrary, maintains that the principle of bivalence admits exceptions, particularly in the case of vague statements. The anti-realist is not thereby maintaining that the principle of bivalence is *false*. He is only saying that one does not know if it is true, and refuses to assert it, even by virtue of his conception of truth as assertibility. Consequently, he is not maintaining that there would be vague facts corresponding to vague statements, nor that there would be vague objects. If he admitted this he would be conceding to the realist the conception of a correspondence of statements to a reality transcendent in respect of our means of recognition. From this point of view, realist and anti-realist are in agreement in saying that vagueness is not a feature of reality, but of our knowledge. But they say it is the name of radically different conceptions of truth. For the first, vagueness is a feature of our knowledge because reality cannot itself be vague. For the second, vagueness is a feature of our knowledge because it cannot be a feature of anything else, for no reality transcendent to our knowledge exists.[39] But this partial agreement between realism and anti-realism is the reason why a realist like Frege and an anti-realist like Dummett can agree on the fact that vague predicates are incoherent. For the one, they are incoherent because reality must *necessarily* be non-vague. For the other, they are incoherent because vagueness points to the fact that there are undecidable statements. For the one, vagueness must always be able to be eliminated, because it is not a feature of reality. For the other, it cannot be eliminated because it is a necessary feature of our knowledge. Dummett does not maintain that this is a good thing; he admits that it is an unavoidable evil.[40]

Which side will the champion of a semantics of vagueness in terms of degrees take here: that of the realist or that of the anti-realist? As in the theory of meaning (Chapter 6), it all depends on the criterion of realism adopted. Let us go back to the criteria of realism acknowledged by Dummett (§ 6.5): (I) acceptance of the principle of bivalence; (II) the truth-conditional conception of meaning; (III) the transcendent character of truth in respect of verification. The semantics of vagueness in terms of degrees rejects (I): in this sense, it is in accordance with anti-realism. It rejects neither (II) nor (III). In the first place, this semantics is truth conditional and in accordance with the Tarskian schema 'S is true iff p'. This schema is true if and only if S has the same degree of truth as p, and is true in a definite way in this case, in an indefinite way in another case; but in yet another case, the degree of truth value of S will be determined by the degree of truth value of its component sentences.[41] In other words, when S is a vague sentence, the (T) convention and the truth-conditional schema do not cease to be valid. 'True' itself becomes a vague metalinguistic predicate, as we have already noted above (§ 10.4.2). A semantics of vagueness therefore does not abandon the biconditional schema because vague sentences are not true in a determinate way. To say that a sentence is able not to be true or false in a determined way is to abandon the principle of bivalence. But it is not to abandon the Tarskian schema, because it is possible to say that

> *S is true in conditions* ϕ

and to acknowledge that the distinction between the conditions ϕ and other circumstances is itself vague.[42] In the second place, the degree of truth of a vague proposition is not necessarily accessible to our knowledge (it is not an observational notion, as has been noted in § 10.4.1). In this sense, it is a notion, transcendent in respect of our verification, and therefore 'realist' in sense (III). (I) can therefore be rejected, without rejecting (II) and (III). From the anti-realist point of view, it would be tempting to conclude that this semantics leads to a contradictory position. As in § 6.5, I would rather be tempted to conclude that this shows that realism cannot consist of criteria (I)–(III) conjointly, and that the principle of bivalence by itself is not enough to define realism. I therefore conclude on this point that the semantics of vagueness in terms of degrees is neither realist nor anti-realist in the Dummettian sense, but that it is realist according to criteria (II) and (III). Does this imply that there is vagueness in reality? As we have seen (§ 9.5), the idea that there could be vague objects is difficult to admit, if it means anything. But if we stick to the semantics proposed, there is no reason to admit it. If we assign a vague predicate to objects, either it is applied to a definite degree or it is not applied in a definite way. It does not follow that the *objects* are vague.

Lastly, up to what point does vagueness lead to a modification of classical logic? Most authors acknowledge that classical logic must be modified in one way or another. The modification considered here is more than an extension of classical logic: it implies a rejection of some of its principles. But this modification is local: it concerns essentially vague terms like sorites predicates. It supposes that we are able to circumscribe the phenomenon of vagueness and that it does not infect all logic. It implies not a radical but a partial revision of classical logic.

—— PART 4 ——
The domain of logic

── 11 ──

THE PROVINCE OF LOGIC

11.1 The problem of the demarcation of logic

11.1.1 The problem of the nature of logical constants

The problem of the demarcation of logic is, in the first place, the problem of knowing what distinguishes logic from other disciplines: is it, according to a traditional conception, a science radically different from the others, prior to them, which would contain their underlying principles? Or is it only one science among the others, distinct from them only because it deals with truths of a more general or of a more particular kind? Let us call this problem the problem of *external* demarcation: what is the boundary-line between the domain of the logical and the domain of the extralogical? There is, however, another problem, concerning the *internal* demarcation of logic: among the so-called 'logical' systems, is there one system (or are there several systems) which would, better than the others, represent 'logic' as such? The first problem is about the identity of logic. The second problem is about its uniqueness.

Although they are distinct, these problems are not independent of one another. For how can we say that logic is distinct from other disciplines because it has certain features or because it answers certain criteria, without using as a point of reference one or several systems of logic that are supposed to have these features or to answer these criteria? And how can we elect one or several systems of logic as representative of the domain of logic in general, without determining what logic *is* and what distinguishes it from other disciplines?

We need a framework for analysis in order to compare various criteria of demarcation of the logical from the extralogical and to give an answer to the problem of whether there is only one logic or whether there are many. But it is dubious whether one can adopt a completely neutral framework that would not presuppose any answer to the questions of internal demarcation and of the external demarcation. In what follows, I shall take up the framework I have already used and developed in several cases, and I shall try to show how it is possible, within this framework, to give several possible answers to these questions about the demarcation of logic.

In the foregoing, I have identified the problem of the demarcation of logic with the problem of knowing what is a *logical constant*. A logic is a certain kind of language, closed under a relation of deduction, and allowing us to determine the truth conditions of certain propositions. The class of truths is itself relative to certain primitive expressions of the language, called the logical constants. Delimiting this class is delimiting the scope of a logic, that is what kind of truths and what kind of inferences are admissible according to this logic. And to give a criterion of demarcation for logical constants comes down to giving a criterion that would allow us to fix their *meaning* within the language. Now there are, as we have seen in Chapter 2 with propositional constants, two canonical ways of giving the meaning of logical constants: through the *semantics* for these constants, that is through the *truth* conditions of the propositions within which they occur, and through their *syntax*, that is through a set of *inference rules* delimiting the inferences in which they occur. These two ways of sorting out the logical constants can be put into correspondence respectively with two traditional conceptions of logic: as a science of truths, and as a science of inferences. One of the questions that I want to ask here is the following: are these two ways of fixing the meaning of logical constants equivalent? Do they determine the same class? If so, what are the consequences that we are allowed to draw about the nature of logic? If not, what is the right conception?

We have encountered the problem of the choice of a logic with the distinction between *classical* logical constants and *non-classical* logical constants. Thus it has been asked in what sense the classical quantifiers were 'classical', as compared to substitutional quantifiers and second-order quantifiers (Chapter 4) and whether traditional 'terms' could be preferred to these (Chapter 3). It has been asked in what sense identity can be a classical logical constant (Chapter 9). It has been asked whether the modal operators of necessity or of possibility were logical constants (Chapter 7). It has been asked whether the intuitionist logical constants could supplant the classical logical constants under the semantical anti-realist hypothesis (Chapter 6). Finally it has been asked whether a vagueness operator could be introduced as a logical constant (Chapter 10). In each case, I have assumed that these languages could be given a coherent semantical treatment, provided there were some adjustments of the Tarskian mould, and that there was, *in this sense*, no reason to refuse to call them 'logics'. But I have not thereby accepted the thesis that *any* logical constant is admissible.

In this chapter, I shall give only a partial answer to the question: 'Is there only one right logic?' and to the question whether classical logic can be revised. A more satisfactory answer to the question whether we should speak of a plurality of logics must await a more precise determination of the criteria of logical constanthood. I shall deal mainly in this chapter with the problem of external demarcation, and I shall come back to the problem of internal demarcation in the next chapter.

Finding a criterion of demarcation for logic is, to a large extent, finding a criterion of demarcation for the logical constants. But how should we start on this investigation?

11.1.2 The traditional criteria

It can be supposed that whatever the class of constants defined as 'logical', the set of logical truths and of logical inferences should bear the characteristics usually attributed to these truths and inferences.

Thus it is often said that logical truths and inferences are distinct from other truths and inferences because they are *formal*, or because they are true or valid independently of the content of the terms that occur in them. As Ryle said, they are 'topic neutral'. But what does one mean by that? Does one mean that logic is formal because it does not bear upon any object (that logic is totally abstract), or because it bears upon all objects (that it is perfectly general), or because it bears upon a special type of objects (so-called 'formal' objects)? How should we understand here the relationship between form and content?

It is also said that logical truths and inferences are *necessary*. An inference from premises A, B, to a conclusion C is said to be valid if and only if the premises being true, the conclusion *must* be true. But how should we understand this necessity? Are logical truths true because they describe immutable states of the universe (they are true 'in all possible worlds'), and if so what distinguishes them from laws of nature? Or are they true because they are the products of certain conventions responsible for their necessity?

It is also said that logical truths and inferences are *a priori*: we can recognise them independently of experience and of empirical facts, either because they describe non-empirical facts, or because they do not describe any *facts* at all – they are thus said to correspond to *norms* that we accept. But what is *a priori* knowledge, and in what sense is the logical *a priori* distinct from other forms of *a priori* knowledge (such as the apriority usually attributed to mathematical knowledge, for instance)?

Another characteristic of logical truths which comes more or less with the other features is that they are *obvious*. Obviousness is, to a large extent, a psychological or subjective property, and therefore a very relative one. But we should account for this feeling of self-evidence that comes with logical truths.

Finally, philosophers often say that logical truths and inferences have the characteristics just mentioned because they are *analytic*, analyticity being the property formed out of the conjunction of the properties of formality, necessity and apriority. But what does it mean to say that a truth or an inference is analytic?

These notions are notoriously obscure, but apart from the last one, which is often invoked as a philosophical explanation of the others, each of them is well entrenched within our intuitive conception of logical truth. Every conception of logical truth that would imply a rejection of these characteristics would have to carry the burden of proof. Correlatively, we can conjecture that every authentic criterion of the demarcation of logic will have to justify one or other of these characteristics. As Ian Hacking (1979) says 'Without the idea of analyticity, who would care about what logic *is*?' This does not imply, as we shall see, that analyticity is, by itself, the criterion that we need. Nevertheless, if there exists such a criterion, it will have to involve the properties that we usually attribute to analytic statements.

11.1.3 Metatheoretical criteria

Instead of trying to circumscribe the domain of logic from general properties difficult to define such as analyticity, one can rather try to formulate some criteria by using *prima facie* clearer properties, such as the metatheoretical properties that logicians themselves establish about the systems that they study. I shall enumerate some of these properties.

The least that one can expect from a logical system seems to be *consistency* or *non-contradiction*. Aristotle claims, in *Metaphysics* Γ, that the law of non-contradiction $(-(A \& -A))$ is the minimal condition of rational argumentation, and in this sense of logic in general[1]. By definition, from two contradictory propositions, one can infer anything (*ex falso sequitur quodlibet*), and to reject the law of contradiction from a system of logic is to accept that anything can be derived from anything. (Some logicians and philosophers object to the requirement of non-contradiction, but I leave aside this point here – see, however, § 12.7 below.) In general a system S is said to be *consistent* or *non-contradictory* in the *relative* sense if and only if no formula of S and its negation is a theorem of S, and a system is said to be *consistent* in the *absolute* sense if and only if at least one formula of S is not a theorem of S.

Consistency warrants that not all the formulas of a system are theorems. *Completeness* is the property of a formal system that guarantees us that all the formulas we want as theorems or as logical truths are actually theorems or logical truths. There are in fact several notions of completeness, and this term sometimes designates absolute consistency, which is also called 'strong' completeness[2]. The notion we are interested in here is *semantical* or *weak* completeness. A system S is said to be *complete* in this sense if and only if (1) every logical truth of S is a theorem of S, and (2) if every theorem is a logical truth. It is sometimes said that S is *sound* when it satisfies the second condition and simply complete when it satisfies the first. Completeness is essential for establishing the equivalence between the two notions, syntactic and semantic, of logical consequence. Completeness gives us, to take up Dummett's phrase, a 'justification of deduction' (see above § 6.4.2): if, on the one hand, we possess a syntactic characterisation of logical consequence, we have only an intuitive justification of our inference rules, and the soundness theorem (2) guarantees that this justification is not only intuitive, and if, on the other hand, we have a semantical notion of logical consequence, the completeness theorem – in the sense of (1) – guarantees that all logically valid formulas can be proved from the rules, and thus that we can *know* that they are valid.[3].

Another property closely related to completeness is *compacity*. Under its semantic version, compacity holds if every finite subset of a set Γ of formulas of a system S has a model (is true under one interpretation), then Γ has a model, and if, if Δ is a logical consequence of Γ, then Δ is a semantical consequence of a proper subset of Γ. Under its syntactic version, compacity warrants that every syntactical derivation of a formula Δ of S is finite. This property is closely related to completeness, and guarantees this latter property because, by definition, a formal derivation contains only a finite number of inferences, and each inference has only a finite number of premises. If compacity fails, there is thus no possibility of showing that completeness holds. In this sense the notion of compacity is at least as important as the notion of completeness, because since a number of theories admit a finite number of axioms it seems possible that a logic cannot prove all the logical consequences of these theories, whereas a theory that is both complete and compact can give us such a proof.[4]

Decidability is another property of a formal system. It is said that a system S is *decidable* if and only if there exists an effective procedure that allows, for every arbitrary formula of S, one to determine whether or not it is a theorem. This definition depends upon the notion of 'effective procedure', for which there is no precise definition, but which can be understood in the following sense: a procedure is effective if and only if it stops after a finite number of steps involving previously defined operations. For instance in propositional logic, the truth-table method is an effective procedure.[5]

Finally a system can have the *Löwenheim–Skolem* property. It is said (under one of the versions of this theorem) that a system S has this property if and only if, for every finite set X of formulas of S, if X is satisfiable, then X is satisfiable in the domain of positive natural integers. In other words (for some particular case) if a formula of S has a model it has a *denumerable* model. The Löwenheim–Skolem theorem belongs to model theory; it concerns the cardinality of the models which make a logical formula true, and it has some important consequences, which I shall examine below, for the relationship between logic and mathematics.

These are not the only metatheoretical properties that one can envisage. But it can be asked whether any one, or several, of them are necessary and sufficient for the characterisation of a system as 'logical'.

The question is now the following: what are the relationships between these metatheoretical properties of logical systems and the general properties of logic mentioned above, and can an analysis of these relationships allow us to formulate a criterion of demarcation for logical constants? I shall envisage several possible criteria in turn.

11.2 Analyticity and logical truth

As I remarked above, many philosophers have tried to formulate a criterion of demarcation for logic by using the notion of analyticity. The thesis that logical truths are analytic belongs to a long tradition, from Leibniz to Carnap, including Kant, Bolzano, and Frege.[6] This tradition, however, is not homogeneous: there are many concepts of analyticity. For Leibniz analytic truths are truths of reason, true 'in all possible worlds'. For Kant, a judgement is analytic if the predicate is contained in the subject, or if its negation is contradictory. To oversimplify, one can say that the recent history of the notion bears the mark of two main features. The first is that the term 'analytic' has been applied more and more to linguistic entities, such as sentences or statements, instead of thought contents or judgements. The paradigmatic expression of this view is the logical positivists' thesis according to which analytic truths are a species of linguistic truths. The second feature is the appearance, in the twentieth century, of two extreme positions: logicism, on the one hand, in the Fregean or in the Russellian sense, according to which mathematical truths are reduced to analytical truths via the reduction of the former to logical truths; and conventionalism, on the other hand, according to which analytical truths are linguistic and true by virtue of linguistic conventions. The failure of logicism as a reduction of mathematics to logic has been largely responsible for the disrepute of the logicist criteria of logical truths, but the notion of analyticity has not been rejected none the less. For the fact that mathematics is not, in the logicist sense, analytic can serve as a negative criterion to sort out the specificity of logical truth, which can still be characterised as a kind of linguistic truth, thus allowing a reformulation of the logicist thesis as the thesis that mathematical truths are a species of conventional truths.[7] I shall leave aside the specific problem of logicism, in order to deal only with this latter characterisation, due to Carnap.

Carnap formulates the analytic/synthetic distinction as a distinction between statements true by virtue of the meanings of the terms which they contain, and statements true by virtue of extralinguistic empirical facts. For him, there are two kinds of analytic truths: logical truths proper, such as

(1) Fido is black or non-black

and non-logical analytic truths, such as

(2) Every bachelor is unmarried.

The former are true by virtue of the meanings of logical constants ('or', 'not'), while the latter are true by virtue of the meanings of the descriptive terms ('bachelor', 'unmarried').[8] Let us suppose that we accept the concept of analyticity as 'truth by virtue of meaning alone'. The problem then arises of how we can distinguish truths in the style of (1), which we can call analytic in the narrow sense, from truths in the style of (2), which we can call analytic in the wide sense.[9] Carnap says that (1) is true by virtue of the *semantical rules* of the language in which 'or' and 'not' occur as logical constants, and that in this sense (1) is 'L-true', that is 'true in all possible worlds' (or 'state-descriptions' – see § 1.1.2.2). He also says that (2) is true by virtue of 'meaning-postulates' or 'conventions' that we accept as governing the descriptive terms 'bachelor' and 'unmarried'. In this sense, Carnap does not see any difficulty in the fact that (2) can, by the effect of other conventions, cease to be analytical with respect to certain conventions and become analytical with respect to other conventions (if, for instance, we decide to call a 'bachelor' a married man who lives separated from his wife). Everything is a matter of the decisions and of the linguistic rules that we accept.[10]

But it is difficult to see how the notion of 'semantical rule' or of 'meaning postulate' allows us to discriminate the *logical* analytical truths from analytical truths in the wide sense, since both are the product of linguistic conventions, and are in this sense arbitrary. Nothing prevents us, according to Carnap's conception, from choosing other semantical rules and thus other logical constants: 'It cannot be the logician's task to prescribe to those who construct systems which postulates they must adopt. They are free to choose their postulates, guided not by their beliefs about facts of the world, but by their intentions about meanings'.[11] It follows that there is no objective criterion of demarcation of logical constants.

We have already encountered this difficulty (§ 2.3.1) with Prior's connective 'tonk': if the meaning of a logical constant is fixed only through conventional inference rules, how can we rule out weird or contradictory constants such as 'tonk'? Carnap's conception does not allow us to answer this question, because it does not tell us *which* conventions are admissible. Carnap, presumably, excludes conventions leading to contradictions such as those for 'tonk'. But he does not tell why, in general, a convention is admissible, or why it should be ruled out.

This objection from arbitrariness is one of those addressed to Carnap by Quine in his famous paper 'Two dogmas of empiricism' (Quine, 1953). As Quine remarks, if we say, following Carnap, that a statement is analytic if and only if it is analytic in a language L by virtue of the semantical rules for L, we only define 'analytic-for-L', relative to a given language, and we do not define analyticity in general, for any language whatsoever. And if logical constants are themselves relative to the semantical rules of L, while they could change according to other rules or meaning postulates, how could our criterion of demarcation of these constants be invariant across languages? Carnap's answer is that indeed this criterion is not invariant, although it is relative. This begs our very question: can there be a non-relative and objective criterion for logical constants?

11.3 Logical truth and logical form

11.3.1 The substitutional conception of logical truth

We are thus led to look for a criterion of demarcation of logical truth that would be independent of the Carnapian criterion of analyticity. It seems more promising to say that logical truth and inferences are formal. What does it mean? According to Quine, mainly this: a sentence is true because of its form if and only if all the sentences of the same *form* or of the same *logical structure* are true, and an inference is valid if and only if all the inferences which have the same structure are valid. For instance the inference

> (3) If the weather is fine, there are many tourists; the weather is fine, therefore there are many tourists

is said to be valid because whatever sentences are substituted for the sentences 'the weather is fine' and 'there are many tourists', the resulting inference will be equally valid, because the structure

> if p, then q; p; therefore q

stays invariant across the substitutions for the propositional variables. In other words, a logical truth or inference that is logically valid is a truth *that remains such under all substitutions of its non-logical constants.* Quine favours this 'substitutional' definition of logical truth for two reasons.[12]

First, it implies that truth-bearers are sentences, since only linguistic entities, such as sentences, can lend themselves to substitutions. The fact that logical truths have a structure does not imply that their bearers are sentences, since intensional entities, such as Propositions, can be structured (§ 1.2.3). Nevertheless, linguistic entities are excellent candidates for being structured entities. One can see all the advantages that a defender of Tarski's theory of truth can draw from this conception, since for him the truth-bearers are sentences, and truth can be, in a formal language, defined from the logical structure of its sentences.

The substitutional conception has also, it seems, another advantage. It allows us to sort out the truths and inferences that we consider as true (valid) by virtue of the meanings of their terms, though we are not prepared to call them logical truths or inferences. This is the case of (2) as opposed to (1) and of

> (4) Milicent knows that life is short; *therefore* life is short.

as opposed to (3). (4) is valid by virtue of the meaning of 'knows that', whereas we can discern a structure in (3).

11.3.2 Logical form

The substitutional definition of logical truth, however, is no more illuminating than the definition through analyticity, since saying that logical truths remain true under all substitutions of *non-logical* constants presupposes a previous determination of *logical* constants. Until the class of these constants has not been delimited, Quine's definition is bound to be as arbitrary as Carnap's.

Quine (1970), however, proposes to extend the notion of structure to grammatical structure: 'A logical truth is a sentence the grammatical structure of which is such that all the sentences which share its structure are true.'[13] But what, then, must count as an identity of grammatical structure? Must grammar, in the sense of the determination of the class of grammatically correct sentences, have authority upon logic? Quine proposes the following criterion: grammatical particles, are, unlike lexical expressions, those that are substitutable, *salva congruitate* (without a loss of grammaticality) with expressions from a *finite* class. Lexical expressions, on the contrary, are interchangeable with the expressions from an infinite class. For instance in the sentence 'The philosopher thinks or does not think', one can substitute for 'philosopher' and 'thinks' an infinity of terms of the lexicon, whereas only a finite set of constructions (for instance 'and', if . . . then' and so on, can be substituted for 'or'. The proposed definition accentuates the dependency of logical truths upon language. But the price paid for this is a considerable extension of the notion of logical truth, since, ultimately, all grammatical constructions become 'logical forms' (we have seen, in § 4.4, that some linguists are ready to accept this). The demarcation becomes as difficult as before, since it supposes the demarcation of the class of grammatical sentences, which is bound to be, however it is determined, extremely large.

Tarski had seen this difficulty, when he wrote in 1935:

> [The division of all terms of the language discussed into logical and extra-logical] is certainly not quite arbitrary. If, for example we were to include among the extra-logical signs the implication sign, or the universal quantifier, then our definition of the concept of consequence would lead to results which obviously contradict ordinary usage. On the other hand, no objective grounds are known to me which permit us to draw a sharp boundary between the two groups of terms. It seems to be possible to include among logical terms some which are usually regarded by logicians as extra-logical without running into consequences which stand in sharp contrast to ordinary usage. In the extreme case, we could regard all terms of the language as logical. The concept of *formal* consequence would then coincide with that of *material* consequence. (Tarski, 1956, pp. 418–19)

Must we conclude then that we cannot delimitate logical constants except by enumerating them in an arbitrary list? The notion of logical constant is relative to the notion of logical form, the latter being itself relative to our account of inferences within a particular language. Let us suppose, for instance, that we have to account for the 'logical form' of the sentences of a natural language. As Davidson says:

> Much of the interest of logical form comes from an interest in logical geography: to give the logical form of a sentence is to give its logical location in the totality of sentences, to describe it in a way that explicitly determines what sentences it entails and what sentences it is entailed by. The location must be given relative to a specific deductive theory; so logical form itself is relative to a theory. The relativity does not stop here, either, since even given a theory of deduction there may be more than one total scheme for interpreting the sentences we are interested in and that preserves the pattern of entailments.

The logical form of a particular sentence is, then, relative both to a theory of deduction and to some prior determinations as to how to render sentences in the language of the theory.[14]

It follows that there is not *one* single logical form for a natural language sentence. To take an excessively simple example, a syllogistic inference such as

(5) All the *A*s are *B*s, all the *B*s are *C*s, therefore all the *A*s are *C*s

can receive a propositional logical form such as

(5′) $A{\rightarrow}B$, $B{\rightarrow}C$, therefore $A{\rightarrow}C$

or a quantificational form such as

(5″) $(\forall x)(Ax{\rightarrow}Bx)$, $(\forall x)(Bx{\rightarrow}Cx)$, therefore $(\forall x)(Ax{\rightarrow}Cx)$

On the one hand, the validity of (5) is relative to the choice of the logical forms (5′) or (5″). On the other hand, these two formalisations equally preserve the validity of an argument. In other cases, the choice of a logical form will affect the validity of an argument. A widely studied case is the case of intuitively valid inferences involving adverbial modifiers, such as:

(6) Livingstone walks in the jungle
   Therefore Livingstone walks.

We can present (6) as a propositional inference of the form

(6′) (In the jungle) Livingstone walks
   Therefore Livingstone walks

by treating the adverb 'in the jungle' as a sentence operator, or by treating the adverb as a place-holder within a two-place predicate '(*x* walks, *y*)' with

(6″) Walks (*Livingstone, In the jungle*)
   Therefore Walks (*Livingstone*)

Either way, we cannot account for the validity of (6′)–(6″) as a matter of *form*, since we cannot know whether (6′) is valid unless we know the meaning of 'in the jungle', and since (6″) is plainly invalid in predicate logic. According to Davidson's celebrated analysis of adverbial modification, the verb of action 'walks' is not a one-place predicate true of an object, but a two-place predicate true of an object and of an event. Thus the logical form of (6) must involve a quantification over this event (*x*), and the modifier itself must be treated as a predicate of the event:

(6‴) $(\exists x)$(Walks (*Livingstone, x*)) & In the jungle (*x*)
   Therefore $(\exists x)$ (Walks (*Livingstone, x*))

(6‴) is thus valid according to the usual rules of predicate logic (provided, however, that we accept a two-sorted quantification over events and people).[15] The choice of a translation scheme in 'logical form' will vary on the one hand according to the *expressive powers* of the logical language, and on the other hand according to the way this language guarantees the properties of deduction. If we emphasize the expressive power, our choice of logical form will be motivated by the need to account for a maximum number of intuitively valid inferences and we shall be tempted to widen the class of logical constants accordingly. For instance we may, with respect to (4), add 'knows that' to the list of our logical constants. If we follow this strategy, nothing prevents us, in principle, from widening the list *ad libitum*. But there is a price: that the properties of the corresponding theory of deduction diminish accordingly. For instance, is a logic with an operator 'knows that' consistent and complete? Is the requirement of expressivity always compatible with the requirement of completeness, according to which our deductions must be stable and warranted? From this point of view, (6''') preserves the classical constants and reconciles the two requirements. But these often conflict with one another. To take up again example (5), one knows that these inferences in propositional form will always be decidable, and the same is true of monadic quantificational forms. But this will not be the case for the *dyadic* predicate calculus.[16]

We can, using a distinction due to Quine, and taken up by Gareth Evans,[17] distinguish two kinds of theories of logical form, and therefore of logical constanthood. The one is *immanent* to a given language, and prescribes deductive properties relative to a background logical theory, and the other is *transcendent*, is not relative to a given theory of deduction, and determines which expressions *should be* treated as logical constants. The foregoing considerations tend to show that there is no transcendent definition of logical constants, but that there are only immanent definitions. This is Tarski's and Quine's position. Does it imply the consequence of the conventionalist account according to which the list of logical constants is arbitrary or relative to our particular interests? No, because the claim that there is no general criterion of demarcation of logical constants does not imply that we should choose any list we like. There are in fact, as we shall see, very strong reasons to limit the list to the classical logical constants of first-order logic.

11.4 The paradigm of first-order logic

11.4.1 Quine's criterion

Classical first-order logic is often called 'standard' or 'canonical'. What are the reasons for this privilege? We often content ourselves with justifications such as the following: 'First-order logic is at the same time the simplest, the most powerful and the most applicable of modern logic'.[18] But these criteria are vague and relative. The propositional calculus is obviously simpler, structurally speaking, than predicate logic. Furthermore, it is, unlike (*n*-adic) predicate logic, decidable. On the other hand, predicate logic, although it is more powerful (in the sense of more expressive) than propositional logic (it allows us to prove more theorems), is less powerful than modal logic, or second-order logic, which allows us to represent quantifications over properties or sets. If, however, the 'power' of a logic means that it has a greater number of metatheoretical properties, first-order logic is more powerful than modal logic or second-order logic, as we shall see. Applicability is a very relative notion.

If we restrict ourselves for the moment to the opposition between first-order and second-order logic, we can say that there exists at least one distinguishing formal criterion: the former is complete, whereas the latter is not. First-order logic is complete in both senses (1) and (2) above: it is complete in the narrow sense since all valid formulas can be proved by a standard proof procedure (this was established by Gödel 1930), and sound in the sense that only valid formulas can be proved in it. Second-order logic, on the contrary, although it is sound, is not complete (this was shown by Gödel's *incompleteness* theorem in 1931). One can say that this a deep, and not a merely 'technical' difference, for, as we have seen above, the completeness of a system is the property that allows us to know that if some formulas can be proved with certain inference rules, these formulas can be known to be true. This feature acquires its importance when first-order logic is compared to second-order logic. The latter, unlike the former, allows us to represent the propositions of mathematics and of set theory, and this has a greater expressive power. Its proof procedure, however, is incomplete. Therefore the completeness theorem allows us to differentiate first-order logic from mathematics. Many writers have thus proposed to consider completeness as the distinctive property of logic itself. Thus Kneale writes:

> It is easy to distinguish the restricted calculus of propositional functions which is known to be deductively complete from the theory of sets (or the corresponding higher-order functional calculus) which has been shown to be not only incomplete by incompletable, and it seems reasonable to say that the former should be called logic and not the latter. For the word 'logic' is connected traditionally with discussions of rules of inference; and while it is strange to apply it to any axiomatic system such as that of Frege, it is even more strange to apply it to a system in which the consequences of the axioms are not all accessible by inference from the axioms. Yet that, as we can now see in the light of Gödel's theorem, is what Frege did when he undertook to reduce arithmetic to logic. Where he noticed only a difference of levels, there is in reality a gulf that may properly be taken as the boundary of logic.[19]

Is completeness sufficient to demarcate logic, and in this sense does it limit the province of logic to first-order? No, since there are many logics with more expressive resources than first-order logic that are nevertheless complete, such as the logic that admits a quantifier 'There are undenumerably many x' or such as so-called 'normal' modal logics[20].

It is, however, possible to establish the discontinuity between first and second order differently, by considering another property of first-order logic, the Löwenheim-Skolem theorem. Second-order logic does not have this property: there is at least one formula of second-order logic the models of which are interpretations in non-denumerable models.[21]

There is, according to Quine, a strong link between his own views about logic, and in particular his own substitutional definition of logical truth, and the Löwenheim–Skolem theorem. Quine (1970) remarks that there is another definition of logical truth than the substitutional definition, namely the *model-theoretic* definition: a given statement (or more precisely, a statement-schema) is valid if it is satisfied by all models. But models are sets, or sequences of sets. Now, not every statement determines a set. There are some statements, such as the statement expressing Russell's paradox (the set of all sets that are not members of themselves is a member of itself):

$$x \, \varepsilon \, x \equiv -(x \, \varepsilon \, x) \text{ (where 'x' is the mentioned set)}$$

which determine no set. And there are some sets, such as the one that gives rise to Grelling's paradox – the set of all the object-language statements which do not satisfy themselves – which are determined by no statement.[22] From the Löwenheim–Skolem theorem, however, two other theorems can be drawn, which show the equivalence of the substitutional definition of logical truth and of the model-theoretic definition, provided that the object-language is rich enough to express the arithmetic of natural whole numbers:

(I) if a schema is true for all the substitutions of statements of elementary arithmetic, then it is satisfied by every model;

(II) if a schema is satisfied by every model, then it is true for every substitution of a statement.[23]

In other terms, as Quine shows, a schema is provable if and only if it is valid (true under all its interpretations) if and only if every substitutional instance of this schema in a language that is rich enough is true. The equivalence of validity and provability is warranted by the completeness theorem. This result holds only for first-order logic. Therefore this logic is characterised by a close link between, on the one hand, the Löwenheim–Skolem theorem and the completeness theorem, and on the other hand, by the correspondence between the substitutional and the model-theoretic definitions of logical truth. Thus there is a 'remarkable' coincidence between the definition of logical truth and the restriction of this definition to first-order logic.

It follows that the conjunction of completeness and of the Löwenheim–Skolem property allows us to limit the arbitrariness of the substitutional definition of logic. As we have seen above, this definition is not sufficient to demarcate the class of logical constants, since we can apply the substitutional definition to any kind of constant. But the constants of first-order logic alone reveal such a strong correspondence between the substitutional and the model-theoretic definitions. Therefore, Quine concludes, we have a strong argument to restrict the application of the substitutional definition. Correlatively, this justifies a maxim about logical form, which Quine calls 'the maxim of minimum mutilation': do not exhibit *more* logical form than is needed to justify the validity of inferences: '*Where it doesn't itch, don't scratch*'.[24] As we have seen above, several different logical forms may represent one single inference as valid, but we should always choose the form that commits us minimally, that is the simplest. Now the simplest structures are those of first-order logic. We thus conciliate pragmatic adequacy with (meta-) theoretical adequacy.

Quine has other arguments to induce us to stick to first-order logic. These are based on his objectual definition of quantification (what I have called in Chapter 4 above 'Quine's thesis'). Quantifying over sets, properties or attributes – as in second-order logic – involves losing the very meaning of quantification, which supposes that we can identify the objects on which we quantify. We have seen above the limits of this thesis and its difficulties, and I have admitted, against Quine, that substitutional quantification, quantification over attributes (Chapter 4) and quantification into modal contexts (Chapter 7) do not involve any major semantic incoherence. But we see better now the price we have to pay if we accept other kinds of quantification than first-order quantification. If we leave aside substitutional quantification, the ontological 'inflation' created by second-order and modal quantifications involves a loss of the correspondence between the substitutional and the model-theoretic definitions of logical truth. The price paid is thus a weakening of the concept of logical truth. It is a characteristic fact of modal logic, for instance, that we are led to prefer for it a definition of logical truth in terms of models and of interpretations, as we have seen in Chapter 7. From a Quinean point of view, this is a very significative fact, because the more we move away from the ontological canons prescribed by first-order logic (to be is to be the value of a variable, and the first-order variables are variables over *individuals*), the more our definition of logical truth loses its chance of being 'pure'.

What the foregoing remarks seem to show is that the more expressive a logic is, the more it deals with a rich domain of objects, the less is it likely to preserve the close link between such metatheoretical properties as completeness and the Löwenheim–Skolem theorem. If we really care about this equilibrium between metatheoretical properties and expressivity, then we have, it seems, a strong reason to limit the domain of logic to first-order logic.

Now, although Quine's definition of logical truth can be understood as an explanation of what it is for (first-order) logic to be 'formal', logic for Quine is by no means formal in the sense of being 'topic neutral', since he rejects the distinction between truths that are true by virtue of meanings alone and truths that are true by virtue of the way the world is. A logical truth is for Quine at least partly true by virtue of the way the world is.[25] Since first-order logic involves quantifiers and variables, and since these carry an ontological weight, logic is in this sense descriptive of the world. Yet for Quine ontology itself is always relative to a background theory, according to his doctrine of 'ontological relativity'. Quine offers two reasons for this thesis. The first one, which I shall only mention, is the indeterminacy of translation, which goes with the *inscrutability of reference*: our referential apparatus is indeterminate with respect to various ways by which we can partition the objects of experience.[26] The other reason is more closely tied to the themes of this chapter. It has to do with the Löwenheim–Skolem theorem. This theorem says, as we have seen, that if a theory has an ontology (if it has models), this ontology must be an ontology of denumerable objects. This is true even of theories that purport to represent non-denumerable universes of objects (this fact is known as 'Skolem's paradox'[27]). Must we conclude from this that Pythagorism, the thesis that the only objects that exist are natural numbers, is true? No, because an ontology of natural numbers has not necessarily an arithmetical interpretation: we cannot say, in any absolute sense, that the objects of a theory are numbers, or that they are sets, or bodies, or whatever, except relatively to a background theory.[28] Thus the Löwenheim–Skolem property runs deeply in Quine's views of the relationships between logic and ontology, and in his limitation of logic to first-order logic.

11.4.2 Granger's criterion

Now, if we accept Quine's argument that first-order logic has these remarkable properties, why should we accept that these are the most remarkable properties that a logic can have, and why could not we try to restrict logic to an even narrower domain? After all, although first-order logic is complete and has the Löwenheim–Skolem property, it is not decidable: there is no effective or mechanical procedure to evaluate the truth or validity of first-order formulas in general. On the contrary, first-order logic *is* decidable, and it alone has this property. This criterion has been proposed by Gilles Granger, who justifies it by a certain conception of what it is, for a given discipline, to be formal.[29]

Like Quine, Granger considers that the completeness criterion is not enough to allow us to delimit the logical from the extralogical. The incompleteness of rich systems, such as second-order logic, justifies only apparently the distinction between logic and mathematics, for we can make this distinction rest on other facts such as the appearance of the notion of infinite in the latter. Indeed it is possible to show, as Tarski did, the completeness of systems dealing with objects that are traditionally included among mathematical objects, such as the algebra of real numbers, the algebra of complex numbers, and of Euclidean geometry, from which none the less the general concepts of whole number and of a set of points are absent.[30] Granger therefore proposes to keep the criterion of decidability only, joined to completeness. The fact that the propositional calculus is, unlike quantification theory, decidable, allows us to limit the logical activity of thinking 'within the circle of formulations which can be directly controlled through a finite number of steps'[31] But decidability alone is not enough, because the 'mathematical' theories proved complete by Tarski are decidable too. Granger proposes therefore another criterion to the effect that the domain of logic is reduced to propositional logic alone. Unlike the former, this criterion is ontological: it requires that the very *objects* of logic be propositions or statements, that is *linguistic objects*. In the propositional calculus, the only objects are statements susceptible of being true or false, or objects *'of whatever kind'* (*'objets quelconques'*), understood independently of any determination. Only this part of logic rests both upon objects and statements through a reduction of objects to statements, allowing us to interpret the calculus directly as a *metalanguage*. On the contrary, as soon as one goes from propositional to first-order logic, logic deals not only with objects 'of whatever kind', but with objects under a certain determination:

> The predicate calculus already opens to us a determinate world in which individuals and their properties – of, if one prefers, elements and classes – are picked out. Only the propositional calculus, therefore, deals with the object in general, with the virtual features of the object, and only in this universe form and content appear as actually indiscernible.[32]

Granger intends to identify logic with the domain where content – that is objects – is reduced to a mere form. According to him, the form/content distinction is a relative distinction, not an absolute one, and it admits several degrees. His conception rests upon a certain view of knowledge in general. Knowledge always introduces a duality between *operations* and *objects*, which is most perceptible in mathematics. In mathematics, for instance, the notion of *group* designates originally a set of operations upon numerical objects; within the theory of groups, however, these objects have been treated as rules independent from their original operations.[33] The same duality holds for every kind of knowledge, which is thus always a certain relation between form (operations) and content (objects). In this sense, it is possible to speak of a certain notion of *formal content*. Propositional logic deals with a very specific relation between form and content: within this logic an object is nothing else than the *invariant of a system of operations*. We are thus at the 'zero degree of content', since content is reduced to the system of operations, and therefore to form alone. The 'content' of propositional logic is 'the complex of rules which define the system'.[34] Granger's definition of logic is very close to a definition given by Gonseth: 'Logic is the physics of objects of whatever kind', it deals only with objects 'without preliminary determination', that is with *formal* objects.[35]

Granger's criterion has two consequences. The first one has just been mentioned: logic does not deal with objects in the sense of objects within a *world*, but only with propositional objects, which are the mere products of a system of operations. It follows from this that the more a logic determines the characters of its objects, the less formal it is. This is in agreement with the consequences that we have drawn above from Quine's criterion. Granger's criterion however, rules out first-order quantifiers as logical constants, since they involve a world composed of individuals and properties, and thus imply that we move one step further along the scale of the form/content relation (quantificational logic could thus be taken as the 'degree 1' of this relation). On the other hand, Granger's criterion agrees with Quine's about modal logic: only *propositional* modal logic is logic proper, since modal operators can be interpreted as operators on statements or as metalinguistic operators (this corresponds to Quine's 'first degree of modal involvement', see § 7.2), whereas quantified modal logic introduces essential properties of objects, and is thus no more, according to the Aristotelian terminology, than an 'apophantic' logic of statements.[36]

The second consequence, according to Granger, is that we have no reason to object to the identification of the zero degree of the form/content relation with the fact that propositional logical truths are *analytic*. Granger's concept of analyticity is the Kantian, and not the Leibnizian or Carnapian concept: a statement is analytically true if it bears on no object, and a statement is synthetic as soon as it bears on a *possible* object or content of experience. This implies that the truths of quantificational logic are, in this sense, synthetic. The validity of the propositions from other parts of (what is usually called) 'logic' than propositional logic depends upon their contents:

> This is not to say that the theorems of the predicate calculus, for instance, are not universally valid; but their validity is determinate for those models which are already specific variants with respect to the *colourless* model which corresponds to the shadow of the formal content of the propositional calculus. Therefore, this content has already been, in a certain way, detached from its form, even if it was actually constituted *a priori*. In the case of the propositional calculus, however, nothing obscures the transparency of the relationship between the operation and the object. The system is decidable, and its content is absolutely the inverse of its form, I shall therefore propose a definition of analyticity in the strict sense which would correspond to the zero degree of formal content. A piece of knowledge expressed within a *complete and decidable* symbolic system would be analytical.[37]

Thus the completeness property implies only a partial degree of formality of a logic, whereas the decidability of the propositional calculus means that it is fully formal.

11.4.3 The degrees of formal content and Lindström's theorem

Granger's conception of logic, as he himself emphasises, and as can be seen from the metaphor of 'colourless objects', is strongly reminiscent of Wittgenstein's *Tractatus*. For Wittgenstein the propositions of logic are tautologies, which as such do not represent any state of the world, and the logical constants do not represent anything: 'My fundamental thought is that the "logical constants" do not denote anything. That the *logic* of fact *could* have no denotations.'[38] The feature is closely related to the fact that, in the *Tractatus*, Wittgenstein does not include the quantifiers among the logical constants: they are reduced to conjunctions and disjunctions or atomic or elementary propositions (see above, § 4.3.2.2). Only propositional connectives are logical constants, which have no 'counterparts' in the world, since they do not represent any object (see § 5.2.1). Now this reduction can only be performed if the universe of objects is supposed to be finite, or when it is presumed that all the objects denoted in these conjunctions or disjunctions are susceptible of having a name. And, as Quine notes, within a finite universe, every ontological consideration loses its force, since when quantifiers can be reduced to such conjunctions or disjunctions, the *referential apparatus* of logic disappears.[39]

Granger himself does not propose any such reduction. But the fact that he assimilates logic to propositional logic actually implies that every ontological concern disappears, and with it every semantical concern, apart from concerns about the truth or falsity of propositions. As soon as a logic has a referential apparatus, it involves an ontology, and in this sense it outlines a possible objectual content, thus ceasing to be formal.

Granger's criterion seems to me to be too strong, and to have unwelcome consequences, for the following reasons. Let us suppose, provisionally, that we can accept his notion of 'formal content' and the correlative idea of a hierarchy of levels of the form/content relation. A first difficulty is that the dividing line between logic and mathematics comes too low in the hierarchy of formal contents. When Granger wants to characterise the formal content of mathematics as opposed to the formal content of logic, he needs to use the criterion of the completeness of a theory instead of his official criterion of decidability, for he says that the distinguishing mark of mathematics is that they can be represented within a second-order logical system, which is incomplete. As he rightly points out, what is at stake with the logicist reduction of arithmetic to logic is not a reduction of the former to propositional logic; such a reduction would have been indeed 'truly radical', but it was never envisaged by the logicist, whose problem was the problem of the difference between a system which, like Frege's, used the notion of set and for which there was no explicit distinction between first order and second order, and a first-order system.[40]

A good criterion of the demarcation of logic, however, is not necessarily or only a criterion of the demarcation between logic and mathematics, but also, according to Granger, a criterion of what it is for a given discipline to be 'fully' formal. As we have seen, Granger proposes two such criteria: on the one hand the metatheoretical criterion of the decidability of a theory, and on the other hand the ontological criterion according to which a truly logical theory deals only with linguistic 'objects'. Now, let us suppose that we interpret substitutional quantification as a quantification over *expressions*. Under this interpretation, there would be no reason to object, according to Granger's criterion, to a characterisation of *substitutional* quantificational logic as 'logic proper', and thus no reason to confine logic within the bounds of propositional logic alone.

This seems to imply that the metatheoretical criterion of decidability is much less important than the ontological criterion. We can see this in another example. Decidability is the privilege of propositional logic. But although first-order logic is *in general* undecidable (according to Church's 1936 theorem), there are *some* sets of quantificational formulas that *are* decidable: formulas of the *monadic* predicate calculus and therefore of syllogistics (according to a result of Löwenheim, 1915) on the one hand, and on the other hand certain specifiable sets of quantificational formulas.[41] Would Granger say that these kinds of quantificational formulas belong to 'logic' according to the decidability criterion? The problem here concerns in part the meaning that we attach to the term 'decidability'. In so far as we are talking only of decidability *in principle*, Church's theorem is enough, since it establishes that quantificational logic is undecidable in principle. But if we mean by 'decidability' decidability *in practice*, the specifiable formulas of quantificational logic for which we have decision procedures have a right to be included among the formulas of 'logic proper'. This is not, however, the end of the matter, for if we restrict ourselves to decidability in practice, it is not even true that propositional logic is decidable: according to certain results in the theory of 'computational complexity', the validity of some propositional formulas cannot be established, since the algorithms are too complex to be performed.[42] Moreover, there is not, according to 'Church's thesis' any *definition* of decidability in terms of the notion of an effective procedure. It seems, then, that the decidability criterion is bound to be imprecise.

In the absence of a rigorous formal criterion, a defender of Granger's position is led to rely upon his ontological criterion. In a sense, Granger agrees with Quine: he admits that first-order logic carries an ontological weight, since it has more 'content' than propositional logic, which carries no ontological weight. The idea that there are degrees of 'formal content' can indeed be used for Quinean purposes, and translated into Quine's terminology of the 'ontological commitments' of a given theory: we could say that the more a logic carries ontological commitments, the more it becomes 'contentful', and the less it is 'formal'. For instance, a 'free' logic without existence assumptions seems to have 'more content' than a logic which presupposes the existence of the objects of quantification[43]; quantified modal logic carries more ontological commitments than first-order predicate logic, a modal logic with second-order quantifiers carries even more commitments. We would thus ascend the scale of a formal ontology. Our view of the 'form' involved in a logic would then be annexed to our particular views about ontology, to the kinds of objects we are prepared to accept, and to the level of formal content we are prepared to assign to these objects. But what reason would there be, if we follow this path and take seriously the notion of degrees of form, to deny that the various forms are *logical* forms, and to restrict the domain of 'pure' form to propositional logic? Prior once expressed this feeling in the following terms:

> What I am inclined to say is that the term 'logic' admits of a strict and a loose sense. In its strictest sense, logic studies the properties of implication and universality; in a looser sense, it concerns itself with principles of inference generally, in all sorts of fields. But there is a difficulty in this account. As I mentioned earlier, even the truth that all feathered animals breathe air *can* be used as a principle of inference, or ought we to talk about not only a logic of time, a logic of obligation, a logic of knowledge, and things like that, but even a logic of organic life? Well, in principle, I don't see why not. . . .
>
> I do not want to be able to say, though, that there is some kind of gradation in these things – that there is somehow *more* point, for example, in talking about a logic of time and tenses than there is in talking about a logic of organic life. The truth is that if there are parrots there will always have been parrots, even if it is *not* reducible to a special case in quantification theory – I don't myself think it *is* so reducible – is nevertheless *more* like a logical truth (or even more a logical

truth) than the truth that all feathered animals breathe air. But I don't think that that there's anything better to be said here than that some subjects do in fact have more order, more structure, more form, than others – that some subjects are more capable than others of being handled by means of a formal symbolic calculus – and in these cases it is more proper than in others to speak of a 'logic' of the thing. . . . In any case the important point is that these things are a matter of degree, and the only way to discover whether a given field can be handled as a logic, that is as the subject of a calculus, and how far it can be so handled, is to try it out and see what happens. You can't settle the question *a priori*.[44]

To accept the idea of degrees of formality at face value thus involves a very loose or pragmatic attitude towards the problem of the demarcation of logic, and therefore a denial that we can formulate a rigorous criterion of demarcation. The only way to block this attitude is, as we have seen, to point out that the stronger a logic is in terms of its ontological content, the weaker it is in terms of its 'interesting' metatheoretical properties. Now if we care about these properties, which ones are we going to choose? If we choose the decidability property, we limit logic to propositional logic, which has almost no expressive power, and we have seen that the decidability criterion is not as precise as it should be. If we choose a combination of completeness and of the Löwenheim–Skolem property, we limit logic to first-order quantification theory, but this choice is not, at least if we take it for Quinean reasons, free from certain ontological motivations. It is difficult, however, to consider Quine's criterion as perfectly objective, since the same metatheoretical properties hold for different systems than standard first-order logic, which have a different ontology: for instance *substitutional second-order quantification theory* has both an important expressive power and the conjunction of the completeness and of the Löwenheim–Skolem properties.[45] It thus satisfies Quine's metatheoretical strictures without satisfying Quine's ontological strictures. Quine's choice, therefore, is not forced on us even if we accept his metatheoretical criterion.

In order to reduce our growing feeling of arbitrariness, we can try the following suggestion: a system has a better chance of being the incarnation of 'logic properly so-called' if it realises an equilibrium or a balance between its expressive powers and its metatheoretical properties. In this sense, first-order logic exhibits such a balance. There is in fact an argument, that is independent from Quine's, to select first-order logic for its special status among the other systems, which can be drawn from an important theorem of metalogic – the Lindström theorem.

Lindström's theorem belongs to a branch of model-theory, 'abstract model theory', which reverses the usual order of research in metatheory: instead of investigating, for a given logic, its various characterising properties, one tries first to consider abstractly these metatheoretical properties, in order to see, in a second step, whether such or such a logical system satisfies the given properties.[46] One starts from a semantical conception of logic: every language L determines a set of structures, or of models that verify its sentences, and must therefore allow the identification of the models that verify the same L-sentences. One must also consider the question whether the models of a logic L are isomorphic; that is whether L is *categorical*. One of the basic requirements for a logic is that the second condition implies the first. The strength of a logic can be measured by the fact that the first implies the second.[47] These investigations have led in particular to the following result, known as *Lindström's theorem*: first-order logic is the only logic for which both the Löwenheim theorem and the compacity theorem or the completeness theorem hold. This result is also true of every logic containing first-order logic or which is an extension of it. (It must be noted here that by 'first-order logic', one must understand the logic that has '−', '&' and '∃' as logical constants (with their ordinary meaning), but *not identity* – a fact that would exclude the usual logic of identity (Chapter 9) from first-order logic as such.)

Lindström's theorem has this remarkable feature: it allows us to unify the properties that we have considered separately to characterise first-order logic, and to isolate this logic among the class of other systems to which one can attribute one or the other of these properties. For instance a logic with the quantifier 'There are finitely many xs' (called 'weak second-order logic') has the Löwenheim–Skolem property, but not the compacity property. A first-order logic to which the 'generalised' quantifier 'most' is added has none of these properties.[48] To take another example given by Hodges (1983, p. 84): in 1965, Ax and Kochen have shown that, within a logic using set-theoretic notions, for every positive integer d there is only a finite number of primes that contradict a certain conjecture of Artin on d, without, however, giving the primes in question; in 1969, however, Cohen has given a proof of the same result which did not use any set-theoretic resources, but allowed an identification of the prime numbers. Therefore a proof given in a richer logic can be correct without being informative: this leads us to favour a weaker logic.

Such properties as Lindström's theorem allow us, without invoking ontological considerations, to consider first-order logic as more central than other systems, and thus as realising the desired balance of expressive and metatheoretical strength. But we cannot consider this as conclusive, and conclude that these metatheoretical properties are sufficient to give us the criterion that we want and the good demarcation of the true domain of the logical. I have, moreover, mainly considered here the distinction between *classical* first-order logic and other systems such as second-order logic; I have not dealt with the distinction between classical and *non-classical* logics such as intuitionist logic, and in this sense the considerations so far are very partial. But even if we extend (as we shall have to) our examination to these, it is unlikely that a metatheoretical criterion alone will suffice. The metatheoretical properties must be justified themselves by a philosophical argument, and a good criterion of the demarcation of logic has to be philosophical.

11.5 Proof-theoretic versus semantic criteria for logical constants

11.5.1 A proof-theoretic criterion

We have attempted, until now, to find an objective criterion of demarcation of logic by reading into various metatheoretical properties of logical systems the general properties of formality and of analyticity that are commonly attributed to the logical truths and inferences. But the results are moot. On the one hand various metatheoretical criteria can be made compatible with various notions of analyticity and of formality. On the other hand a certain amount of agreement on the metatheoretical criteria is compatible with scepticism about the very characterisation of logic as 'formal' and 'analytic'. Moreover the metatheoretical criteria do not deliver by themselves any objective and uncontroversial delimitation of the realm of logic. We should not, however, conclude from this that the task of providing a demarcation line simply eludes us. Let us then try to state again our problem.

The main lesson that we can learn from the attempts to select a certain system – or a set of systems – as the incarnation of logic is that we cannot make this selection without attempting to say what logic *is*. The answer, in most general terms, is obvious enough: logic establishes certain *truths* by *proving* them, it rests upon a certain relation between truth and proof. This, after all, is what the completeness property is about. The question is: how does a proof establish the truth of the conclusion in a 'logical' argument or inference? Why is the proof justified? The intuition lying under such characterisations of logic as 'analytic' or 'formal' is that a logical proof is justified because the sentences that feature in it and in the conclusion have a certain *meaning*. They have a certain meaning, like all sentences, because of the meaning of the terms that occur in them, and some of these terms have a special status. These are the logical constants. If we knew, therefore, how the meaning of logical constants is determined, we would have an answer to the problem of the justification of logical inferences. To say what is the justification of logical truths and inferences is to say what logic is, and from this justificatory account we can hope to select the most appropriate system on the map of the various 'logical' systems. This kind of strategy for answering the question of the choice of the 'right' logic is essentially Dummett's (as it was presented in Chapter 6): first give the general requirements for a theory of meaning, then proceed to give an account of the meanings of logical constants in conformity with this account, in terms of which logical deduction could be said to be justified and its proper domain selected.

Now one might say here that this strategy already begs two questions: why should we suppose that logical proofs are in need of any justification? And why should we suppose that there is something special about the meanings of logical constants? The first supposition would be that there is some sort of independent foundation of logic, and the second would just amount to acknowledging that logical truths are true by virtue of meanings alone, that is analytic. I do not think, however, that the strategy involves these presuppositions, since posing the question of the justification of logical inferences and trying to give an account of the meanings of logical constants does not imply in advance that we shall give a positive answer to the question or that we shall find such an account. What the strategy *does* imply is that we have the intuition that logical inferences have a certain warrant and that logical terms have a meaning. As I said above, scepticism about the grounds of the intuitions is not enough to dispel the intuitions themselves.[49] I shall address the worries about the general strategy in the next chapter. My concern here is to attempt to see how it can work.

Let us come back, then, to the general characterisation of logic as a discipline establishing certain relationships between proof and truth. Although this characterisation is unobjectionable, one can lay the emphasis on either aspect when attempting to give a definition of logic. One can, on the one hand, say that logic is essentially a science of *truths*, which, in so far as it is also about proofs and inferences, is concerned to preserve, through these proofs and inferences, a particular property, truth. In this sense, truth is more important than proof, which is just, so to say, a means for an end. This conception was Frege's. He took truth to be the central notion of logic, in the particularly strong sense that the 'basic laws' of logic had to be *absolutely true* and that logic had to describe them. Logicians have now withdrawn this absolutist conception of logic, to retain only the notion of truth *relative* to a language (Chapter 5). But the *semantical* conception of logic, according to which proof is to be defined mainly in terms of the notions of truth and validity, has not thereby been abandoned. But one can think, on the other hand, that this point of view is erroneous, or at least partial, and put the emphasis on proof instead. Thus Dummett finds 'retrograde' the Fregean conception of logic as a theory of the laws of 'being-true' as well as the focus on truth in logic:

> The representation of logic as concerned with a characteristic of sentences, truth, rather than of transitions from sentences to sentences, had highly deleterious effects both in logic and in philosophy. In philosophy it led to a concentration on logical truth and its generalization, analytic truth, as the problematic notions, rather than on the notion of a statement's being a deductive consequence of other statements, and hence to solutions involving a distinction between two supposedly utterly different kinds of truth, analytic truth and contingent truth, which would have appeared preposterous and irrelevant if the central problem had from the start been taken to be that of the character of the relation of deductive consequence. The distinction between kinds of truth led in turn to a distinction between kinds of meanings, ordinary empirical meaning and the special kind of meaning possessed by analytic statements. . . . The first to correct this distorted perspective, and to abandon the false analogy between a formalization of logic and axiomatic theory, was Gentzen. By replacing the axiomatic formalization of logic by sequent calculi, Gentzen showed how it was possible to formalize logic solely by a specification of rules of inference, without any outright postulation of logical truths.[50]

But the suggestion that logic is a science of inferences rather than a science of truths can itself be understood in two ways. On a weak interpretation, it can mean that proof is more important than truth, in the following sense: logical inferences are to be characterised primarily in *syntactic* or proof-theoretic terms rather than in *semantical* or model-theoretic terms. This does not imply that the semantical definition of inference is wrong, but that the notions of truth, validity and the other semantic notions have a derived or secondary status with respect to the proof-theoretic notions. On a stronger interpretation the suggestion means that truth and the other semantic notions are inappropriate to define logical inference, which should be defined in proof-theoretic terms alone. On this more radical view, truth should be defined in terms of proof, and the semantic notions should simply disappear from an account of logic.

What is at stake in this opposition between a semantical and a proof-theoretic definition of logic is nothing else than the conflict between a 'realist' and an 'anti-realist' conception of logic, in Dummett's sense. A realist conception of logic is, *prima facie*, committed to a semantic account of logic, since it takes the meanings of logical sentences as determined by their (transcendent) truth conditions. On the realist conception, a logical inference is justified by the meanings of the sentences that feature in it, and the meanings of these sentences are in turn determined by their transcendent truth conditions. An anti-realist conception, on the other hand, tends to favour a syntactical account of logic, since it takes the meanings of logical sentences as determined by their verification or their assertion conditions. Now these assertion conditions, in the logical case, are nothing else than the conditions by which we prove, or infer, certain conclusions from given premises. Different accounts of the meanings of logical constants seem to follow from these antagonist conceptions. A realist will say that their meanings are determined by the truth conditions or the sentences in which they occur, and he will favour a truth-theoretic or a model-theoretic analysis of these meanings. He will also say that the truth conditions of these sentences in some sense justify their meanings, and therefore their logical inferences. An anti-realist will say that the meanings of logical constants are fixed by their *inference rules*, which are just, in the particular logical case, their assertion conditions. He will also say that the particular way in which these inference rules are introduced provides a justification of their meaning, and therefore of logical inferences. The anti-realist, however, is not bound to accept the radical thesis according to which one should eliminate the semantic notions of truth and of logical consequence in order to replace them by the syntactic notions of theoremhood and of deducibility. We have already encountered this radical thesis when we have discussed Prior's 'tonk' connective: according to the thesis, the meanings of logical constants are completely determined by their corresponding deduction rules. As we saw, the major objection to the radical thesis is that the deduction rules do not *by themselves* warrant a correct definition of the meanings of logical constants, since we must also be sure that our constants are not, like 'tonk', contradictory, and we must impose certain restrictions on deducibility to the effect that a language in which some new constants are introduced must be a *conservative* extension of the original language (§ 6.4.2). This requirement, as we have seen, is integral to Dummett's anti-realist programme. An anti-realist can then hold the less radical thesis that rules of deduction *obeying certain restrictive conditions* can fix the meanings and the list of the admissible logical constants. In the remainder of this chapter I want to examine the credentials of such a proposal. I am not concerned here by all the implications and consequences of this proposal for the anti-realist, but only by the claim that there can be a syntactic, or proof-theoretic criterion of logical constants, independent of a semantic criterion, which would render the semantic notions derivative and secondary.

Several writers have proposed to take the proof-theoretic concept of deduction as the central concept of logic, and to assimilate the 'province' of logic to the domain determined by Gentzen-type systems. Logical constants are thus introduced by natural deduction rules similar to those presented in § 2.2.2 above.[51] Such a proposal has been advanced by Kneale (1956) and more recently by Hacking (1979). I shall consider only Hacking's version and call it *criterion H*. According to Hacking, an expression of a language L is a logical constant if and only if it is completely determined by the introduction and elimination rules for it in a *sequent calculus* for L. Sequent calculi belong to the family of Gentzen's natural deduction systems, although they differ from the system presented in § 2.2.2 by the fact that the hypotheses do not appear as 'discharged', but are introduced directly at the left of the deduction sign '$\vdash$' within strings of formulas called 'sequents'.[52] Logic is the domain determined by a system of deduction rules if and only if the deducibility relation obeys the following conditions:

1. it must be *reflexive*, that is such that for any formulas A, $A \vdash A$;
2. it must have the property of *'dilution'* or *'weakening'*, that is be such that the adjunction of one or more premises to an inference does not affect the deducibility relation:

    If $\Gamma \vdash \Theta$, then $\Gamma; A \vdash \Theta$ and $\Gamma \vdash A, \Theta$

    (where 'A' and 'Γ' and 'Θ' are finite sets of formulas);
3. it must be *transitive*: if $A \vdash B$ and $B \vdash C$, then $A \vdash C$.

These three conditions on '$\vdash$' do not by themselves determine any logical constant. They correspond to what Gentzen calls *structural rules* of a deduction system. For instance

$$\frac{\Gamma \vdash \Theta}{\Gamma, A \vdash \Theta} \qquad \frac{\Gamma \vdash \Theta}{A, \Gamma \vdash \Theta} \qquad \frac{\Gamma \vdash A, \Theta \quad \Gamma, A \vdash \Theta}{\Gamma \vdash \Theta}$$

are respectively the rules of dilution to the right and to the left and the 'cut' rule. The rules that introduce the logical constants proper are called by Gentzen *operation* rules, which are the elimination and introduction rules. For instance, here are (in sequent notation) the operational rules for '&':

$$\frac{\Gamma, A \vdash \Theta}{\Gamma, A \& B \vdash \Theta} \quad \frac{\Gamma, B \vdash \Theta}{\Gamma, A \& B \vdash \Theta} \quad \frac{\Gamma \vdash A, \Theta \quad \Gamma \vdash B, \Theta}{\Gamma \vdash A \& B, \Theta}$$

The resulting system, Gentzen's 'sequent calculus' has what is called the 'subformula property': all the formulas that feature in the derivations are subformulas of a formula featuring in the conclusion,[53], and all the operational rules allow us to go from less complex formulas to more complex formulas. The cut rule alone can have a less complex conclusion than its premises. In 1934, however, Gentzen proved a theorem (the *Hauptsatz*, or 'main theorem') according to which a derivation using the cut rule can be transformed into a so-called *normal* derivation, where the cut rule does not appear. The *Hauptsatz* is, in this sense, called the 'normalisation theorem' or 'cut elimination' theorem. It owes its importance to the fact that it allows the proof of other results in proof-theory, such as the consistency of a system or its completeness. First-order logic is shown to have these properties.[54]

According to Hacking, the cut elimination property is especially important, since it guarantees that the definitions of logical constants through operational rules are *conservative*. For instance the definition for 'tonk' is not conservative. According to criterion *H*, the domain of logic is the domain circumscribed by constants introduced by operational and structural rules that have the subformula property, are conservative with respect to the conditions (1)–(3) above, and have the cut elimination property.[55] This proof-theoretic conception has, for Hacking, three important consequences.

First, criterion *H* justifies the limitation of logic to first-order logic. Logic is restricted to what it was for Russell: the ramified theory of types, without the simple theory of types and the axiom of reducibility, which involve a second-order logic. In this sense, this conception is in agreement with Russell's logicism.[56] Criterion *H* implies that logic must have the Löwenheim–Skolem property, and therefore agrees with Quine's criterion. Hacking also notes that it agrees with Lindström's result.[57]

Second, criterion *H* allows us to demarcate classical logic from certain non-classical logics (with the important exception of intuitionist logic, to which I shall come back below). Thus the weakening property holds only for *deductive* logic, but not for the so-called *inductive* logic. The weakening property means that a deductive inference keeps the same conclusion whatever premises are added to it. This is not the case for inductive inferences, for which the addition of one or more premises changes the conditions of validity. In general, an inductive argument is an argument that allows us to go from particular propositions as premises (or from a conjunction of such propositions to a general conclusion, or from a statistical generalisation of a property over a set of individuals to the instantiation of this property in a given individual). For example an argument of the latter kind has the form:

> Most *Fs* are *Gs*
> *x* is an *F*
> therefore *x* is a *G*.

The conclusion is not a deductive consequence of the premises, since it can only be made 'probable' by them. Adding further premises can invalidate the argument. For instance if one adds the following two premises:

> Most *F* & *Hs* are *Gs*
> *x* is an *H*

the conclusion *may* not follow from the premises, since it is less probable. Hacking concludes from this that inductive logic is not 'logic' at all. At least we should say that if there is such a thing as 'inductive logic', its rules will differ from those of deductive logic. I shall not, however, deal with this notoriously obscure and controversial topic.[58] The weakening property implies that there is a *stability* of deductive reasoning or what can be called their *monotonous* or *cumulative* character. Now this property fails to hold in reasonings where premises are said to be true *ceteris paribus*, and are considered as *default* assumptions which one might replace, in the light of new informations, by other alternative assumptions. Such 'default' reasoning has been widely studied in the context of artificial intelligence, and various 'non-monotonic' logics have been proposed in this field, which do not obey the monotonicity condition.[59] According to criterion *H*, these 'logics' should not count as 'logic' at all.

Criterion *H* also rules out modal logic. Hacking notes that Gentzen-type natural deduction rules with the cut elimination property can be given for modal systems such as *T*, S_4 and S_5. But these systems lose the elimination property for the weakening rule. Thus for the following rules of S_4

$$\frac{\Gamma, A \vdash \Theta}{\Gamma, \Box A \vdash \Theta} \qquad \frac{\Box \Gamma \vdash A}{\Box \Gamma \vdash \Box A}$$

the rule on the right is such that the sequent at the top must begin with an operator '□'. We must, therefore, impose restrictions, in modal logic, on the cut elimination property. According to Hacking, this means that modal logic, unlike first-order logic, has a metalinguistic character, since the fact that one step is valid in a proof depends upon the form of the sentences used in the derivation.[60]

Third, and finally, Hacking holds that criterion *H* justifies the idea that logic is the province of *analytic* propositions. Logical truths are analytic by virtue of the meaning of logical constants, which are fixed by inference rules meeting the appropriate conditions. But a worry might arise here: analyticity is a *semantic* property, which applies to logical *truths*, whereas criterion *H* is framed in terms of *proof-theoretic* properties, so how can criterion *H* be a criterion of analyticity? To answer this question we need to see how, for Hacking, proof-theoretic notions are related to semantical ones.

Hacking does not want, through criterion *H*, to get rid of semantic notions, but only to give them a derived status. He does not want to say that the inference rules for logical constants *completely* determine their meaning. A being who would have no logical concept could not define logical constants: one must *already* have something like, for instance, the concept of a conjunction in order to apply the rule for conjunction.[61] Hacking thus does not hold the radical thesis mentioned above, which we have rejected in § 2.2.2 in consideration of the *tonk* connective. To take up the terminology used in § 2.3.1, for Hacking the inference rules do not *define* the meaning of logical constants, although they *characterise* it. Moreover, if Hacking held the radical thesis, his conception would be open to the following devastating objection raised by Putman.[62] Let us consider the translation, given in § 6.5 of the classical connectives into intuitionistic connectives. If the operational rules 'fixed the meaning' of the classical connectives, one could accept all these rules, and nevertheless *use the connectives in their intuitionistic sense*. Therefore these rules do not 'give' the meaning of the connectives. Hacking, however, refuses this consequence of his criterion. His thesis is, rather, that *if* the classical (bivalent) notion of truth is presupposed for the sentences of a language in which figure only elementary sentences of the form '*Pa*', '*Pb*', and so on, *then* once the logical constants are introduced by means of Gentzen-type inference rules one can determine or 'read off' the semantics of these constants from the inference rules.[63] Let us, for example, consider the left and right introduction rules for the sign '→':

$$\frac{\Gamma, A \vdash B, \Theta}{\Gamma \vdash A \to B, \Theta} \quad \frac{\Gamma \vdash \Theta, A \quad B, \Sigma \vdash \Omega}{\Gamma, \Sigma, A \to B \vdash \Theta, \Omega}$$

These rules preserve the following property of the sequent: if all its antecedent formulas are true, at least one of the subsequent formulas is also true. From this and the left introduction rule, we conclude that when either *A* is false or *B* is true, then *A* → *B* is true; for in the case in which all the formulas in Γ are true and all the formulas in Θ are false, only then will the rule preserve the intended property. From the right introduction rule, we conclude that if *A* is true and *B* is false, *A* → *B* is false; for only in the case in which all the Γ are true and all the Θ and Ω are false does the rule preserve the property. We can thus recover the truth table for '→' from the inference rules.[64] Hacking claims that in *this* sense the inference rules 'determine' the semantics of the constants. Semantics thus becomes a 'by-product' of proof-theory.[65] We can say, therefore, that the propositions that can be derived from such a system of rules are analytic once they are *interpreted*.

11.5.2 A semantic criterion

Hacking's conception of logic has the undeniable merit of giving a clear and precise meaning to the thesis that logic is a science of inferences. Although

Hacking himself does not draw any particular consequence in favour of the anti-realist programme, his account seems to bring some grist to the anti-realist's mill if it shows that the proof-conditions of logical statements are more important than their truth conditions. But does it favour the anti-realist programme? And does criterion H really imply that the proof-theoretic notions override the semantic ones?

In the first place, criterion H hardly favours the anti-realist programme if this programme implies – as it should, according to Dummett – that *intuitionist* logic should be chosen instead of classical logic. On the one hand, as we have just seen, Hacking presupposes a classical framework and a bivalent concept of truth. On the other hand criterion H is neutral between classical logic and intuitionist logic, since a Gentzen-type system of rules satisfying the required conditions can be given for intuitionist logic as well. For instance, for negation, one can show that the rule *ex falso sequitur quodlibet* and the rule of *reductio ad absurdum* are complete with respect to the intuitionist concept of negation:

$$(EFSQ) \ \frac{\Gamma \vdash A \quad \Gamma \vdash -A}{\Gamma \vdash B} \qquad (RAA) \ \frac{\Gamma, A \vdash B \quad \Gamma, A \vdash -B}{\Gamma \vdash -A}$$

RAA is based on the idea that we can conclude $-A$ if we *know* that B implies a false statement, in opposition to the classical introduction rule for '$-$', based on the semantic version of the principle of excluded middle, according to which A *or* $-A$ must be true.[65] A sequent calculus is, in this respect, as neutral between a classical and an intuitionist reading of the logical constants as a Tarskian theory of truth (§ 6.5). Criterion H thus fails to demarcate the domain of logic as *classical* first-order logic.

In this second place, criterion H hardly supports the claim that semantic notions such as truth or validity are only derivative or a 'by-product' of proof-theoretical notions. Hacking himself admits that the inference rules determine the meaning of the logical constants only if a certain classical concept of *truth* is presupposed. And what is the property that the inference rules of a sequent calculus are supposed to preserve if not truth? In such a calculus, a derivation is correct if and only if it has the *semantic* property of allowing us to go from antecedent formulas that are true to subsequent formulas that are also true. Without the notion of truth, the rules are only strings of signs devoid of any meaning. One can see this by coming back once again to Prior's *tonk* connective. The reason why this connective is incoherent is not only syntactical, but semantical: the introduction and elimination rules that are associated with it do not correspond to any assignation of truth values. For the *tonk* introduction rule (§ 2.3.1), if it must preserve the truth of sentences in which the connective figures, requires that '*A tonk B*' be true when A is true and B is false, whereas the *tonk* elimination rule requires that '*A tonk B*' be false when A is true and B is false. This shows that the semantics of *tonk* cannot be coherently established. The fact that its syntax, through the inference rules, is also incoherent is a closely related fact, but nothing allows us to say that the syntactical or proof-theoretical inconsistency is responsible for the semantical inconsistency, once we realise that the problem with *tonk* sentences is that we cannot assign to them any coherent truth conditions.[66]

There is thus no reason to draw, from criterion H, the conclusion that proof-theoretic concepts override the semantic ones. The most we can say is that they are parallel, since to every inference rule corresponds an assignment of truth values. This is well attested by the fact that a natural deduction system can be formulated in *semantic* terms, with the familiar system of Beth's 'semantic tableaux'. This system, often called the 'tree method' for validity, rests upon the semantical idea that a formula is true if and only if it has a model, and valid only if it is satisfied in all models. One determines whether a given formula is satisfiable or valid by looking for a counter-example, or a counter-model of the given formula, and by checking whether this counter-model is realised – that is by trying to falsify the formula. Every connective or operator is introduced through deduction rules written down in tableau or 'tree' form, which summarise the semantic evaluations given by the corresponding truth tables. For instance, the usual truth functional connective '$\rightarrow$' receives the rules:

$$\text{(I)} \quad A \rightarrow B \qquad\qquad \text{(II)} \quad -(A \rightarrow B)$$
$$\underset{-A \qquad B}{\diagup\quad\diagdown} \qquad\qquad\qquad\qquad A$$
$$\qquad\qquad\qquad\qquad\qquad\qquad -B$$

which are just the characteristic lines of the truth table for '$\rightarrow$': the first rule means that '$A \rightarrow B$' can be rewritten as '$-A \lor B$', and the second rule means that '$-(A \rightarrow B)$' is '$A \,\&\, -B$'. Every given formula to be tested for validity or satisfiability is decomposed, through the rules, into various subformulas until we reach atomic formulas. The resulting 'tree' is a 'semi-evaluation' or a 'model set' of the formula, or of the inference. A formula is satisfied if and only if its tree does not contain any formula together with its negation on one 'path' of evaluation of its subformulas. A formula is valid if and only if the negation of its conclusion, together with the conjunction of its premises have a counter-model. For a very simple example, let us consider the following inference

$$p \rightarrow (q \rightarrow r) \models (p \rightarrow q) \rightarrow (p \rightarrow r)$$

(where '$\models$' denotes the semantic relation of consequence). The tree resulting from negating the conclusion and evaluating it is

(6')   1. $p \rightarrow (q \rightarrow r)$ [premise]

2. $-((p \rightarrow q) \rightarrow (p \rightarrow r))$ [negation of conclusion]
3. $\quad p \rightarrow q$ [rule (II) on 2]
4. $-(p \rightarrow r)$ [rule (II) on 2]
5. $\quad p$ [rule (II) on 4]

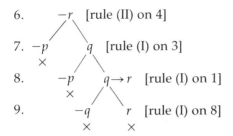

6. $-r$ [rule (II) on 4]

7. $-p$ q [rule (I) on 3]

8. $-p$ $q \to r$ [rule (I) on 1]

9. $-q$ r [rule (I) on 8]

This semantic tableau gives a counter-example to the inference from (1) to (2), as shown by the fact that every terminating 'path' is 'closed' because it contains contradictory atomic formulas (this is indicated here by a cross). Therefore the initial inference is valid.[67]

The rules (I) and (II) are the counterparts of the introduction and elimination rules in a natural deduction system (although they are not introduction or elimination rules; they are, so to speak, verification and falsification rules). This correspondence is not accidental: one can show that the existence of a counter-model in a semantic tableau system corresponds to the existence of a derivation in a system of natural deduction rules or in a sequent calculus.[68] Like the latter, the decision procedure through tableau rules has the subformula property (or its reverse: one goes from more complex to simpler formulas). The completeness of the propositional calculus and of the predicate calculus can be proved in the tableau system, and the Löwenheim–Skolem theorem too. What Hacking aims to achieve through criterion H can be achieved with a semantic natural deduction system.[69]

Hacking, therefore, has not shown that a purely syntactic criterion could be given for logical constants. In fact the foregoing remarks suggest that one can give a semantic criterion as well, and this is the kind of criterion that I want to put forward. Christopher Peacocke (1976) has formulated such a criterion. To formulate a semantic criterion for logical constants, however, it is not enough to transpose simply criterion H into semantic terms. Criterion H, as Peacocke shows, suffers from a difficulty that is common to any purely *extensional* reading of the deducibility relation captured by the criterion, since every constant that would have the same operational rules or the same truth conditions as a classical logical constant would itself be a logical constant. Let us suppose, for instance, that we introduce a two-place connective '$\$$' which would mean in English the same thing as:

$$(\ldots \& \ldots) \vee -(\text{the teachers are ill-paid})$$

'$\$$' has exactly the same inference rules and the same truth conditions as those of the usual connective '$\&$': '$A \$ B$' is true if and only if A and B are true, and false otherwise (this example is similar to the one we have considered in §2.3.1 with the connective 'flop'). In other words, the inference and the truth conditions of '$\$$' do not allow us to define its meaning in the case where the teachers are not ill-paid.

Consequently, they are not sufficient, even if necessary, to classify '\$' as a logical constant. Peacocke suggests that what we need further is to have a knowledge *a priori* of the fact that the sentences containing the constants meet the required deducibility or truth conditions. The fact that the teachers are ill-paid is a regular and constant fact, but it is an empirical fact that could fail to obtain and which is not necessary. But what about a case where '\$' would be formulated (like 'flop') thus:

$$(\ldots \& \ldots) \vee -(7 + 5) = 12?$$

'$(7 + 5 = 12)$', being an arithmetical truth, is presumably *a priori*. The answer is that in this case indeed '\$' would have just the same inference and truth conditions as '&', since the second conjunct, being *a priori*, would always be true. There would, then, be no reason for not interpreting '\$' as meaning the same as '&' (just as we saw in § 2.3.1 that 'flop' meant the same as '&').[70]

Peacocke, therefore, proposes to reformulate criterion *H* in two ways. The first involves a *semantic* reading of the criterion in terms of Tarskian truth theories, according to which an expression is a logical constant if and only if it satisfies sequences of objects. The second requires that we know *a priori* which sequences of objects are satisfied by the sentences in which the given expression figures. More precisely Peacocke's criterion (let us call it criterion *P*) is the following:

> α is a logical constant if α is non complex and, for any expressions $\beta_1, \ldots, \beta_n$ on which α operates to form expressions $\alpha (\beta_1, \ldots, \beta_n)$, given knowledge of which sequences satisfy each of $\beta_1, \ldots, \beta_n$ and of the satisfaction condition of expressions of the form $\alpha (\gamma_1, \ldots, \gamma_n)$, one can know *a priori* which sequences satisfy $\alpha (\beta_1, \ldots, \beta_n)$, in particular without knowing the properties and relations of the objects in the sequences.[71]

As we have seen (§ 4.2.1), the apparatus of sequences can be used to formulate the truth conditions of sentences with propositional connectives. For instance, given that we know which sequences satisfy *A* and that any sequences satisfies $-A$ if and only if it does satisfy *A*, we can know *a priori* which sequences satisfy $-A$: just those that do not satisfy *A*. Thus '$-$' is a logical constant according to criterion *P*. For existential quantifiers, we say that if one knows which sequences satisfy *A* and knows the satisfaction conditions of existentially quantified sentences, one can know *a priori* which sentences satisfy x_iA (i.e. all the sequences differing from a satisfier of *A* in at most the *i*th place). As Peacocke notes, there is an important difference between propositional constants and quantifiers, since for the former we need only consider which sequence satisfies a given expression formed out of a propositional connective, whereas for the latter whether a given sequence satisfies an open sentence depends in part on whether *other* sequences satisfy the open sentence.[72] Thus Granger's insistence that there is a difference between the propositional and the predicate calculus with respect to their 'degree of formality' is here partly vindicated, though criterion *P* does not rule out the quantifiers as truly *logical* constants.

Unlike criterion H, criterion P is semantical. Unlike it, it rests upon an intensional (epistemic) notion of aprioricity. Doubts can arise about this notion: first, because it is not clear what *a priori* knowledge is; and second, because if we set up a condition for a good criterion of logical constanthood that such a criterion would *explain* the properties of logical truths such as aprioricity, it should not, as here, *use* this very notion. To answer the first doubt, one can say that the notion of aprioricity here involved is tolerably clear. For instance criterion P will rule out a classification of so-called 'attributive' predicate modifiers such as 'large' or 'tall' as logical constants, on the grounds that if one knows which sequences satisfy a given predicate ϕ and if one knows which objects satisfy in a given circumstance 'tall', one does not know *a priori* which sequences satisfy large ϕ (for instance if one knows that Mao Zedong and Gary Cooper were men and tall, one does not know *a priori* which objects are tall men; Deng Tsao Ping and Mickey Rooney, for instance, could satisfy both predicates relative to other people, such as pygmies).[73] The second doubt is well motivated if our aim were to *define* the aprioricity of logical truth through such criteria as H or P – but it is not our aim; such criteria are meant to *elucidate* these notions, not to define them. We shall, in the next chapter, try to say more about the aprioricity of logical truths, but we should note here that criterion P helps to elucidate another notion commonly associated with logical truths, their topic neutrality, since, as Peacocke observes, the criterion speaks of *any* expression $\beta_1, \ldots, \beta_n$ to which a constant α is applied, regardless of what things they are true of. The requirement of aprioricity is meant to imply that whatever objects and features of objects are concerned we shall know that they satisfy the given expressions.[74]

What are the consequences of P for the demarcation of logic? Just like H, it does not rule out intuitionist logical constants: as we have already noted, since it is formulated in Tarskian model-theoretic terms, it is as neutral as Tarski's truth theories with respect to the choice between classical and intuitionist logic. Indeed there can be an intuitionist reading of the condition of *a priori* knowledge of sequences of objects, which the intuitionist might want to limit to the finite case, although the notion of knowledge does not imply that we favour this intuitionist reading.[75] Identity will not, however, count as a logical constant by criterion P, if it is a primitive notion of our language, since from a knowledge of what objects satisfy an identity statement $a = b$, we shall not know *a priori* which sequences satisfy an open statement like $x = y$, unless we somehow fix the stock of these objects.[76] The same thing can be said about such quantifiers as 'most' or 'many'. The more we move away from clear cases (such as propositional connectives) of *a priori* knowledge of sequences, the more it is difficult to count a constant as truly logical. As already noted, this confirms, in other terms, Granger's idea of degrees of formality. What about modal operators? Criterion H ruled them out (see above). Criterion P does too. As Peacocke notes, when '□', for instance, is a candidate logical constant, we do not know *a priori* the satisfaction conditions of □ $(\beta_1, \ldots, \beta_n)$. The issue turns upon whether we could quantify over possible worlds in order to give extensional conditions of satisfaction for modal formulas. Criterion P by itself does not settle this.[77]

The main thing, therefore, achieved by criterion P is not that it gives us, in terms of the distinction above (§ 11.1.1) a solid internal demarcation for logic, but that it gives us an important external demarcation of logic through a *semantic* account of logical constants. To introduce a logical constant is not simply to show that it obeys certain inference rules subject to proof-theoretical criteria (such as conservative extension, or cut elimination). It is to show that the inference rules preserve, for every possible inference, a certain property. Which one? It can only, if the preceding remarks are correct, be *truth*, according to the traditional definition of the validity of an inference; an inference is valid if it obeys rules that preserve truth in the passage from premises to conclusion. In other words, it is not enough to say that a principle of inference is valid if every manner by which one establishes its premises can be transformed into a manner by which its conclusion is established. This means that although truth cannot go without proof, proof itself cannot go without truth. It follows that the anti-realist line of argument sketched above, according to which the assertion conditions alone, under the form of proof-theoretic inference rules, *by themselves* fix the meaning of logical constants, cannot be correct. If one considers the principles by which one fixes the meanings of logical constants as particular *justifications* of deduction, this means that, in the end, such a justification has to be *semantical*.[78] Now this does not block another anti-realist line of argument. For if the anti-realist accepts that a justification of deduction is semantical, and therefore must use the notion of truth, he is not debarred from trying to explain this notion in terms of assertion conditions, or from limiting the domain of logic to intuitionist logic. Anti-realist *revisionism* is not blocked once we accept criterion P and its consequences. But at least our acceptance of a semantic criterion implies that logic cannot be defined only as a science of inferences, and that it should at least be a science of truths. In so far as the realist favours this semantical account, realism is a metaphysical position that harmonises well with the semantical criterion for logical constants.

I shall try, in the next chapter, to further this issue and to show how it can be settled in favour of the realist. What can we conclude here from our quest for a demarcation criterion of the 'province' of logic? I have attempted first, following Quine, to formulate a criterion without using the properties traditionally ascribed to logical truths, such as topic-neutrality and analyticity. But the substitutional definition alone leaves us without a precise criterion. We have therefore tried to formulate our criterion in terms of the metatheoretical properties of formal systems. But although these criteria favour a limitation of logic to first-order logic, they do not by themselves trace precise boundary lines. In every case, I have found that the metatheoretical criteria had to lean upon philosophical characterisations, be they ontological or epistemological. This does not imply, however, that the business of determining logical constants is a purely arbitrary or relative matter. If the foregoing is correct, logic does not begin only when there exists a certain relation between sentences which we call inference, which has a certain degree of formality, and which can be represented within a certain language that has certain expressive properties. Inference and logical form have to be constrained by certain stable and identifiable properties. These properties follow from the way we fix the meaning of logical constants. I have considered two principal ways of fixing this meaning – a proof-theoretic and a semantical one. Both imply that the deduction relation must have certain formal properties, but they do not force us to choose a particular logic, although they imply that first-order logic has *more* of the desired formal properties than others. In this sense, we can take seriously the idea that 'logical' and 'logical constant' are epithets that admit degrees, although there are constraints on our moving away from a central core, constituted by first-order logic. The choice of a central core for the domain of logic, however, is not a determinant of, but determined by, the way we fix the meanings of logical constants, and I have admitted, with Peacocke, that any such criterion must be semantical. The question whether logic should be confined to classical systems, or revised, will depend upon how we formulate these semantic constraints on the meaning of logical constants.

—— 12 ——

LOGICAL NECESSITY

12.1 Three paradoxes

It will be convenient, to introduce the topics of this chapter, to start off with three paradoxes.

The first paradox comes from Lewis Carroll's famous story of Achilles and the Tortoise.[1] In the story Achilles proposes to the Tortoise to consider the following three propositions:

(A) Things that are equal to the same are equal to each other.
(B) The two sides of this triangle are things that are equal to the same.
(Z) The two sides of this triangle are equal to each other.

Achilles says that if one admits that (Z) follows logically from (A) and (B), then one *must* admit that (Z) is true. Someone, however, can accept the conditional proposition

(C) If (A) and (B) are true then (Z) is true

without accepting (A) or (B) (although Achilles is right to say that such a person had better abandon Euclid and take up football). Achilles and the Tortoise both agree that someone could accept (A) and (B) without accepting (C). The Tortoise adopts the latter position, and challenges Achilles 'to force him, logically, to accept (Z) as true'. The story suggests that Achilles will never succeed. The Tortoise does not accept (C), but he is ready to do so when Achilles asks him to. Once again, Achilles asks him to accept (Z). But the Tortoise reiterates his point that it is possible to accept (A), (B) and (C) without accepting the proposition

(D) If (A) and (B) and (C) are true then (Z) is true.

But the process can go on indefinitely without the Tortoise ever accepting (C).

It is not easy to draw the moral of the story, and several interpretations of it have been proposed. One of the morals is that one must distinguish the *true propositions* of logic (theorems, logical truths) such as (A) and (B) on the one hand, from the *rules of inference* such as (C) on the other. If one transforms, as the Tortoise does, the inference rules into propositions, one generates an infinite regress, which never allows us to infer logically anything. It is one thing for a proposition to be a conditional of the form 'If p then q', and it is another thing, for this very same conditional, to be a *rule* of logic: 'From p, to infer q'.[2] Although this last proposition can be written as a proposition of logic ('$p \vdash q$' or '$\vdash p \rightarrow q$'), its status as an inference rule is distinct from its status as a proposition. Achilles wants the Tortoise to accept (Z), because otherwise 'Logic would take [him] by the throat and force

[him] to do it.' Now a possible interpretation of the story is the following. One can say that two conceptions of logical necessity conflict here: the one, Achilles', according to which necessity would be an *intrinsic* feature of the propositions of logic, in so far as they are, like (C), tautologies, or universally valid expressions; and the other, the Tortoise's, according to which if there is here some kind of necessity, it is not an *intrinsic* feature of the propositions of logic, but an extrinsic feature of these. According to the latter conception, logic only states what is the case, or what implies what. But it never tells us that people *must* accept certain things if they accept other things. 'Whatever *Logic* is good enough to tell me is worth writing down', says the Tortoise. But all that he writes on his notebook is *another* conditional sentence. If the Tortoise is right, the propositions of logic do not force anything upon us, and they do not infer anything for us. It is *we* who, because we consider certain propositions as rules or conventions, commit ourselves to perform the 'necessary' inferences. In other words, Achilles adopts what may be called a *realist* view of logical necessity, whereas the Tortoise adopts a *conventionalist* view of this notion.

The second paradox is the one we have called above 'Mill's paradox' (§ 6.4.2): it is often said that, for an inference to be valid, the conclusion must be already 'contained' within its premises; but if the conclusion is already present in the premises, it is trivial, and we can learn nothing from it. So how can an inference be both valid and informative?[3]

The third paradox is the so-called 'sceptical' rule-following paradox adduced by Saul Kripke from Wittgenstein's considerations about rules.[4] As Kripke formulates it, this paradox arises from our attempt to account for what it is that constitutes a person's following a certain rule. For instance what constitutes my following the rule for addition by 'plus' or '+'? Presumably my past uses of the rule and my intentions to conform to them. But no such rule is predetermined simply by extrapolation from the previous cases in which I have applied '+' to numbers, since there are always infinitely many functions which accord with a given list of instances of such additions. How do I know, for example, that I follow the rule for 'plus' and not a distinct deviant rule (call it 'quus') according to which $x + y$ gives the usual results when x and y are smaller than 57, but gives the result of 5 otherwise? The sceptical suggestion is that no amount of facts or of dispositions about my previous uses can determine *which* rule I follow (or what meaning my words have, or what concepts are used).

The three paradoxes are distinct, but the problems that they raise are connected. Carroll's paradox bears on the very status of the propositions of logic as necessary propositions: is it legitimate to confer on them this status and what makes them necessary? Mill's paradox bears on the possibility of logical inference. It concerns not the necessity of logical inferences, but their related property of being apparently *a priori*: if a logical inference is known to be valid, that is if to recognise the truth of the premises is always to recognise the truth of the conclusion, how can we fail to know *a priori* that is it so, and in this sense how can such knowledge be of any use to us? How can logical knowledge be surprising?

The problem arises because the way we can be surprised by the truth of a logical conclusion obviously differs from the way we can be surprised by the truth of an empirical statement (such as, for instance, the statement that a given combination of chemical substances leads to an explosion). We have the intuition that we do not learn logical truths or principles by experience (although Mill himself attempted to show the falsity of this intuition) and that we have an *a priori* knowledge of them; nevertheless, how can they be fruitful and have a cognitive content? Wittgenstein's paradox (or Kripke's, since it is a disputed matter whether Wittgenstein actually formulated it) bears on the status of rules in general, but logical rules are a prominent case. It raises the problem of how the *content* of those rules can be determined. In particular is this content determined by an understanding of independent logical *facts*, or is it determined by the mastery of proper *practices*? And can our understanding of these facts or practices explain our particular uses of the rules? Formulated in this way, the problem is closely tied to the one we have been dealing with before, of how to determine the meanings of the words that have an 'essential' occurrence in logical truths or laws, namely the logical constants. An answer to the question whether we can determine the meanings of the logical constants and of the rules in which they figure will also amount to an answer to the question whether the deductive practice which rests upon them is itself *justified*, and a 'sceptical' answer, according to which there is no such justification will conflict with a non-sceptical answer according to which these rules can be, one way or another, justified.

The three paradoxes thus confront us with a family of problems that can be formulated in the following way:

(a) Are logical truths and laws necessary? If so, of what nature is this necessity?
(b) Are logical laws analytic, and if so in what sense?
(c) Are logical laws *a priori*, and if so in what sense?
(d) What is it to follow a logical rule?
(e) What is the meaning of logical constants?
(f) Are logical truths and laws in need of a justification, and if so which?
      To which we should add:
(g) What choice of a logic is induced by our answers to (a)–(f)?

These questions are among the most fundamental in the epistemology of logic, and any proper philosophical account of the nature of logic must deal with them. But the task of giving an integrated and coherent answer to all these questions is certainly very hard, and in many cases philosophers have been dealing with only some of these questions, generally by focusing on either one of them. I shall not be able, in what follows, to give the systematic answer that the questions require, but I shall attempt to trace out more fully some of their connections, with the hope of giving an overall map of the possible positions and of their respective defects and merits.

12.2 The realist-cognitivist conception of logical necessity

Achilles' conception of logical necessity is the most natural and the most usual: the propositions of logic are necessary because they are *objective* in the sense that they describe a universe of facts or of situations that could not fail to exist. This idea is also present in the Leibnizian (or neo-Leibnizian) idea of a necessary proposition as a proposition that is 'true in all possible worlds'. On this conception logical truths consist in a special category of non-empirical, non-natural facts bearing on an independent reality. Frege is clearly a representative of this conception, which seems, to his eyes, to be the only possible way of justifying the objectivity of logical laws, since they describe the 'laws of being-true' belonging to a realm of true 'thoughts' that are independent of the sensible world (see § 1.2.1). This conception is both 'Platonistic', since it postules a universe of objects or entities (propositions, objects, truth values) that are responsible for the truth of the propositions of logic, and realist in Dummett's sense (Chapter 6), since the logical truths are such that there is something *by virtue of which* they are true. For Frege, logical necessity is grounded within things themselves.[5] For instance the axioms of arithmetics are for him *absolutely true*, and cannot be the effect of some hypotheses that we accept. Two images are usually associated with this realist conception.

The first is the image of the logician as a scientist who *discovers*, just in the same way as natural scientists do, the logical truths and the laws of logic. For Frege, logic is a scientific description of a universe that we do not create because it is 'universal', in the sense that it describes not only the laws of the 'logical universe', but also the laws of the universe as a whole (§ 4.1.1).[6]

The second image is that of the observation of the logical demonstrations by a 'spectator' who plays a purely passive role in, for instance, the way in which a certain decision procedure is applied to a formula of the predicate calculus: the procedure is entirely predetermined, even in the cases where it is effective, as if it were only unpacked by the calculus which renders it explicit.[7] If the spectator were not present, things would be just the same. The realist conception of necessity associated with these two images is commonly called 'cognitivist'.[8] Cognitivism (with respect to logical truths) is the view according to which to the necessary truths of logic (and of mathematics) correspond a universe of *facts*, which, though they are distinct from the empirical facts of experience, are nevertheless real, knowable and discoverable.

The cognitivist realist (to whom I shall also refer as a 'strong' realist or as a 'Realist') has a natural answer to the Tortoise's question: like Achilles, he does not understand why one could refuse to infer what one is told to infer, unless one is victim of a particular sort of blindness; it is impossible to fail to infer what has to be inferred, of all eternity. As Frege says: 'The question why and with what right we acknowledge a law of logic to be true, logic can answer only by reducing it to another law of logic. Where it is not possible, logic can give us no answer.' And

Frege suggests that any person who would refuse (as the Tortoise does) a law of logic would illustrate 'an hitherto unknown form of madness'.[9]

The cognitivist realist has also an answer to Mill's paradox. Because logical truths describe a certain reality, they have, as Frege says, a cognitive value. For Frege, the fact that propositions of logic are 'analytic' does not mean that they are empty or devoid of cognitive content. Frege criticises Kant precisely on this point. According to the Kantian criterion of analyticity, logical truths are analytic because 'they say nothing else about the predicate but what was already contained in the subject' and consequently they have no cognitive value. For Frege, on the contrary, the very fact that logical (analytic) truths involve logical laws and logical deductions referring to an objective realm of facts, means that they are neither sterile nor unproductive. The deductions are productive since they allow us to discover facts, and the mathematical deductions based upon them describe an objective reality too. Logic itself describes objective truths. Thus if arithmetic is logic, and is, in this sense (analytic), it is not empty. The universal applicability of logic is precisely what gives to its propositions (and to the mathematical propositions that derive from it) a cognitive value. A logical inference is informative and fruitful, since the conclusion is contained in the premises 'like the plant in the seed, and not like the beam in the house'.[10]

12.3 Conventionalism and logical necessity

12.3.1 Moderate conventionalism

A strong realist explains the necessity, aprioricity, and analyticity of logical truths by invoking a special ontology of Objects, Concepts and Propositions. This view is open to a common objection addressed to any Platonist ontology of this kind: the Objects, Concepts or Propositions alluded to are queer entities that we do not usually encounter, and that can hardly be known other than through a certain form of specific intuition. This is apparently what Frege means when he says that we have to 'grasp' (*Fassen*) the laws of being-true. But what kind of cognitive act is this 'grasp'?[11] The cognitivist is bound to make the knowledge that we have of logical and mathematical entities very mysterious. This, however, is not the only problem with this view. Another problem is, as was noticed about the Tortoise, that the true propositions of logic cannot be put on the same footing as the propositions that describe something about the world. The propositions of logic are not descriptions of anything, but *rules* of descriptions, that is guidelines about what we *count* as a description of a state of affairs. They do not 'correspond' to any fact, but are the expressions of *conventions* that we have adopted. According to this conventionalist view, logical necessity is not imposed upon us by reality, but comes from ourselves and from the way we use our language: a proposition is necessary because we have decided that we shall not count it as false, and to *confer* this meaning on it. Our recognition of logical necessity becomes a particular case of our recognition of our own intentions about meaning.[12] This kind of necessity is not grounded in the way the things are, but is the product of our attitudes towards linguistic statements.

Conventionalism is the thesis that the necessary truths of logic derive from conventions or rules that we have chosen to adopt, and can be *reduced* ultimately to these conventions and rules. This is, in particular, Carnap's position (§ 11.2). We have already seen, on several occasions (Chapters 2 and 11), the difficulties that confronted the conventionalist thesis according to which we can introduce and define logical constants by means of conventions or of 'meaning-postulates'. Now conventionalism encounters two further difficulties, which are specific to the claim that logical necessity can be reduced to conventions.

The first difficulty has been forcefully exposed by Quine in his famous paper 'Truth by convention'. In logic there is an infinity of theorems and tautologies. Only a finite number of rules of description (or of 'semantical rules' or 'meaning-postulates') can be *primitive* rules. The other rules must be derived from these. But we are thus directly led to the infinite regress of Carroll's paradox, which is generated by the Tortoise's conventionalist position: 'If logic is to proceed *mediately* from conventions, logic is needed for inferring logic from the conventions.[13] This can be seen from the following example given by Quine. Let us suppose that we use Lukasiewicz's axiomatisation of the propositional calculus (the axioms (A_1), (A_2) and (A_3) of § 2.2.2 above) to derive the true sentence: 'If time is money then time is money.' Let us suppose, then, according to the conventionalist hypothesis, that we have the following conventions:

(I) Let all results of putting a statement for 'p', a statement for 'q', and a statement for 'r' in (A_1) be true.

(II) Let any expression be true which yields a truth when put for 'q' in the result of putting a truth for 'p' in 'if p then q' (i.e. the rule of *modus ponens*).

(III) Let all results of putting a statement for 'p' and a statement for 'q' in 'If p then if $-p$ then q' or 'If if $-p$ then p then p' be true (respectively (A_2) and (A_3)).

Putting 'Time is money' for 'p', we can derive '$p \to p$' from (I)–(III) thus:

(A) (1) $p \to (-p \to p)$ [by (III)]
(2) $(-p \to p) \to p$ [by (III)]
(3) $(p \to (-p \to p)) \to ((-p \to p) \to (p \to p))$ [by (I)]
(4) $((-p \to p) \to p) \to (p \to p)$ [by (II) applied to (3) and (1)]
(5) $p \to p$ [by (II) applied to (4) and (2)]

Quine identifies the conventions upon which logic is supposed to rest with the decision to treat all the instances of the axioms (A_1)–(A_3) as true, and all the applications of the *modus ponens* as truth preserving. But in order to derive the truth of a specific statement from a general convention, we need to make a logical inference, and this leads us to an infinite regress. Namely, when we derive q from p and $(p \rightarrow q)$ on the authority of (II) – that all applications of *modus ponens* are truth preserving – we *infer* from (II) and from the premise that p and $(p \rightarrow q)$ are both true the conclusion that q is true. Quine suggests that this is the very regress into which we are led if, like the Tortoise, we refuse to consider certain propositions – the logical laws – as imposed upon us independently of our explicit choices. In other words, the derivation of logic from conventions is circular, since logic is true by convention only *given logic*.[14]

The second difficulty for the conventionalist view is that it does not allow us to find a satisfactory solution for Mill's paradox. According to Carnap, the thesis that the tautologies of logic are true by convention goes with the thesis that they do not have any informative content: they all say the same thing, that is nothing.[15] It follows that a logical inference, in so far as it is valid by virtue of logical laws, is but an explicitation of what is already contained in the premises, and thus can teach us nothing.

To avoid these difficulties, two strategies can be adopted. The first one consists of radicalising the conventionalist thesis, by holding that logical truths are not indirect, but *direct* expressions of conventions. This is Wittgenstein's position, which I shall examine now. The second strategy consists in rejecting conventionalism altogether. This is Quine's position, which I shall examine later.

12.3.2 'Radical' conventionalism

Among contemporary philosophers, Wittgenstein has been the most constant upholder of the thesis that logical truths are best conceived as rules or conventions. Against Frege's cognitive realism, Wittgenstein holds that the propositions of logic are *rules*, which do not correspond to any pre-existing universe of facts. No more than the rules of a game ('the bishop does not move like the horse') these rules do not describe anything or correspond to anything. These are conditions, or 'preparations' for description, which have only a normative status. Wittgenstein's doctrine of logical truths is an integral part of his theory of 'grammatical' propositions. These are 'autonomous', that is they owe nothing to any independent reality. Only an illusion, or a well-entrenched philosophical myth, can make us believe that these propositions describe a distinctive universe of facts: 'To a necessity in the world corresponds a rule of grammar.'[16] Where we see the particular effect of the 'hardness of the logical must' (the *must* that Achilles pretends to follow), there is only a rule that we have decided to follow, the 'constraining' force of which is due only to the power of a convention.

Dummett has suggested that Wittgenstein's conventionalism differs from Carnap's conventionalism because for the latter the logical necessity of a given statement is an *indirect* expression of a convention, whereas for the former it is always the *direct* expression of a convention:

> That a given statement is necessary consists always in our having expressly decided to treat that very statement as unassailable; it cannot rest on our having adopted certain other conventions which are found to involve our treating it so.[17]

According to Dummett, Wittgenstein's conventionalism is 'radical' or 'full blooded' since it does not accept that there could be an indirect connection between the statements that we accept as necessary and the conventions upon which they are founded. Wittgenstein seems to reject the distinction between primitive rules and derived rules. It follows that, every time we are dealing with a particular application of a logical rule within an inference, it is *this* very rule, and not a more primitive rule, that is responsible for our acceptance of a given proposition as true. Wittgenstein holds this view because he believes that to think otherwise would commit us to the idea that a logical rule could guide, so to say, at distance, its applications:

> How do I know that $(\exists x)fx$ follows from fa? Is it that I as it were see behind the sign '$(\exists x)fx$' the sense lying behind it, and see from that that it follows from fa? Is *that* what understanding is?[18]

To think in this way (that is to think that there exists a predetermined meaning of '$(\exists x)Fx$', which would guide in advance the conclusion 'Fa'), would amount to the thought that there can be 'hidden connections' within logic. But 'one cannot dig behind the rules, because there is nothing behind them.'[19] Wittgenstein criticises systematically the doctrine of a 'meaning-body' (Bedeutungskörper), according to which there exists, behind every sign, some sort of hidden meaning which determines in advance all the possible applications of this sign, and he considers this doctrine as an expression of the realist-cognitivist view of logical necessity. Thus

> Whoever calls '$--p = p$' (or again '$--p \equiv p$') a 'necessary proposition of logic' (*not a stipulation about the method of presentation* that we adopt) also has a tendency to say that his proposition proceeds from the meaning of negation.[20]

To this Wittgenstein opposes the idea that the rules of inference confer directly their meanings to the signs, without these possessing any meaning independently of the rules through which they are stipulated.

The notions of logical necessity and of logical consequence are therefore for Wittgenstein *non-objective*: all the logical truths are true by virtue of conventions, not by virtue of facts given prior to the conventions. The fact that logical rules are 'arbitrary' means, for him, essentially this: that their necessity does not originate in any fact, and can in no way be *discovered*; it must be (in Crispin Wright's phrase) *invented*, and recognised as such.[21] It is therefore meaningless to say that the premises of a demonstration 'necessitate' their conclusion, if one means by this that a logical inference unfolds a piece of information already contained within these premises. Any assertion to the effect that a given conclusion is 'necessary' has nothing to do with the previous assertion of the necessity of an inference rule. One can see, then, how it is possible to answer Lewis Carroll's paradox: the logical 'must' invoked by Achilles is neither inexorable nor irrevocable. Wittgenstein seems here to side with the Tortoise.

Mill's paradox can also be solved along these Wittgensteinian lines. According to Wittgenstein, to accept the proof of the conclusion of a logical or mathematical inference is to confer a new meaning on it, precisely by adopting a new convention: 'The proof creates a new concept' or 'a new paradigm'.[22] Wittgenstein seems to mean here that if, for instance, we accept the proposition that $2 + 2 = 4$ on the basis of, say, counting on our fingers, and later come to accept that $2 + 2 = 4$ on the basis of the Leibnizian proof of this proposition (which uses only the rule of substitution of identicals and definitions),[22] we thereby change the meaning of '$2 + 2 = 4$', and we would again change its meaning if we proved it by using the Peano axioms and by translating it into the notation of *Principia Mathematica*. According to this view, the conclusion of a logical inference is *never* contained in the premises. Thus Mill's paradox cannot arise. Unlike the positivist conventionalist, Wittgenstein takes a logical proof as being intrinsically fruitful and informative, since it provides a new criterion of the truth of its conclusion.

The radical conventionalist answer to Carroll's paradox and to Mill's paradox seems to have extraordinary and unwelcome consequences. In the first place, as Dummett observes, 'it makes proof fruitful at the cost of robbing it of that feature which we take as making it compelling':

> It leaves unexplained the power of proof to induce us to change the meanings of expressions of our language in the way that it represents a proof as doing. On the ordinary view of proof, it is compelling just because, presented with it, we cannot resist the passage from premises to conclusion without being unfaithful to the meanings that we have already given to the expressions employed in it; whereas, on the [radical conventionalist] view, its function is precisely to seduce us into such unfaithfulness. . . . One of the most obvious objections to the Wittgensteinian view, as I have stated it, is that a proof normally proceeds according to already accepted principles of inference, and that, therefore, by giving a proof we cannot be affecting any alteration of meaning, since the possibility of such proof was, as it were, already provided for by our linguistic practice, namely by our acceptance of those principles employed in the course of it.[24]

In the second place, can Wittgenstein really hold the view that the necessary propositions of logic are, as 'grammatical rules', under no control at all of any fact or of any reality? Wittgenstein's 'anti-cognitivism' about logical necessity can be compared to Hume's anti-cognitivism about causal necessity: Hume holds that causal necessity is not in the world, but is only a projection of our beliefs and expectations about future events, while Wittgenstein holds that logical necessity is not in the world (and not in *any* world), but is the (direct) product of our intentional decisions. For Wittgenstein logical truth and logical necessity find their source *in us*. It does not follow, however, as many commentators have remarked, that logical necessity is under the control of no reality at all, and that it can be reduced to a form of contingency, since 'in us' means 'within our nature' and 'within our forms of life'.[25] In this sense, Wittgensteinian conventionalism accepts the idea that our conventions are under the constraint of some sort of facts, in so far as the rules that we accept conform to the data of our 'natural history'. This is why it would be much better to characterise Wittgenstein's view as a *naturalistic* conventionalism, rather than as a radical conventionalism. Nevertheless his view is that there is no absolute *justification* of our logical rules in the sense of their being grounded in a reality external to our practices.

Now the *prima facie* objection to this view is that our acceptance of truths, axioms or inference rules cannot be *entirely* conventional in this sense. For instance, does the fact that some systems of logic are consistent, complete and decidable depend entirely upon our nature and upon our conventional choices? Could our nature make it the case that a contradictory set of axioms or of inference rules (such as those that govern Prior's *tonk* connective) hold? That a system of axioms, such as those of Peano arithmetic or of Lukasiewicz's propositional calculus, is consistent seems to be a fact that we do not *invent*.[26] It also seems to be a fact to which we are constrained, and not the expression of a choice. What does a logician do who learns from one of his colleagues that a deductive system that he has built is inconsistent? Will he go on and use his system as before? No, he will make adjustments in order to achieve consistency.

To this objection the Wittgensteinian can answer that such metatheoretical properties of our logical systems as consistency, completeness, decidability and so forth need not be viewed as objective properties of these systems, but are just intrinsic properties of their being constituted by rules. In this sense the requirement of consistency is just the same as the requirement that a calculus must be performed according to certain rules: 'Why must not rules be inconsistent? Because otherwise they would not be rules.'[27] In other words, when we discover that an inconsistency arises within a logical system, the situation is the same as when we discover that the rules of a game conflict, for instance that they systematically benefit one player. There is nothing special about consistency, in so far as it is an intrinsic feature of a working set of rules or conventions. This is why Wittgenstein refuses to attach any particular significance to metamathematical results: they are just mathematical results like others, and we should not be under the illusion that because consistency, completeness and so on are 'meta-' properties they should serve to found or to justify our logical or mathematical systems. Moreover, the very fact that a given system is inconsistent does not prevent us from using it. Let us suppose that a community actually uses a system of signs (arithmetical or logical) that happen to be inconsistent, but the inconsistency of which has not been proved. There is nothing absurd in the supposition that such an inconsistent system of signs can be used, have practical effects, and so on, and thus can belong to a certain 'form of life' (as a matter of fact, the supposition is not so far-fetched: 'naïve' set theory was in use before it was discovered that it leads to paradoxes). Now could we say to the members of this community, on the basis of our knowledge of the inconsistency of the system, that they are *wrong*? The Wittgensteinian seems here committed to the view that there is no straightforward affirmative or negative answer to this question. If we met individuals who would accept logical systems that are, by our criteria, inconsistent (for instance if they believed that $2 + 2 = 5$, or that q does not logically follow from $p \& q$), the only thing we could do would be to attempt to force them to accept *our* own criteria, and not to try to persuade them that $2 + 2$ is 'actually' 4, or that q 'really' or 'in fact' follows from $p \& q$. One of Wittgenstein's main doctrines, is, according to Crispin Wright, the doctrine 'that logic and mathematics are antecedent to truth.'[28] It is the thesis that logic and mathematics, as rules, delimit the domain of sense, before any further determination of the truth conditions of their statements. It follows that if some people reach some conclusions that we can deem as false, but insist that these conclusions have been reached through logical rules, there is, in Wright's phrase, 'no olympian standpoint from which we could discern who gives the right answer'.[29]

The nature of Wittgenstein's position here depends upon the kind of solution that he gives to the 'sceptical paradox' that Kripke attributes to him.[30] According to Kripke, scepticism about rule-following is the thesis that there is no fact about me, or about my past dispositions that distinguishes my following a given rule (for example, addition) and my following another deviant rule (for example, as above, 'quaddition') or my following no rule at all. The 'sceptical solution' to this problem is, according to Kripke, given that there is no fact about our following rules (or meaning anything), that we should replace our intuitive idea that our rules have objective application conditions by the idea that their application conditions are solely determined by the practice of the community to which we belong. Since the sceptical paradox concerns the very notion of our meaning something by a sign, the sceptical solution consists in giving up the idea that our sentences have *truth* conditions and in admitting that they have instead *assertibility* conditions, which can be described in terms of the actions and dispositions of a community.

It is however, a much disputed matter whether Wittgenstein himself was a sceptic about rules in Kripke's sense, and whether he advocated the 'sceptical solution' that I have just outlined. I shall not attempt to venture into these controversial matters. I shall follow Crispin Wright in his suggestion that there are four main themes that can be uncontroversially attributed to Wittgenstein in his 'rule-following considerations':[31]

> (i) our own understanding of a rule does not exceed what one can explain (following a rule is not a matter of following a rail or a route already traced for us);
> (ii) it might be preferable, in describing one's most basic rule-governed responses, to think of them as informed not by an intuition, but a kind of decision (following a rule is not a matter of cognition);
> (iii) supposing that grasping a rule is a matter of coming to have 'something in

mind', how am I supposed to recognise what its requirement are? (following a rule is not a matter of interpretation);

(iv) the foundations of language and of rule-governed institutions do not consist in our having internalised autonomous and explanation-transcendent rules, but in primitive dispositions of judgement and action (following a rule is a practice).[32]

As Wright notes, all these themes are negative, and it is difficult to build upon them any positive doctrine. On the negative side, it is clear that Wittgenstein's considerations about rules are directed against the realist-cognitivist conception of logical rules: the epistemology of rule-following does not require that we understand anything that would be beyond the reach of our actual capacities, and in particular it does not require that we grasp, by some act of intuition, any evidence-transcendent instruction. This much suffices to classify Wittgenstein as an *anti-realist* about logical necessity. But is it enough to classify Wittgenstein as an anti-realist about meaning and truth in Dummett's sense? As it was presented in Chapter 6, Dummettian anti-realism consists basically in two doctrines. The first is that the meaning of a sentence or expression is epistemically constrained by the requirements of our understanding this sentence or expression, and that our understanding consists in grasping the assertion conditions of a sentence or expression. The second doctrine is that truth itself is epistemically constrained, and should be defined in terms of assertibility. To borrow a phrase from John Skorupski, we can call these doctrines respectively 'the epistemic conception of meaning' and 'the epistemic conception of truth'.[33] Dummett holds that the first doctrine leads us to the second: that because meaning is understanding assertion conditions, truth should be defined in terms of assertibility. But although Dummett considers himself as giving justice to Wittgenstein's dictum 'meaning is use', it is not obvious that the dictum itself, and Wittgenstein's own remarks on rules, justify that we attribute to him, as Kripke does, the thesis that understanding is constituted by a grasp of assertion conditions, nor the thesis that truth is to be equated with assertibility. It is difficult to attribute to Wittgenstein the first thesis because he rejected the idea that meaning and understanding have to be constituted by some key or central concept. It is difficult to attribute to him the second thesis because it does not follow, from the fact that logic is 'antecedent' to truth, that there is no such thing as the truth of our assertions, or that truth is to be defined as assertibility.

Similar remarks can be made about the other positive doctrine that one is tempted to attribute to Wittgenstein on the basis of Dummett's interpretation quoted above, namely 'radical conventionalism'. As we have characterised it above, radical conventionalism holds, on the one hand, that logical truths *are* conventions, and, on the other hand, that the acceptance of a conclusion from a logical proof need not be faithful to the meaning of antecedent premises or rules. Now the first claim, if it is taken to mean that logical truth *can be reduced* to conventions, is certainly open to the Quinean objection to conventionalism in general, namely that logical truths can be reduced to conventions only by presupposing those very truths. But when Wittgenstein says that we should better think of logical truths as rules or conventions, does he intend to give an account of the *origin*, or of the *ground* of logical necessity? Does he try to explain this notion in terms of more fundamental ones? This is very dubious, since he is concerned to point out a 'grammatical' difference between two kinds of statements – those that are descriptive and those that have the character of rules – but he is not trying to say what makes it the case that they are rules, or how they are acquired or determined.[34] In this sense Wittgenstein can agree with Quine that the concept of convention is hardly an explanatory concept.

We should, therefore, be very cautious in trying to force Wittgenstein's analyses about logical necessity into a positive set of doctrines. What is, however, uncontroversial is that he attempts to destroy a certain pervasive overall picture of logical necessity, the 'strong realist' or Realist picture, according to which the normative character of logical truths or laws is to be explained by their correspondence to a certain objective realm of facts, and our understanding of a sentence consists in our grasping its objective truth conditions, this grasp being itself constituted by a kind of intuitive epistemic relation. This, as I have suggested, points in the direction of an anti-realist conception of meaning. In so far as the Realist aims to *justify* logical truth, Wittgenstein's criticism of the Realist picture is also a criticism of the very idea that such a justification is possible. This, as we shall see, points in the direction of a holistic view of logical inference. But it remains to be seen how the realist/anti-realist debate can be settled on the grounds of more positive doctrines. This is what I shall attempt to do now, by envisaging the conflict between a holistic and a molecularist conception of logical inference, and the bearing it can have on the notion of the analyticity of logical truths.

12.4 Holism and analyticity

12.4.1 The holistic conception of inference

Let us, then, return to the problem of accounting for logical inferences, as it was posed by Carroll's and Mill's paradoxes. The solutions given to these paradoxes by strong realism and radical conventionalism are extreme. The Realist solves the first paradox by assimilating logical necessity to the truth of propositions describing necessary facts, and solves the second by supposing that logical inference are totally predetermined by those necessary facts. The radical conventionalist solves the first by assimilating logical necessities to conventions resting on our own decisions about what to count as true, and solves the second paradox by removing it from any influence of meanings and truths given in advance. But both conceptions of logical necessity deprive logical inferences of one of their two fundamental features by accounting for the other. The Realist accounts for the constraining character of logical rules, but – although Frege insisted upon the fruitfulness of logical truths – it treats our activity of drawing a conclusion as the purely passive recognition of an already given law, and in this sense a logical inference can hardly bring us *new* information. The radical conventionalist, on the other hand, accounts for the fruitfulness of logical inferences, but deprives them from any constraining character.

Let us consider again the inference (*A*) above. Apart from the fact that the conclusion '$p \to p$' is utterly obvious, can we say that it is contained in advance in the premises? No, since we *draw* the conclusion by means of rules and axioms. Should we say, then, that these rules are conventionally introduced? No, because we do not accept them on this particular occasion or for the sake of drawing this particular conclusion. They certainly belong to our deductive equipment before we have to make this inference. This does not speak against the conventionalist view in general, since under its moderate, Carnapian form, it is consistent with the idea that an inference is made in accordance with already accepted general conventions. But it is inconsistent with the idea that the rules we use are the *direct* expressions of explicit new conventions. In any case, it seems difficult to dissociate these rules from our global inferential practice.

The correct, intermediate position between the two extreme theses seems to be the position described by Dummett in the quotation above: our *total* linguistic practice justifies our inferences, but these are nevertheless fruitful, because we can, through them, reach conclusions that we could not have reached before. Dummett considers that such a position amounts to some form of *holism* about meaning, according to which one cannot explain the meaning of an individual sentence in a language without taking into account the meanings of *all* the sentences of the language, nor explain the validity of any inference without taking into account all the other inferences that we accept.[35]

Holism in this sense underlies Quine's criticism of conventionalism: if logical truths are conventional, they can only be so given logic itself. No valid inference performed according to the rules of logic can establish *directly* and autonomously the truth of its conclusion. The rules that seem to be applied directly at one stage of an inference are in fact justified by the background of the other accepted rules. In this sense, we cannot be said to invent them; they are imposed upon us, not by any form of logical predetermination (as strong Realism implies), but by our overall practice.

According to Dummett, holism is both a theory of meaning and a theory of the justification of deduction.[36] To justify a deduction is to explain why it is necessary. As a theory of meaning holism is the thesis that an individual sentence has no isolated meaning apart from the meaning of all the other sentences of a language. As a theory of logical inference, holism is the thesis that a logical inference is never justified in isolation, but only against the background of our total inferential practice. This is why, according to Dummett, holism must admit that a justification of deduction is always *circular*. For a particular logical inference is justified if it can be shown that it is valid relative to the rules of deduction of a certain logical system. But one must then show that this system is complete (§ 11.3.1). To prove completeness, however, one must use the inference rules themselves, that is one must suppose that they are justified. But these are precisely the rules that we intend to justify through a completeness theorem. According to most logicians, this kind of circularity is not vicious. This situation is perfectly described by Goodman:

> Deductive inferences are justified by their conformity to valid general rules, and general rules are justified by their conformity to valid inferences. But this circle is a virtuous one. The point is that rules and particular inferences alike are justified by being brought into agreement with each other. *A rule is amended if it yields an inference we are unwilling to accept; an inference is rejected if it violates a rule we are unwilling to amend.* The process of justification is the delicate one of making mutual adjustments; and in the agreement achieved lies the only justification needed for either.[37]

This is also in the spirit of Quine's position: our logical rules cannot be justified by individual conventions, independently of the whole set of logical rules that we adopt.

According to Dummett, this holistic position can account for the informativity of logical inferences, but it does not explain why they are legitimate: our global inferential practice sustains the validity of our particular inferences, but the fact that these inferences belong to a general practice can hardly be said to 'justify' them. In this sense holism does not provide us with any true justification of deduction. On the contrary, it is inspired by an anti-foundationalist view of logic, and must reject the idea that logical truths can be *necessary*. Such is, indeed, Quine's position. For him the criticism of the notion of logical necessity goes hand in hand with a criticism of the correlative notion of *analyticity*.

12.4.2 Quine's criticism of analyticity

Quine's semantic holism is based on the thesis that it is impossible to draw a sharp dividing line within a language, between the sentences that are true only by virtue of the meanings of the terms that occur in them, and the sentences that are true only by virtue of experience or facts, that is between *analytic* and *synthetic* truths. As we have seen (§ 1.4.2, 12.2), Quine's rejection of this distinction is closely tied to his criticism of the notions of meaning and of identity of meaning: to withdraw the analytic/synthetic distinction amounts to withdrawing the very idea that the judgements about an identity or a difference in meaning can themselves have a sense.

According to Quine, the notions of analyticity, of necessity and of aprioricity interlock in a circle. When we talk about logical truths and inferences, they can be linked together as follows. To say that B logically follows from A is to say that if A is true them B *must* be true (or is necessarily true). But it is also to say that the corresponding conditional *if A then B* is analytic, or true by virtue of meaning. And it is also to say that such a conditional is known *a priori*, and in this sense, immune to revision. Thus the notion of analyticity that Quine attacks involves these three notions: the traditional metaphysical notion of necessity, the notion of truth by virtue of meaning alone, and the notion of *a priori* truth, or of truth known independently of experience.

Like Wittgenstein, Quine rejects realism and cognitivism about logical necessity. As we have seen (§ 7.4) he holds that the notion of *de re* necessity, or of a necessity in the world, is meaningless. He therefore has no sympathy for the thesis that logical truths are necessary because they are grounded in a universe of special facts. But he does not hold that logical truths are not based upon facts. On the contrary, logical truths are, like all other truths, true by virtue of the way the world is. In other words, they are true by virtue of empirical facts, although they answer to much more general facts than those of other disciplines. In other terms Quine holds a form of empiricism about logic. Is he, however, an empiricist in the sense of Mill, who held the extreme view that all logical and mathematical truths can be reduced to truths about experience?[38] No, for Quine rejects any form of reductionism as a 'dogma of empiricism'. His empiricism rests mainly, as we have seen above (§ 1.4.2) on the 'Peircian' verificationist thesis that the meaning of a statement is the difference that its truth would make for possible experience. Combined with epistemological holism, according to which our statements face the tribunal of experience collectively and not individually, verificationism leads to the idea that there is no determinate meaning for any individual statement, and thus to semantic holism (which is one of the central features of Quine's thesis of the indeterminacy of translation).

Quine's rejection of the analytic/synthetic distinction implies that there are no grounds for a sharp distinction between statements that have the status of 'grammatical rules' or of 'meaning-postulates', and statements that have the status of descriptions of facts. His holism implies that this distinction is simply *relative*. In some contexts, some statements can function as rules; in other contexts they are merely reports of factual contents. It does not follow from this that there are no conventional truths, but only that these are not only or always conventions:

> The lore of our fathers is a fabric of sentences. In our hands it develops and changes, through more or less arbitrary and deliberate revisions of our own, more or less directly occasioned by the continuing stimulation of our sense organs. It is a pale grey lore, black with fact and white with convention. But I have found no substantial reasons for concluding that there are quite black threads in it, or any white ones.[39]

Quine's rejection of the notion of analyticity implies also that there is no logical truth or rule which is *a priori* in the sense of being absolutely unrevisable. This is the gist of a famous passage of 'Two dogmas of empiricism':

> It becomes folly to seek a boundary between synthetic statements which hold contingently in experience, and analytic statements, which hold come what may. Any statement can be held true come what may, if we make drastic enough adjustments elsewhere in the system. Even a statement very close to

the periphery can be held true in the face of recalcitrant experience by pleading hallucination or by amending certain statements of the kind called logical laws. Conversely, by the same token, no statement is immune to revision.[40]

Not only can every logical rule be revised, but every statement can acquire the status of a rule. The distinction between necessary and contingent truths does not disappear, but it becomes a distinction of degree. According to conventionalism, on the contrary, the distinction between conventional and non-conventional truths ought to be a sharp one. Quine's gradualism involves the rejection of this conventionalist thesis.

If, therefore, we want to adopt Quine's holistic solution to Mill's paradox, we must also adopt his solution to Carroll's paradox, which implies that we reject the idea that there are necessary, *a priori* and analytic truths in an absolute sense. But, as I have suggested in the previous chapter, I do not intend to defend a conception of logical truth at the cost of giving up these notions.

12.5 The analyticity of logical truths

12.5.1 Molecularism and harmony

An anti-realist response to Quinean holism will, in general, rest on the following three claims:

(a) Contrary to what semantic holism implies, logical truths have a special status. They are true by virtue of the meanings of the logical constants that figure in them, and the meaning of these constants is fixed by deductive rules, independently from the meanings of other terms in a language.
(b) Contrary to what holism implies, logical inferences are not justified by our overall inferential practice, but because the rules that govern them obey certain particular characteristics.
(c) If one accepts (a) and (b), there is a reasonable sense in which one can claim that logical rules have a conventional character, and that they are analytic.

A first step in the anti-realist argument has to deal with the main basis of Quinean holism, the thesis of the indeterminacy of translation (§ 1.4.3). I cannot here deal with such an intricate issue, but a few remarks are in order.[41] In principle, Quine should not be opposed to the idea that a determinate meaning can be given to *some* logical constants, since he holds that propositional connectives can be translated, and thus be given a meaning, in a situation of radical translation. But he holds that when we come to quantifiers, translation is indeterminate, and reference inscrutable. So Quine has to deny that logical constants in general can be given precise meaning–conditions, and an anti-realist must resist this claim, just as he must resist Quine's scepticism about meaning in general. The anti-realist position on this score is well expressed by Crispin Wright:

> Quine, like Socrates, seems to have supposed that the absence of any clear, non-circular definition of a concept somehow calls its propriety into question. The proper response is that it does nothing of the sort, provided there is independent evidence that the concept is teachable and is generally well understood. A sceptic about the intelligibility of a concept does not have to be answered by a rigorous explanation of it: it is enough to supply unmistakable evidence that the concept *is* well-understood.[42]

Secondly, in order to assess claim (a), the anti-realist will claim that the meaning of logical constants consists in the assertion conditions of the sentences in which they figure, which is their *inferential role*. He will say that to grasp the meaning of a logical constant is to know how it behaves in logical inferences, and that this involves in particular knowing from what sentences a sentence containing a constant can be inferred (that is how the constant behaves in the premises of an inference), and what sentences can be inferred from it (that is how the constant behaves in the conclusions of inferences). As Dummett says, the inferential role or meaning of a constant is constituted in the *conditions* or *grounds* of its use, and in the *consequences* of using it.[43] Now this thesis can be given a clear technical sense if one formalises logic within a Gentzen-type natural deduction calculus (§ 2.2.2 and 11.5.1 above): for the elimination rules of a constant (or equivalently, in a sequent calculus, its 'right' introduction rules) specify the grounds of the sentences containing it, whereas the introduction rules (or equivalently its 'left' introduction rules) specify the consequences of these sentences. So the meaning of logical constants can be said to be given by their natural deduction rules (see § 11.5.1 above)

Now, as we know from our discussion of the connective *tonk*, inferential rules must not be introduced in an arbitrary way: they must correspond to certain specific requirements. According to Dummett's *molecularist* conception of logical inference (§ 6.3.2, 6.4.2) these are as follows:

1. The requirement of the *separability* of logical rules: each rule governing the meaning of a logical constant must have an independent content, and must be understood independently from the other rules.
2. The requirement of the *molecularity* of rules: every new introduction of a logical constant must yield a *conservative extension* of the class of assertible sentences in the language (§ 6.4.2); in other words we must not introduce rules that would be derived from rules that are *more complex* than those we already have.

Dummett (1973, 1990) and Tennant (1987) hold that these requirements correspond to the proof-theoretical condition of the *harmony* of natural deduction rules. The basic idea is the following. The only acceptable inferences are those that introduce a close correspondence between on the one hand the assertion conditions of a sentence, and on the other hand the consequences that can be drawn from the assertion of this sentence. In a Gentzen-type system, the harmony of rules is simply the expression of the fact that these rules obey what Gentzen called the 'inversion principle', that is the parallelism between the introduction rules and the elimination rules for a constant such as '&':

$$(\&\text{-introduction}) \quad \frac{A \quad B}{A \& B} \qquad (\&\text{-elimination}) \frac{A \& B}{A} \quad \frac{A \& B}{B}$$

The justification for an elimination rule consists in the existence of an effective method to transform the justifications of the assertions of premises into the justifications of the assertions of their conclusions, which in turn implies that the basic meaning of a logical constant is given by its *introduction* rules, since the elimination rules are only derived from the introduction rules, which they conservatively extend. This 'reduction procedure' can be represented thus:

$$(B) \qquad \frac{\dfrac{P_1 \qquad P_2}{C_1 \qquad C_2} \qquad P_i}{\dfrac{C_1 \ \& \ C_2 \qquad C_i}{C_1}} \rightarrow$$

The case of '&' is of course the simplest. The harmonic rules for the other constants are more complex. The harmony condition is also expressed by Gentzen *Hauptsatz* and the various 'normalisation' or cut-elimination theorems, according to which we can eliminate all the detours consisting of an introduction followed by an elimination (§ 11.5.1).[44]

If we impose such constraints on our deductive rules, then it is not true that *any* rule can justify a particular inference, but only harmonic ones. We can thus combine the two features of deductive inferences: through the use of inference rules, the *creativity* of proofs, and through harmony and the principle of conservative extension, the *faithfulness* of our conclusions to the meanings of the constants contained in our initial rules.

According to Dummett these requirement amount to a *justification* of logical rules and of deductive inference, according to the anti-realist claim (b). Since our logical constants have a separable meaning, fixed independently of other terms of the language through their associated inference rules, such rules are not justified by our overall linguistic practice, as is the case for the holist. Because the inferential rules for the constants are not accepted through a previous acceptance of other rules, they are in this sense primary and provide the grounds for our logical practice.

This is not the only consequence that the anti-realist can draw from his proposal. The requirement that logical rules must satisfy the harmony condition comes down to the requirement that logical proofs should be *direct, normal* or *'canonical'*, which implies in turn that we give a constructivist or intuitionistic account of logical truth, by defining truth in terms of 'direct' assertibility. Indeed, as Tennant argues, if one accepts the claim, encapsulated in schema (B) above, that there is an effective method for turning justifications of the assertion of the premises of a valid inference into the justification of its conclusion, then one has to give up classical logic. For instance Tennant argues that if one has a fragmentary language with only '$\vee$' and '$\rightarrow$' as propositional operators, the introduction and elimination rules for these operators do not permit the derivation, as a theorem of the classical logical truth $(p \rightarrow q) \vee (q \rightarrow p)$, because we do not always have an effective method to justify an assertion of $p \rightarrow q$ or to justify an assertion of $q \rightarrow p$. But if we add to our language the classical negation operator '$-$' we can derive this logical truth. This shows that the addition of classical negation produces a *non*-conservative extension of the deducibility relation on the original fragment, and that if the principle of harmony is respected, classical logic should be dropped.[45]

The anti-realist notion of assertion condition can thus be reformulated in terms of the notion of canonical proof. For instance in the intuitionist definitions of logical constants of § 6.4.1 above the notion of 'grounds for asserting A' can be replaced by the notion of 'having a canonical proof for A'. Dummett himself, as we have seen, sides with intuitionist logic. Tennant advocates another system, intuitionistic relevant logic (on relevant logic see § 12.7.2).[46]

12.5.2 Conventionalism vindicated?

We have already seen, in Chapter 11, how such a proof-theoretical account of the meanings of logical constants could be used to support the claim that logical truths are analytic (§ 11.5). The anti-realist can also counter, on the basis of this account, Quine's argument against conventionalism, and reinstate the view that logical truths are conventional. This is what Tennant (1987a) argues.

Let us consider again Quine's argument, in 'Truth by convention' (§ 12.3.1). It depends upon a certain conception of proof, and upon a particular kind of formalisation of logic, through an axiomatic system (Lukasiewicz). When he makes the particular derivation (A) above, Quine in fact supposes that when we prove the truth of a conclusion from premises by using a conventional truth (here the truth that instances of *modus ponens* are always truth preserving), this presupposes in turn that we verify, step by step, the truth of the various sentences involved in an inference. It is precisely because we need to appeal to the truth of the very statements that express the conventions that we use that a regress arises. But this is a very artificial account of logical proof. It seems much more natural to say that, when we deduce a conclusion from certain premises, we assert the truth of these premises on the basis of certain warrants, then assert the truth of the conclusion on the basis of a proof from these premises, *without verifying at each step whether the principles we use are true*. This feature of deductions emerges clearly from a natural deduction framework. In a Gentzen-type system, Quine's cumbersome derivation (A) would take the much simpler following form:

(A′)
$$\frac{\quad\quad\quad\quad\quad}{p}\text{(1)}$$
$$\frac{\quad\quad\quad\quad\quad}{p \to p}\text{(1)}$$

where we assume that p for the sake of argument, then infer, by the rule of $\to$-introduction or of conditional proof, that *if p, then q*, thereby 'discharging' our initial assumption. In such a derivation there is no need to suppose the truth of the premise, since the assumption is discharged. If, unlike Quine, we express our logical conventions as natural deduction rules corresponding to each logical constant, and not as general axioms, we can say that these conventions are responsible for the truth of the conclusion, *without being antecedents of a logically true conditional with that conclusion as consequent*. According to Tennant, Quine's regress argument becomes spurious:

> For it is now clear that the sense in which the truth of individual logical truths 'follows from' conventions is *not* the same as that in which the consequent of a logically true conditional follows from the antecedent. It would be better to speak of logical truth (and indeed consequence in general) as *arising from* or *flowing* from the conventions in question. For we are interested in truth (and now, more generally, consequence) by convention, not in what follows from the truth *of* conventions. It may be true that a certain convention holds: but we cannot hold that a certain convention *is true and logically implies* individual logical truths. Conventions are not truth-bearers. Rather they regulate truth-bearers: they are the means whereby the truth-bearers assume, shift, and deposit their loads. There is no circularity, and no uncovered case, in an account of conventions as the source of all logical truth.[47]

On this view, the rules that introduce logical constants are not themselves logical truths: as rules and conventions, they are neither true nor false. We come here close to Wittgenstein's doctrine that logic (logical conventions) are antecedent to truth.

12.5.3 Minimal realism

But we can agree with these remarks about the nature of proof without agreeing with the conventionalist consequences that Tennant draws from them. Such a conventionalist view can only be accepted if we presuppose that the meaning of logical constants can only be given in proof-theoretical terms, that is if we overlook the fact that our logical rules are valid if and only if they are *truth*-preserving. Now we have seen in § 11.5.2 that a purely proof-theoretical or syntactic criterion for the logical constants could not be correct precisely for this reason. It follows that conventionalism, understood as the thesis that logical truths can be *reduced* to conventions cannot be true. Unless he wants to renounce altogether the idea that logical deduction stands in need of a justification, the anti-realist must accept that our natural deduction rules must be justified. For this he needs a soundness theorem, and for this again he must presuppose the truth of the laws of logic. In this sense the Quinean holist is right. But it does not follow that he is right in holding that logical rules do not stand in need of justification, and that logical constants do not have a separate meaning. In fact, it can be argued that some of the molecularist requirements on logical constants are compatible with doctrines that are constitutive of holism and realism in the theory of meaning.

In the first place, the anti-realist molecularist requirements for the logical constants are quite compatible with a holistic view of meaning for *non*-logical constants in a language. Take a typical holistic account of language such as that given by a Davidsonian theory of meaning for a natural language (§ 6.2), whereby the meaning (reference and truth conditions) of isolated expressions and sentences depends upon the meanings (reference and truth conditions) of all the other expressions and sentences of the language. This holistic account can work for the language as a whole without being true of the logical constants of the language. In fact the *recursive clauses* of a theory of truth are molecular, since they go recursively from the simple semantic elements to complex elements according to the hierarchy of complexity required by molecularism.[48] Each recursive clause of a truth-theory can be isolated from the others and considered as a definition fixing the meaning of each logical constant, and thus as giving an 'analytic truth'. As Davidson himself points out:

> A theory of truth does not yield a definition of logical consequence or logical truth, but it will be evident from a theory of truth that certain sentences are true solely on the basis of the properties assigned to the logical constants. The logical constants may be identified as those iterative features of the language that require a recursive clause in the characterization of truth and satisfaction.[49]

It follows that, on Davidson's own account of a theory of truth:

> A truth definition does not distinguish between analytic sentences and others, except for sentences that owe their truth to the presence alone of the constants that give the theory its grip on structure: the theory entails not only that these sentences are true, but that they will remain true under all significant rewritings of their non-logical parts.[50]

The recursive clauses in question can be rewritten as natural deduction rules for the constants (see § 11.5.2). There is then, on this score, a strict parallelism between a semantical account, such as that given by a theory of truth, and a syntactical account, such as that given by a natural deduction system.

Furthermore, Davidson's conception of a theory of meaning is perfectly compatible with the thesis according to which the meaning of a sentence or expression (in particular of a logical constant) is determined by its *inferential role*. For the axioms of a T-theory do not by themselves determine the meaning of the sentences of a language; this meaning is also determined by the kind of *proof* available for the T-sentences. According to Davidson, a T-theory must not only determine truth conditions for sentences, but also *inference* conditions for these sentences:

> [It is an error] to think that all we can learn from a theory of truth about the meaning of a particular sentence is contained in the biconditional demanded by Convention T. What we learn is brought out rather in the *proof* of such a biconditional, for the proof must demonstrate, step by step, how the truth value of the sentence depends upon a recursively given structure. . . . There is no giving the truth conditions of all sentences without showing that some sentences are logical consequences of others.[51]

Of course this does not establish that those proofs, according to Davidson, must conform to the constructivist's standards of 'canonical' proof, as the anti-realist molecularist would want it. But it shows that at least *some* of the molecularist's requirements are available to someone who holds a holistic view of meaning, and in particular the requirement of the *separability* of logical constants.[52]

In the second place, the 'anti-realist' view about the meaning of logical constants, according to which their meaning consists in their assertion conditions and in their inferential role, is quite compatible with a *realist* view of truth as transcending our cognitive powers of verification. We have seen, in Chapter 5, how the anti-realist moves from the thesis that meaning is constituted by assertion conditions (what I have called above, with John Skorupski, the 'epistemic conception of meaning') to the thesis that truth itself should be defined in terms of assertibility ('the epistemic conception of truth'). But, as Skorupski has argued, the epistemic conception of meaning does *not* entail the epistemic theory of truth.[53] To see this, let us suppose that the epistemic conception of meaning is true. Then the meaning of a sentence S will be determined by its assertion conditions, and the content of S will be that its assertion conditions obtain, that is the content of S will be identical to the content of *it is assertible that S*. But if so, *not-S*, and *it is not the case that it is assertible that S* must have the same assertion conditions, and therefore the same content. But this is obviously false: for instance 'The Loch Ness monster does not exist' and 'It is not the case that it is assertible that the Loch Ness monster exits' do not have the same content. There is no general equivalence between assertibility and truth, because even if we can equate a statement and its assertibility with respect to a given state of information, we cannot equate this statement and its assertibility with respect to another, larger state of information. This is particularly true for empirical statements, which are 'defeasible' and can be refuted in the light of new evidence. In other words, it may well be that what we understand when we understand the meaning of a sentence, are its assertion conditions, but it does not follow that the sentence is true because it has these assertion conditions: it can have truth conditions that outstrip our cognitive capacities.

The recognition of this basic point leads us to envisage a position that could combine certain features of the anti-realist account of logical constants and of logical inference with a realist account of truth and a classicist conception of logic. This is the conception put forward by Christopher Peacocke (1986, 1988, in press), who holds the following views:

1. The meanings of logical constants consist in part in their assertion conditions and inferential role.
2. Logical deduction can be justified and can partly answer certain molecularist requirements.
3. Nevertheless, truth is not to be reduced to assertibility, and we should not give up the realist concept of truth, nor adopt logical revisionism.

I shall label this position 'minimal realism': realism, because it rests on a realist account of truth, minimal because it agrees with the anti-realist about some of the epistemic requirements on meaning.[54]

Peacocke's analyses are based on a general theory of the content of thoughts and of concepts, with which we cannot deal here. According to this theory, there are two dimensions of the content of a thought or of a sentence: the condition that leads a thinker to accept this content (or its 'acceptance conditions') on the one hand, and the truth conditions of the content on the other. Peacocke holds that in general the acceptance conditions for a given content *determine* its truth conditions. Let us see what this means for the particular case of sentences containing logical constants.

What are, for instance, the acceptance conditions of sentences containing a conjunction? These are the principles by which a thinker understands conjunction. According to Peacocke these principles are to be 'primitively obvious' in the sense that someone who genuinely understands the meaning of conjunction recognises immediately the validity of certain inferences involving these principles, whereas other principles are only derivative and not immediately recognised. Peacocke calls the former 'sense-determining', and the latter 'sense resultant'. For the case of conjunction, the 'obvious' and sense-determining principles are the usual introduction and elimination rules for '&'. Now Peacocke holds that the very principles we find 'primitively obvious' *are* precisely those that determine the truth conditions of the sentences involving conjunctions, and the validity of these inferences. In other words, if someone accepts as obvious such inferences as the inference from '*A* & *B*' to *A* and to *B*, these inference forms are also truth preserving and they determine the classical semantic value for '&'. A principle that is not primitively obvious for conjunction, on Peacocke's account, is for instance the familiar equivalence between A & B and $-(-A \lor -B)$. For the conditional the rule of *modus ponens* or conditional proof can be considered as primitively obvious, whereas such principles as Peirce's law $(((A \rightarrow B) \rightarrow A) \rightarrow A)$ are derivative and not obvious. The cases of other constants (such as negation, disjunction or quantifiers) are more complex. But Peacocke holds that for all these there are a set of basic principles that are immediately recognised as norms for the logical constants and determine the meanings of the constants, and in turn their semantic values and the truth conditions of the sentences in which they figure.[55]

How far is this conception different from a conception according to which the meanings of logical constants are determined by their 'conceptual' (psychological) role, such as Harman's (compare, in particular, the notion of the 'obviousness' of a principle with Harman's notion of 'immediate implication' above § 2.5.3)? And how far is this conception distinct from the anti-realist view that the meaning of logical constants is given by their proof-theoretic natural deduction rules? I have indeed criticised, at the end of Chapter 2, Harman's notion of 'immediate implication' for being too psychologistic, and for inducing us to confuse the impression that a given inference is valid with its being actually valid. Similarly, I have argued that the meaning of the logical constants cannot consist wholly in their conceptual or inferential role, and that this meaning should be primarily determined by their semantic contribution to truth conditions (§ 11.5.2). But this does not imply that the psychological or conceptual roles associated with a given constant do not play any role in the determination of the meanings of those constants. In particular, if we take these roles as permanent across the subjects' responses, and as obvious for anyone who is presented with inferences containing those constants, then we shall have grounds for taking them as normative acceptance conditions for the logical concepts involved, that is as conditions that *any* rational subject should recognise. And if we can set the appropriate correspondences between the inferential roles of the logical constants and their semantic values, then we shall have grounds for acknowledging the plausibility of Peacocke's conjecture – that normative acceptance conditions determine truth conditions in this particular case.[56]

If this is correct, the requirements that are held by anti-realists to be constitutive of the meanings of logical constants and sufficient to justify logical principles involving those constants – the molecularist requirements of harmony and of conservative extension – *can* be available for a realist who holds that the meaning of logical constants has to meet primarily semantic criteria of truth-preservingness. For that, the realist has to claim that a constant that is introduced in conformity with such requirements must also be truth preserving. Peacocke calls this claim 'the Semantic Constraint'.[57] To show that a requirement of conservative extension is not only compatible with, but also depends upon this Semantic Constraint, Peacocke argues as follows. If we have a sound and complete logic LC for a language L, and if a new constant δ conforming to a set of rules $P(\delta)$ is introduced into this language, then if there is a semantic assignment that validates the rules $P(\delta)$, then these rules $P(\delta)$ conservatively extend LC over L. Suppose we can derive a certain conclusion B from certain sentences $A_1 \ldots A_n$ of the unextended language according to LC and $P(\delta)$. Since LC is sound and since the rules $P(\delta)$ are sound, then under the given assignment of δ, in any model in which $A_1 \ldots A_n$ are true, B is true. Now since LC is complete, B can also be derived from $A_1 \ldots A_n$ according to LC. If follows that conservative extension holds in this case. It does not, hold, however if LC is sound but not complete. For instance, if LC is second-order logic, then there are sentences that can be true but not provably so. This shows, according to Peacocke, that the molecularist require-ment of conservative extension for logical constants is available for a realist, but that it cannot be accepted in any case. It cannot be accepted, in particular, in the cases where truth cannot be equated with provability or assertibility. All this is in agreement with Peacocke's criterion for logical constants, which we have discussed at the end of Chapter 11, according to which the proof-theoretical principles for the constants have also to answer semantical principles.

A realist, therefore, can accept certain molecularist requirements. But he will not follow the anti-realist in holding that these requirements are everywhere mandatory, for this would lead him, with Dummett and Tennant, to reduce truth to assertibility, and to opt for logical revisionism in favour of an intuitionistic logic. According to Peacocke's minimal realism, the realist need not be a holist with respect to logical constants, and he does not need to reject the idea that logical principles should be justified. He will hold that the meaning of logical constants is determined by a set of minimal rules, which fix their contribution to *truth*, and not only to inference conditions, and which are primitively obvious for anyone who grasps their sense (the 'sense-determining principles'). Thus logical deduction will be justified, without this justification being given through principles that lead us to assimilate truth to assertibility and to adopt a non-classical logic.[58] In other words, there can be, contrary to what Dummett claims, a *realist* justification of logical deduction. This means that the principles by which we determine the meanings of logical constants are relatively independent of the conception of truth one adopts.

This minimal realism (or 'molecular anti-constructivism', as Peacocke calls it) is still programmatic, and I shall not detail the specific proposals on which it rests. But it should at least be considered as a coherent option in the logical space of the different accounts of logical necessity that we have so far examined. But we still have to develop some of the consequences of this minimal realism for the aprioricity of logical truths.

12.6   In what sense are logical truths *a priori*?

On the minimal realist position just outlined, there is a set of basic principles by which the meaning of logical constants is determined, and in this sense, they can be said to determine a set of *analytic* truths, or truths by virtue of meaning (see also

§ 11.5). We have seen above that this notion of analyticity is still compatible with a holistic theory of meaning such as Davidson's. Because the principles that determine the meanings of logical constants are 'primitively obvious' they are known and understood non-inferentially, independently of experience, and are, in this sense, *a priori*. Because they express acceptance conditions for the logical concepts involved, they can be said to be *normative* in the sense that they represent rules that anyone should follow if he is to reason logically. According to minimal realism, logical truths do not answer a world of trans-empirical or transcendent facts by virtue of which they would be necessary, as is the case for the strong, cognitivistic or Fregean, Realist. But if this is so, in what sense can the minimal realist position be different from the conventionalist brand of anti-realism such as Tennant's position sketched in § 12.5.2 above, according to which the analyticity, apriority and normativity of logical truths consists only in their being conventions that we have decided to accept?

The answer lies in the fact that although there are, for a minimal realism, epistemic constraints on the meaning of logical concepts (this is why this realism is *minimal*), it does not follow that logical truths are true 'by virtue of meaning alone', and that meaning consists only in assertibility conditions or that truth reduces to assertibility (this is why we have a minimal *realism*). Logical truths can still be true in virtue of 'the way the world is', since a logical truth will be true because its meaning will also be given by a disquotational T-sentence, and will be expressed in *semantical* terms. And logic itself will be used to derive the validity of the semantical properties of the logical constants. So the minimal realist will agree with Quine's criticism of conventionalism on that score.[59] But he will disagree with Quine in holding that logic can still be justified by a basic set of primitive principles.

The minimal realist can also agree with the basically Wittgensteinian point that logical truths express norms, which do not correspond to any reality or to any 'rigid' universe of facts. In this sense he can also be a minimal conventionalist. But he will not draw the conclusion that these truths are only 'conventional', because the fact that logical concepts obey certain normative acceptance conditions, by virtue of which we take them as correct, does not imply that the meaning of the sentences in which they figure consists only in their assertion conditions. As we have seen, the normative acceptance conditions of logical constants (the conceptual or inferential roles determined by their meaning giving principles) determine their *truth* conditions, and these truth conditions can hold without being recognised by us. What does it mean to say that logical concepts can figure in judgements that are *a priori*, normative and universally true? To see this, consider the case of negation. A primitively obvious principle governing this constant is that a sentence A cannot be true while its negation $-A$ is also true. In other words, someone who understands negation cannot rationally accept such sentences as

London is pretty and London is not pretty.

This means that a thinker cannot sincerely believe such a proposition, and that it would be irrational for him to assent sincerely to it. Of course there can be circumstances where it is possible to attribute to him such a belief: circumstances where, for instance, he believes successively that London is pretty and then that London is not, after all, pretty; or circumstances where he mistakes London for another town. But someone who would sincerely assert both conjuncts simultaneously would be irrational.[60] In this sense, he would not conform himself to the *norm* that is expressed by the incompatibility of a sentence and its negation, or his concept would not be the concept of negation. This way the usual natural deduction rule of negation-introduction

$$(-I) \quad [A] \quad [A]$$

$$\cfrac{B \qquad -B}{-A}$$

is a primitive rule. But, as we have seen, such a principle or rule can only be valid if it determines the correct truth function of negation. An intuitionist will of course object that this determines the *classical* concept of negation, not the intuitionist one, and he will not accept such derivative principles as the inference of A from $--A$. Nevertheless, he would have to admit that a minimally rational thinker has to accept such a principle as $(-I)$.[61] I want to suggest that it is in this sense that logic is normative: it determines principles one ought to believe as *true* (and not only as assertible or justifiable), such as the principles that if X believes that p then X believes that p is true, and does not believe that p & not-p is true. Logic determines what it is minimally rational for us to believe, and such minimal principles on the coherence and consistency of our beliefs are both normative, in the sense that they state what it is correct to believe, and *a priori*, in the sense that such truths do not depend upon our experience or upon empirical facts (I shall come back to this normative status of logical truths with respect to our psychology in Chapter 13).

Finally, how does this position help us in solving the Wittgensteinian rule-following problem stated at the beginning of this chapter? This problem was that there does not seem to be any *fact* that could settle which rule a thinker is following when we attempt to ascribe to him the possession of certain concepts or rules. To answer fully this so-called 'sceptical challenge' – if it is indeed such a challenge – would need a lot more space than it is possible to use here, but we can at least outline the bases of a solution. In the light of the preceding remarks, it can be agreed that the rules of logic, being normative, do not answer to any fact, and thus that the meanings of logical concepts are not justifiable by the holding of any natural, or non-natural facts. But if the understanding of these concepts rests on some primitive principles, then their meaning is not subject to the kind of indeterminacy that is supposed to appear with such examples and the 'quus' function mentioned above (§ 12.1). Indeed the very fact that a thinker takes those principles as primitively obvious prevents us from saying that he does not know *which* logical rules he is following, or that he does know whether he is following rules at all. This is certainly not enough to rule out all the 'sceptical doubts' that can be adduced here, but it points towards the way of a non-sceptical account of the possession of logical concepts.[62]

I have attempted to give an account of logical necessity that addresses the main questions (a)–(f) listed at the end of § 12.1 above. I have not, however, dealt explicitly with the last question (g), about the choice of logic that this account can induce. Without an answer to this question of whether logic can be revised, an account of logical necessity is incomplete.

12.7 Can logical rules be revised?

12.7.1 Absolutism and relativism in logic

Let us return to the problem, mentioned only briefly in Chapter 11, of an internal criterion of demarcation of logic. There are several possible answers to the question: 'Which logic is the "right" logic?' Let us try to give a taxonomy of the possible answers. The position according to which this question should be answered affirmatively can be called, in Van Heijenoort's phrase, *absolutism*, and the position according to which we should give a negative answer can be called *relativism*.[63] Each of these positions admits of subdivisions. According to *conservative* absolutism, only classical logic is the right logic. According to *revisionist* absolutism, only one non-classical logic (for instance intuitionistic logic, or relevance logic) is the right logic. On the relativist side, one can say that there is no logic which is the 'right' one, because the idea that a logical system is the 'right' one does not make sense: for the idea of the 'rightness' of a logical system is only relative to our interests, which can vary. Let us call this position *instrumentalism*. But one can also say that there is no right logic, because several logics can be equally right, or because every logic can be the right one (this position is difficult to distinguish from instrumentalism). Let us call this position *pluralism*. One can then draw the following table of these various positions:[64]

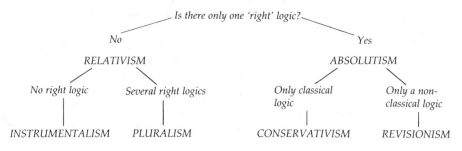

In order to be complete, this table should include two distinctions which cannot figure in it. On the one hand one must distinguish (as above § 7.1, 11.1) the non-classical logics that are *extensions* of classical logic, from non-classical logics that are considered as rivals with respect to classical logic. From this point of view, one can subscribe to classicism and at the same time accept the idea that such logics as modal logics are legitimate extensions of classical logic (this is the position adopted in Chapters 7 and 11, which stands in between conservatism and pluralism). On the other hand one must distinguish the thesis according to which the rivalry between classical logic and non-classical logic is genuine and real, from the thesis that this rivalry is only apparent. Someone who holds this second thesis can refuse the very distinction between conservatism, revisionism and pluralism, in holding that it is not even possible to draw these two last distinctions, since it is impossible to compare classical notions with non-classical notions. This thesis can lead to a form of radical conservatism or to a form of radical pluralism.

To give a full answer to all these questions would imply that we examine the variety of reasons one might have to reject classical logic, the various possible forms of deviation or of extension, and the various systems into which they are incorporated. I shall limit myself to a small number of examples, dealing only with the principle of non-contradiction and the principle of the excluded middle.

Quine's philosophy will, here again, serve as a lever, since Quine offers radical answers to each of the preceding questions. For Quine holds that:

(A) *All* logical laws are *in principle* revisable.
(B) The rivalry between classical and 'deviant' logics is only apparent.

Thesis (A) is typically expressed in the passage from 'Two dogmas of empiricism' quoted above (§ 12.4.3), and seems to be a direct consequence of his rejection of the analytic/synthetic distinction: it implies a form of pluralism according to which all the laws of classical logic should be changed. Thesis (B), on the contrary, seems to imply that we cannot really change our logic, since there is no jurisdiction higher than classical logic to *judge* the real nature of such a change. This position goes in the direction of absolutism and conservatism. Many commentators see here a contradiction, but it is only a characteristic tension of Quine's holistic position, for which all logical laws could be in principle revised, while we should also resist such changes and keep classical logic at the centre of our conceptual scheme. Be it as it may, I want to reject (A) and (B), and to hold that not all logical laws are revisable, and that there is a genuine rivalry between logics.

12.7.2 Is there a rivalry between the logics?

Let us deal first with the problem of rivalry. I have held above that the principle of non-contradiction formulated under the form 'no statement can be both true and false', is *a priori*, and necessary, as a maxim of normative rationality. As we have seen this principle corresponds to the natural deduction rule of 'absurdity', *ex falso sequitur quodlibet*: from a contradictory pair of statements, p & $-p$, one can infer anything. On this rule rests the notion of consistency of a formal system. But, whatever its centrality to our theory of logic, this rule, seen from another angle, is rather unnatural: in fact it is one of the 'paradoxes of material implication' (§ 7.1). If we want to say about the very concept of implication that it is such that anything cannot imply anything, this rule is objectionable. This is precisely the objection raised by those logicians who aim at forging a concept of implication such that only the *relevant* consequents of their antecedents can be logical consequences of these.[65] These logicians do not agree that anything at all can be derived from a contradiction. They do not for that reject the absurdity rule as such, but they reject the classical reasoning which leads to it:

(1) p & $-p$ [premise]
(2) p [by (1) and &−elimination]
(3) $-p$ [by (2) and &−elimination]
(4) $p \lor q$ [by (2) and $\lor$ −introduction]
(5) q [by (3) and (4), and the rule of disjunctive syllogism]

The rule of disjunctive syllogism is the rule

$$\frac{p \qquad\qquad -p \lor q}{q}$$

and it is precisely this rule that is criticised by the 'relevance' logicians. This rule is nothing else than a version of *modus ponens* (through the equivalence between $(-p \lor q)$ and $p \to q$; this is why it is sometimes called *modus ponens for* '$\lor$'). By rejecting this last principle and its application, the relevance logician denies that a contradiction implies anything. As Michael Dunn says, you would not want that a contradictory information about the colour of your car, which would be stored one way or another in the computer of the FBI could lead it to infer the conclusion that you are Public Enemy Number One.[66] Consequently, the relevance logician argues, one needs to reformulate the principles of material implication so that p can imply q only if q is *relevant*, one way or another, with respect to p. For instance, in Anderson and Belnap's system of relevant logic,[67] the following propositional axioms are found:

(I) $A \Rightarrow A$
(II) $(A \Rightarrow B) \Rightarrow ((C \Rightarrow A) \Rightarrow (C \Rightarrow B))$
(III) $(A \Rightarrow (B \Rightarrow C)) \Rightarrow (B \Rightarrow (A \Rightarrow C))$
(IV) $(A \Rightarrow (A \Rightarrow B)) \Rightarrow (A \Rightarrow B)$

In this system (which is only one among a variety of possible systems of 'relevance logic'), the sign '$\Rightarrow$' does not have the same meaning as the classical '$\to$', and in particular the equivalence between '$p \to q$' and '$p \lor q$' does not hold. '$\Rightarrow$' therefore, is not the classical material conditional, and it does not correspond to the classical concept of implication or validity, but only to the concept of *relevant* implication. This system is complete and decidable. Given these distinctions, it is no longer true that, through the use of the rule of disjunctive syllogism, anything can be inferred from a contradiction. What the relevantist logician is in fact looking for is a natural deduction rule for '$\vee$' according to which the rule of $\vee$-introduction becomes *harmonious*, in the sense of the preceding paragraph, with the elimination rule of disjunctive syllogism, and *conservative* with respect to this rule. The problem posed by disjunctive syllogism is that the statement $p \vee q$ can have been introduced (as in the derivation 1–5 above), by $\vee$-introduction. But to infer q from $p \vee q$ and from $-p$ can be legitimate only if we accept that the inference from p and $-p$, to q is itself legitimate. But this is precisely what is in question. One can see, then, that the relevantist logician's preoccupations are not different from those of a molecularist theorist of meaning.

Other logicians go even further, and reject the principle of contradiction and the rule *ex falso sequitur quodlibet*. They propose 'paraconsistent' logics, in which (A & $-A$) can be a theorem, although it is not *always* a theorem. Their aim, in particular, is to account for the fact that certain paradoxes and antinomies have 'veridical' character, in spite of their contradictoriness. Thus Newton da Costa has proposed a paraconsistent system with the following axioms:[68]

(1) $A{\rightarrow}(B{\rightarrow}A)$
(2) $(A{\rightarrow}B){\rightarrow} ((A{\rightarrow} (B{\rightarrow}C)){\rightarrow}(A{\rightarrow}C))$
(3) $A{\rightarrow}(B{\rightarrow}(A\&B))$
(4) $(A\&B){\rightarrow}A$
(5) $(A\&B){\rightarrow}B$
(6) $(A{\rightarrow}C){\rightarrow}((B{\rightarrow}C){\rightarrow}((A\vee B){\rightarrow}C))$
(7) $A{\rightarrow}(A \vee B)$
(8) $B{\rightarrow}(A \vee B)$
(9) $A, A{\rightarrow}B \vdash B$
(10) $-- A{\rightarrow}A$
(11) $A \vee -A$
(12) $B^{(n)}{\rightarrow}((A{\rightarrow}B){\rightarrow}((A{\rightarrow}-B){\rightarrow}-A)$
(13) $A^{(n)}\&B^{(n)}{\rightarrow}((A{\rightarrow}B)^{(n)}\& (A \&B)^{(n)}\& (A \vee B)^{(n)})$

where 'A is an abbreviation for a sequence '$-(A \& -A) \& \ldots -(A \& -A)$'. Here '&', '$\vee$' and '$\rightarrow$' all have their classical meanings. The question is whether '$-$' can also have its classical meanings. This system is complete and decidable.

Can the rejection (or the modification?) of the principle *ex falso sequitur quodlibet* by relevance logic and paraconsistent logic count as a real revision of classical logic? Quine holds that the revision is only apparent:

> What if someone were to reject the law of non-contradiction and so accept an occasional sentence and its negation both as true? An answer one hears is that this would vitiate all science. Any conjunction of the form '$p\&-p$' logically implies every sentence whatever; therefore acceptance of one sentence and its negation as true would commit us to accepting every sentence as true, and thus forfeiting all distinction between true and false.

In answer to this answer, one hears that such a full-width trivialization could perhaps be staved off by making compensatory adjustments to block this indiscriminate deducibility of all sentences from an inconsistency. Perhaps, it is suggested, we can so rig our new logic that it will isolate its contradictions and contain them.

My view of this dialogue is that neither party knows what he is talking about. They think they are talking about negation '−', 'not'; but surely the notation ceased to be recognizable as negation when they took to regarding some conjunctions of the form 'p & −p' as true and stopped regarding such sentences as implying all others. Here, evidently, is the deviant logician's predicament: when he tries to deny the doctrine he only changes the subject.[69]

Quine uses the same argument about intuitionist logic. When the latter rejects the principle of the excluded middle, $A \lor -A$, it only changes the meaning of the connectives, and in particular the meaning of negation. $A \lor -A$ then means '*A has been verified or A has been refuted*'. If Quine is right, there cannot be any real *translation* of the intuitionistic connectives into the classical ones (such as the translation presented in § 6.5 above), and the same would be true about relevance logic or paraconsistent logic. These logics, according to Quine, do not revise, and thus do not refute, classical logic; by changing 'the doctrine' they only 'change the subject'.

To see whether Quine's view is right, let us, for the time being, leave aside paraconsistent logic, and let us refer to the 'deviations' represented by relevance logic and intuitionist logic. In view of the meaning of logical constants adopted so far here, it is undeniable that that relevance logic changes the meaning of '→' when it uses '⇒' instead, and that intuitionist negation changes the meaning of '−', for the rules that fix the meanings of the connectives differ. But does it follow that there is a radical intranslatability between these logics and classical logic? No, because we are in fact dealing with the notion of implication in relevance logic, and with the notion of negation in intuitionist logic. It does not follow that those logics change 'the subject' by 'changing the doctrine', because the *reference* of the connectives is held constant, whereas their *meanings* change. One can have a different doctrine about validity from the classical doctrine, but we are still talking about validity and about *truth*. Of course the intuitionist has another notion of truth, truth as assertibility, but intuitionism is still dealing with truth, as we have seen from the realist/anti-realist debate about logical constants. In this sense, there can be a dialogue between the classicist logician and the intuitionist logician.[70]

Is it on the other hand, possible to talk, as Quine does, of a *complete* or total change of meaning of the connectives in the 'deviant' logics? No, since the relevantist logician does not assert, contrary to what Quine implies, the truth of 'p & −p'. He only refuses the absurdity rule that goes with it. Moreover this rule is valid in intuitionist logic, even though the intuitionist rejects other rules that go with negation, such as '− −$p \vdash p$'. It is still true that, in both systems – the classical and intuitionist – *no statement is both true and false*. One can only speak here of revisions that are *more or less* strong. What relevance logic and intuitionist logic have in common is that they are *weaker* systems than classical logic. Thus intuitionist logic is weaker than classical logic, in the sense that all the theorems of the former are also theorems of the latter, but the converse is not true (every inference provable intuitionistically is also provable classically, but some classical inferences are not provable in intuitionist logic).[71]

Let us now return to paraconsistent logic. Does it assert the *falsity* of the principle of non-contradiction? It is important here to distinguish paraconsistent logics from the so-called 'dialectical' logics, which are based on the idea that there are *real* contradictions *in things*. These logics may rest on considerations that are similar to those of the logicians who are ready to accept that there are exceptions to the principle *ex falso sequitur quodlibet*. But their other motivations are notoriously obscure. Although it is clear that paraconsistent logics *are* logics in the usual sense of the term, it is much less clear about 'dialectical logics'.[72] Paraconsistent logics, just like relevance logic, are based on the idea that the deductive powers of classical logic are too strong when one accepts the principle *ex falso sequitur quodlibet* without restriction. This leads them to accept that, in *some* important cases, $A \& -A$ can be a theorem. But does it follow that they adopt a different attitude from the classicist's with respect to the *metatheoretical* principle of non-contradiction? No: refusal of the fact that $A \& -A$ entails anything is based on the same requirement as the classicist logician when he rejects logics that lead to contradictions. It is the requirement that we should *keep control over our inferences*. The classical logician intends to reject every theory that would produce *any* contradiction. The paraconsistent logician intends to accept *some* 'interesting' contradictions (in particular those that contain paradoxes and antinomies), but he does not intend to accept *all* contradictions. In this sense, he tries, just as the classical logician, to control our deductions, and his general attitude does not differ from the attitude of the classical logician. As Tarski already remarked:

> I do not think that our attitude toward an inconsistent theory would change even if we decided for some reason to weaken our system of logic so as to deprive ourselves of the possibility of deriving every sentence from any two contradictory sentences.[73]

In other words, to accept, with the relevantist or the paraconsistent logician, a weakening of the laws of classical logic does not amount to a withdrawal of the requirements upon which the latter is based, as a *logic*.

12.7.3 To what extent can logic be revised?

Can we accept Quine's thesis (A), that all logical laws are in principle revisable? Quine holds, as we have seen, that for pragmatic reasons having to do with the necessity of preserving the coherence of our theory of nature, we can most of the time refuse revisions. I want to agree with Quine that we should reject the two extreme positions: radical absolutism, according to which we should not change any logical laws, on the one hand; and radical pluralism, according to which every logical law can be changed, on the other hand – but for somewhat different reasons than Quine's pragmatist reasons.

Each one of these extreme positions rests upon a dubious assumption, according to which a logic is associated with a certain structure of thought, a certain interpretation of reality, or a *conceptual scheme*, expressed by this logic. According to absolutism, there is only one conceptual scheme, and it cannot be revised or replaced by other schemes. According to pluralism and relativism, there is a plurality of such schemes. Is it possible to talk of such logical conceptual schemes? Donald Davidson has given strong reasons to suspect the notion of a conceptual scheme in general.[74]

Davidson has argued, in the first place, that the notion of a conceptual scheme presupposes a dualism between, on the one hand, a system of concepts, of theories, or of languages, which organise a given or reality, and, on the other hand, this unorganised given or reality. But does such a contrast make sense, and is there any conceptual, theoretical or linguistic intermediary between our sentences and reality? In the Tarskian conception of truth defended in Chapter 5 above, this contrast does not make sense, and our sentences are true without the interposition between them and reality of schemes that they would 'fit'.

In the second place, and in so far as the notion of a conceptual scheme is associated with that of a language (here of a logical language), is it possible to talk of conceptual schemes that would be different from our own, and *incommensurable*, as Quine supposes them to be in the case of deviant logics? Now, we can talk in this way only if we can *translate* these languages into our own. But a language can be translated only if there is already, for it and our own, a common ontology. But we can only give sense to failures or translation if they are *local* or partial, but not global. As Davidson says: 'A background of successful translations is required to make those failures intelligible', and 'talking of different points of view makes sense, but only if there is a common coordinate system onto which they can be placed: thus the existence of a common system refutes the thesis of a dramatic incompatibility'.[75] In other words, we can translate a language (logic) into another only if there is, for these languages (logics) a background of common, and stable, truths. I shall not spell out the whole Davidsonian argument here, or the tacit departure that it implies from Quine's thesis of the indeterminacy of translation.[76] But it should be noted that it rests upon an extended use of the principle of charity (§ 6.2.1, see also below § 13.4.2). Not only should we try to maximise agreement when we translate logical constants, but we are bound to do so. It might also be asked whether a rejection of the scheme/content dualism is consistent with the acceptance of the analytic/synthetic distinction in § 12.5 above, given that the rejection of the first dualism is advocated by Davidson on the basis of the second dualism. But it should be remembered that we have accepted the idea of the analyticity of *logical* truths only, because of the separability of logical constants only, and not for a whole language.

The background of common, unrevisable truths that we have to presuppose consists, in particular of those that have the status of *a priori*, necessary and normative logical principles. In this sense we can say that the non-classical logics must share with classical logic a *generic* concept of truth, which is neutral with respect to the various interpretations that they give. This generic concept is expressed by Tarski's equivalence principle '*S* is true iff *p*' which, as we have seen (§ 6.5), is compatible with an intuitionist logic. It could be shown that it is also compatible with a relevance logic.

It follows that a verdict of total revision of logic is impossible, since it can only be settled against such a background of common principles. A verdict of total irrevisability, however, is also impossible, since even a judgement about the 'recalcitrance' of a principle supposes that some principles are not put into question.[77] I conclude, therefore, that a partial revision of classical logic is possible, but that, in any case, the kind of radical revisionism that is adopted by the logicians and philosophers who would replace a non-classical logic with a classical logic is impossible. Nor should it be said that this position is inspired by a form of holistic account of the justification of logical principles, according to which these are justified only by our overall practice. On the minimal realist position exposed above, there can be an epistemic justification of *classical* principles. In this sense conservatism is not simply forced upon us. To complete the *a priori* argument based on the criticism of the notion of conceptual scheme and on the principle of charity, one should examine in each particular case whether such or such a revision is justified, and whether it is partial or global. I have held that in the case of relevance logic, intuitionist logic and paraconsistent logic, we should not accept global revisions. I shall not examine here the sources of other possible deviations, such as quantum logic.[78] But if the argument given here is coherent, the extent to which one should revise classical logic should be much less than has often been claimed.

The conception here defended admits that we can have good reasons to accept partial revisions, and that the rivalry between classical logics and non-classical logics (at least those that are not extensions of classical logics) is real. In this sense this conception concedes to the pluralist that there may not be only one 'right' or 'correct' logic. But this notion of 'rightness' or 'correctness' itself has to be questioned. If by it we mean 'correct to describe a universe of facts', we fall back into the Realist, descriptivist or cognitivist illusion, according to which a logic has to represent such a universe. To say that there can be more than one correct logic does not amount to the suggestion that there could be different descriptions of a 'logical reality' from those that we in fact have, and which could be incommensurable with our own. This point of view is fallacious on two counts. On the one hand it is suggested that logic could, through a different scheme, describe another reality than that described by our scheme. But if the scheme/content dualism is incoherent, this suggestion is itself incoherent. On the other hand, in suggesting that logic could *describe* better, or differently, some reality, one supposes that logic has to describe something. But logic does not describe a world, be it empirical or transcendent. It establishes norms, and its propositions have the status of rules. It does not describe anything. But it does not thereby cease to deal with *truths*. This is where the position advocated here differs from a straightforward Wittgensteinian position. On the latter position, because logical rules are norms, they cannot, strictly speaking, be true or false, because normative statements do not correspond to a world of facts. On the present position, however, it does not follow, from the thesis that logical rules express norms, that they cannot be truths, because the fact that they express rational, justified, norms implies that they can be true without being verified by us. The norms are norms of truth. This is because, in the minimal realist view, there is an intimate link between normative acceptance conditions and truth conditions. But it remains to be seen how these rational acceptance conditions function with respect to the actual psychology of subjects.

——— 13 ———

LOGIC AND RATIONALITY

13.1 Logic and psychology

The story of Achilles and the Tortoise has, in addition to the various morals that have been drawn from it in the preceding chapter, a further moral. If the Tortoise does not want to infer from the propositions that Achilles gives to him the conclusion he would like him to infer, it is, it seems, because logic in itself cannot force him to infer those conclusions. In order to perform the *act* of inferring those conclusions, that is to *accept*, or to *recognise* that the truth of the conclusion follows from the truth of the premises, the Tortoise needs also to *believe* that if a given proposition *A* is true, then another proposition *B* is true also. But logic in itself is only a set of 'written' propositions, which does not tell anything about the *reasons* one might have to believe the truth of some premises or the truth of some conclusions on the basis of these premises. Lewis Carroll himself excelled, in his logic manuals, in giving examples of logical arguments based on absurd or exotic premises.[1] An argument is valid even though we do not believe for one minute the truth of its premises, provided that the conclusion is also true, and given that it is derived according to the rules of logic. But logic does not give us any reason to believe the truth of these propositions. The Tortoise's point is even more radical: logic does not give any reason to believe in its own rules either. The psychological act of inferring, the belief that this can be inferred from that, is something different from the fact that a series of propositions is written in a logic book. In other words, logic is a description of certain entailments, but it does not say anything about the psychology of reasoning, or about the psychological reasons that we have for recognising the validity of an inference.[2] The psychology of reasoning studies the various ways in which we actually believe certain propositions on the basis of others. But logic is not about our beliefs. For instance the rule of *modus ponens* does not tell us that if we *believe* that *p*, and if we believe that *if p then q*, then we *believe* that *q*.

This point is welcome for the Fregean Realist who believes that logic describes a universe of necessary facts that are independent of our psychological representations, but it can also be welcomed by the Wittgensteinian who insists that the 'hardness of the logical must' is nothing other than the constraint imposed by the rules that we have accepted. Logic is normative, not descriptive, with respect to our beliefs: it does not tell us what we believe or how we believe, but what we *should* believe. And what we should believe is something different from a *causal* mechanism through which our acts of inference would be explained. This, however, poses a problem for those who, like Frege and Wittgenstein, insist on the *normativity* of logic. For how can logical rules be norms for our reasonings, if they cannot, by definition, bear on the psychological states through which we make our actual reasonings? What is the relation between the norm and its application, between it and that for which it is supposed to be a norm? What is the relationship between our intuitive judgements that such or such an argument is valid or invalid, and the canons by which logic establishes the validity of arguments in general, or between what the medievals used to call *Logica Utens* (the set of our informal judgements about validity) and *Logica Docens* (the formal rules described by the logician)? To say that logic is normative is not enough. We have to say why it is so.

The answer sketched in the preceding chapter is that logic is normative in the sense that it is a theory about our rational beliefs and judgements, which prescribes the forms of this rationality. But the problem that we need to solve is the following: on the one hand as a *normative* theory of rationality, logic does not need to answer the descriptive question whether we are actually rational when we make inferences, but on the other hand it must, as a *theory* of rationality, help us to answer this question, that is to evaluate our descriptions of rationality. We must therefore examine more fully the relationships between logical norms and the psychology of actual reasoning. We shall thus come back to some of the problems encountered in Chapter 2.

13.2 Psychologism versus anti-psychologism

Psychologism in general is the thesis according to which logic describes the actual psychological processes of reasoning. But there are various forms of psychologism. The strongest version is the naturalist or reductionist psychologism, according to which logical laws *are* laws of human psychology – 'the laws of thought' – in the sense that they can actually be derived from the way we actually think. They are, in this sense, laws of our *nature*. One of the clearest expressions of this thesis is Stuart Mill's view that 'logic is not a science distinct from psychology'. For Mill, the law of non-contradiction is but 'a generalisation from experience', the 'ground' of which is our experience that a belief and the contrary belief exclude each other.[3] In a similar spirit, Alexander Bain held that

> The law of Excluded Middle . . . is simply a generalisation of the universal experience that some mental states are destructive of other states. It formulates a certain absolutely constant law, that the appearance of any positive mode of consciousness cannot occur without excluding a correlative negative mode; and the negative mode cannot occur without excluding the correlative positive mode. . . . Hence it follows that if consciousness is not one of the two modes it must be in the other.[4]

This thesis has two immediate consequences. The psychologist has no difficulty in accepting the first: logic is not a normative discipline which says what we ought to think, but a natural science of how we in fact think. The second consequence is more problematic for the psychologist: if logic is a description of 'the laws of thought', how are logical mistakes possible? To this the psychologist can answer that we sometimes reason badly because of factors that are extrinsic to those psychological laws (for instance lack of attention). He also has an *a priori* response to this question, which Mill (but not all writers in this vein) does not hesitate to endorse: the laws of thought are not necessary laws, but they are contingent and variable. If it were the case that what we consider, in the present state of our psychology, as 'mistakes' or as exceptions to those laws, are systematically and constantly reproduced in our reasonings, then we should have to conclude that the laws of our psychology have changed.[5]

A weaker form of psychologism consists in holding that although logical laws find their origin in mental operations, they rest upon psychological acts that acquire, with respect to their origins, an autonomy and an independence by which they come to be detached from their mental origins, to become leading principles of our conduct of reasoning. This was Peirce's position. For him, a belief is a disposition to act or a mental habit, reinforced by the evolutionary habits of the species. 'In the long run' these habits become identical for all, and can play a normative role by becoming severed from what was previously believed.[6] At a certain stage of the enquiry, we cease to take into account the particular ways by which we have arrived at certain conclusions through certain inferential acts, and we begin to take those forms of inference as general rules of conduct.[7] This is why Peirce can declare that logic is a normative science which does not raise the question of what *is*, but of what *must* be. Like ethics and aesthetics, logic states the goals and ideals of conduct and action, and thus of thought (since for Peirce logical inference is, like any kind of thought, a form of action). Although this position is psychologistic because it gives a natural origin to our logical thought, Peirce in the end gives a definition of logic that is surprisingly close to the anti-psychologistic definition.[8]

Anti-psychologism denies that logic has anything to do with psychology, and that its normative character can be accounted for through any kind of psychological origin of its laws. Nevertheless, anti-psychologism has, just like psychologism, degrees. One of the clearest expressions of anti-psychologism seems, on the face of it, to be Kant's famous statement:

> Certain logicians suppose . . . that there are *psychological* principles in logic. But to accept such principles would be as absurd as taking morality from life. If we took the principles from psychology, that is from observations about our understanding, we would merely see *how* thinking occurs and how it is under manifold hindrances and conditions; this would therefore lead to the cognition of merely *contingent* laws. In logic, however, the question is not of *contingent* but of *necessary* rules, not how we think, but how we ought to think.[9]

Kant, however, adds: 'The rules of logic must be derived from the necessary laws of our understanding', and he defines understanding as the power of rules in the *faculty of thinking*. Many commentators have held here that even though Kant admits that those laws can be thought 'apart from their applications or *in abstracto*', they had to be considered as springing from acts of consciousness. In fact, as Husserl noted, such statements can be accepted by a psychologist who would consider the necessary laws of understanding as psychological.[10]

Because of this ambiguity in the Kantian position, one considers in general that Husserl and Frege are the most radical and uncompromised representatives of anti-psychologism. I shall here leave aside Husserl's views. Among the many criticisms of the psychologist thesis to be found in Frege's work, two of them are prominent:

(a) Psychologism cannot account for the *objectivity* of logical laws, because the subjective representations (ideas, images) that are held by the naturalist psychologist to be the basis of these laws are necessarily *private*, whereas logical laws are *public* and accessible to everyone; logic deals with a universe of thoughts that cannot be reduced to representations (§ 2.2.1).
(b) Psychologism cannot account for the *necessity* of logical laws, for these subjective representations vary from one person to another; but the idea of a variable law is a nonsense.[11]

The source of these criticisms, as we have seen, is Frege's conviction that logic describes an immutable universe, the universe of the 'laws of the being-true', the Platonic 'third world' independent of our representations and our signs. Only the existence of such an autonomous world of thoughts, which are necessarily true and independent of our minds, can warrant the distinction between truth (validity) and recognition of truth (validity), a distinction that is systematically ignored by psychologists (§ 2.5.3). The Fregean position, however, runs into at least three difficulties.

First, it is not obvious that it can be directed against every form of psychologism. Criticism (a), for instance, does not seem to apply to Peircian psychologism as described above, since Peirce does not assimilate our logical beliefs to particular *private* representations, but to habits of action that are *public* and common to all mankind as a species.

Second, the Fregean position (and in general every position according to which a norm consists in the truth of a theoretical proposition corresponding to it) implies that logic is absolutely normative by virtue of its *descriptive* character, that is, as we saw in the preceding chapter, because it describes a universe of necessary *facts*. The realist-cognitivist conception of norms presupposes that a norm can be objective only through its reference to objects or to facts. But it can be thought that the very notion of a norm does not imply any form of description of facts.

Third, Frege's concern to cut radically logic from any psychological datum has the consequence that our relationship with logical laws becomes mysterious: we happen to know them by virtue of a form of intuition (§ 12.2), but it is difficult to figure out how they could be used in actual reasoning.[12] What Frege, and the anti-psychologists in general, leave in the dark is the way in which logic can become *applied*, since they assimilate any applied logic, or any 'art of thinking' (as the Port Royal logicians called it) to a lapse into psychologism.[13]

13.3 The psychology of reasoning

13.3.1 Is the psychology of reasoning psychologistic?

Frege and Husserl rejected the close connection between psychology and logic that was prevalent at the end of the nineteenth century. During the same period, the scientific psychologists distanced themselves from the associationism upon which naturalistic psychologism was based, and from philosophy in general. In this context, anti-psychologism, according to which logic has nothing to do at all with psychology, helped in reconciling the two sides by separating them: to the scientific psychologists was given the psychology of reasoning, to the philosophers pure logic as a theory of the universal validity of reasonings. As Elliot Sober says, 'while the psychologists were leaving, philosophers were slamming the door behind them'.[14]

No contemporary psychologist today holds the form of naturalistic psychologism against which Frege levelled his criticisms. The behaviourism that was prevalent during the first part of the twentieth century was notoriously unable to account for the superior intellectual faculties of thought, and even less, in its more physicalist versions, to produce the sought-for reductions of mental states to behavioural dispositions. In this sense the Fregean argument comes out as stronger: logic does not describe the laws of human psychology in the narrow associationist or behaviourist sense. Nevertheless the psychology of reasoning is a very fruitful branch of contemporary psychology. But it rejects explicitly the kind of psychologism criticised by Frege: it rejects the idea of the subjective character of representations and associationist reductionism. In this sense the Fregean argument is weakened: on the one hand the psychologist no longer bases his hypotheses on the introspective and private character of subjective representations, which would vary from one subject to another, but on his attempts to analyse the objective and testable invariants of representations; and on the other hand, he no longer aims at reducing logical laws to combinations of atomic representations, but tries instead to envisage the *psychological reality* of the abstract schemes of inference described by the professional logician.

Neither of the two schools that have dominated the psychology of reasoning in the twentieth century can be called psychologist in Frege's sense. The first, Piagetian developmental psychology, studies the stages that occur in the formation of concepts and judgements during childhood and adolescence. Logic is, for Piaget, the correct description of the state of equilibrium reached by logical thought at its ultimate stage of formation in the adolescent. But the genetic steps in this developmental process, even if they contain virtually the equilibrium laws reached at an ulterior stage, are the product of mental operations which 'pure' logic itself does not *describe*. In this sense Piaget is explicitly opposed to the conceptions according to which logic is 'the mirror of thought'. The problem, however, is to know whether the mental 'operations' *through which* logic is constituted (but with which it should not be identified) coincide with the structures of logic itself, and to what extent.[15] The second school, cognitive psychology, rests upon the information-processing model. An information-processing model in psychology must show how inputs are transformed into outputs, and how the intermediaries in such a system transfer information. The inputs and the outputs differ from one cognitive task to another (for instance in visual processing and in conscious judgements), and in this sense there will be no reduction of the 'superior' to the 'inferior' (to use the language of the nineteenth century). The entities on which the information processing is based will be *inner representations*. Whether they are considered as propositional, imaginistic or of any other nature, these representations are supposed to be *objective* media, which are transformed, through an information-processing mechanism, into other representations, to produce outputs, which, at the most general level, produce behaviour. According to one of the most influential cognitive models, this information is processed through structured *symbolic entities*, namely sentences, or analogues of sentences of a language. The transformation of representations will be performed by *inferential processes* operating on these inner symbolic entities. The question arises whether these inferential processes are identical to the inference rules of logic, and to what extent.[16] The Piagetian model and the cognitive model thus raise similar problems. But these problems are distinct from those raised by the classical psychologistic thesis, since it is no longer asked whether the genetic, or informational, processes describe logical rules and explain the fact that they are rules, but rather it is asked whether the logical rules themselves can describe these processes. Contemporary psychology is not committed, at this level, to reductionism, for it does not purport to reduce the representations of valid inference given by logic to psychological representations or processes. In fact cognitive psychology postulates an autonomous level of representation that is intermediate between the usual descriptions that we give of mental states and the physiological processes that subserve these states (it is, in particular, one of the assumptions of the 'functionalist' view in the philosophy of mind that there is such an intermediate level at which mental states can be studied).[17] Given, therefore, that contemporary psychologists do not attempt to explain the nature and the objectivity of logical laws by the holding of psychological laws, they are not committed to psychologism in its traditional form. They are, however, committed to a different form of psychologism, when they hypothesise that logical laws can have a 'psychological reality'. But this form of psychologism is much more plausible than the classical forms of this thesis.

13.3.2 'Mental logic'

Several contemporary schools in the psychology of reasoning have proposed the hypothesis that the mind contains, in a certain sense, a logic. But which kind of 'logic' is this? And in what sense can it be said to be 'in' the mind? Is it innate or acquired? And in what sense is it responsible for our capacity to reason 'logically'? Let us call, following Johnson-Laird (1983), the generic doctrine of these psychologists 'the doctrine of mental logic'. There are several versions of it, which differ according to: (1) what kind of logic is considered as 'specific' to the mental processes of reasoning; (2) whether it is innate or acquired; and (3) the *medium* of internal representations or operations involved in the exercise of the capacity of reasoning.

One form of the doctrine is Piaget's. According to Piagetian psychology, the 'mental logic' that is present in the human mind is a system of *operations*, characterised by the sixteen possible truth functions of propositional calculus, and the 'INRC' group of transformations, which define the relationships between these truth functions. When Piaget characterises logic as a logic 'of operations', he naturally uses certain constructivistic metaphors; his basic style of presentation, however, is algebraic.[18] The logic of mental operations is not innate. It is shaped through a series of stages, during which children construct operations through an interiorisation of their own actions, and a reflection upon them. The medium through which these operations are constructed is neither a language nor a system of symbols, but what Piaget calls 'operational schemes', which include concepts, strategies and processes necessary for reasoning, and which include, for instance, a strategy of systematic variation of one factor while the others are held constant, or a procedure to construct the set of possible permutations of a collection of elements. At the earlier stages of the development of intelligence, the operational schemes and the operations are only partial, and the 'logic' of the child is only, so to say, a proto-logic. Only at the last stage, with the adolescent, can we find the full set of operations of the INRC group and of the associated schemes. There is then an 'equilibrium' between the various operations, and the constituting logic meets the constituted logic, as it can be described by the propositional calculus. The problem, under the Piagetian hypothesis, is whether we can talk, for the stages that are intermediate between the first acquisitions of logic and the terminal stage of equilibrium, of an interiorisation of the logical operations of the propositional calculus *itself* (for instance disjunction or conjunction). In particular, do the experiments about the perception and conceptualisation of physical equilibria described by Piaget (for example Piaget and Inhelder, 1955) show that children 'possess' the mastery of such and such an operation at such and such a stage, or do they show that they have acquired something else, which is rather the set of extralogical operational schemes and heuristics described by Piaget himself?[19] And how can we attribute to them these competences independently of their linguistic capacities, as Piaget does when he insists on the primacy of the interiorisation of perceived and lived schemes? For these reasons, his results are often considered as ambiguous and inconclusive.

Several writers have formulated versions of the doctrine of mental logic quite different from Piaget's (Osherson, 1975; Braine, 1978; Rips, 1982). They use a syntactic presentation of logic, derived mainly from a Gentzen-type system of natural deduction rules, and they suppose that the representational medium in which inferences are performed (as mental processes) is a *mental language* in which the premises are translated, and to which rules of inference are applied (as logical rules) in order to derive, in this mental language, certain conclusions. The logical mental language, however, is only one of the components of this model, which describes a subject's *competence*. It can be supposed that this competence is innate, although the hypothesis is not always explicit. In any case it is not developmentally acquired, as in Piaget.[20] The second component of the model is a *performance* component, including two programmes: (a) understanding processes that determine the information accepted from premises, and (b) routines and strategies that allow the construction of lines of reasoning.[21] In other words, it is not supposed that the mind applies *directly* the list of the inference rules that it 'possesses'. The rules by themselves do not wear, as it were, their conditions of application on their sleeves. Something like a 'control system' is required, to guide the subject in his inferential strategies to construct a proof of a conclusion from given premises.

For instance, in one of the most developed models, 'ANDS' ('A Natural Deduction System'; Rips, 1982), reasoning begins by constructing a proof in the working memory. The proofs have two components or 'trees': an *assertion tree* and a *subgoal tree*: The first encodes a demonstration in a natural deduction system. The second describes the reverse pathway from the conclusion to the premises. The inferential routines control the actions of the system by putting new assertions and new subgoals in the memory. Each routine is a set of conditions that must be verified on the memory trees to determine whether the routine applies. If the conditions are fulfilled, then a series of actions are performed which modify the trees in a particular way. Thus for the usual *modus ponens* rule, ANDS has two routines.

R_1 (*modus ponens*, backward version)
  conditions: 1. current subgoal: q
      2. the assertion tree contains *if p then q*
  actions: 1. set up the subgoal to infer p
      2. if the subgoal is achieved, add q to the assertion tree

R_2 (*modus ponens*, forward version)
  conditions: 1. the assertion tree contains the proposition $x = if p then q$
      2. x has not been used by R_1 or R_2
      3. the assertion tree contains p
  actions:
      1. add q to the assertion tree

The procedure can be implemented in a computer program.

We can see that the Chomskyan[22] distinction between a competence and a performance component shows that logic, as a vocabulary and as a set of inference rules, is not sufficient by itself to warrant the intelligence of an agent, which involves the capacity to have a goal-directed behaviour. The 'heuristic' component of the system looks much more like the 'techniques' of deduction and of calculus given by logicians in their manuals, which are not statements of formal rules, but rather *resolution procedures* that facilitate the mechanical application of rules.[23] Rips constructs testing procedures for his model, which allow him to establish a correspondence between the possibility of deriving conclusions with help of the various routines and the probability of the subjects reaching these conclusions when they are given specific problem-solving tasks.

Under this version, the doctrine of mental logic poses several problems. The first concerns the logic that is supposed to mirror the psychological competence of the agents. From the psychological point of view, the choice of a natural deduction system rather than, for instance, an axiomatic system, is justified, for the latter is psychologically implausible: some derivations from axioms can involve a great number of steps, and thus increase the complexity and tractability of the reasoning task, whereas the application of natural deduction rules involves a smaller number of steps (see, for instance, the contrast between derivations (A) and (A') of Chapter 12). This is why Gentzen claimed that his rules were 'more natural' than those of an axiomatic system.[24] Nevertheless, a system of 'natural' deduction rules is not natural unless we have some justification for assuming that the meanings of propositional connectives, for instance, are close to their meanings when they are involved in psychological processes of reasoning. This is why several writers have proposed that our basic logic should be revised in order to 'naturalise' it even further. For instance, Braine (1978) proposes a system of 'natural logic' in which (among other things) the rule of →-introduction is absent, because he considers that our mental logic does not contain any truth-functional conditional (see § 2.4.2). But where should this naturalisation process stop? Why should we keep classical rules, and why should not we use relevance logic instead, on the grounds that it is more natural? Should the mental logic include a temporal logic, a deontic logic, and so forth?

A second problem concerns the very idea of a mental language, whether or not it is innate. This notion has often been invoked by cognitive scientists and philosophers of mind (its most famous proponent being Fodor, 1975, 1987). But it raises notorious difficulties. If the sentences through which we perform inferences in daily life get their meaning through an inner linguistic code made up of mental sentences, and if meaning in general is, according to the hypothesis, a matter of there being symbolic representations internal to agents, then the inner linguistic code itself has to be interpreted, and the internal representations must have a meaning; otherwise they would be only syntactic marks devoid of content. But how do these internal representations get their content? From their being translated into another linguistic code of mental sentences that would 'interpret' the first? Or are we to suppose that inside the head there is a little agent who interprets and understands the contentless symbols? But who is going to interpret his interpretation? Another little agent? The threat of a regress obviously arises. The general difficulty with the language of thought hypothesis seems to be that it is not enough, to account for the fact that an agent believes a certain proposition p, to say that this proposition must, in some way, be 'written' into his mental language, as if it were on an internal register or in a special box. Something more is required to explain the fact that the agent represents to himself his belief that p; this fact cannot simply be explained by saying that one or more sentences are inscribed into his mental language. This is another version of Lewis Carroll's problem: the Tortoise cannot believe that p simply by adding new propositions to his list.[25] The psychologist can solve this problem in part by saying that the subject does not simply *store* a set of internal representations in his head, but that he also uses this set through specific processes of understanding and through various heuristics that account for the specific strategies of reasoning in his actual performance of reasoning. But this does not explain why the logical competence is represented in the first place, why the inner symbols have a meaning. The Carroll point is precisely that a *list* (wherever written) of propositions and of rules is by itself inert, and does not tell us how the subject can understand these propositions and rules, and use them in actual reasoning.

Last but not least, the doctrine of mental logic itself encounters the problem of error: human beings often make logical mistakes or paralogisms, and are often unable to recognise the validity or the invalidity of a number of arguments. But the rules of a mental logic belonging to the subjects' competence are suposed to be valid; so how can there be logical mistakes if such rules are internalised? The origin of these errors can always be traced back to the performance level and to the heuristics, which can be fallible though the rules of a mental logic themselves are not supposed to be fallible, since they are internalised in the subject's psychology. But what are we to say about logical mistakes that are almost universally reproduced? Must we say that the mind contains some invalid rules? As we saw above (§ 12.3.2) we can perfectly accept the idea that a system could function with invalid inference rules. If so, how can it be supposed that these rules are isomorphic to those of a valid logical system in the usual sense?

Logical mistakes and paralogisms are common. A number of them are taxonomised in logic manuals under the heading of 'fallacies'.[26] Recently psychologists have undertaken a systematic study of some of these mistakes, in particular as they occur in conditional propositional reasoning. The most famous of these psychological experiments is Wason's *selection task* (Wason, 1968). In it, subjects are given four cards, one side of which is open to view, the other side is hidden. On the visible side of the cards are written the following symbols:

E 4 K 7

The subjects are informed that each card has a number written on one side, and a letter on the other side. The experimenter then presents the subjects with the following generalisation or rule:

> (1) If there is a vowel on one side of the card, then there is an even
> number on the other side

which is of the form *if p then q*. The subject is asked to select the cards that have to
be turned over (in whatever order) to find out whether the generalisation is true or
false. In the display of cards above, the subject is presented with the following
situation:

> E (*p*), K (*not-p*), 4 (*q*), 7 (*not-q*)

To solve the problem, one must make an elementary piece of propositional
reasoning: (1) that the rule must be false if the E card were paired with a number
other than 4; (2) that it is logically necessary to turn over any card that would
falsify the hypothesis. The correct decision consists in choosing the cards E and 7,
which represent the combination *p* and *not-q*, that is the situation in which the
conditional (1) is false. One should infer, by *modus ponens*, that the card E must
have an even number on its back if the hypothesis is true, and therefore that E
must be chosen. And one should infer, by *modus tollens* (*if p then q, but not-q, then
not-p*), that the card 7 must not have a vowel on its back, and thus that it should be
chosen. You should also infer that there is no need to turn over the cards K and 4,
since no matter what there is on their backs, they do not correspond to the
falsifying situation *p and not-q*.

Now the results of the experiments show the following:

(a) Fewer than 10 per cent of the subjects give the correct solution (most of them
    choose the E and 4 cards, or the E card only).
(b) These selections are resistant to change, that is most of the subjects stick to
    their initial choices even when they are shown that these are inconsistent with
    a logical evaluation of the task.
(c) The results are much better when the selection task is reproduced in other
    versions in which more 'realistic' or more 'familiar' materials than letters and
    vowels are presented on the cards, for instance names of city and modes of
    transportation such as:

| Grenoble | | Paris | | Train | | Car |

for the rule:

> (2) When I travel to Grenoble, I take the train.

In such cases, the percentage of correct answers is much higher (up to 60 per
cent). It has been observed, however, that it is not the case for every kind of
'realistic' material;
(d) When the rule is presented under the form *p and not-p* (for instance if it is, for
    the cards above, 'If there is a vowel on one side, then there is not an even
    number on the other side') then most subjects choose the correct combina-
    tion, E and 7.[27]

It is rather difficult to interpret these results. Do they show that the subjects are systematically unable to perform simple conditional reasonings, and that they are, in this sense, irrational (in particular in the light of (b))? The results (c) and (d) seem to point towards possible explanations. Some psychologists (Evans and Lynch, 1973) have argued that (d) shows that the subjects have a 'matching bias', a tendency to select the items that will match the items presented in the rule. This bias may be explained by linguistic and pragmatic factors in the initial presentation of the task (Evans, 1989). Other writers (Johnson-Laird and Legrenzi, 1972) focus on (c), the facilitation of the task when realistic material is present. This suggests *either* that, if there is a mental logic, this logic is more sensitive to the contents than to the form of the propositions, *or*, if we take the mental logic to consist only in *formal* rules and operations, that there is more to human conditional reasoning than these formal rules, *or* that the very hypothesis of a mental logic is false. This last hypothesis is the path followed by the writers who suggest that human reasoning is not a matter of formal rules at all, but rather that it involves the manipulation of entities such as *schemes*, *images* or *models*, which are far less abstract and symbolic than symbolic signs and rules.[28]

13.3.3 Mental models and syllogistic reasoning

Johnson-Laird (1983) adopts a form of this latter hypothesis. He believes that the hypothesis of a mental logic is false, and that one can account for natural reasoning without supposing that subjects have internalised a logical system of rules of inference: 'There can be reasoning without logic. And, more surprisingly, there can be valid reasoning without logic.'[29] To a large extent, we have already encountered this view with Harman (§ 2.5.3). Both Johnson-Laird (§ 2.5.2) and Harman attempt to redefine or to change the usual logical rules in order to give a psychologically more plausible account of reasoning. In this sense, as we have seen, Harman distinguishes the notion of *argument*, which is applicable, according to him, to inferences codified in a logical system, from the notion of *reasoning*, which concerns our inferences in the psychological sense. For Harman, the *deductive* inference rules are not the same as the inference rules, which operate at the level of *reasoning* itself. In particular, reasoning must, according to Harman, include some rules for the *revision* of our beliefs. But logic itself (deductive logic, but also inductive logic) cannot account for our rules of revision of beliefs.[30] But I shall leave aside Harman's views to concentrate on Johnson-Laird's proposals.

According to Johnson-Laird's theory of 'mental models', reasoning is not a matter of *syntactical* inference rules or of analogues of those rules, but a matter of *semantical* rules or of analogues of those rules, through which the subjects construct mental models of the premises of a reasoning and attempt to find mental models of the conclusion. We have already seen how the rules operate in propositional reasonings (§ 2.5.2). The results of Wason's selection task, in particular the subjects' better performance with realistic materials, can thus be interpreted in the light of the fact that they find more easily counter-examples to the proposed rules by constructing models or situations representing the contents of the various propositions, and by using in these cases the semantic fact that a conditional is true if its antecedent is true and its consequent is false.[31] Johnson-Laird's theory, however, is mainly based on an account of syllogistic inferences.

Let us suppose that we are given a pair of syllogistic premises, and that we are asked to find a conclusion on the basis of these premises (it is, in the psychologist's vocabulary a 'W-task': *which* conclusion follows from the premises?, by contrast with an 'Y/N-task': does the conclusion follow from the premises, *yes or no?*):

> A) Some bookmakers are not crooks
> All mafiosi are crooks
> Therefore . . .?

According to Johnson-Laird, one first interprets the premises, by constructing a mental sample corresponding to a representation of particular bookmakers, crooks and mafiosi. The mental models of the two premises can be described thus:

> (1) bookmaker
> bookmaker
> _____
> (bookmaker) = crook
> crook
>
> (2) mafioso = crook
> mafioso = crook
> (crook)
> (crook)

These diagrams are only representations of the models, and the words serve only to differentiate the exemplars of kinds of individuals. The identity between two exemplars is marked by a '=' (thus 'bookmaker = crook' represents a bookmaker who is a crook). In (1) the bookmakers mentioned above the line are those who are not crooks, and similarly below the line there is a crook who is not a bookmaker. The parentheses indicate that there can be a bookmaker who is not a crook. Once the premises are represented, one constructs a model combining the informations contained in them, such as:

> (3) bookmaker
> bookmaker
> _____
> (bookmaker) = crook = mafioso
> crook = mafioso
> (crook)
> (crook)

To get the appropriate conclusion for (A), one tries to read from this model the relationships that hold between the two 'external' terms: bookmakers and mafiosi. Two conclusions are possible:

> Some bookmakers are not mafiosi
> Some mafiosi are not bookmakers

and only the first is valid. To be sure that this conclusion follows, one must check that there are no alternative models of the premises that would make this conclusion false.[32]

Johnson-Laird compares his theory with others and holds that it accounts for the actual performances of the subjects. It can account in particular for what is called the 'figural effect' in syllogistic reasoning: the subjects have a tendency to reason better according to what syllogistic figure is concerned (for instance 51 per cent give the right answer with the first figure, 48 per cent for the second figure, but only 21 per cent for the third). The explanation of this fact lies, according to Johnson-Laird, in the greater number of alternatives that have to be manipulated in the second and third figures to reach the result, and in the greater capacity of memory needed.[33]

Although it is ingenious, the procedure of mental models recalls the traditional resolution procedures for syllogisms. In a certain sense, Aristotle himself used semantical methods and 'models' in his theory of the syllogism, and the role of 'crook' above is clearly the role of the middle term of Aristotelian syllogistics. Aristotle had clearly seen the privileged, 'more scientific', role, of the first figure, which calls for a lesser number of counter-examples.[34] In a certain sense too, the familiar Venn and Euler diagrams can be interpreted in a psychological way as analogues of mental constructions.[35] Johnson-Laird, however, insists rightly on the fact that none of the traditional methods rests on a mechanical *effective resolution procedure* such as his, and that none of them accounts so well for the experimental findings. Moreover, while the construction of mental models through counter-examples has strong affinities with similar methods of construction of counter-examples such as Beth's method of 'semantic tableaux' (§ 11.6.2), Johnson-Laird rightly points out that the latter does not require, unlike the former, any translation into a formal language (such as the predicate calculus) at all, and he suggests that in many cases people are not systematic in their use of mental models, and may use 'quick and dirty' heuristics rather than follow rigid rules.[36]

As I have already observed, the notion of 'mental model' is somewhat ambiguous. Sometimes it seems to play the role of a heuristic construction that is actually used by subjects when they perform inferences, sometimes it seems to belong to their competence. Sometimes it seems to be a purely psychological notion (a mental model in this sense is a real representation in the mind), sometimes it is closer to the non-psychological representations of abstract situations that logicians themselves call 'models' (a mental model in this sense is a partial description, for heuristic purposes, of mental processes the real nature of which is left indeterminate).[37]

Finally, one may ask whether the theory of mental models is really different from the theory of mental logic. The construction of mental models does not involve the use of traditional logical inference rules, but other specific rules (how to construct the premises, how to integrate them, how to find counter-examples). Nevertheless, these latter rules, as we have seen, bear a strong similarity to classical rules, and must conform to the properties of classical syntax even if the medium of representation is not a symbolic medium. For instance the sign '=' must be such that the two items flanking it refer to the same object. In this sense the manipulation of mental models is rather similar to the manipulation of propositions. If it is the case, Johnson-Laird has not given us any reason to think that the mind does not use any logic, but has only formulated a *semantical* version of the thesis of mental logic. To this he could answer, according to the suggestions above, that on the one hand the construction of mental models is often a sort of tinkering, and that on the other hand mental models are not real entities *in* the mind but only posits or postulated entities that are useful for the description of psychological process. But such an answer would reduce the systematicity and the psychological force of this account.[38]

Other kinds of hypotheses have been proposed to account for the properties of conditional propositional reasonings and other kinds of reasonings. Some writers invoke the presence of 'pragmatic schemas', others invoke certain kinds of deontic rules involving 'social contracts' tacitly accepted by subjects. I shall not detail these proposals.[39] In spite of the impressive progress of the psychology of reasoning, one must conclude that the psychologists' attempts to assess the 'psychological reality' of certain rules or schemes, whether or not they are borrowed from logic, are not deeply probing. Even if it is shown that there is a certain amount of isomorphism between psychological schemes or rules and abstract logical structures, the degree of isomorphism is not clearly established. Jonathan Evans has proposed the interesting hypothesis that not one, but two sorts of processes occur in reasoning: on the one hand 'heuristic' processes through which aspects of the information contained in a problem are selected as 'relevant', and on the other hand 'analytic' processes in which inferences are drawn from this information. But it is not always clear where a process of either type begins and where it ends: if, as Evans (1984, 1990) suggests, human reasoning is a 'mixture' of reasoning and biases, it will be very difficult to sort out what belongs to the 'analytic' part and what belongs to the 'heuristic' part.

Two facts at least emerge from these empirical investigations into the psychology of reasoning: logic in itself does not describe, or at least cannot describe *directly*, the processes of natural reasoning (as if the logical rules could be simply transposed to the psychological level); but it cannot codify either something that would be *totally* distinct from the actual conduct of human reasoning (as if logic were only an abstract play from arbitrary rules). The problem is whether these two facts can be reconciled and how.

13.4 Normative rationality and empirical rationality

13.4.1 Logic as a theory of normative rationality

I have already suggested in the preceding chapter that logic is a normative theory of rationality. But this can be understood in at least two senses. The first sense derives from the first fact above: logic does not describe the real states and processes of our psychology (beliefs, thoughts, representations) that occur when we reason. It does not follow that those states do not exist, when we say that someone reasons 'logically' or 'illogically', but it follows that these states are not *causally* responsible for the fact that our reasonings are logical or illogical. What logic 'describes' – if it is a description at all – are the *norms*, *canons* or *criteria* that allow us to evaluate an inference as correct or not. To use a Wittgensteinian vocabulary, the 'grammar' of the adjective 'logical' is that of an *evaluative* term (just as 'good' or 'beautiful'), which determines a property that our inferences must have, and not of a descriptive term (such as 'red', 'hirsute', or 'triangular'), which would determine a factual property about the way we reason. The illusion consists in believing that logic describes certain facts, as a painting or a map does. As we saw, there are two avatars of this descriptive illusion: Fregean Realism, according to which logic is normative because it describes necessary fact; and psychologistic realism, which either (in its strongest form) reduces norms to natural and empirical laws of the mind or (in its weakest version) 'realises' the norms in the psychological representations. But if logic is truly normative, logical rules are, according to Wittgenstein's favourite characterisations, instructions, prescriptions or orders.

Logic is normative in a second sense, closely linked to the first. Once again after a Wittgensteinian metaphor, logic is a standard, or a measuring instrument, according to which we evaluate whether inferences are correct. This corresponds to the second fact noted above: our norms must be applied, they would not be norms if they were inapplicable to *some* reality that in some sense conforms to them and which they help to explain. Normativity does not bear so much here on the evaluation or on the prescription of actions, but on the explanation or the prediction of events. Logic is normative because it sets a number of principles without which we could not explain why agents have a certain competence and why they perform logical inferences in such and such a way. This kind of rationality is not an empirical rationality. When we say that it is empirically true or false that subjects are rational, we are investigating whether *in fact* agents are rational in their deductive behaviour, whereas when we ask what are the principles by which we evaluate the rationality of agents, we are investigating *by what right* we can impose on them a rational or an irrational behaviour. The thesis that the very concept of rationality is a normative concept is the thesis according to which any judgement about the actual rationality or irrationality of an agent must presuppose that some principles or maxims apply *a priori* to the behaviour of the agent, and that these principles themselves cannot be tested empirically, because

any test about actual or empirical rationality can be framed and evaluated only in the light of these *a priori* principles.

A number of writers have held that the interpretation of the behaviour of an agent presupposes the ascription to this agent of logical principles governing his deductive competences. Their argument can be called, after Stich (1985), 'the argument of the inevitable rationality of believers', or the argument of the *necessary presumption of rationality*.

13.4.2 The presumption of rationality

Quine (1960), in his analysis of radical translation (§ 1.4.3), has insisted on the necessity of a presupposition of rationality on the part of the agents whose language is being translated. The chief presupposition takes the form of the 'principle of charity', according to which we must assume that agents are rational. In the context of translation, the principle of charity is threefold: (1) it concerns the *truth* of beliefs: we are likely to prefer translations that 'maximise agreement' between the beliefs of the speakers whose language we translate and our beliefs; (2) it concerns the *rationality* of beliefs: we must suppose that the aliens' beliefs are consistent and non-contradictory; (3) the principle rests on a methodological conservatism about *logic*: a correct translation must preserve classical logical laws (cf. § 12.7.2). It follows that any context in which we would be led to attribute an irrational or illogical belief to a native speaker is suspect by definition, because attributions of beliefs in these cases may come from our incapacity to translate. This is why Quine holds that such conceptions as Lévy-Bruhl's theory of 'pre-logical mentality' are only 'myths injected by bad translators'.[40]

Davidson, in the context of his theory of radical interpretation (§ 6.2), makes a much more extensive use of the principle of charity than Quine. He takes it not only as a general methodological maxim, but also as an *a priori* principle of the attribution of thought contents and the interpretation of behaviour. According to Davidson, the principle of charity is the principle that *most* of a speaker's beliefs must be true and consistent, if we are to interpret his utterances and actions. Charity is not only a regulative maxim for translation, but also a constitutive normative principle on thoughts and beliefs: a thought would not be a thought if it were not supposed to be true and rational in the first place.[41]

Dennett (1978, 1987) has held a similar conception about what he calls *intentional systems*. According to him, when we ascribe beliefs, desires and other intentional states with content to a being (man, animal, machine) we must presuppose that this being is an 'intentional system'. An intentional system is a completely rational system: its beliefs and other states

> are those that it ought to have, given its perceptual capacities, its epistemic needs, and its biography. . . . Its desires are those it ought to have, given its biological needs and the most practicable means of satisfying them. . . . And its behaviour will consist of those acts that it *would be rational* for an agent with those beliefs and desires to perform.[42]

Here the idealisation bears on three kinds of constraints: logical, cognitive and biological. Let us consider only the first. Dennett develops the point that was put forward in the preceding chapter (§ 12.6): the very concept of belief, or of 'propositional' thought cannot be ascribed meaningfully to a given creature if we do not suppose that (a) if X believes that p, then he believes that p is true, and (b) there is large degree of consistency and coherence among its beliefs. For human agents (a) is in general true on the basis of sincere and reflexive assent to sentences meaning that p. This linguistic capacity, however, is not a necessary feature of beliefs, and is apparently absent in animals or machines. This does not prevent Dennett from saying that we must ascribe to these creatures a minimal logical competence to interpret them:

> I alleged that even creatures from another planet would share with us our beliefs in logical truths; light can be shed on this claim by asking whether mice and other animals, in virtue of being intentional systems, also believe the truths of logic. There is something bizarre in the picture of a dog or mouse cogitating a list of tautologies, but we can avoid that picture. The assumption that something is an intentional system is the assumption that it is rational; that is, one gets nowhere with the assumption that entity x has beliefs p, q, r, . . ., unless one also supposes that x believes what follows from p, q, r, . . .; otherwise there is no way of ruling out the prediction that x will, in the fact of its beliefs p, q, r, . . . do something utterly stupid, and, if we cannot rule out *that* prediction, we will have acquired no predictive power at all. So whether or not the animal is said to *believe* the *truths* of logic, it must be supposed to *follow* the *rules* of logic. Surely our mouse follows or believes in *modus ponens*, for we ascribed to it the beliefs: (a) *that there is a cat to the left*, and (b) *that if there is a cat to the left, I had better not go to the left*, and our prediction relied on the mouse's ability to get to the conclusion. In general there is a trade-off between rules and truths; we can suppose x to have an inference rule taking A to B or we can give x the belief in the 'theorem': *if A then B*. As far as our predictions are concerned, we are free to ascribe to the mouse either a few inference rules and many logical beliefs, or many inference rules and few if any logical beliefs. We can even take a patently non-logical belief like (b) and recast it as an inference rule taking (a) to the desired conclusion.[43]

We can now apply these ideas to the problems about the psychology of reasoning that we have met so far. In view of the fact that there is a necessary presumption of rationality, the psychologists' attempts to establish the psychological reality of logical rules and to evaluate the deductive rationality of agents are bound by such a presumption. No more than Dennett's mouse, the subjects have 'in their heads' such logical rules as *modus ponens*. These rules do not describe any beliefs that subjects would accept, consciously or not, but are principles without which we could not explain or predict their inferential behaviours. There are two senses in which one can say that a creature 'accepts' the rules of logic. In a strong sense, it can be said that x accepts a logical rule if he assents consciously to it and takes it as a *leading principle* of his investigations and future inferences, or if he 'possesses' this rule as an unconscious or tacit representation internalised in his cognitive equipment. In a weak sense, X accepts a logical rule if he 'follows' it, that is if his behaviour can be described as *conforming* to the rule.[44] Dennett holds that, in the context of psychological explanation, only the weak sense is required, and that it is neither necessary to suppose, with the theorist of a mental logic, that the rule has any psychological reality in the mind, nor to suppose that all the inference principles that we follow are conscious and reflexive. According to such a view, Johnson-Laird's mental models are instrumental artefacts for the description of a deductive competence, and do not necessarily have real counterparts in the minds of the agents.

If this view is correct, the very question of the rationality of agents receives a categorical answer: rationality is an *a priori* feature of any form of psychological explanation dealing with contents of thoughts. We cannot avoid, when we try to explain deductive behaviour, the attribution to agents of a *general* logical competence. It follows that the psychologists' empirical researches cannot show that they are rational or irrational *in the empirical sense* of the term 'rational'. Such results as those of Wason's selection task no more show that agents are irrational when they fail to give the correct results, than the capacities of individuals to reason by constructing mental models show that they reason rationally. Rationality is a necessary condition of psychological explanation, and not a descriptive feature that could be best tested empirically.

13.4.3 Idealisation and description

The argument from the presumption of rationality says that we must consider the agents as being *a priori* rational. But it does not tell us *what form* this rationality must take, or what exact principles or norms of rationality we must accept *a priori*. Let us repeat that, by definition, a norm does not describe the real behaviour of individuals, but the behaviour that they should have. This counterfactual is usually completed by saying that it is the behaviour that they should have *if certain ideal conditions were realised*. In other words, it is supposed that the norms of rationality are those that *an ideally rational agent* would follow, by opposition to, or at least by abstracting from, the rules that a real and imperfect agent actually follows.

The concept of idealisation is familiar in ethics, where, under one of the most usual interpretations of the rules of theoretical morality, one supposes that the rules concern the conduct of perfect agents, who would not be subjected to the vicissitudes to which real agents are subjected. But this concept is equally familiar from disciplines that are not *prima facie* 'normative', such as natural science, where idealisation is present in the process of explanation and of prediction of real events. Thus in physics 'ideal' models describe laws governing the behaviour of physical bodies by abstraction from a number of real physical parameters. For instance, the theory of 'ideal gases' describes the conditions of temperature and pressure of gases independently of some real features that limit, in concrete situations, these descriptions. The opposition between the ideal norm and the description of reality is no less familiar from the theory of rational action. For instance, the 'normative' theory of decision hypothesises that agents obey two ideal principles of rationality which form the kernel of the 'Bayesian' theory of decision: (a) that agents should always have a consistent set of beliefs about the probable states of the world and a coherent set of preferences, and (b) that they should always act in order to choose the action that has for them the greatest 'expected utility'. But the real choices of individuals do not always conform to these principles. In economics, for example, where ideal conditions of competition and markets are defined, idealisations play an important role; in linguistics models of grammatical competence describe the knowledge an ideal speaker would have of his own language.[45]

But talk of idealisation is not enough to say which norms should be accepted. Here appears what might at first sight look like a paradox. On the one hand, a norm or an ideal is abstract, and would cease to be so if it were to describe real situations, or be inductive generalisations from these situations. On the other hand, a norm or an ideal cannot be totally abstract, up to the point where it could not be said *of what* they are norms or ideals. If it were the case – if the norms were, so to say, free-floating over and above the factual world – we would be free to invent any formal scheme, and to decide that it is 'normative' by virtue of its abstract character. In answer to this, it can be said that logic, as a formal discipline, could just be normative in this very sense. But it is not abstract to the point that it is arbitrary. This feature is reflected in various conceptions of the domain of logic that we have considered. Even according to a conception such as Granger's (§ 11.4.2), where logic is the 'zero degree' of formal content, logic outlines the figure of a system of possible operations. According to a less austere conception, the domain of logic is mainly the domain of first-order logic, and individuals and properties as well as operations are the possible 'formal objects'. According to a richer conception, logical constants are added according to whatever degree of formality or structure is required by a given area of discourse (see Prior's quotation in § 11.4). On any one of these views, then, the various 'possible' objects and degrees of form are not free from any reference to a universe of objects. Indeed, in Quine's view, logical truths, although formal, are nevertheless truths about the world.[46]

Idealisation, therefore, is not absolute. It comes in degrees, according to whether we require of our normative principles that they move away from a certain kind of reality. It follows that one cannot draw a sharp distinction between a purely normative theory and a purely descriptive theory of rationality. This seems to be true of any theory of rationality, whether it concerns action, probability judgements or deductive reasoning.[47] In the case at hand – the problem of the purported rationality or irrationality of our deductive inferences – our normative principles can be convincing only if we consider the ways people *in fact* reason, and this is a matter of an experimental description of psychological aptitudes and performances. But we have seen, from the argument of the presumption of rationality, that such an experimental description can only be set against a background of idealisations about the purported rationality of agents, or at least about the logical beliefs that they should have. The results of Wason's selection task could not be evaluated and formulated if one did not suppose in the first place that the agents *should* follow an elementary piece of conditional propositional reasoning.[48] The question here is not whether a set of normative logical principles is needed, but *which* set of principles one must admit. An idealisation, it seems, falls between two extremes: a maximal and a minimal idealisation. A maximal idealisation involves the norms that a *perfect*, or *optimal* agent should follow, if he were not impeded by the ordinary empirical limitations that weigh upon the real agents. Such an idealisation is, for instance, encountered in the 'pure' theory of decision, which describes the actions of a perfect agent. A minimal idealisation is that postulated by Davidson and Dennett: agents are capable of being rational, in the sense that they have coherent intentions, beliefs and desires. The problem is to know whether we must adopt *as much* rationality as is prescribed by the maximal theory of rationality, or *less*, and *more* than what the minimal theory prescribes. There is a solution to this problem, namely that given by Rawls about idealisations in moral theory: we must attempt to find a 'reflexive equilibrium' between various norms and various descriptions, and the reflexive equilibrium method is a method for finding the appropriate level of normative theory (§ 2.3.2).

This conception has been, for the psychology of reasoning, explicitly defined by Jonathan Cohen (1981, 1986) on the basis of an argument quite similar to the one we have considered for propositional connectives. One of the difficulties raised by the psychological hypotheses examined above is the following. In the problem-solving tasks for deductive reasonings presented to the subjects in experiments, it is in general supposed that these subjects understand the premises of the arguments they are given. But on what bases can we say that they understand these arguments, if not because they have some kind of pretheoretical *intuition* about the meanings of the logical constants involved in those arguments? As we saw above, even if we accept the hypothesis that this intuitive understanding is due to the translation of the premises into a logical mental language, we are still at pains to explain how subjects understand this mental language, and the postulation of another mental language in which the first is itself translated would involve us in an infinite regress. This problem is more general: it concerns any translation of the sentences of ordinary language into a logical language with a canonical syntax and a canonical semantics. Such a translation cannot be performed in a mechanical and direct way, without any use of our ordinary intuitions about the meanings of connectives and other logical signs. To be assured, for instance, that the meaning of connectives such as 'or' or 'if . . . then' is, or is not, the meaning prescribed by the usual truth-functional rules, we must rely upon previous knowledge of the meanings of these connectives. This is why the meaning of the logical constants can only be *characterised* by their deductive rules, without being totally *defined* by them (§ 2.3.1).

The relationship, then, between a normative theory of rationality in general (and of deductive rationality in particular) on the one hand, and the descriptions that we can give of inferential behaviour on the other hand, is the following, according to Cohen. We start from the intuitions that agents have about the validity or invalidity of given arguments. We idealise these intuitions through a logical theory describing the ways rational agents should reason. This theory prescribes the general form of this rationality. We then test the normative theory by confronting it with our initial intuitions. If it accords with these, we conclude that it is the correct theory from which we can construct an empirical or factual theory of psychological reasoning. If it does not agree with them, we modify our initial theory accordingly, perhaps by lowering the degree of idealisation of the norms adopted in the first place, until a sufficient adjustment is reached between the norms and the intuitions.

To take up one of Cohen's examples, let us suppose that we had to evaluate the validity of the following inference:

(A) If Pascal owns a rusty Peugeot, he is poor, and if he owns a Rolls-Royce, he is rich

----

Either, if Pascal owns a rusty Peugeot, he is rich,
or if he owns a Rolls, he is poor

Our intuitions are that this inference is invalid. But our normative theory adopts the principles of the propositional calculus, according to which this inference has the form

(A') $\dfrac{((p \to q) \mathbin{\&} (r \to s))}{((p \to s) \vee (r \to q))}$

and is valid. This conflict between our normative theory and our intuitions shows that we had better choose another normative theory (maybe relevant logic, if we say that the antecedent of a conditional must be relevant for the truth of its consequent). This new theory would then be tested against other intuitions, and modified accordingly. Does it follow that we must change systematically our normative theory, that is classical logic? No, because all of our intuitions do not go against it, and even if most of them were to go against it, our changes of norms should arise *against* this theory, which would then keep its strong normative status.

We could, however, adopt the reverse procedure: we can start from the procedure prescribed by the propositional calculus, and predict that such inference schemes as (A') must be valid. Noticing, then, that one of its instances (A) is not intuitively valid, we could envisage a modification of our theory. Such a procedure of balancing happens in all the cases where we realise that classical logic does not prescribe all the forms of valid arguments that we encounter in ordinary reasoning. We are thus led to propose non-classical extensions of classical logic, or even to envisage more drastic revisions. But, once again, this does not imply that a *total* revision of our classical principles is possible, since it is still possible to defend 'conservative' approaches, such as that described in § 2.4.2 above about the meaning of connectives.

The reflexive equilibrium method in logic is quite well described by Goodman in the quotation given in § 12.4 above, in the context of our discussion of holistic theories of inference. Cohen draws from this application of the method of the theory of deductive rationality an argument to the effect that it is inevitable to assume that agents are rational. He distinguishes two kinds of theories about the deductive competence of agents: a normative one, which determines what reasonings are correct; and a factual one, which systematises our intuitions. Both theories, however, will be idealised and will be in harmony with each other:

> [The] factual theory of competence will be just as idealised as the normative theory from which it derives. And though it is a contribution to the psychology of cognition it is a by-product of the logical or philosophical analysis of norms rather than something that experimentally oriented psychologists need to devote effort to constructing. It is not only all the theory of competence that is needed in this area. It is also all that is possible, since a different competence, if it actually existed, would just generate evidence that called for a revision of the corresponding normative theory.
>
> In other words, where you accept that a normative theory has to be based ultimately on the data of human intuition, you are committed to the acceptance of human rationality as a matter of fact in that area, in the sense that it must be correct to ascribe to normal human beings a cognitive competence – however often faulted in performance – that corresponds point by point with the normative theory.[49]

The parallel between logic and ethics (one could add: aesthetics), encountered on several occasions, acquires here its full significance. Both are normative theories. But they are not so in the sense that normative principles fall from the skies. Just as moral truths are not revealed, logical truths are not revealed: they are not written on the 'Tables of the Law'. They do not come, as Frege thought, from a world of 'the being-true' (Frege held the same view about the Good and the Beautiful). They come from idealisations that we make from our inferential or moral practices, from our ordinary judgements. In this sense logic is a theory of the norm of truth. We do not need to invoke a 'logical original sin' to account for the fact that people are, most of the time, illogical or irrational. They are such sometimes, perhaps very often, but not always. But they cannot but be rational, if they are to be understood.[50]

13.5 Ideal versus minimal rationality

13.5.1 The limits of idealisation

The procedure of reflexive equilibrium applied to logical rationality offers the choice, as I have said, between two kinds of principles: maximal and minimal. But do we need the maximal principles at all?

Most of the normative theories based on deductive logic lead to ascriptions of rationality that are so strong that it is improbable the corresponding principles could ever be applied to real agents. Let us, to begin with, consider the norm of consistency among beliefs discussed in § 12.6. A logical system must be consistent. If logic describes the beliefs that an ideally and optimally rational being should have, this being should never hold any pair of contradictory beliefs: his belief system should be perfectly consistent. I have held, in § 12.6, that it is dubious that anybody could consciously hold two contradictory beliefs. Now if we accept the notion of a 'tacit' or 'implicit' belief, even that of unconscious belief, there does not seem to be any obstacle to the idea that we could contradict ourselves in our system of beliefs.[51] If, however, we consider not the beliefs that an agent really has, but those that an *interpreter* might ascribe to him, do we not have good reasons, in some circumstances, to ascribe contradictory beliefs to people? A *strong* version of the principle of charity, according to which contradictions should *never* be ascribed, seems to be unrealistic.

Another dubious idealisation consists in ascribing to perfect agents a form of *logical omniscience*, according to which such an agent should be able to deduce *all the logical consequences of his beliefs*, and to know all the logical truths that are logical truths. But there is an infinity of logical consequences of any given proposition, and an infinity of logical truths, so that only an infinite being could fit this ideal state. Such an excess of idealisation does not affect only first-order logic. Hintikka (1962), for instance, has proposed a system of epistemic logic in which all the beliefs of an individual must be *closed under deduction*.[55] It follows that an agent should infer all the consequences of his beliefs, whatever they might be. But it is a feature of human psychology that we infer only those propositions that are for us informative and relevant, and not those that are trivial (§ 2.5.2).[53] From the point of view of *our* psychology, a 'perfect creature' who would deduce from a proposition p a trivial set of conjunctions $p \& p$, $(p \& p) \& p$, $((p \& p) \& p) \& p$, and so forth, would resemble more a logical idiot than a god. We could even wonder whether he has any beliefs at all, since the notion of belief does not only imply the existence of an inferential net from some beliefs to others, but also a limitation of the set of accepted beliefs.[54]

There are, therefore, good reasons to doubt that the maximal rationality models could give us the *right* idealisations. One can, from this observation, adopt more or less radical positions: either by rejecting totally the notion of ideal rationality, or by lowering systematically the standards of rationality in order to satisfy more realistic descriptions of our inferential practices.

13.5.2 Are norms empirical?

The first kind of solution has been defended by Stich (1985, 1990), who holds that the theory of rationality in general, and the theory of deductive rationality in particular, are empirical theories just like other empirical theories in psychology, the experimental results of which show that humans are *as a matter of fact* irrational. According to Stich, it is simply false that our attributions of beliefs and other intentional states presuppose the rationality of agents. There is nothing incoherent in the description, in intentional terms, of a person having contradictory or irrational beliefs. For instance, in Wason's selection task, most of the subjects really believe that the cards E and 4 must be turned over. They understand the conditions of the problem and what they are asked to do. Nevertheless, their beliefs are contradictory. Other experiments about 'belief perseverance' or 'cognitive dissonance' seem to establish similar data.[55]

Cohen's argument, according to Stich, leads us to grant a *factual* rational competence to individuals that exactly coincides with the *normative* theory of rationality. This 'virtuous' circularity seems to be so convenient that we may wonder whether it is not *ad hoc*. Moreover, this theory seems to be strongly idealised: are not the competences of individuals very disparate? Confronted with these differences, the upholder of the reflexive equilibrium method can, according to Stich, choose only two strategies. Either he relativises his norms, maybe by ascribing distinct competences to individuals, or he adopts a kind of 'majority rule' by choosing the 'normal' or 'average' normative theory. On the first hypothesis, the very concept of norm disappears (for an individual norm is no more a norm). On the second hypothesis, it is inadequate (for nothing obliges us to believe that the correct theory is the one held by the majority). According to Stich, when a psychologist evaluates the logical competences of subjects, he compares these to the standards of deduction accepted by experts. Their competence is as much an empirical fact as the fact that one can deviate from the norms can itself be an empirical fact.[56]

One can agree with Stich that the model of a perfect logical competence is too strong, for the very reasons that have been given above. But does it follow that rationality or irrationality are empirically testable properties? We cannot ascribe contradictory beliefs to individuals without presupposing *some* interpretative system, and a logical system is part of an interpretative system. Let us suppose, for instance, that someone holds (truly) that sentence (a) is true and that sentences (b) and (c) are false

(a) If Gina lives in Florence, then she lives in Italy.
(b) If Gina lives in Salzburg, then she lives in Italy.
(c) If Gina lives in Florence, then she lives in Austria.

It can easily be verified, however, that such an individual would nevertheless have a contradictory system of beliefs, if the conditional 'if ... then' were interpreted in the truth-functional sense.[57] We can avoid this contradiction if we do not interpret the conditional in this sense. Irrationality here is a feature injected by bad translators. This seems to be the case for Wason's selection task. For instance, Cheng and Holyoak (1985) have suggested that the subjects' conditional reasoning in such tasks can be accounted for by the presence of 'permission schemas' of the form 'if an action is to be taken, then some deontic precondition must be satisfied', which facilitates the resolution of a task when such a deontic element is present. If it is indeed the case, we may speculate that some form of deontic logic will be useful for representing that nature of the problem and its solution, or at least, if one is reticent about the use of a 'logic' in such reasonings, that some deontic knowledge is involved. Psychologists themselves are much more cautious than Stich about the issue of the empirical or non-empirical character of rationality in these tasks. For instance Jonathan Evans declares: '*If* [my italics] conditional reasoning implies the possession of formal logical rules, then I do not believe that people are rational.'[58] But the issue of whether formal rules are indeed involved is, as we have seen, moot. If the empirical results of a selection task are better explained by the presence of some form of cognitive illusion rather than by the presence or absence of a mental logic of sorts, then it is just as illegitimate to diagnose a form of irrationality here as it can be, for instance, with visual illusions: we do not say, of a person who is victim of such an illusion, that she is irrational. We could just as well, as Cohen suggests, interpret the empirical results as coming from a bad application of our normative theories.[59]

Finally, it is wrong to say that the reflexive equilibrium procedure leads us to a relativisation of our norms or to the use of a sort of majority rule that would cancel them. To *weaken* a norm, so that it becomes compatible with conflicting intuitions, is not to suppress it, but it is to change it, or to adopt a new one. This does not mean that it must lose its status as a *norm*. There is, however, no reason why reflexive equilibrium could not lead us, after a series of adjustments, to the conclusion that agents are irrational, if all of our previous attempts produce a systematic disagreement between our intuitions and our norms. The presumption of irrationality could then be discharged.[60] But this does not imply that it was false in the first place as a normative principle. A norm can be taken as 'false' only if one forgets that, in a sense, it is neither true nor false, unlike empirical generalisations. I cannot, therefore, find how Stich's position differs from those psychologistic positions that we have previously found unacceptable.

13.5.3 Minimal rationality and the paradox of the norm

The second solution mentioned above consists in systematically weakening the rules of ideal deductive rationality. The ideal model of rationality seems to be unrealistic in any case, so why should we try to impose it in the first place, at the price of a series of adjustments required by the fact that it is unfit for accounting for the real performance of agents? So, it is argued, we would save ourselves time and effort if we tried directly to find realistic norms instead of trying to test the competence of a perfect rational agent. For instance, many problems arise in the normative theory of decision when we try to adopt the principle of maximisation of expected utility without restriction, and there exist several manners of reducing such idealisations.[61] Thus a number of economists have criticised optimal models and proposed instead a theory of 'bounded' or 'limited' rationality for agents who are 'less than rational'.[62] What, however, will guide our choice of normative standards in the case where we fix the standards of rationality as 'less than perfection'?[63]

Cherniak (1986) has explored systematically the options of such a theory of 'minimal rationality'. His basic hypothesis is that we are *finite* agents, endowed with finite cognitive resources (in particular in memory). We are not capable of perfect consistency in our belief systems, and we have no logical omniscience that would allow us to deduce all the consequences of our beliefs. Thus Cherniak proposes the following rules of *minimal* rationality:

(a) *A minimal general rationality condition*: if A has a particular belief-desire set, A would undertake some, but not necessarily all, of those actions that are apparently appropriate.
(b) *A minimal inference condition*: if A has a particular belief-desire set, A would make some, but not all, of the sound inferences from the belief set that are apparently appropriate.
(c) *A minimal consistency condition*: if A has a particular belief-desire set, then if any inconsistencies arose in the belief set, A would sometimes eliminate some of them.[64]

Adopting such *ceteris paribus* principles does not imply, according to Cherniak, that one comes back to a form of psychologism, according to which these principles would cease to be norms. For instance, the fact that a person does not perform, at a given moment, a particularly obvious inference prescribed by our normative theory (such as, for example, an instance of *modus ponens*), does not imply that this person is so irrational that he does not have the corresponding beliefs and desires.

> As an example, I may have established earlier that $p \rightarrow q$; I may have been using it in other proofs, and so on. And I may now have just proved p; I may have been using it subsequently, and so on. And it may be that I must see that q is true before some other desired proof can be completed, but I may not have recognized it yet. Nonetheless, I can still qualify as believing p. Minimal normative rationality splits the difference between ideal and minimal descriptive rationality.[65]

In other words, the fact that my cognitive attitudes do not allow me to infer the correct conclusion does not imply that I am not rational, or that I should not be presumed to be so.

A theory of minimal rationality, therefore, does not withdraw the presumption of rationality; it simply relocates it. For a descriptive theory of rationality cannot fail, in ascribing to an intentional system beliefs, desires or intentions, to use normative notions. To *describe* an agent as having beliefs is already, in a minimal sense, to explain his cognitive competence, and to *rationalise* this competence, that is to reveal a structure in which this competence is made rational from the point of view of the agent. To give a propositional content to an agent's belief is to describe his propositional attitude as an attitude that, in certain circumstances, is apt to cause, and in this sense to rationalise, the agent's behaviour. In this sense, every attribution of a content involves a normative element, and is not simply descriptive of the psychology of the agent.[66]

Cherniak, however, holds that the presumption of rationality, as it is understood by Quine, Dennett and Davidson, that is as a principle of charity, implies the ascription of a strong form of rationality. Cherniak criticises in particular Quine's argument (taken up by Davidson) that logic is necessarily involved in any translation manual and in any interpretative practice. According to Quine, as we saw, 'Fair translation preserves logical laws' and we must adopt the rule 'Save the obvious'.[67] According to Cherniak, this amounts to ascribing a particularly strong form of rationality, since every agent must accept logic, in the sense that it would be impossible for him to reject *any* logical truth.[68] In other words, the principle of charity would have the absurd consequence that any agent 'accepts' or 'possesses' a logic – namely classical logic.

If this is indeed a consequence of the principle of charity, it is not difficult to show that it is absurd. According to Cherniak, a finite human agent cannot be rational to the point that he accepts all the logical truths and consequences of his beliefs, and all the logical truths of logic. This is evident, in particular, from the theory of 'computational complexity', a branch of the theory of algorithms, which studies the decidability *in practice* (and not in principle, unlike metalogic) of logical calculi, and the combinatory problems posed by the practical feasibility of algorithms.[69] A number of algorithmic problems, which are decidable in principle, proved in fact to be 'computationally intractable', since real-world finite systems are unable to solve these problems because of the 'computational explosion' that would result from the carrying out of *all* the calculations necessary for the solution of the problems. I have already observed, in my discussion of Granger's criterion of the demarcation of logic (§ 11.4.2), that the fact that a system is undecidable in principle (for example first-order logic) does not imply that there are not a number of heuristic procedures, which would allow us to find decision procedures for a limited number of classes of formulas. The converse holds: a system that is decidable in principle, such as a truth-functional propositional logic, may be undecidable in practice. As Cherniak remarks, a consistency test for a set of 138 propositions using the truth-table method, or even one using more efficient algorithms, would take twenty billion years on a machine capable of verifying the conjunction of all these propositions on a line of a truth table in the time it takes a light ray to traverse the diameter of a proton![70] Indeed we cannot ascribe to a man the 'possession' of logic in this sense, for the metatheoretical adequacy of a logic does not imply its practical adequacy. It was, as we saw (§ 11.3), a Wittgensteinian point that the metatheoretical properties of a calculus do not imply anything about the real psychological competence of agents. In this sense, Wittgenstein was right to assert that metalogic is of no use when we want to understand what it is for somebody actually to follow a logical rule, and there is no contradiction in the fact that a subject reasons according to a contradictory system: 'an inconsistency is not the germ which shows a general disease'.[71] Of course, to suppose that *all* the properties of a logic could be transferred to the psychology of a real agent would be as absurd as to suppose that the fact that a set of axioms is adequate for number theory implies that the system is realised in our psychology and that we should count according to it.

But does the principle of charity have such absurd consequences? I do not think that the fact that logic is incorporated into our translation manuals or our interpretations means that we intend to impute to the agents a possession, in the strong sense, of a logical competence somehow realised in their psychology. The principle of charity does not mean that the interpreter is bound to ascribe a perfect logical knowledge to agents *as a matter of fact* about their psychology. All kinds of situations can arise in the course of interpretation, which might lead an interpreter to abandon the 'obvious' that he tried, in the first place, to save. An interpretation procedure, as Davidson conceives it, is more a gradual process of adjustment and fit than the definitive imposition of some form of knowledge or understanding on the agents. For instance, an interpreter may decide that, all things considered and on the basis of a series of interpretative attempts, an agent whom he had first charitably interpreted as not contradicting himself, *has* in fact contradictory beliefs.[72] In fact Davidson's principle of charity is quite similar to Cherniak's minimal rationality requirement: it prescribes that *most* of the beliefs of the agents are true, and that *ceteris paribus* the agent follows logical truths. In other words, it is a weak, and not a strong, principle of normative rationality. The fact that a logical norm is required for the interpretation of a certain deductive competence does not imply that the agents do possess a real system of states corresponding to the ideal set of inferences prescribed by the norm. We have already encountered above this apparent paradox, which we may call the *paradox of the norm*: on the one hand, the norm, being ideal, does not describe any real logical fact about the psychology of agents; but on the other hand, it must be tested against the facts, and revised even when it is minimal. *The norm never 'corresponds' to any fact, but it must agree with the facts.*

Now it might be thought that this commits us again to some sort of descriptive fallacy about the status of logical rules, similar to that which was denounced about the Realistic view of logical truths. When we say that rationality is 'ideal' (whether maximally or minimally so), are we not saying that an ideally logical being would follow rigid rules, whereas a real being conforms himself only imperfectly to the hardness of the logical must? Do we not confuse a norm, which is neither true nor false, with a true description of a universe of ideal *facts*? I do not think so. 'Ideal' does not mean ideal *reality*. An ideal rationality does not describe any fact, psychological or other, and in this sense the rules of minimal rationality are still *rules*, and do not say truths about real subjects. The paradox of the norm, however, is not a genuine, but only an apparent paradox, which arises only when we suppose that the norm must 'agree' with the facts in the sense of the unique correspondence of a true statement with a reality. Agreement here means the result of a process of reaching an equilibrium between the normative standards and the observed facts. There is no reason to believe that such an agreement or equilibrium can be attained in only one way. It can be the result of many trade-offs between norm and experience.[73] We cannot presuppose in advance what the exact form of this result will be (this is why the principles of minimal rationality are bound to be rather imprecise), but we must presuppose their general form.

13.6 Between the 'psychological wash-basin' and the laws of 'being-true'

Frege accused the psychologism of his age of dissolving logic into a 'psychological wash-basin', and he advocated a strong form of Realism to cure this psychologistic disease. But it may well be that the cure was worse than the disease. The position I have attempted to defend rejects both Frege's cognitive Realism and psychologism: logical truths are not true by virtue of a universe of rigid facts, or *because* we think in such and such a way. The present position is nevertheless compatible with the weak form of psychologism that is assumed by most contemporary research in the psychology of reasoning: logical truths and rules might turn out to have a 'psychological reality'. In this sense, the hypothesis of a 'mental logic' is a respectable one, even if it is far from having been empirically established. But I have held that the very enterprise of giving an empirically adequate account of our deductive practices cannot be carried out without the adoption of normative principles of rationality. These principles need not be maximal; they had better be minimal, since it would be more costly to presuppose that human agents can perform the deductions that are valid according to logic. They need not be exclusively logical principles, for they might include rules that are not readily describable as logical rules. But they need to be normative and ideal, in the sense that we must postulate that agents behave *as if* they followed those rules or principles if we want to interpret them at all. It does not follow, however, that the logical competence of agents is merely an instrumental or heuristic feature of our interpretations, but only that the normative preconditions of the interpretation of rational or logical behaviour are not to be confused with the end-product of these interpretations. The choice between the various rules is not fixed once and for all: it is a matter of adjustment between our normative standards and empirical descriptions. If we did not take into account such an equilibrium method, we would always run the risk of wondering whether our rules are *too ideal* or *not ideal enough*.[74]

When one says, therefore, that logic is a 'theory' of reasoning, one says something that is both correct and incorrect. On the one hand, logic is, as Peirce said, a theory 'of the stable laws of our beliefs', in the sense that it gives us the general and structural principles of deductive reasoning. I have, in this book, left out the problem of the relationship between deductive and inductive reasoning. But the same thing could be said about the latter. On the other hand, logic is not a theory at all, since its laws do not bear on any reality. It does not state any truth about the world, but it sets the norms of truth.

CONCLUSION

> In a Muslim story, a fallen champion saw a Crusader wielding against him a magic invincible sword bearing the name of God: 'Sword!' he cried 'can you strike a true believer? Do you not know the name on your blade?' 'I know nothing but to strike straight', the sword replied. 'Strike then, in the name of God!' Logic is not partisan, and knows nothing but to strike straight; but the sword is invincible, when it wears the Maker's name. (Geach, 1969, p. 81)

For my part, I ignore which name is written on the blade, and I do not even believe that there is a name on it. If logic is indeed an instrument, it is not at the service of any cause. But the story is otherwise right: logic is not partisan. It does not commit us to any particular ontology, because it does not describe a world, but only prescribes the most general conditions of such a description. In this sense it is formal. I have held that the 'formal contents' of logic rest on an ontology that is only minimal. By 'minimal' I do not mean that the ontological commitments of logic are those prescribed by extreme nominalists and upholders of ontological economy, but rather that logic is neutral with respect to a number of ontological issues. Thus a theory of truth, as it is formulated through a Tarskian conception, is 'modest' and 'non-substantial'. In modal logic, the 'essentialism' that is pre-scribed by logical semantics is minimal too, and 'possible worlds' are not genuine parts of the world. The logical theory of identity only states the constraints of any theory of the individuation of substances.

Such an ontological minimalism is closely linked to the other characterisation of the story: logic knows nothing but to strike straight. It is a normative and a prescriptive discipline, the truths of which have the status of rules. In this sense it is not what Wittgenstein called a 'hyperphysics', which would describe a universe of rigid realities. I have, however, tried to show that the characterisation of logical truths as rules does not imply that they are mere conventions that we would be free to choose or to change at will.

With Dummett, we can characterise realism as a thesis that does not bear on the reality of particular entities for such and such a subject matter, but about the objectivity of the judgements or of the statements that we can articulate in any particular field. In so far as these judgements have a meaning and a content, realism is a semantic thesis about the meanings of these judgements. It can, as we saw, be associated with three theses: adherence to the principle of bivalence for the sentences of a given class, adoption of a truth-conditional semantics for the language in question, and acceptance of the possibility that truth transcends our means of verification and of use of the sentences of the language. None of these theses is by itself sufficient for realism, nor do they imply each other. But in so far as anti-realism of the Dummettian kind rejects them all, a full-blooded realism can be characterised as the conjunction of the three theses. The realism defended here is not a full-blooded one, but it is realism nevertheless.

The realist thesis in the philosophy of logic rests upon the traditional conception of logic as a science of truths. Logic is not only in charge of setting the rules of valid inference, it must also explain why inferences are valid. The correct explanation is that an inference is valid if it preserves a certain property, the semantic value of truth of the propositions figuring in a given inference. In this sense, the logician analyses those features that, in the sentences of a language, systematically determine the truth of these sentences. These structural features are those of logical form, and logical inferences are said to be valid by virtue of the recurring presence of logical constants. From this point of view, a certain conception of the form of a theory of meaning for a language in general involves a certain conception of logic. The realist favours a semantical definition of logical constants, the meanings of which are determined by the truth conditions of sentences. The anti-realist favours a syntactical definition of the constants, the meanings of which are determined by their inferential roles. But I have tried to show that these two approaches are not exclusive, and can be combined into an overall realist view of inference and truth, which, however, falls short of the strongest realist commitments.

Realism in logic also involves a certain view of the justification of the validity of logical laws. I have followed Dummett in holding that a merely 'technical' justification (through the proof that the laws are complete) was not sufficient, and that a 'holistic' justification was not sufficient either. We must, in one way or another, try to explain the fact that the propositions of logic have a special, irreducible status. Traditionally this specific status is characterised by the idea that logical truths are analytic, necessary and *a priori*. Although these characterisations are often obscure, I have not seen any reason to reject them, provided we can have a clear account of them. I have identified the analyticity of logical truths with the fact that deduction is constrained by certain formal principles. This led us to grant a relative privilege to first-order logic, which, in a sense, is the incarnation of the more formal part of the domain of truths. The analytical nucleus of rules, which can be put into correspondence with the logical constants, is, within a language, autonomous. To grant this autonomy means that one cannot introduce any constant into one's language. Every new constant must be such that its rules preserve the truths of the inferences in which it appears. This 'molecularist' requirement can be taken up by a realist, in so far as it obeys a semantical constraint.

Now the adoption of a semantical criterion of demarcation for logic is not sufficient by itself to determine a position as realist or not, if full-blooded realism entails adoption of the principle of bivalence. We have seen several cases where the principle can indeed be put into question legitimately. But none of the revisions considered seems to justify a radical form of revisionism with respect to classical logic (such as intuitionism). If logic cannot be so radically revised, it is not because it would describe a world that would be *the* world, and which other systems could describe better or otherwise. To take seriously the normative character of logic, the fact that it knows only to 'strike straight', is to admit that it does not describe any reality. In this sense our realism cannot be Fregean extreme Realism, but it is compatible with the thesis that logic determines the ideal normative acceptance conditions of sentences, the conditions that a rational agent is disposed to accept. It is because we accept certain ideal norms that our statements have truth conditions. A logical rule is the statement of a leading principle that an agent must follow if he is to be rational. If logical laws are necessary and *a priori*, it is in this sense. This kind of rationality is not psychological, as the recognition of the validity of an inference does not imply that it is actually valid. Actual validity concerns logic only. The rationality of real agents is different from the normative rationality incarnated by logical rules. But the former can only be evaluated in the light of the latter. Neither is logic the incarnation of rationality itself. But it sets its minimal criteria.

NOTES

Notes to the introduction

Bibliographical references

Haack (1978), Grayling (1982) and Sainsbury (1991) are among the introductory books that cover similar ground to this one. Quine (1970), although idiosyncratic, is still the best introduction. The books that have most inspired my style of approach are Blackburn (1984) (although it is concerned with the philosophy of language) and Davies (1981). I have used principally the following manuals: Jeffrey (1967, 2nd edn 1981), Hodges (1977), Quine (1950), Lemmon (1965), Newton-Smith (1985), Scott *et al.* (1981), Guttenplan (1986) and especially Tennant (1978). For an introduction to metatheoretical treatments see Kleene (1967), Hunter (1971) and Grandy (1977).

1. 'The Art of Thinking' refers to Port Royal. '*Vernunftslehre*' is Wolf's and Thomasius's term, '*Wissenschaftslehre*' is Bolzano's. One could also cite J. F. Lambert's *Neues Organon* as belonging to this tradition of a general logic in the wide sense.
2. Dummett (1973, preface; 1978, p. 442).
3. Russell used the phrase 'philosophical logic' to designate the general study of logical form in *Our Knowledge of the External World* (1914). See Sainsbury (1991, p. 1).
4. This is most clear from Strawson (1985, pp. 49–60), for instance.
5. In this sense Gabbay and Guenthner (1983–6) contains a panorama of classical logic (vol. I), of its extensions (vol. II), and of its alternatives (vol. III).
6. See, for instance, Hintikka (1962), Schlesinger (1984, pp. 4–5). The paradox of the omniscient knower is alluded to in Chapter 13 below.
7. Hintikka (1973, p. 1).
8. On Beth's theorem, see Tennant (1986); on Craig's theorem, see Putnam (1975, ch. 14).
9. On this distinction, see Peirce (1930–58, vol. II, pp. 188–90).
10. Grice (1986, p. 64).
11. The distinction between various levels of analysis is here inspired by Davies (1981, p. ix) and by the current distinction between a 'meaning-theory' (a semantics) for a language and a 'theory of meaning', along Davidsonian lines. For the articulation between the purpose of a theory of meaning and the classical metaphysical and epistemological problems in the philosophy of logic, see in particular Dummett (1991, preface).
12. Wiggins (1980, p. 3).

Notes to Chapter 1

Bibliographical references

Gochet (1972) is the most complete discussion of the notion of proposition in logic. Nuchelmans (1977) contains useful historical information, but is purely doxographic. The best introduction to Quine's position is Quine (1970). Haack (1974) is useful. The contemporary seminal articles are Cartwright (1962), Geach (1968, pp. 166–74), Lemmon (1966), Blackburn (1975) and Stalnaker (1976, 1984). See also the references given to Chapter 8.

1. I have borrowed these characterisations from Gochet (1972, p. 18), although his list of the uses of propositions is different from the one suggested here. In particular, Gochet includes an 'ontological use' of propositions, which seems to me more an abstraction from the various uses.
2. See Quine (1934: 'Ontological remarks on the propositional calculus'), in Quine (1976, p. 129); and the analyses of Gochet (1972, pp. 22–3).
3. I have analysed the differences between the theories of Frege and those of Carnap and Church in Engel (1985, ch. 2). See also Burge (1979).
4. See Frege (1892) in Frege (1952). I do not say here *why* Frege made this distinction. His argument is examined in § 8.1 below.
5. 'What is distinctive about my conception of logic is that I begin by giving central place to the content of the word "truth", then immediately introduce a thought like the one to which the question "is this true?" applies' (Frege, 1969a, p. 272; English translation, p. 253).
6. According to the most common interpretations of Frege. None the less, it is not always certain that meanings are always entities for Frege. See Engel (1985, ch. 2).
7. See 'Der Gedanke', in Frege (1956). This problem has received particular attention since Kaplan (1977) and Perry (1977).
8. Frege (1966, p. xvii).
9. See 'Der Gedanke' in Frege (1956), pp. 191–2.
10. This is the principle of 'compositionality' (see § 6.1). See particularly the letter to Husserl of 1891, in Frege (1976, pp. 96–7).
11. The example in question comes from a letter from Frege to Jourdain in 1914. See Frege (1976, p. 127). The formulation of the intuitive criterion has been suggested by several authors, in particular Evans (1982, p. 19).
12. See Van Heijenoort ('Frege on sense identity' and 'Sense in Frege'), in Van Heijenoort (1986).
13. The use of the idea in contemporary logic goes back to Carnap (1956, p. 9), who instead of 'possible worlds' talks about 'state descriptions' (a state description is a set of sentences that contains only atomic sentences or their negations, and gives a complete description of a possible state of the universe). The modern use of the notion goes back to Hintikka, Kanger and Kripke. See the references given in Chapter 7.
14. This conception is notably that of Stalnaker (1976, 1979, 1984). See also Lewis (1983).
15. Stalnaker (1979; 1984, ch. 3).
16. See Lewis (1972), Montague (1968: 'Pragmatics'), in Montague (1974, ch. 3), Stalnaker (1972).
17. See for example, Granger (1979, pp. 116–17).

18. Wittgenstein (1922, 6. 127): tautologies all say the same thing, that is to say nothing (6. 11).
19. Stalnaker (1984, p. 54).
20. Carnap (1956, p. 56).
21. On the other hand, this defect is a virtue when one is dealing with propositions as *contents of propositional attitudes*, because the contents of propositional attitudes are less easily assimilable to linguistic entities such as sentences. See Chapter 8. This shows the difficulty there is in making the four roles indicated above apply to propositions.
22. An ordered pair is an ordered set (i.e. where the order of the elements cannot be changed $\langle x, y \rangle$ of objects so that if $\langle x, y \rangle = \langle z, w \rangle$, then $x = z$ and $y = w$. Wiener gives the set-theoretic definition $\{\{x\}, \{y, \phi\}\}$ where 'ϕ' is the empty category, Kuratowski gives the definition $\{\{x\}, \{x, y\}\}$. See Quine (1960, p. 258).
23. The conception of propositions as ordered n-uples goes back to Russell (1903); for modern authors who endorse it, see Kaplan (1989) and Donnellan (1974). See the comments in Gochet (1972).
24. Davidson, 'True to the facts' (1969), in Davidson (1984, ch. 3), Church (1943), Quine, 'Three grades of modal involvement', in Quine (1976, pp. 163–4). See Chapter 8 below. The argument is also found in Gödel ('Russell's mathematical logic', 1944), in Benacerraf and Putnam (1983, p. 450), which is why it is often called 'the Church–Gödel argument' (Burge, 1986a, p. 108). The name 'slingshot argument' was coined by Barwise and Perry (1983).
25. Frege (1952, p. 111).
26. The formal version of the argument can be given in the following way (see Davidson, 1984, p. 19; Burge, 1986a, p. 108). The argument presupposes three premises: (a) that sentences have a denotation or reference, and that this is a truth value; (b) that sentences are composed of expressions and that their denotation is a function of the denotion of these component expressions (principle of compositionality); and (c) that three logically equivalent sentences have the same denotation. Then the following four sentences have the same denotation:

    (1) R
    (2) $(\iota x)(x = 0) = (\iota x)(x = 0 \ \& \ R)$
    (3) $(\iota x)(x = 0) = (\iota x)(x = 0 \ \& \ S)$
    (4) S

    where the expressions of the form '$(\iota x)(\ldots)$' are singular terms (Russellian definite descriptions). (1) is logically equivalent to (2), as (3) is logically equivalent to (4). Consequently, by (c), (2)–(3) and (3)–(4) respectively have the same denotation, (2) and (3) are only different in the singular terms '$(\iota x)(x = 0 \ \& \ R)$' and '$(\iota x)(x = 0 \ \& \ S)$' respectively. But since, by hypothesis, R and S have the same truth value, and S and R have the same denotation, it follows that these singular terms have the same denotation and that (2) and (3) also have the same denotation. Consequently (1)–(4) have the same denotation.

    Burge (1986a) discusses the question of knowing if the Church–Gödel argument is really Frege's. I will not discuss this point and will still call the slingshot argument 'Fregean'.
27. Davidson (1984, p. 42). See also § 6 below.
28. See Føllesdal (1983), Barwise and Perry (1981).
29. See Barwise and Perry (1983).

30. Barwise and Perry (1981).
31. The comment is made, notably by Hornstein (1986, p. 171). This is particularly clear in the analysis of what Barwise and Perry call 'scenes'. These are *perceived* situations, corresponding to completive clauses with 'naked' infinitives, like 'John saw [Mary leave]' or 'Russell saw [Moore wink]', where the structure of the scenes is that of the infinitive clauses concerned (Barwise and Perry, 1983, pp. 183ff., and the presentation in Gochet, 1983). See §8.3.
32. For example, Haack (1978, p. 75). A *token* of a sign customarily designates the particular physical occurrence of this sign, while its *type* designates the category of these occurrences. The *type/token* distinction comes from Peirce.
33. Strawson (1950: 'On referring'), in Strawson (1971). See Lemmon (1966).
34. Lemmon (1966), Haack (1978, p. 80).
35. Geach (1968, p. 255: 'Assertion').
36. Strawson (1950: 'On referring'), in Strawson (1971).
37. See, for example, Quine (1969, pp. 35, 68). See Chapters 4 and 7 below.
38. Quine (1960, ch. 1 and 2), Gochet (1986). See Chapter 13 below.
39. Quine (1977). See Blackburn (1975a).
40. Quine (1970, ch. 1). The notion of analyticity must be added to these ideas. It will be examined in Chapter 12 below. According to Quine, it presupposes the notion of synonymy as much as that of proposition in the majority of definitions that are given of it.
41. Quine (1970, ch. 1). See Gochet (1972).
42. Quine (1970, pp. 25–6).
43. Quine (1960, ch. 2; 1970; ch, 1), Gochet (1986, ch. 2).
44. See, in particular, Hornstein (1985).
45. Blackburn (1975), to which this section owes a great deal.
46. Davidson (1967): 'Truth and meaning', in Davidson (1984, p. 20).

Notes to Chapter 2

Bibliographical references

Haack (1978) is a good introduction to the problems of this chapter. On the semantics of propositional logic, see Hodge (1978: tree method, elementary treatment) and Scott *et al.* (1981: more advanced treatment). On natural deduction, see Lemmon (1965), Tennant (1978) and Newton-Smith (1985). On 'tonk', see Wagner (1981), Hart (1982), Harman (1986a, 1986b) who have influenced me much.

1. It is in fact a question of *schemas of axioms*: the letters 'A', 'B', etc. of A_1, A_2 and A_3 are not real symbols of propositional calculus, but metavariables that make it possible to obtain axioms from this calculus for all appropriate substitutions of propositional variables 'p', 'q', 'r', etc.
2. For an overall presentation of the rules of natural deduction, see Prawitz (1965). Here I have followed the notation of Scott *et al.* (1981). It can be reformulated in the 'multiple conclusion logic' of Shoesmith and Smiley (1978), see Harman (1986a).
3. Completeness, in the semantic sense (every tautology of a formal system is a theorem of this system), is usually distinguished from completeness in the sense of soundness

(all theorems of a system are tautologies). For an overall presentation, cf. Hunter (1971). See Chapter 11 below.

4. Belnap (1962), see Haack (1978, p. 32).
5. Rawls (1970, pp. 48–51) especially pp. 51–2, where Rawls himself makes the comparison between moral theory and logic.
6. See McCawley (1981, p. 18).
7. See Anscombre and Ducrot (1983), for instance.
8. See Lewis (1973), Nute (1980).
9. See the work by O. Ducrot; Anscombre and Ducrot (1983).
10. See Kneale and Kneale (1962, pp. 128ff.).
11. A causal context is usually thought not to be extensional because it is not truth functional (the truth value of sentences governed by the operator 'cause' is not a function of the truth value of their component parts in the sense of truth-functional connectives; when the connective 'if ... then' has its causal sense, the falsity of the antecedent is not sufficient to ensure the validity of the conditional), and because the singular coferential terms are not substitutable *salva veritate* in these contexts. See Davidson (1980, ch. 7). See § 6.2.2 below.
12. Grice (1975), McCawley (1981), Jeffrey (1965, 2nd edn, 1980).
13. Strawson (1986, p. 236).
14. Grice's analysis is far from being the only possible pragmatic analysis. But it has the advantage of being compatible with the truth-conditional conception of meaning (see Chapter 6). Cohen (1972, 1977) has pointed out that Grice's analysis fails when a conditional has a conditional as antecedent. Grice's analysis is not the only analysis of conditionals which preserves the idea that they have truth conditions. Jackson (1987) has given an analysis in terms both of truth conditions and assertion conditions (the 'supplemented theory of indicative conditionals') which is, in general, more powerful than Grice's.
15. Harman (1986a, p. 126).
16. Harman (1986a, p. 118). See Fodor (1975) for a general definition of functionalism in philosophy of mind; Johnson-Laird (1983, ch. 1). 'Conceptual role' semantics have notably been set out by Harman (1982).
17. Johnson-Laird (1983, ch. 2). A closely related theory is Kamp's 'semantics of discursive representations' (Kamp, 1981).
18. Bar Hillel and Carnap (1952); see also Jeffrey (1965, 2nd edn, 1980, pp. 10–11), Johnson-Laird (1983, pp. 34–8).
19. Johnson-Laird (1983, p. 47).
20. The procedure of proof by 'semantic tableaux' (currently known as 'tree method') comes from Beth (1955). For a presentation, see Smullyan (1968), Jeffrey (1981) and Hodges (1978). See § 11.2 below.
21. Harman (1986a.), pp. 11–12).
22. See Peacocke (1986). Frege, in his critique of psychologism, has made the most explicit use of this type of argument (see Chapter 13).

Notes to Chapter 3

Bibliographical references

An excellent introduction to syllogistics can be found in Gunther Patzig's article, 'Syllogistic', *Encyclopaedia Britannica* (1975) vol. 17, pp. 890–8; and also in Patzig (1963) and Granger (1976). Geach (1962) is still the classic work, when it comes to comparing traditional logic and modern logic; Geach (1975) is penetrating and profound; Strawson (1973) is useful and so is Van Heijenoort (1986, ch. II). On Frege, see Dummett (1973, 2nd edn, 1980), and for more recent evaluations, Hintikka and Haaparanta (1986). Zaslawsky (1981) has an original conception of asymmetry of subjects and predicates which he compares with the focus/theme in linguistics. On Sommers's work, see Engelbretsen (1987, 1988).

1. Frege (1883, I, § 32).
2. See Spade (1982, pp. 194–5).
3. Sommers (1982, p. 2).
4. Leibniz, in this sense, was as much a 'naturalist' as a 'constructionist'. He believed in the existence of a logical form immanent in natural language *and* in the possibility of an ideal language.
5. Sommers (1982).
6. *De Interpretatione*, § 6. See the analyses in Granger (1976, ch. 1).
7. *De Interpretatione*, § 5.
8. Geach (1962) and Strawson (1971, 1973), in particular, have stressed this thesis. See Zaslawsky (1981).
9. Geach (1968, 2nd edn 1972, p. 47).
10. See Van Heijenoort (1974: 'Subject and predicate in Western logic', reprinted in Van Heijenoort, 1986, pp. 17–34.
11. Sommers (1982, p. 16).
12. See *Opuscules et fragments inédits*, ed. Couturat (1966) p. 67; and *Philosophische Schriften*, ed. Gerhardt, vol. VII, p. 211 (quoted by Bouveresse, 1986, pp. 80–1, to whom the analyses in this chapter owe much).
13. Sommers (1982, p. 16).
14. Here, I am following the analyses of Dummett (1973, 1980) without raising the exegetic problems. See also Engel (1985, ch. 1).
15. See, for example, 'Funktion und Begriff', English translation in Frege (1952).
16. Dummett (1973, p. 10), Sommers (1982, pp. 13–14).
17. See Geach (1962), Strawson (1973), Engel (1985, pp. 39–40).
18. See Geach (1980, p. 282; 1975, p. 151), Bouveresse (1986, pp. 97–8).
19. On this problem, see Bouveresse (1985; 1986, p. 95).
20. Geach (1962, 1975); Strawson (1973).
21. Sommers (1982, p. 45).
22. Dummett (1981, pp. 268–80; 1973, pp. 28–9), Geach (1975, p. 146), Bouveresse (1986, p. 94). But it seems to me that, from a Dummettian point of view, Bouveresse is confusing analysis and decomposition of a proposition here.
23. Lakoff (1972), McCawley (1972, 1981). Careful note will be taken of the fact that 'natural logic' does not have the same meaning here as in Chapter 2 above.
24. Here, I am indebted to the analyses of McCulloch (1984, pp. 111–12).

25. See Quine (1940), which uses a procedure taken from Shönfinkel (1924). See Van Heijenoort (1967, pp. 355–66). See also 'Algebraic logic and predicate functors', in Quine (1976, ch. 28), Van Heijenoort (1986, pp. 57ff.).
26. McCulloch (1984, p. 117). This point is ignored by Bouveresse (1986) who considers the same objection.
27. Sommers (1982, ch. 13–14, and pp. 52–3).
28. Sommers (1982, p. 53).
29. McCulloch (1984).
30. This detracts not at all from the strength of the arguments for a combinatory or algebraic logic without variables, that is to say from the idea that it might be possible to give truth conditions without reference conditions (I am indebted to M. Boudot for this point). Englebretsen has criticised Geach's and Strawson's asymmetry thesis along Sommersian lines. See Englebretsen (1987, 1988).
31. Kaplan (1986, p. 113) in fact notes it.
32. For an analysis of Frege's views on this point, see Dummett (1981, ch. 3).
33. Sommers (1982, p. 3).
34. Fodor (1975).

Notes to Chapter 4

Bibliographical references

Introductions to Tarskian theories of truth for the predicate calculus can be found in Quine (1970), Haack (1978), Platts (1979) and Guttenplan (1986a), whom I have followed here, together with Tennant (1978). For more precise presentations see Mendelsson (1964) and Grandy (1977). Natural deduction systems for the predicate calculus can be found in Lemmon (1965), Tennant (1978), Scott *et al.* (1981, vol. 2), Newton-Smith (1985) and Guttenplan (1986a). For presentations in terms of semantic trees, see Smullyan (1968), Jeffrey (1965), Hodges (1978), Scott *et al.* (1981) and Bonevac (1989). Quine (1950) and Quine (1969) are good introductions to his theory of quantification. About substitutional quantification, see in particular Gottlieb (1980), Dunn and Belnap (1968), Marcus (1962) and Parsons (1978). On second-order logic, see Grandy (1977) and Boolos and Jeffrey (1981). About Russell's theory of descriptions, see Linsky (1967, 1977) and Neale (1990). I have not dealt here with the large literature on existence and free logics. See in particular Lambert (1991) and Lambert and Van Fraassen (1972). McCawley (1981) is an excellent introduction to the linguistic problems about quantification; see also Hornstein (1981). On Montague, see Dowty *et al.* (1981). On generalised quantifiers, Barwise and Cooper (1981).
1. Dummett (1973, pp. 89–90). Contrast, however, with Goldfarb (1979).
2. Van Heijenoort (1967).
3. See Goldfarb (1979, p. 352), Van Heijenoort (1986, p. 45).
4. The question whether Frege and Russell had a 'semantics' in the contemporary sense of the term is a disputed one; see Goldfarb (1979), Van Heijenoort (1986, pp. 43–53).
5. For an illuminating analysis on these points, see Bouveresse (1980a).
6. Van Heijenoort (1986, pp. 43–53).
7. Löwenheim, 'Über Möglichkeiten im Relativkalkul' (1915), English translation in Van Heijenoort (1967).

8. On Herbrand's work, see Van Heijenoort (1986, pp. 99–121) and Golfarb's preface to Herbrand (1967).
9. Dummett (1973, p. 8) and Chapter 2.
10. Quine, 'Existence and quantification', in Quine (1969).
11. Strawson (1980) see also Strawson (1985).
12. 'Der Wahreitsbegriff in den formalisierten Sprachen' (1930), in Tarski (1956, 2nd edn 1983, pp. 152–278). Tarski's presentation concerns the calculus of classes, and not the predicate calculus. The presentation here is similar to Guttenplan's (1986), and Tennant's (1978).
13. Tennant (1978, pp. 25ff.). I am indebted to Tom Baldwin here.
14. Tennant (1978, pp. 25–27); see also Gochet and Gribomont (1990, p. 300).
15. For an exposition of relative truth theories, see Grandy (1977), Tennant (1978, p. 29). See also Chapter 7 below.
16. I have used the presentation in Scott *et al.* (1981, vol. 2).
17. See in particular, Quine, 'Existence and quantification' in Quine (1969).
18. Quine (1969). The connections between Quine's theses are clearly articulated by Marcus (1988).
19. Quine (1953, 1960). For an analysis of Quine's criterion, see for instance Gochet (1986).
20. Quine (1969, pp. 99–100).
21. Quine (1953, ch. 4: 'Identity, ostension and hypostasis'; 1969).
22. See in particular Quine (1969, p. 97).
23. For analyses of Russell's theory of descriptions, see Linsky (1967, 1977) and Neale (1990).
24. Quine (1953, pp. 8ff.; 1960, pp. 181ff.).
25. See for instance 'The scope and language of science', in Quine (1976, pp. 228ff.).
26. Strawson (1950).
27. See in particular Lambert and Van Fraassen (1972), Lambert (1991) and Schock (1968).
28. G. Evans, 'Pronouns, quantifiers and relative clauses' (1977), in Evans (1985, pp. 81–7).
29. See Dummett (1973, p. 405).
30. Frege (1883, p. x), Dummett (1980, ch. 19).
31. Evans (1985, pp. 85–6).
32. Frege (1969, p. 67, English translation p. 60).
33. Marcus (1961, 1962, 1967), Kripke (1976), Linsky (1977, pp. 153ff.), Gottlieb (1980), Davies (1981, ch. VI), Parsons (1978).
34. On non-existent objects, see Parsons (1980) and Lambert (1982).
35. See Haack (1978, pp. 49ff.).
36. Quine (1969, p. 65).
37. Kripke (1976, p. 355) criticises Wallace (1972) and Tharp (1971) on this point. See Davidson, 'In defense of Convention T' (1973) in Davidson (1984, p. 67, and especially notes 6 and 8).
38. Kripke (1976, § 5), Davies (1981, pp. 144–48).
39. See in particular Marcus (1961, 1962, 1981) and Bonevac (1986).
40. Quine (1970, pp. 66–7).
41. Strawson (1973, p. 7).
42. Strawson (1974, p. 33).
43. Boolos (1975, pp. 518–19).
44. See, for example, Boolos (1975, p. 511) and Boolos and Jeffrey (1975, 2nd edn 1989, p. 198).

45. Quine (1970, p. 68).
46. Boolos (1984).
47. Sommers (1982, ch. VII).
48. Quine (1960, pp. 157–61); on the notion of logical form, see below, Chapter 11.
49. See, for instance, McCawley (1972, 1981) and Lakoff (1972).
50. Quine (1960, pp. 138–41).
51. McCawley (1981, p. 98), Vendler (1967).
52. See for instance Récanati (1986).
53. Quine (1950, p. 293); see Hintikka (1974, 1975), McCawley (1981, pp. 447–8) and Boolos (1984).
54. Boolos (1984).
55. Wiggins (1980), Davies (1981, pp. 124ff.), Platts (1979, pp. 100–4).
56. Evans (1977, 1982, p. 155), Davies (1981, pp. 124ff.). Neale (1990) proposes a similar analysis for all quantifier phrases, among which he includes descriptions.
57. McCawley (1981, p. xiii).
58. Montague (1974), see Dowty et al. (1981). I follow here some remarks by Van Heijenoort (1986, pp. 49–50).
59. See Hornstein (1981) and Barwise and Cooper (1981), for instance.

Notes to Chapter 5

Bibliographical references

Presentations of the themes in this chapter will be found in Haack (1978) and Grayling (1982). The best compendium on the idea of truth is still Pitcher (1965). Blackburn (1984) has influenced me considerably. On the semantic theory of truth, see Quine (1970); on redundancy, see Mackie (1972), Williams and Horwich (1990). Dummett's 'Truth' (1959, 1978, ch. 1) remains a classic. See also Dummett (1973), Soames (1984) and Baldwin (1989) have influenced me even if I do not follow the thesis of the second. Martin (1970, 1984) are indispensable collections on the Liar Paradox.

1. On the distinction between definition and criterion of truth, see Russell (1910, ch. 12) and the comments by Haack (1978, pp. 88–91).
2. Wittgenstein (1922), Russell 'The philosophy of logical atomism', in Russell (1956).
3. Molecular propositions, according to Wittgenstein, do in fact contain logical constants that do not represent anything, and therefore cannot 'correspond' to entities of the world. I will come back to this doctrine in Chapters 11 and 12.
4. For a defence of the notion of fact, see Taylor (1976, 1985), Forbes (1987) and Mulligan, Smith and Simons (1984).
5. This is Strawson's diagnosis of Austin, in Pitcher (1965, p. 44).
6. The formulation is borrowed from Blackburn (1984, p. 239). My debt to Blackburn for the formulations in this chapter must be obvious.
7. See Dancy (1985, p. 113).
8. For a general presentation of Peirce's conception, see, for example, Hookway (1985). In another sense, Peirce's theory is more commonly defined as verificationist. Peirce took explicit care to distinguish his position from James's, by calling his position

'pragmaticism'. For a useful analysis of the various theories of truth, see Lehrer (1970), Haack (1978) and Grayling (1982).

9. For example, the conception of Davidson (1982), which is both a correspondentist theory of truth and a coherentist theory of knowledge.

10. Blackburn (1984, p. 227). In its traditional form, the paradox of analysis maintains that an analysis is either false or trivial. Either the *analysandum* (the expression to be analysed) and the *analysans* (the expression which analyses) are synonymous, in which case the analysis is trivial, or they are not, and the analysis is false.

11. Frege's argument is in his article 'Der Gedanke' (Frege, 1956). See Dummett (1973, ch. 13).

12. In 'Der Gedanke', Frege seems to support the first position. In another text (Frege, 1976, p. 24) he seems to support the second. For a detailed analysis of Frege's positions on truth, see Burge (1986).

13. Ramsey, 'Facts and propositions' (1927), in Ramsey (1978, p. 44). Wittgenstein (1952, App. 1, § 6).

14. See Quine, 'Truth and disquotation' (1970), in Quine (1976); and Quine (1970, p. 10). The truth-predicate is a technique of 'semantic ascent' from things to discourse about things.

15. Ramsey (1978, p. 45: 'Facts and propositions').

16. Prior (1971); Prior's theory is elaborated in Williams (1976), which is the best general treatment. Grover, Camp and Belnap (1975) are the authors of the expression 'prosentential theory'. Mackie's theory of the 'simple truth' goes in the same direction (Mackie, 1972).

17. See, notably, the comments by Haack (1978, pp. 127–34).

18. Dummett, 'Truth' (1959), in Dummett (1978, pp. 4–5).

19. Dummett, 'Truth', in Dummett (1978, pp. 5–6 and xxi).

20. Dummett, 'Truth', in Dummett (1978, pp. 6–7).

21. Dummett, 'Truth', in Dummett (1978, pp. 2–3).

22. I owe these formulations to Blackburn (1984, pp. 231–2). Dummett's analyses aimed to establish a verificationist theory. See Chapter 7.

23. Tarski (1956, ch. VIII); Tarski (1944) in Feigl and Sellars (1949, pp. 52–84).

24. Tarski (1944, p. 71).

25. Quine (1976, p. 161). The use of the sign '⌢' in order to form 'structural names of expressions' was introduced by Tarski (1956, p. 172); see also Quine (1960, p. 143).

26. Carnap (1963, p. 61), Ayer (1936), Quine (1960, p. 24). On positivist definitions of truth, see Hempel (1935).

27. Popper (1972, pp. 318ff.).

28. See Tarski (1956, pp. 265–6). For a synthetic presentation, see Grandy (1977, ch. IX).

29. Davidson, 'In defense of Convention T' (1973), in Davidson (1984, p. 65).

30. Tarski (1956, p. 406).

31. Field (1972). I do not follow Field's presentation here, but take my lead from Blackburn (1984, pp. 264ff.) and Soames (1984).

32. Blackburn (1984, p. 265) (see Tarski, 1956, pp. 192, 404).

33. Field (1972, p. 96).

34. Field (1972, p. 99). He is inspired by Kripke's 'causal' theory of reference (Kripke, 1972); see Chapter 10 below.

35. This objection is made by Leeds (1978) and repeated by Putnam (1978).

36. This second objection was raised by Soames (1984, p. 419).

37. Tarski (1956, p. 418).
38. Carnap (1942, p. 11).
39. Lehrer (1970, p. 46).
40. Haack (1978, pp. 101–2). There is, however, a simple solution to this problem (as T. Baldwin reminded me): if truth values other than the true and the false are acknowledged, it is possible to select a set of values as *designated*, and it is in terms of this idea of designated value that ideas such as that of logical consequence are defined. The equivalence of

    it is designated that p = p

    is then valid for all multivalued logics.
41. Popper (1972, p. 323). Popper's conception is correspondentist when he develops his idea of verisimilitude, or of approximation to truth. I do not analyse this point.
42. Davidson, 'True to the facts' (1969), in Davidson (1984, p. 48).
43. Davidson (1984, p. 43). The analogy between Davidson's conception and Austin's (1950) on this point will have been noted.
44. Davidson (1982, p. 309). See also Davidson (1984, ch. 13 and 15).
45. Recent defences of the redundancy conception of truth are Soames (1984), Field (1986), Baldwin (1989) and Horwich (1990). I cannot do justice here to their arguments, but the following remarks are in order. They generally consider that Tarski's theory is deflationary in the sense that it amounts to the redundancy conception, via the equivalence principle, and that there is no more to be said about truth than what the truism 'it is true that *p* iff *p*' says. The position advocated here comes close to these conceptions in so far as it admits that Tarski's theory does not define truth or allow any further substantial conception, but parts company with them by claiming, with Davidson (see, in particular, his 1990) that a Tarskian theory can say more about truth by being used within an empirical account of the meaning of the sentences of a natural language, along the lines of the programme analysed in Chapter 6 below. In his 1990 paper, however, Davidson claims that he now rejects the idea, set out here, that a Tarskian theory of truth is, in an important sense, 'correspondentist'. The divergence between him and the theories quoted above rests upon the *importance* of the concept of truth in theories of meaning, mind and action. If the 'deflationary' theorists are right, truth does not play an essential role in these theories, and we had better formulate them without this concept. On the view advocated here (and in Chapter 13), truth *has* an important role to play, in particular, since it is a normative concept that figures essentially within the rational explanation of meaning and action.
46. Russell, 'On denoting', in Russell (1956, p. 47).
47. The usual distinction between 'semantic' paradoxes such as the Liar and syntactic paradoxes (for example, Russell's paradox about the set of all the sets which do not contain themselves) comes from Ramsey.
48. The first theory in this sense seems to be Bochvar's (1939); see Skyrms (1970) and the articles in Martin (1970). The presentation of *MR* adopted here is taken from Burge, in Martin ('Semantical paradox': 1982, p. 87).
49. See Martin (1970, 1982).
50. Kripke (1975, p. 60).

51. For example, Kleene's three-valued logic, which is similar to Lukasiewicz. See Kleene (1952) except for material implication;

A \ B	A t	$\rightarrow$ i	B f
t	t	i	f
i	t	i	i
f	t	t	t

52. Kripke (1975, pp. 66–79). Kripke borrows the idea of 'foundation' from Herzberger (1970).
53. Kripke (1975, pp. 80–1). See Burge in Martin (1982, p. 88). Burge himself develops a theory according to which the truth predicate varies with the context of utterance. See also Parson's comments in Martin (1984, p. 41).

Notes to Chapter 6

Bibliographical references

Davidson (1984), Evans and McDowell (1976), Platts (1979), Peacocke (1981a), Davies (1981), Dummett (1978, 1991) and Wright (1986a) are the best introductions to the themes of this chapter. There is a vast literature on anti-realism: McGinn (1980), Appiah (1986) and Luntley (1988) are very useful. On the intuitionist position in the philosophy of mathematics, see the essays in Benacerraf and Putnam (1983). On intuitionist logic, useful introductions can be found in Scott *et al.* (1981, vol. 2), Heyting (1966) and Dummett (1977).

1. See, in particular, Frege (1893, vol. 1). This section owes a great deal to McDowell (1976).
2. Frege (1893, vol. 1, § 32, p. 50). On the interpretation of this passage, see Wiggins (1981), Engel (1985, p. 68).
3. On Tarski's concept of truth in a structure, see Hodges (1986).
4. Evans and McDowell (1976, pp. x–xi).
5. Blackburn (1984, pp. 282–3), from where I borrowed the example.
6. See, in particular, Foster (1976) and the discussion in Davies (1981, ch. 1 and 2).
7. McDowell (1976, p. 57).
8. Davidson's seminal text is 'Truth and meaning' (1967) in Davidson (1984). His programme is also formulated in 'Semantics for natural languages' (1973), 'Radical interpretation' (1974), 'In defense of Convention T' (1973), all in Davidson (1984), and Davidson (1981).
9. See § 2 above. For a comparison of Davidson's and Quine's views, see Davidson (1984, ch. 15–16).
10. See Davidson (1984, ch. 9–12), Engel (1988).
11. See, on this point, 'In defense of Convention T', in Davidson (1984).
12. For an analysis of this question, see Evans (1981), Davies (1981, ch. IV), Wright (1986a, ch. 6).
13. See Davidson (1984, ch. 12); 'Reply to Foster', ch. 15 ('Reality without reference').

14. See § 2 above. More precisely, Church's argument, as Quine reinterprets it (see § 8.4), purports to show that every context that is 'transparent' (where the co-referential singular terms are intersubstitutable *salva veritate*) is truth functional.
15. Blackburn (1984, p. 287).
16. See Chapter 8. Montague (1974) and Lewis (1972) suggest truth-conditional theories of this type.
17. See 'In defense of Convention T', in Davidson (1984, ch. 5).
18. Davidson, 'The logical form of action sentences' (1967), in Davidson (1980).
19. Blackburn (1984, p. 289).
20. Davies (1981, ch. 2; 1986, pp. 128–9).
21. Davies (1981), Blackburn (1984, pp. 289–93).
22. Davidson (1984, pp. 34–5).
23. See Dummett (1973, 1978, 1981).
24. See Dummett (1982). On the independence of semantic anti-realism in relation to scientific instrumentalism, see Tennant (1987).
25. Wright (1986a, preface) suggests such a programme in favour of anti-realism. See also Dummett, 'The reality of the past', in Dummett (1978).
26. See, for example, Dummett (1978, pp. xxxiii, 146, 175, 228, 274, 315 and 358) quoted by Wright (1986a, p. 318).
27. McGinn (1980) challenges Quine and Dummett on this point; according to him, Dummett contraposes on (a) while Quine 'detaches'. On this argument, see Tennant (1987a, p. 20).
28. See Dummett (1976, p. 70).
29. This is the principal argument of Dummett (1975).
30. Dummett (1975, pp. 129–32).
31. Dummett (1975, 1976, pp. 79–80).
32. See Dummett (1978, pp. xxi–xxii).
33. Dummett also adds a theory of the 'force' of assertions, that is to say of their pragmatic conditions. See Dummett (1976).
34. See McGinn (1980), McDowell (1987).
35. Dummett (1975, pp. 81, 89).
36. This conception is present in Dummett himself (Dummett, 1973, p. 299; see Evans, 1982, p. 95) and in Blackburn's 'projectivism' (Blackburn, 1984).
37. See Wright (1986a, pp. 47ff.), Appiah (1986, pp. 21–2).
38. Here I follow the presentation by Scott *et al.* (1981, vol. 2). See also Dummett (1977).
39. For example, Scott *et al.* (1981, vol. 2, p. 166).
40. Mill (1843), Dummett (1978, p. 300).
41. See Chapter 12 below, where this point is developed.
42. *Tractatus* 6. 1251.
43. Dummett (1978, pp. 300–1).
44. Dummett (1978, pp. 290–2).
45. On the idea of conservative extension, see Dummett (1978, pp. 221–2, 302–3, 315–17). See also the discussion in Chapter 12 below.
46. See Shoenfield (1967, p. 41), Barwise (1977a, p. 36).
47. Dummett (1977, pp. 363–4).
48. Dummett (1978, pp. 316–17).
49. According to a result due to Gödel (1933). See Putnam (1978, pp. 26–8) and McDowell (1976).

50. Dummett (1976, pp. 107–8; 1981, p. 441). See McDowell (1976, p. 55).
51. Wright (1986a, pp. 318 and 343ff.).
52. Wright (1986, p. 318), McDowell (1976).
53. Bilgrami (1986).
54. On this problem, see Davies (1981), Wright (1986a, ch. 6).

Notes to Chapter 7

Bibliographical references

Hughes and Cresswell (1968) remains the most accessible introduction to modal logic. I have partly followed Scott *et al.* (1981, vol. 2) and Forbes (1985), which is also the best introduction to the philosophical problems of modal logic. Marcus (1981, 1986) are excellent syntheses. For more advanced textbooks, see Chellas (1980) and Hughes and Cresswell (1985), which treat modal logic in terms of model theory and frames. On the criticism of Quine, see Gochet (1986). I have tackled some of the problems of this chapter in Engel (1985). A fine analysis of the problems in the last part of this chapter is Pariente (1982). For a useful collection see Loux (1979).

1. These paradoxes have been discussed by the Megarians. When Philo of Megara suggested his concept of material implication (§ 2.4.2), Diodorus contrasted it with a concept of strict implication close to the latter; see Vuillemin (1984). See
   C. I. Lewis (1918). Strict implication is denoted by the sign ' $\dashv3$ ' which has the meaning of 'necessarily implies'. None the less, there are also paradoxes of strict implication:

   $$\Box p \to (q \dashv3 p)$$

   (a necessary proposition is strictly implied by every proposition)

   $$\Box - p \to (p \dashv3 q)$$

   (an impossible proposition strictly implies every proposition).

   It is these paradoxes that are the modal equivalent of the rule *ex falso sequitur quodlibet*, which have convinced logicians of the relevance of formulating their own concept of implication (see § 13.6).
2. On Aristotle's modal syllogistics, see Granger (1976).
3. In Lukasiewicz's three-valued logic, the third value is the indeterminate or the possible, which the following tables supply:

A \ B	A & B			A \ B	$A \to B$			A \ B	$A \vee B$		
	t	i	f		t	i	f		t	i	f
t	t	i	f	t	t	i	f	t	t	t	t
i	i	i	f	i	t	t	i	i	t	i	i
f	f	f	f	f	t	t	t	f	t	i	f

   where 't^*' is the 'designated' value, that is to say the value such that the expressions which take it uniformly count as tautologies.
   The problem from which Lukasiewicz starts in order to formulate his three-valued

logic is that of 'contingent futures'. See Lukasiewicz (1920), Vuillemin (1984) or Bull and Segerberg (1983), for a historical analysis and an introduction (Hughes and Cresswell, 1968).

4. The 'model-theoretic' tradition originated with Carnap (1956), who suggests a concept, comparable to that of 'possible world', the concept of state description, within the framework of an intensional logic (see § 1.2.2). But the real point of departure is Kripke's 1963 article, which is the clearest formulation of the basic concepts.

5. Causal logic studies causal modalities such as 'it is causally necessary that'; deontic logic modalities such as 'it is permitted', 'it is forbidden', 'it is obligatory', etc. The most usual temporal logics (called 'Priorian') treat operators of time – 'it is past', 'it is present', 'it is future (true in the future)' – as modal operators comparable to 'necessarily'. Again, it might be possible to cite the logic of norms, epistemic logic, the logic of imperatives, conditional logic. See the references at the end of the chapter.

6. See Hughes and Cresswell (1968), Forbes (1985, p. 17). Via the 'reduction schemas' one system is obtained from another, S_5 implies or 'contains' S_4 and B, S_4 and B imply T.

7. Vuillemin (1984). The master argument of Diodorus of Megara is the famous argument discussed in antiquity which concludes at a form of 'logical' fatalism, starting from the following premises, regarded as contradictory by Diodorus:

(a) The past is irrevocable.
(b) From the possible to the impossible the consequence is not good.
(c) There are possibles that will never be realised.
(d) What is, cannot be, while it is.

8. Quine, 'Three grades of modal involvement' (1953), in Quine (1976, pp. 158–76). On the *de re/de dicto* distinction, see Kneale (1962).

9. Carnap (1956) initiated the Leibnizian metaphor; but it could not be concluded from it that these concepts correspond to those of Leibniz's philosophy. See Mates, *The Philosophy of Leibniz* (1986).

See Forbes (1985, pp. 5–8). Take, for example, the following invalid inference:

$$\frac{\Diamond p \quad \Diamond q}{\Diamond (p\&q)}$$

(if it is possible that Major be elected and if it is possible that Kinnock be elected, it does not follow that Major *and* Kinnock be elected). Compare this inference with the invalid inference in usual predicate calculus:

$$\frac{(\exists x)\ Fx\ (\exists x)\ Gx}{(\exists x)\ (Fx\ \&\ Gx)}$$

In order to show that this inference is invalid, it is sufficient to present a counter-example, that is to say, a counter-domain in which one x is F but not G.

The operator '$\Diamond$' can be treated as a quantification on a possible world m, '$(x)Pm$' will then summarize 'p is true in a world m' (and likewise for 'Q' and 'q'), and transcribe the propositional inference above in the following way:

$$\frac{(\exists m)\, Pm \qquad (\exists m)\, Qm}{(\exists m)\, (Pm\ \&\ Qm)}$$

The parallelism is striking. The invalidity of the propositional inference is justified by the same process as the one that justifies the invalidity of the quantificational inference, that is to say by looking for a counter-example to the conclusion (a possible world in which it is true that Major is elected and false that Kinnock is). Modal reasoning in terms of possible worlds is thus based on the same search for models, although worlds are substituted for the usual domains of quantification.

10. Lewis (1973, 1985). See Engel (1985, p. 109).
11. Stalnaker (1976, 1984, ch. 3).
12. Adams (1974).
13. See Vuillemin (1984), Knuuttila (1981), for example.
14. Goodman (1954).
15. Goodman (1954, pp. 49–58). Analyses of counterfactual conditionals in terms of possible worlds have been provided by Stalnaker (1984), Lewis (1973) *inter alia*. ·
16. Stalnaker (1984, p. 57). See also Cresswell (1985, pp. 66–7).
17. Quine, 'Reference and modality', in Quine (1953, pp. 139–57); Quine (1953, n. 8; 1960, pp. 169, 197). The reduction of referentiality to extensionality is valid if the slingshot (see § 1.3.2) is accepted. A criticism of this reduction can be based on the distinction, put forward below (§ 6) between two sorts of singular terms, referential and non-referential. It is on this distinction that Barwise and Perry (1981) base their criticism of the argument.
18. Quine (1960, pp. 279–80).
19. Carnap (1946, ch. 5).
20. This is the solution suggested by Smullyan (1948) and repeated notably by Kripke (1972), which is used as a basis for part of his distinction between rigid and non-rigid designators. See later on in § 6. I have analysed these arguments in detail in Engel (1985, ch. 3 and 4).
21. See Hugues and Cresswell (1968, pp. 142–4). In such a system, the converse of these formulas are also valid.
22. See Kripke (1963), Hugues and Cresswell (1968), Forbes (1985, pp. 28ff.).
    A model structure S_5 will be a set of five elements:

    (I) a set M of possible worlds (with one element designated m^*, the actual world);
    (II) a set D of possible objects;
    (III) a function d assigning to every world m a subset $d(m)$ of D constituting the set of objects existing in m; the function d being such that for every object x in d there is a world m in M such that x is in $d(m)$;
    (IV) for every atomic predicate to n-places F and for every world m, a specification of the n-uples of objects of $d(m)$ which are in the extension of F in m;
    (V) for each individual constant an assignation of a referent in D (this clause does not figure in Kripke (1963); it corresponds to the fact that each constant is referential or a rigid designator, in the sense of § 6 below).
    The clauses for the connectives remain those of § 2. One will also have

(VI) an atomic sentence $Ft \ldots t$ is true in a world m iff $\langle \text{Ref}(t) \ldots \text{Ref}(t) \rangle$ is a member of the extension of F in m (and 'Ref' the function assigning to each term its referent, a *constant* function);

(VII) $(\exists x)Fx$ is true in m iff for some a in $d(m)$, $F[a/x]$ is true in m.

(VIII) $(\forall x)Fx$ is true in m iff for every a in $d(m)$, $F[a/x]$ is true in m.

23. Quine, 'On what there is' (1953), in Quine (1953, p. 4).
24. For example, Quine, 'Intensions revisited' (1977), in Quine (1981, p. 118).
25. Quine, 'Worlds away' (1976), in Quine (1981, p. 127); See Chisholm (1967); Salmon (1982, 1986), Forbes (1985, ch. 7).
26. D. Lewis (1968, 1973). For an overall presentation, see Forbes (1985).
27. Forbes (1985, pp. 160–8).
28. See, in particular, Adams (1974, 1979).
29. Marcus (1967). See Engel (1985, pp. 112–13) (in this book I do not make a clear enough distinction between Marcus's form of weak essentialism and the one defended here, following Føllesdal, 1986). See also Gochet (1986, ch. VII).
30. Føllesdal (1986).
31. Føllesdal (1986, p. 176). According to Føllesdal, a singular term can be referentially transparent, but *extensionally opaque*, that is to say, be a substitutable term in an intensional context.
32. Kripke (1980); I have analysed his arguments in Engel (1985).
33. See Engel (1985, ch. III).
34. Kripke (1985). See Engel (1985, ch. VII).
35. Føllesdal (1986), Marcus (1962, 1988), Gochet (1986, ch. VII), Almog (1986).
36. Van Heijenoort (1977, p. 45), Engel (1985, p. 111).
37. See, for example, Boolos (1979), Vuillemin (1984).
38. For example, Boolos (1979) takes '□' in the sense of 'is provable' and proves, in modal logic, certain metalogical results. For a *compendium* of recent results, see Hugues and Cresswell (1985).

Notes to Chapter 8

Bibliographical references

Quine (1956), Kaplan (1968) and Hintikka (1962) are the sources for the problems raised in this chapter. However, I have not dealt with epistemic logic, see Schlesinger (1984). Barwise and Perry (1983) and Cresswell (1985) are two comprehensive and original treatments of the semantics of propositional attitudes. Kripke (1972), Evans (1982) and Salmon (1986) present the neo-Russellian theses of reference. Blackburn (1984, ch. 9) is an excellent introduction.

1. As Salmon notes (1986, p. 12). In what follows, I have taken my lead from the reconstruction of Frege's argument given by Salmon.
2. In 'X believes that p', 'p' is the sentence embedded in the context 'believes that'.

3. Frege, 'Über Sinn und Bedeutung' Frege (1952, p. 23). This Fregean theory has given rise to a vast literature on the problem of knowing if oblique contexts comprising a double, a triple, etc. level (*X* believes that *X* believes that, etc.) must imply a hierarchy of distinct meanings. See Linsky (1974), Dummett (1973, pp. 264ff.) and Parsons (1981). Like Dummett, I think that this problem is largely theoretical, and that it is possible to adhere to two levels of meaning. But we do not need to consider this here.

4. According to Frege's famous expression: *Die Art des Gegebenseins*, (Frege, 1952, p. 23).

5. Mill (1857, p. 33). See Engel (1985, pp. 15–16). Kripke (1980) calls his own theory 'Millian'.

6. According to a distinction by Plantinga (1974, p. 125), who takes it from Carnap (1956).

7. In the *Principles of Mathematics* (1903). It was David Kaplan who, when he took up this Russellian theory (Kaplan, 1977), associated this term with it. It must not be confused with the 'sophisticated' Russellian theory (§ 8.2.3, above). The expressions 'singular Propositions' and 'Russellian Propositions' also come from Kaplan (1975) and are common in the literature (Salmon, 1986; Schiffer, 1987). According to the convention adopted in Chapter 1, I 'dignify' propositions with a capital letter when they are explicitly entities independent of sentences.

8. See, for example, Frege (1976, p. 127). Frege was even more astonished when Russell replied to him that he intended literally to say that the mountain itself was a component of the proposition.

9. Carnap (1956, § 13).

10. Church (1950).

11. Frege (1952, p. 23).

12. The most famous example from the pragmatic point of view is Donnellan (1966), who distinguishes two uses of definite descriptions, one 'referential', the other 'attributive'.

13. Kripke (1980, p. 79).

14. Here I have followed Blackburn (1984, p. 330).

15. This point is well brought out by Schiffer (1987) and Jacob (1991).

16. According to the distinction made by Salmon (1986, p. 45), who speaks of 'a modified naïve theory' for the sophisticated theory.

17. According to Russell's famous analysis, 1905 (1956, p. 52).

18. In this case, the proper names are 'logically proper names' or 'genuine' in the sense of Chapter 7. See, for example, Russell (*The Philosophy of Logical Atomism*, in Russell (1956), pp. 193ff.).

19. Quine, 'Quantifiers and propositional attitudes' (1956), in Quine (1976, pp. 185–96).

20. Quine (1976, p. 189).

21. Davidson, 'On saying that' (1968), in Davidson (1984, p. 108).

22. A semantic analysis of these sentences has been put forward particularly by Barwise (1981) and by Barwise and Perry (1983), who construct verbs of perception as implying relationships to 'scenes' that are 'situations' in the sense of § 1.3.3. For a criticism of this theory, from a Davidsonian point of view, see Higginbotham (1982).

23. Quine (1960, ch. 6), Davidson (1984, pp. 98–9).

24. Davidson states that 'that' has firstly the role of a demonstrative of utterances, and then becomes fixed as a means of introducing subordinate clauses. It is not possible to play on the same ambiguity in French. But it is not obvious in what way this would be an objection to Davidson's conception, as Schiffer (1987, p. 125) suggests, since Davidson's theory is not a theory of the lexical meaning of 'that', but of its logical form.

25. See Davidson (1984, p. 104, n. 14).

26. However, this objection seems tortuous to Burge (1986b). Schiffer (1987, pp. 131–3) suggests a similar one, originating with Loar.
27. Davidson (1984, p. 166) explicitly suggests extending his analysis of 'to say that' to 'to believe that'. But see Schiffer (1987, pp. 126–31).
28. Schiffer (1987, pp. 133–6). I am not sure that Davidson would disagree with this. He maintains that there cannot be a theory of meaning without a theory of thought (for example, ch. 2 of Davidson, 1984).
29. Salmon (1986).
30. Salmon (1986, pp. 111ff.). An analysis of this type seems to me appropriate to account for what Kripke calls his 'puzzle about belief' (Kripke, 1979), which is intended to show that similar problems arise for Millian and Fregean theories of reference in contexts of attitudes.
31. Salmon (1986, pp. 84–5). A very convincing criticism of this view has been given by Schiffer (1986). See also Jacob (1991).
32. Evans (1982, ch. 1, 6, 7), McDowell (1984, pp. 98–109). In Engel (1985), I have adopted the theory according to which a *minimal* descriptive sense could be accorded to proper names, consisting of a description referring to the noun itself (Chapter 7). This theory now seems to me to be inadequate; but it was an attempt to articulate the idea of *de re* sense appropriate to Evans's and McDowell's neo-Fregean theories.
33. See Russell (1910).
34. On the reference of demonstratives, see Kaplan (1989) and in particular his distinction between the *content* and *character* of a sign; Evans (1982, ch. 6), Peacocke (1983) and Forbes (1986) represent a 'neo-Fregean' theory. What Evans (1982) calls 'Russell's principle' is the thesis according to which 'in order to think of an object or make a judgement about an object, one must know *what* object one is thinking of' (p. 65). What he calls 'Russellian thought' is a thought 'such that it would not be able to exist in the absence of the object or objects on which it bears' (p. 71). The whole of Evans's book on reference is devoted to an attempt to classify Russellian thoughts and to analyse the contents of the information they convey. The problem raised by the difference of reference combined with the identity of descriptions has been particularly advanced in Putnam's 'Twin Earth' thought experiments (Putnam, 1975). The question of the existence of singular Propositions has given rise to a whole debate on the individuation of contents of thought by the subject's environment and by his 'individual' circumstances. The stimulus to literature has resulted from various articles by Burge (e.g. Burge, 1979a). A good analysis of the polemic can be found in Jacob (1987). Blackburn (1984, ch. 9) is an excellent overall discussion.
35. One of the most famous consequences of the Fregean theory of functions and concepts is that existence is a property of a concept, and not a property or a predicate *simpliciter*. See Frege (1883). Russell (1903, Russell, 'The philosophy of logical atomism' (1989), in Russell (1956)) emphasises the same theme.
36. Zaslawsky (1981) is devoted to this subject. See Williams (1982). The best introduction to the logical problems of singular terms and existence is Lambert and Van Fraassen (1972), which is also an introduction to 'free logics'. In a ' free logic', the suppositions of existence of the usual logic are waived and complementary hypotheses introduced to confirm existence. The Meinongian theories have recently been revived and have returned to the forefront of the scene. See notably Parsons (1980) and Lambert (1982). Evans (1982, ch. 10) is an attempt to make his causal theory of reference compatible with the problem of empty names and existential statements

37. Russell began this psychologist turning-point in his theory as early as 1919 ('On propositions', in Russell, 1956).
38. This point is very well brought out by Mackie (1977a).
39. Quine (1960, p. 221).
40. This theory has been principally defended by McGinn (1982).
41. An intensionalist theory of the meaning of attitude sentences is Cresswell's (1985). Cresswell defends the idea that meanings cannot in any case be mental representations, and therefore a form of anti-psychologism in semantics (ch. 6). As he notes (p. 159), this conception can accord with the conception of bifurcation of content, in as much as it is acknowledged that the two forms of contents never meet.
42. For example, Fodor (1975, 1981, 1987).
43. Cresswell (1985).
44. Schiffer (1978) supports a theory of this type (and Evans, 1982, also seems to come under this heading), but any semantics that define sense by mechanisable mental procedures can be classed 'procedural' (see Johnson-Laird, 1983; Suppes, 1984, ch. 7).
45. This thesis has principally been defended by Stich (1983) and Woodfield (1982). Similar themes are adopted by Sperber and Wilson (1986), and by Jacob (1987). Jacob nevertheless emphasises the fact that reports of attitudes have truth conditions.
46. Wittgenstein (1953, II, p. 127).
47. See Woodfield (1982, pp. 259ff.), Stich (1983), Sperber and Wilson (1986) and Jacob (1987).
48. Wittgenstein (1953, II, p. 217).

Notes to Chapter 9

Bibliographical references

Quine (1953, ch. 4), Geach (1962, 1968, ch. 7) respectively describe the absolute theory and the relative theory of identity. Griffin (1977) is a sustained defence of the latter. Kripke (1972) and Wiggins (1980) are classics now. Seminal articles can be found in Munitz (1971). I have used Brody (1980) and Morris (1984). Hirsch (1982) is a study of individuation conditions according to types of objects.

1. Quine (1963, pp. 12–13), Griffin (1977, p. 1).
2. Leibniz (1901, p. 259), Ishiguro (1972, ch. 2).
3. Frege, 'Recension von *Philosophie der Arithmetik* von Husserl', in Frege (1952, p. 120); Frege (1966, II, p. 245).
4. Wittgenstein (1953, § 216). See *Tractatus* 5. 5. 302.
5. Frege (1879, § 8). See Proust (1986, pp. 210ff.).
6. Morris (1984) classes Frege amongst the supporters of 'the metalinguistic' analysis, according to which statements of identity bear on signs.
7. In his theory of concepts, Frege emphasises the fact that the 'is' of identity must not be confused with the 'is' of predication (see 'Concept and object', in Frege (1952). Russell (1903) considered this confusion as the Hegelians' principal error.
8. See Leibniz, *New Essays*, II, 27; Russell, *The Philosophy of Leibniz* (1937); see Ishiguro (1972).

9. Ayer, 'The identity of indiscernibles', in Ayer (1954, p. 12).

10. Brody (1982, p. 11), Wiggins (1980, p. 56), Dummett (1973, p. 544).

11. See Black, 'The identity of indiscernibles', in Loux (1970).

12. See the references in note 8; Russell (1937) accords a pre-eminent place to the doctrine of internal relationships in Leibniz. See Ishiguro (1972).

13. Dummett (1973, pp. 544–5).

14. Quine (1953: 'Identity, ostension and hypostasis', ch. 4), Ishiguro (1972, ch. 1), Cartwright (1971).

15. Marcus (1975), Wiggins (1980, p. 21).

16. Geach (1972, p. 238). The notion of 'sortal' concept originates from Locke's *Essay Concerning Human Understanding*.

17. Geach (1972), Frege (1977, 1966, II, p. 254).

18. On the problem of Theseus' ship, initially in the Sophists, see also Hobbes, *De Corpore*, II, 11; Molesworth, p. 316 (see Engel, 1985a, p. 126). See Chisholm (1971).

19. Wiggins (1980, pp. 19–21), Griffin (1977).

20. Wiggins (1980, p. 47).

21. Wiggins (1980, pp. 30–3).

22. Wiggins (1980, pp. 66–7).

23. Quine, in a review of Geach (1962) (see *Philosophical Review*, 1964, pp. 100–4) makes a clear statement on the absolute character of identity.

24. Marcus (1947). This theorem has been copiously discussed. See Kripke (1972), Salmon (1982) and Forbes (1985).

25. Wiggins (1980, pp. 109–10).

26. Kripke (1972, *passim*). According to Kripke, a statement of identity containing rigid designators is necessary *a posteriori*, and a statement where a description 'fixes' the reference of a term (for example, 'the standard metre of Paris') is contingent *a priori*.

27. Wiggins (1980, pp. 120–2).

28. Wiggins (1980, pp. 117–18).

29. See the Leibniz–Arnauld correspondence and the illuminating comments by Pariente (1982).

30. Wiggins (1980, p. 121).

31. Wiggins (1980, ch. 3). Kripke (1972) and Putnam (1975, vol. 1) have developed this theory of terms of natural species. See Salmon (1982).

32. Wiggins (1980, p. 62).

33. See, in particular, Granger (1987b).

34. Unger (1979) has expanded this point with the intention of concluding that objects do not exist. See Quine (1981, ch. 3), 'What price bivalence?' The relationship between the problem and Chisholm's paradox (§ 7.6) will have been noted.

35. Thom (1982, p. 268).

36. Evans (1982, pp. 176–7: 'Can there be vague objects?', Salmon (1982, p. 245). Salmon's argument differs from Evans's because he does not invoke an operator of indetermination, and notes only that if identity is vague, reflexivity ceases to be valid: an object cannot be vaguely identical to itself.

37. See Noonan (1982).

Notes to Chapter 10

Bibliographical references

Alston (1964) and Haack (1974) give an introduction to the problem of vagueness. The classic texts of Russell (1923), Black (1937) and Waismann (1945) are available for consultation. This chapter is primarily based on Dummett (1978, ch. 15: 'Wang's paradox'), Wright (1975), Fine (1975), Peacocke (1981a) and Sainsbury (1988). McCawley (1981) contains an introduction to the theory of fuzzy subsets. I have not dealt with the method of 'supervaluations' of Van Fraassen (1969) or of Kamp (1975a), which are much disputed works. Fine (1975) is a theory of 'precisification' which keeps classical logic. Peirce is one of the authors who has emphasised a 'logic of vagueness', but without giving a logic in the proper sense of the term. Intuitionist logic and the problem of strict finitism, raised by Dummett (1978, ch. 15) and Wright (1986a, ch. 4), do not figure in this chapter.

1. Van Heijenoort, 'Frege and vagueness' (1986), p. 94.
2. 'Truth value gaps' designate all the circumstances in which a statement is neither true nor false, or can have another value than the true or the false (for example, statements containing empty names).
3. The notion of presupposition was introduced by Frege 'On sense and reference' in Frege (1952). In general, *A* presupposes *B* if *A* is neither true nor false unless *B* is not true. See Strawson (1950), who introduces this idea to solve the problems raised by non-denoting descriptions.
4. See Sperber and Wilson (1986).
5. Frege (1969, p. 133). See Van Heijenoort (1986, pp. 86ff.) and Sainsbury (1987).
6. See, for example, Sperber and Wilson (1986) and Recanati (1986).
7. Sainsbury (1988, p. 9).
8. See Van Heijenoort 'Frege and vagueness' (1986). The principle of completeness can be regarded as an idiosyncratic feature of Fregean logic, linked to his absolutism and his conception of logic as language. In modern logic, logics with 'several sorts' of variables ('many-sorted') can be acknowledged. Kit Fine recently suggested a logic for generic or 'arbitrary' objects (see Fine, 1985).
9. Wright (1976, pp. 226–7).
10. See Barnes (1982) on the Sorites reasonings in antiquity, and Cargile (1969).
11. Sainsbury (1988, p. 7).
12. Peirce is the author who has perhaps most emphasised the philosophic importance of a logic of vagueness and the idea of the reality of vagueness. But although he talks about 'logic' of vagueness, this question is treated more in the framework of his semiotics and his metaphysics and less in the framework of a logical calculus (Peirce envisages a three-valued logic); see Engel (in press).
13. Sainsbury (1988, p. 7).
14. Fine (1975, p. 70).
15. Lukasiewicz (1920). Lukasiewicz suggested this logic in order to treat the problem of future contingents.
16. Dummett (1978, p. 255).
17. Fine (1975, pp. 269–70).
18. Dummett (1978, pp. 261ff.), Wright (1975, 1976).
19. Wright (1975, 1976).

20. Dummett (1978, p. 258).
21. This is a recurrent theme in all Dummett's writings. See, in particular, Dummett (1976), Wright (1986, p. 4).
22. Zadeh (1965); an introduction can also be found in Haack (1978, pp. 162ff.).
23. I have used Forbes's exposition (1985), which he utilises for a treatment of Chisholm's paradox, pp. 169–77. See Peacocke (1981) and Sainsbury (1988).
24. They are valid, but not sound in this sense.
25. Peacocke (1981, p. 125), Forbes (1985).
26. Peacocke (1981). The idea of identity of *qualia* or of sensible qualities is Goodman's (1952): an object x and an object y are of the same colour (e.g. red) to the same degree if the correspondence to that colour of one of them corresponds to the colour of the other.
27. See, for example, Ramsey ('Truth and probability' (1926), in Ramsey (1927) and Jeffrey (1965)).
28. As Haack (1980) notes.
29. Popper (1972).
30. Haack (1980).
31. Wright (1976, pp. 238–9).
32. Wright (1976, pp. 238–9).
33. Sainsbury (1988).
34. Sainsbury (1988).
35. Sainsbury (1988).
36. Sainsbury (1988).
37. Peacocke (1981, pp. 135–9).
38. Wright (1986, p. 319).
39. Dummett (1978, p. 260) rejects as obscure the idea that reality might be vague. But he retracts (1981, p. 440) in order to acknowledge this idea: 'Realism as far as vague properties are concerned has more affinities with the various forms of anti-realism than with the corresponding forms of realism.'
40. Dummett (1978, pp. 264–5).
41. Peacocke (1981).

Notes to Chapter 11

Bibliographical references

Hacking (1979), Peacocke (1976) and Granger (1982) are my main influences in this chapter. Bouveresse (1980b) is useful. Gochet (1986) contains a good account of Quine about the demarcation of logic. On logical versus grammatical form, see in particular Harman (1975), Evans (1976; ch. 3 in Evans, 1985), Lycan (1984) and Sainsbury (1991). On natural deduction, see Prawitz (1965) and Tennant (1978). Two important points of view on these issues have been neglected here: on the one hand that of Paul Lorenzen (1962) and Kuno Lorenz (1968), who propose a 'constructive' semantics for logic, taking into account both the semantic notion of consequence and the proof-theoretic one, and that of Herbrand, who may be considered (Van Heijenoort, 1986) as a proponent of a constructive semantics, although he seems to privilege the syntactical standpoint.

1. Aristotle, *Metaphysics*, Γ, 4.

2. On the various meanings of 'completeness', see Hunter (1971).

3. As Tharp (1975, p. 6) observes.

4. Tharp (1975, p. 6). For an interesting analysis of the importance of compactness and its anticipation by Aristotle, see Lear (1979).

5. The fact that there is no definition of the notion of an effective procedure is known as 'Church's thesis'. In practice, this notion can be reduced to that of computability by a Turing machine, or to the notion of a recursively computable function. See Jeffrey (1965, 2nd edn 1980, pp. 132ff.) and Hunter (1971, pp. 230ff.) for introductions, and for a more advanced treatment, see Jeffrey and Boolos (1975).

6. Proust (1986) gives a history of this tradition and of the different meanings of analyticity within it.

7. See, for instance, Granger (1984, p. 46).

8. Carnap, 'Meaning postulates', in Carnap (1956, pp. 222–9).

9. I borrow this distinction from Haack (1978, p. 173).

10. Carnap (1956, p. 225).

11. Carnap (1956, p. 225)

12. Quine (1970, pp. 49–60). Many writers trace the origins of this conception to Bolzano, see Proust (1986). In Quine's work the definition can be traced back to 'Truth and convention' (1936), as a distinction between terms that have an 'essential' occurrence in a statement (non-logical constants) and terms that have a 'vacuous' occurrence (logical constants). See Gochet (1986, ch. V).

13. Quine (1970, pp. 47–9).

14. Davidson (1980, p. 140).

15. Davidson, 'The logical form of action sentences', in Davidson (1980), ch. 6.

16. See, for instance, Jeffrey (1981, p. 150), who gives a proof in the system of semantic tableaux (see § 11.6) and Quine (1950) for a decision procedure for 'monadic schemas' based on Herbrand 1930s procedures for reducing validity in monadic predicate logic to validity in propositional logic.

17. Evans, 'Semantic structure and logical form' (1976), in Evans (1985, p. 50). See also Quine (1970, pp. 19, 59).

18. Hodges (1983, p. 2).

19. Kneale (1962, p. 741). See also Kneale (1956).

20. Tharp (1975, p. 10). On completeness proofs in modal logic, see Hugues and Cresswell (1984).

21. See, for instance, Jeffrey and Boolos (1975, p. 198).

22. Quine (1970, p. 53).

23. Quine (1970, p. 55).

24. Quine (1960, p. 160) or 'the maxim of minimum mutilation'. One of the best examples of this strategy is Davidson's analysis of action sentences, which uses only first-order resources to express logical form, through a quantification on individual events. See above § 11.3.

25. Quine (1970, pp. 95ff.).

26. Quine (1969, pp. 30–4).

27. Skolem has shown that since the axioms for Zermelo–Fraenkel set theory form a denumerable first-order theory, they have a denumerable model. In this model there are sets that satisfy the predicate 'x is non-denumerable', although they have only (by virtue of the Löwenheim–Skolem theorem) a denumerable number of members. On 'Skolem's paradox', see Resnik (1966), Putnam (1980) and Wright (1985).

28. Quine (1969, ch. 2).
29. Granger (1982, 1987).
30. Granger (1982, p. 368).
31. Granger (1982, p. 366).
32. Granger (1982, p. 368). The notion of an 'object of whatever kind' ('quelconque') comes from Gonseth (1937). Such an object is obtained 'through abstraction and through axiomatisation' from the principles of identity, of excluded middle, and of non-contradiction, which are its only attributes. Logic is a 'physics' of objects of whatever kind, according to Gonseth, because logic deals with the pure and rational existence of objects from a schematisation of their characteristics.
33. Granger (1982, p. 368).
34. Granger (1979, p. 67).
35. Granger (1982, p. 370).
36. Granger (1982, pp. 370–1).
37. Granger (1982, pp. 370–1).
38. *Tractatus*, 4. 0312.
39. Quine, 'Ontological reduction and the world of numbers', in Quine (1976, p. 216).
40. Granger (1982, p. 372).
41. For an analysis of the decision problem for first-order logic, see Dreben and Goldfarb (1979). For monadic predicate logic, Löwenheim (1915), Skolem (1919) and Behnamn (1922) have shown its decidability in principle. Bernays and Shonfinkel (1928) have shown that quantificational formulas prefixed with quantifiers are decidable, and Gödel (1932), Kalmar (1933) and Schutte (1934) have shown that it is also the case for formulas prefixed with quantifiers. Undecidability results are exposed in Lewis (1978).
42. I come back to the theory of computational complexity in § 13.5 above.
43. See Lambert and Van Fraassen (1972), Lambert (1991).
44. Prior (1976, pp. 128–9).
45. I am indebted here to Seymour (1990), who discusses the merits of such substitutional second-order logic.
46. See Lindström (1969), Tharp (1975) and Monk (1976) for a commentary on these results.
47. See, for instance, Martin (1965, p. 87).
48. Monk (1976, ch. 30).
49. See in particular Wright (1986a).
50. Dummett (1973, pp. 433–4).
51. See in particular Popper (1947), Kneale (1956), Prawitz (1965) and Hacking (1979).
52. For a presentation, see Scott *et al.* (1981, vol. 2).
53. See Gentzen (1934), in Gentzen (1969); Prawitz (1965).
54. Hacking (1979, p. 295); for a proof, see for instance Barwise (1977, pp. 36–7).
55. Hacking (1979, p. 304).
56. In the simple theory of types, one has a hierarchy of objects classified into types (type 0: individuals; type 1: classes of individuals; type 2: classes of classes of individuals, etc.). In the ramified theory, a hierarchy of orders is added, according to whether quantification is of the first, or of a superior order. See for instance Quine (1963, ch. II).
57. Hacking (1979, p. 203).
58. See for instance Black (1967) in Edwards (1967), pp. 169–81.
59. See, for instance, Turner (1984, ch. 5).
60. Hacking (1979, p. 310).

61. Hacking (1979, p. 299).
62. See above, § 7.5; Putnam (1978, p. 27).
63. Hacking (1979, p. 300). This is what Hacking calls a 'do-it-yourself semantics'.
64. The example is taken from Peacocke (1976, p. 232, n. 11). See Hacking (1979, pp. 310–11). Hacking claims here that he follows the theory of a 'prelogical' language of Wittgenstein's *Tractatus*, composed of elementary sentences to which logical constants are added to get sentences of greater complexity, the truth conditions of which are a function of the truth conditions of elementary sentences.
65. Hacking (1979, p. 317).
66. Peacocke (1988, p. 167).
67. On the tree method, see Scott *et al.* (1981, vol. 2, p. 167), Jeffrey (1981), Hodges (1977).
68. Beth (1955). For a general presentation of Beth's semantic tableaux, see Smullyan (1968).
69. On the relationship between model theory and proof theory from the standpoint of the natural deduction methods, see Kleene (1967) and Prawitz (1975). See also Sundholm (1981, 1983).
70. Peacocke (1976, p. 229).
71. Peacocke (1976, p. 223); see also Peacocke (1981b, pp. 171–2).
72. Peacocke (1981b, p. 172).
73. Peacocke (1976, p. 232).
74. Peacocke (1976, p. 233).
75. Peacocke (1976, p. 234).
76. Peacocke (1976, p. 234).
77. Peacocke (1976, p. 234).
78. Peacocke (1988, and in press), Engel (in press), see Chapter 12.

Notes to Chapter 12

Bibliographical references

The main sources for this chapter are Quine's 'Truth by convention' (1936) in Quine (1976), Dummett (1975), Wright (1980, 1986), Bouveresse (1987), Tennant (1987a, 1987b), Davidson (1984) and Peacocke (1988). Lewis (1969) contains an illuminating analysis of the notion of convention, but I do not know how far it can be used for an account of logical conventions (see, however, Tennant 1987b). There is an enormous literature on the analytic-synthetic distinction. Pap (1958) is still useful, and for a history of the notion until Carnap, see Proust (1986). Among the contemporary discussions, see Putnam (1962) and Hintikka (1973). Moser (1987) is a useful collection about *a priori* knowledge. On the problem of the plurality of logics, see Haack (1974, 1978) and Van Heijenoort (1986, ch. 11).

1. Lewis Carroll (1895).
2. See, for instance, the common confusion, about the notion of logical consequence, between the notion of implication (valid consequence) and the material conditional, notably in the medieval theory of *consequentiae*; see Kenny and Pinborg (1982, pp. 300–1).
3. Mill (1843, Bk II, ch. III, EI). See Dummett (1978, pp. 300–6), Cohen and Nagel (1934, p. 173).

4. Kripke (1982).
5. This is especially clear in Frege's polemic against Hilbert, in Frege (1976). See Bouveresse (1980).
6. On this conception of logic as a 'universal language', against the conception of logic as a 'calculus', see Van Heijenoort, 'Logic as language and logic as calculus' (1967), in Van Heijenoort (1986).
7. See Dummett, 'Wittgenstein's philosophy of mathematics' (1959), in Dummett (1978, pp. 166ff.). See also Wright (1986a, p. 188).
8. Wright (1980, 1986a), Bouveresse (1987).
9. Frege (1967, p. 14).
10. Frege (1883, p. 24). See Dummett (1978, p. 300; 1973, p. 632).
11. See, for instance, similar objections about such entities as the good, e.g. John Mackie's 'argument from queerness' (1977a).
12. Dummett (1978, p. 169).
13. Quine (1936), quoted after Quine (1967, pp. 93ff.); see Stroud (1981, p. 243).
14. Quine (1936, pp. 90–1).
15. Wittgenstein (1922, 6.2, 6.21).
16. Wittgenstein (1953, § 372).
17. Dummett (1978, p. 170).
18. Wittgenstein (1969, p. 303).
19. Wittgenstein (1969, p. 302).
20. Wittgenstein (1956, p. 106).
21. Wright (1980, p. 392; 1986a, pp. 203ff.).
22. Wittgenstein (1956, p. 82).
23. Leibniz, *New Essays on Human Understanding*, IV, 7. The proof runs:

> *Definitions*: (1) $2 = 1 + 1$
> (2) $3 = 2 + 1$
> (3) $4 = 3 + 1$
> *Axiom*: putting equals for equals, the equality remains
> *Proof*: $2 + 2 = 2 + 1 + 1$ (by df 1)
> $2 + 1 + 1 + 1 = 3 + 1$ (by df 2)
> $3 + 1 = 4$ (by df 3)
> therefore (by the axiom): $2 + 2 = 4$ (QED)

24. Dummett (1978, p. 303).
25. See in particular Stroud (1965), Putnam (1979) and Bouveresse (1987, p. 132).
26. Putnam (1979, p. 88). See also Chihara (1982).
27. Wittgenstein (1969, p. 303).
28. Wright (1980, p. 301), Bouveresse (1987, pp. 126ff.).
29. Wright (1986a, p. 311).
30. Kripke (1982), and the abundant literature thereof: Hacker and Baker (1984), McGinn (1985), Wright (1981), Blackburn (1984).
31. Wright (1989).
32. Wright (1989, pp. 239–43).
33. Skorupski (1988, pp. 503–4; see also Skorupski (in press).
34. Bouveresse (1987, p. 98).
35. Dummett (1978, pp. 302–3), see also Wright (1987, pp. 330ff.).

36. Dummett (1978, pp. 290–7). Dummett observes that the situation for deduction is the reserve of the situation that holds for the justification of induction.
37. Goodman (1954, p. 64).
38. Mill (1843, Bk II, chs 4, 5).
39. Quine, 'Carnap and logical truth' (1964), in Quine (1976, p. 138).
40. Quine, 'Two dogmas of empiricism', in Quine (1951, pp. 42–3).
41. Quine (1974) examines further the translation of the logical connectives, and proposes a method of 'verdict tables' somewhat different from the approach of Quine (1960). See Berger (1980). For a lucid analysis of the various theses and versions involved in Quine's 'indeterminacy thesis', see Kirk (1985). Seymour (1990) rightly points out that a number of the positions I take in this book involve a rejection of Quine's indeterminacy thesis, at least in its strongest versions.
42. Wright (1986a, p. 190). This point is similar to Grice and Strawson (1956).
43. Dummett (1973, p. 221).
44. See in particular Prawitz (1965, 1977), Tennant (1987a, ch. 9), Sundholm (1983) and Kremer (1988). As Dummett (1973, p. 454) remarks, Belnap's analysis of the *tonk* problem (§ 2.3.1) goes clearly in that direction.
45. Tennant (1987a, p. 145), see Peacocke (in press).
46. Tennant (1987a, ch. 6).
47. Tennant (1987b, pp. 86, 88); see also Tennant (1987a, ch. 9).
48. Tennant (1987a, pp. 66–7, 117). See also Blackburn's (1984) distinction between the 'top-down' method and the 'bottom-up' method in Davidson (1984, pp. 273–6).
49. Davidson (1984, p. 71).
50. Davidson (1984, p. 33).
51. Davidson (1984, p. 61). See Tennant (1987a, pp. 70–5), Lower and Le Pore (1981) and Le Pore (1982).
52. Tennant (1987a, pp. 71–5); see also Tennant (1987c).
53. Skorupski (1988, and in press).
54. 'Minimal realism' is not Peacocke's own term. To distinguish his position from Dummettian anti-realism, he calls himself a 'manifestationist' (according to which meaning is manifest in use without consisting in verification conditions; Peacocke, 1987), or, in the context of his discussion of logical constants, a 'molecular anti-constructivist' (Peacocke, in press). On his theory of thoughts and concepts, see Peacocke (1986).
55. Peacocke (1988, p. 161).
56. Peacocke (1988, p. 167 and in press).
57. Peacocke (1988, p. 169).
58. Peacocke (1988, p. 172 and in press).
59. Peacocke (in press). The minimal realist position is, in a sense, compatible with Wittgensteinian conventionalism, in so far as the latter does not involve a *reduction* of logical truths to conventions, but only points out the conventional and normative character of logical truths. Bouveresse (1987, pp. 128–9) characterises Wittgenstein's position as a 'minimal conventionalism' in this sense. Nothing in what is said here is inconsistent with such a minimal conventionalism. If, however, one interprets Wittgenstein as holding that the meaning of a sentence consists in its assertion conditions, and that the meaning of logical constants consists in its inferential rules (as Skoruski, in press, does), then the present position is not Wittgensteinian.

60. The example about London is inspired by Kripke's (1979) famous 'puzzle' about belief. See Marcus (1983). Putnam (1979) holds, in the same vein, that the fact that *a statement cannot be both true and false* is an *a priori* truth in this sense.
61. Peacocke (1988, p. 172; and in press). For a further elaboration about these issues, see Priest (1986).
62. See Peacocke (in press) for an elaboration of this non-sceptical view of rule following.
63. See Van Heijenoort, 'Absolutism and relativism in logic' (1979), in Van Heijenoort (1986, pp. 75–83). Van Heijenoort, however, establishes a close link between the absolutist/relativist distinction and the distinction between an axiomatic and universal-ist conception of logic as language (Frege, Russell) and a semantical conception of logic (Tarski). I have ignored here this interpretation of the distinction.
64. The table here is inspired by Haack (1978, p. 225).
65. On relevant logics, see in particular Anderson and Belnap (1975), Dunn (1983), Tennant (1987a, ch. 17) and Read (1988). Anderson and Belnap's calculus has been called by Church the calculus of 'weak implication'. In other systems of relevant logic, the rule of the transitivity of implication is rejected (see Tennant 1987a, pp. 190ff.).
66. Dunn (1983, p. 163), Belnap (1962). Tennant (1987a) proposes a logic that is a combination of intuitionist and relevant logic.
67. Anderson and Belnap (1975).
68. Arruda (1980, p. 14).
69. Quine (1970, p. 81).
70. As Van Heijenoort (1985, p. 73) remarks.
71. In another sense classical logic is stronger, for if we establish for instance $p \lor q$, this result is weaker than if we had established it intuitionistically, since from the intuitionistic point of view that we have established is $-(-p \& -q)$ or $- -(p \lor q)$, which are classically equivalent to $p \lor q$, but which are weaker *for the intuitionist*.
72. Arruda (1980) distinguishes paraconsistent logics from the so-called 'dialectical logics'. An interesting attempt to formulate what such logics should look like is Dubarle (1972). See also the remarks in Granger (1981).
73. Tarski (1944, p. 77). I owe this quotation to Granger, in Vuillemin (1986, p. 57).
74. Davidson, 'On the very idea of a conceptual scheme' (1974), ch. 13 of Davidson (1984).
75. Davidson (1984, pp. 192, 184).
76. Davidson (1984, pp. 196–7). See n. 41 above.
77. Wright (1980, p. 99; 1986a, pp. 337ff.), Lear (1982) and Bouveresse (1987) remark that this is also Wittgenstein's point of view.
78. On quantum logic see in particular Reichenbach (1944), Putnam (1975) and Dummett (1978, ch. 16). For an introduction, see Haack (1974).

Notes to Chapter 13

Bibliographical references

Sober (1978), Johnson-Laird (1983), Cohen (1981, 1986), Cherniak (1986), Stich (1985, 1990) and Over and Manktelow (1987, 1990) have been my main sources for this chapter. The debate about rationality in deductive reasoning can be usefully compared to the corresponding debates in economics (Simon, 1957) and in the social sciences (Elster,

1978). Goldman (1986) contains a comprehensive account of the relationships between the psychology of reasoning and epistemology.

1. Lewis Carroll (1977).
2. Stroud (1979) draws explicitly this moral from the story of Achilles and the Tortoise.
3. Mill, *Examination of Sir Hamilton's Philosophy* (1874), quoted by McNamara (1986, p. 13).
4. Bain, *Logic* (1843, II, 7.3), quoted by McNamara (1986, p. 7).
5. McNamara (1986, p. 14).
6. Peirce (1930–58, III, pp. 160–1).
7. Peirce (1930–58, I, p. 56).
8. Peirce (1930–58, V, p. 39).
9. Kant (1974, p. 16).
10. Husserl (1970), see Cavaillès (1947, p. 1).
11. See in particular Frege (1966).
12. See, for instance, Frege (1956).
13. As Husserl (1970, p. 160) remarks, Kant distinguished such a logic from pure logic.
14. Sober (1978, p. 169).
15. See for instance, Piaget and Inhelder (1955).
16. For a general presentation of the computational theory of thought processes, see, for instance, Fodor (1975) and Pylyshyn (1984).
17. On functionalism in the philosophy of mind, see, for instance, the various papers collected in Block (1981, vol. 1).
18. See in particular Piaget (1940). The 'INRC' group of operations consists in the logical operations of inversion or negation, and of reciprocity or correlation. For instance, for disjunction, $(p \lor q)$, I or N is $-p \& -q$, R is $-p \lor -q$, and correlation corresponds to duality: $p \& q$. See Manktelow and Over (1990, p. 89). The INRC group is doubly reversible (the inverse of reciprocal operations are reciprocal, and the reciprocals of two inverse operations are inverse).
19. See Braine (1978, p. 5), McNamara (1986, pp. 114–15) and Johnson-Laird (1983, p. 25).
20. Rips (1982) denies that mental logic is innate; McNamara (1986) seems to be more favourable to inneism.
21. This is Chomsky's (1965) classical distinction, See, for instance, McNamara (1986).
22. Rips (1982); I follow Goldman (1986, p. 288).
23. See, for instance, the rules of resolution in Quine (1950).
24. Gentzen (1969).
25. Stroud (1979) uses Carroll's paradox to that effect. On the difficulties of the idea of a mental language, see Dennett (1978, ch. 3) and Blackburn (1984, pp. 51ff.).
26. See, for instance, Hamblin (1970).
27. On the selection task, see Wason (1968), Wason and Johnson-Laird (1970), Johnson-Laird (1983), Manktelow and Over (1987, 1990), Evans (1989) and Stich (1983, 1985).
28. See in particular, for theories along these lines, Johnson-Laird (1983), Cheng and Holyoak (1985) and Cosmides (1989).
29. Johnson-Laird (1983, p. 40).
30. Harman (1986, p. 6).
31. Wason (1968) and Evans (1982, 1989) talk here of a 'confirmation bias'.
32. Johnson-Laird (1983, ch. 4, 5), Goldman (1986, pp. 290–1).

33. Johnson-Laird (1983, ch. 4) analyses this 'figural effect', that is the fact that the performance of the subjects varies according to which syllogistic figure is concerned. For instance the proportion of answers in an experiment where the subjects have received 64 possible syllogistic pairs (and where the difference consists in the proportion of answers of the kind 'no valid answer'), is the following:

Form of the conclusion	Figure of the premises			
	A-B B-C	B-A C-B	A-B C-B	B-A B-C
A-C	51%	5%	21%	32%
C-A	6%	48%	21%	18%

34. See Granger (1976) on Aristotle's 'semantic' procedures.
35. On Venn diagrams, see, for instance, Quine (1950, ch. 15, 16).
36. A semantic tree is an attempt to describe a model of the conclusion of an argument that would be a counter-example of the inference from the premises to the negation of the conclusion. See § 11.5.2 above. But it should be noted that the tree method answers a question Y/N, and not, as the procedure described by Johnson-Laird, a W-question (in this sense syntactical methods are more appropriate).
37. Johnson-Laird (1983) says (p. 146) that there are three kinds of mental representations: images, propositional or linguistic representations, and mental models. But on p. 397, the latter are characterised as 'theoretical entities' posited 'to make sense of inferences'. In one sense the models are 'constructed', in another sense they rest upon conceptual primitives that are 'innate' (p. 411).
38. See, for instance, Rips (1982), Goldman (1986, p. 292) and McNamara (1986, pp. 45ff.).
39. In particular in the works of Cheng and Holyoak and Cosmides quoted above n. 28. For a presentation of those works, see Manktelow and Over (1987; 1990, pp. 111–16).
40. Quine (1976, p. 109).
41. See in particular Davidson (1984, p. 197).
42. Dennett (1978, p. 48).
43. Dennett (1978, pp. 10–11).
44. The notion of a 'leading principle' is taken from Peirce (1930–58, III, p. 161); see above § 13.2.
45. On decision theory, see, for instance, Jeffrey (1981), Suppes (1984) and Davidson (1980, ch. 14). In economics, Simon (1957). Ramsey (1927, pp. 74–5) has already formulated the 'normative' standpoint.
46. Quine, 'Carnap and logical truth', in Quine (1976), see § 12 above.
47. Davidson (1985, p. 89) and Harman (1986, p. 7) emphasise this point. For probability judgements, see Kahneman and Tversky (1982), Goldman (1986, ch. 14).
48. This is implicitly assumed in many descriptions of the task; see for instance, Manktelow and Over (1990, p. 105) and Evans (1989, p. 54).
49. Cohen (1981, p. 231).
50. The situation for human reasoning should not be, in this respect, much different from what it is with animals. See Davidson (1982).

51. Of course such claims are still vague unless the very notion of belief is analysed. On tacit belief, see Lycan (1985).
52. Hintikka (1962, pp. 24–6); see Dennett (1978, p. 20).
53. This is one of the main motivations for the introduction of a principle of relevance such as Grice's (§ 3.5) or Sperber and Wilson's (1986). The question arises, however, whether such a principle is a rule of rationality, as Grice often implies, or a real psychological principle, as Sperber and Wilson emphasise.
54. See, for instance, Charniak and McDermott (1984, pp. 343–4).
55. Stich (1985, p. 255). The experiments of belief perseverance alluded to consist in giving to subjects data that the experimenter reveals later to be false; even after learning that they were wrong, subjects keep their initial beliefs and performances.
56. Stich (1985, pp. 263–5).
57. Ellis (1979, p. 61), Jeffrey (1981, p. 81).
58. J. Evans (1984, p. 465), quoted by Manktelow and Over (1987).
59. Cohen (1981, p. 326). See Thagard (1988) on various forms of reflexive equilibrium.
60. As suggested by Dennett (1978, pp. 11–12).
61. See, for instance, Eells (1982).
62. See, for instance, Simon (1957) and Elster (1980).
63. Dennett (1978, p. 20).
64. Cherniak (1986, ch. 1).
65. Cherniak (1986, p. 25).
66. Davidson (1985, pp. 89–90).
67. Quine (1970, p. 83).
68. Cherniak (1986, ch. 4).
69. On the theory of computational complexity, see Stokmeyer and Chandra (1979) and Lewis and Papadimitriou (1978).
70. Cherniak (1986, pp. 93–4).
71. Wittgenstein (1956), quoted by Cherniak (1986, p. 99).
72. Cherniak misunderstands the meaning of Quine and Davidson's principle of charity, when he ascribes to them the thesis of a strong acceptance of logic in the agents. He is right, however, to insist that the interpretation procedure cannot succeed without hypotheses about the real psychology of agents.
73. It is interesting to notice here that the method of reflexive equilibrium plays no role in Cherniak's analysis of minimal rationality.
74. A conception which has certain affinities with the one proposed here is Ellis's (1979) theory, according to which the laws of logic are 'equilibrium laws' of rational belief systems. Ellis, however, insists too much in my mind on 'maximal' norms of rationality; he does not hesitate to call his position 'psychologistic' and he thus overlooks the normative status of rules. I am aware that the claims of this chapter should be completed by an account of what Ellis calls the 'dynamics' of belief systems, and of the status of normative rules in a theory of belief change (see Harman, 1986; Forrest, 1986). It should be clear, however, that I do not agree with Harman's view that deductive logic has nothing to do with human reasoning. If that position were correct, why should one care about *teaching* logic at all?

BIBLIOGRAPHY

Adams, R. (1974) 'Theories of actuality', *Nous*, 8.

Adams, R. (1979) 'Primitive thisness and primitive identity', *Journal of Philosophy*, 76.

Almog, J. (1986) 'Naming without necessity', *Journal of Philosophy*, LXXXIII, 4.

Alston, W. (1964) *Philosophy of Language*, Prentice Hall, Englewood Cliffs.

Anderson, A. R. and Belnap, N. D. (1975) *Entailment*, vol. I, Princeton University Press.

Anscombe, E. (1959) *An Introduction to Wittgenstein's Tractatus*, Hutchinson, London.

Anscombe, J. C. and Ducrot, O. (1983) *L'argumentation dans la langue*, Mardaga, Bruxelles.

Appiah (1986) *For Truth in Semantics*, Blackwell, Oxford.

Arruda (1980) 'A survey of paraconsistent logic', in Arruda, Churaqui and Da Costa, ed., *Mathematical Logic in Latin America*, North Holland, Amsterdam, 1980.

Austin, J. L. (1950) 'Truth', in Pitcher 1965.

Ayer, A. J. (1936) *Language, Truth and Logic*, Gollancz, London.

Ayer, A. J. (1954) *Philosophical Essays*, Macmillan, London.

Baker, G. and Hacker, P. (1984a) *Language, Sense and Nonsense*, Blackwell, Oxford.

Baker, G. and Hacker, P. (1984b) *Scepticism, Rules and Language*, Blackwell, Oxford.

Baker, G. and Hacker, P. (1985) *Wittgenstein, Rules, Grammar and Necessity*, Blackwell, Oxford.

Baldwin, T. (1975) 'Quantification, modality, and indirect speech', in Blackburn 1975.

Baldwin, T. (1979) 'Interpretation of quantifiers', *Mind*.

Baldwin, T. (1989) 'The truth in the correspondence theory of truth', in Cooper and Engel 1991.

Bar Hillel, J. and Carnap, R. (1952) 'An outline of a theory of semantic information', repr. in Bar Hillel, *Language and Information*, Addison-Wesley, Reading, Mass.

Barnes, J. (1982) 'Medicine, science and logic', in Brunschwicg, Burneyat & Sorabji, ed. *Studies in Hellenistic Theory and Practice*, Cambridge et Maison des sciences de l'homme, Paris.

Barwise, J. ed. (1977a) *Handbook of Mathematical Logic*, North Holland, Amsterdam.

Barwise, J. (1977b) 'An introduction to first-order logic', in Barwise 1977a.

Barwise, J. (1981) 'Scenes and other situations', *Journal of Philosophy*.

Barwise, J. & Cooper, R. (1981) 'Generalized quantifiers and natural language', *Linguistics and Philosophy*.

Barwise, J. and Perry, J. (1981) 'Semantic innocence and uncompromising situations' in *Midwest Studies in Philosophy*, VI.

Barwise, J. and Perry, J. (1983) *Situations and Attitudes*, MIT Press Bradford Books, Cambridge, Mass.

Belnap, N. D. (1962) 'Tonk, plonk and plink', *Analysis*, 22, repr. in Strawson 1967.

Benacerraf, P. and Putnam, H. (1983; 1964) *Philosophy of Mathematics; Selected Readings*, Cambridge University Press.

Bentham, J. Van (1985) *Essays in Logical Semantics*, Reidel, Dordrecht.

Berger, A. (1980) 'Quine on alternative logics and verdict tables', *Journal of Philosophy*, 77, 259–77.

Beth, E. W. (1955) 'Semantic entailment and formal derivability', *Mededelingen van de*

Koninklijke Academie van Wetenschappen Afdeling Letterkunde, NR, 18, no. 13, Amsterdam, 309–42, reprinted in Hintikka 1969.

Bilgrami, A. 1986 'Meaning, holism, and use', in Le Pore (1986b).

Black, M. (1937) 'Vagueness', *Philosophy of Science*, 4.

Blackburn, S. (1975a) ed., *Meaning, Reference and Necessity*, Cambridge University Press.

Blackburn, S. (1975b) 'Propositions', in Blackburn 1975.

Blackburn, S. (1984) *Spreading the Word*, Oxford University Press.

Block, N. (1981) *Readings in the Philosophy of Psychology*, 2 vols, Methuen, London.

Bonevac, D. (1986) 'Systems of substitutional quantification', *Philosophy of Science*.

Boolos, G. (1975) 'On second order logic', *Journal of Philosophy*, LXXXII.

Boolos, G. (1979) *The Unprovability of Inconsistency*, Cambridge University Press.

Boolos, G. (1984) 'To be is to be the value of some variables', *Journal of Philosophy*, LXLI.

Boolos, G. & Jeffrey, R. (1975, 2nd edn 1989) *Computability and Logic*, Cambridge University Press.

Bouveresse, J. (1980a) 'La philosophie et les fondements', *Archives de philosophie*, 43, 1.

Bouveresse, J. (1980b) 'Frege, Wittgenstein, Dummett et la "Nouvelle querelle du réalisme"', *Critique*, 399–400.

Bouveresse, J. (1980c) 'Qu'est-ce que la logique?', in Delacampagne, C. and Maggiori, R. ed., *Philosopher*, Fayard, Paris.

Bouveresse, J. (1983) 'Le problème de Ramsey', *Histoire, épistémologie, langages.*

Bouveresse, J. (1986) 'Théorie de la proposition atomique', in Vuillemin 1986.

Bouveresse, J. (1987) *La force de la règle*, Minuit, Paris.

Braine, M. (1978) 'On the relation between the natural logic of reasoning and standard logic', *Psychological Review*, 85, 1–21.

Brody, B. (1980) *Identity and Essence*, Princeton University Press.

Bull, J. & Segerberg, K. (1983) 'Basic modal logic', in Gabbay and Guenthner 1983, vol. 2.

Burge, T. (1979a) 'Sinning against Frege', *Philosophical Review*.

Burge, T. (1979b) 'Individualism and the mental', *Midwest Studies in Philosophy*.

Burge, T. (1986a) 'Frege on truth', in Hintikka and Haaparanta 1986.

Burge, T. (1986b) 'Davidson on saying that', in Le Pore (1986b).

Cargile, J. (1969) 'The sorites paradox', *British Journal for the Philosophy of Science*, 20.

Carnap, R. (1942) *Introduction to Semantics*, Cambridge University Press.

Carnap, R. (1956) *Meaning and Necessity*, Chicago University Press, 2nd edn (1st edn 1947).

Carnap, R. (1963) 'Intellectual autobiography', in P. A. Schillpp, ed., *The Philosophy of Rudolf Carnap*, Open Court, Evanston, IL.

Cartwright, R. (1962) 'Propositions' in Butler, ed., *Analytical Philosophy*, vol. I, Blackwell, Oxford.

Cartwright, R. (1971) 'Identity and substitutivity' in Munitz 1971.

Cavaillés, J. (1947) *Sur la logique et la théorie de la science*, 2nd edn 1976, Vrin, Paris.

Carroll, L. (1895) 'What the Tortoise said to Achilles', *Mind*, 4.

Carroll, L. (1977) *Symbolic Logic*, ed. W. Bartley III, Potter, New York.

Charniak, C. and McDermott, D. (1984) *Artificial Intelligence*, Addison-Wesley, New York.

Chellas, B. (1980) *Modal Logic*, Cambridge University Press.

Cheng, P. W. and Holyoak (1985) 'Pragmatic reasoning schemas', *Cognitive Psychology*, 17, 91–416.

Cherniak, C. (1986) *Minimal Rationality*, MIT Press, Bradford Books, Cambridge, Mass.

Chihara, C. (1983) 'The Wright-Wing defense of Wittgenstein's philosophy of mathematics', *Philosophical Review*, XCI, 1.

Chisholm, R. (1967) 'Identity through possible worlds, some questions', *Nous*, 1.

Chisholm, R. (1971) 'Problems of identity', in Munitz 1971.

Chomsky, N. (1965) *Aspects of Syntactic Theory*, MIT Press, Cambridge, Mass.

Church, A. (1943) 'Review of Carnap 1942', *Philosophical Review*, 52.

Church, A. (1950) 'On Carnap's analysis of statements of assertion and belief', *Analysis*, 10, 5.

Church, A. (1951) 'A formulation of the logic of sense and denotation', in Henle, P., ed., *Structure, Method and Meaning*, Liberal Arts Press, New York.

Church, A. (1956) *Introduction to Mathematical Logic*, vol. I, Princeton University Press.

Cohen, L. J. (1972) 'Remarks on Grice's analysis of logical particles in natural language', in Y. Bar-Hilell, ed., *Pragmatics of Natural Language*, Reidel, Dordrecht.

Cohen, L. J. (1977) 'Can the conversational hypothesis be defended?', *Philosophical Studies*, 31, 81–90.

Cohen, L. J. (1981) 'Can human irrationality be demonstrated experimentally?', *The Behavioural and Brain Sciences*, 4.

Cohen, L. J. (1986) *The Dialogue of Reason*, Clarendon Press, Oxford.

Cohen, M. and Nagel, E. (1934) *An Introduction to Logic and Scientific Method*, Routledge, London.

Cooper, N. and Engel, P., eds (1991) *New Inquiries into Meaning and Truth*, Harvester, Hemel Hempstead.

Cosmides (1989) 'The logic of social exchange: has natural selection shaped how humans reason?', *Cognition*, 31, 187–276.

Cresswell, M. J. (1985) *Structured Meanings*, MIT Press, Bradford Books, Cambridge, Mass.

Dancy, J. (1985) *An Introduction to Epistemology*, Blackwell, Oxford.

Davidson, D. (1980) *Essays on Actions and Events*, Oxford University Press.

Davidson, D. (1982) 'A coherent theory of truth and knowledge' in Le Pore 1986b.

Davidson, D. (1984) *Inquiries into Truth and Interpretation*, Oxford University Press.

Davidson, D. (1990) 'The structure and content of truth', *Journal of Philosophy*, LXXXXVII, 6, 279–328.

Davidson, D. and Harman (eds) (1972) *Semantics of Natural Language*, Reidel, Dordrecht.

Davidson, D. and Harman (eds) (1975) *The Logic of Grammar*, Dickenson, Encino, Cal.

Davies, M. (1981) *Meaning, Quantification and Necessity*, Routledge, London.

Davies, M. (1986) 'Tacit knowledge, and the structure of thought and language', in C. Travis ed., *Meaning and Interpretation*, Blackwell, Oxford.

Dennett, D. (1978) *Brainstorms*, MIT Press, Bradford Books, Cambridge, Mass.

Dennett, D. (1987) *The Intentional Stance*, MIT Press, Cambridge, Mass.

Donnellan, K. (1966) 'Reference and definite descriptions', *Philosophical Review*, 75.

Donnellan, K. (1974) 'Speaking of nothing' *Philosophical Review*, 83.

Dowty, R. *et al.* (1981) *An Introduction to Montague Grammar*, Reidel, Dordrecht.

Dreben, B. and Goldfarb, W. (1979) *Solvable Classes of Quantificational Formulas*, Addison-Wesley, Reading, Mass.

Durable, D. (1972) *Logique et dialectique*, Larousse, Paris.

Dummett, M. (1959) 'Truth', *Proceedings of the Aristotelian Society*, LIX, 141–62, reprinted in Dummett (1978), pp. 1–24.

Dummett, M, (1973) *Frege, Philosophy of Language*, Duckworth, London.

Dummett, M. (1975) 'What is a theory of meaning? (I)' in S. Guttenplan ed., *Mind and language*, Oxford University Press, Oxford.

Dummett, M. (1976) 'What is a theory of meaning? (II)', in Evans and McDowell (1976).

Dummett, M. (1977) *Elements of Intuitionism*, Duckworth, London.

Dummett, M. (1978) *Truth and Other Enigmas*, Harvard University Press.

Dummett, M. (1981) *The Interpretation of Frege's Philosophy*, Duckworth, London.

Dummett, M. (1987) 'Replies', in Taylor 1987.

Dummett, M. (1991) *The Logical Basis of Metaphysics*, Harvard University Press, Harvard.

Dunn, M. (1983) 'Relevance logics' in Gabbay & Guenthner 1983, vol. III.

Dunn, M. & Belnap, N. (1968) 'The substitution interpretation of quantifiers', *Nous*, 2.

Edwards, P. (1967) *Encyclopedia of Philosophy*, vol. 3, Macmillan, London.

Eells, E. (1986) *Rational Decision and Causality*, Cambridge University Press.

Ellis, B. (1979) *Rational Belief Systems*, Blackwell, Oxford.

Elster, J. (1978) *Sour grapes*, Cambridge University Press.

Engel, P. (1985) *Identité et référence*, Presses de l'École normale supérieure, Paris.

Engel, P. (1988) 'Radical interpretation and the structure of thought', *Proceedings of the Aristotelian Society*, 88.

Engel, P. (in press) 'Holisme, mólécularité et constantes logiques'.

Engelbretsen, G. (1988) *Essays on the Philosophy of Fred Sommers*, Edwin Mellen Press, Queenston, Ontario.

Engelbretsen, G. (ed.) (1987) *The New Syllogistic*, Lang, New York.

Evans, G. (1982) *The Varieties of Reference*, Blackwell, Oxford.

Evans, G. (1985) *Collected Papers*, Oxford University Press, Oxford.

Evans, G. and McDowell, J. (ed.) 1976 *Truth and Meaning*, Oxford University Press, Oxford.

Evans, J. (1982) *The Psychology of Deductive Reasoning*, Routledge, London.

Evans, J. (1984) 'Heuristics and analytic processes in reasoning', *British Journal of Psychology*, 75.

Evans, J. St. B. (1990) *Bias in Human Reasoning*, Erlbaum, Hove and London.

Evans, J. St. B. T. and Lynch, J. S. (1973) 'Matching bias in the selection task', *British Journal of Psychology*, 64, 391–70.

Fauconnier (1976) *Étude de certains aspects grammaticaux de la quantification et de l'anaphore en français et en anglais, thèse*, Université de Paris VIII.

Fauconnier (1984) *Espaces mentaux*, Minuit, Paris. English trans., *Mental Spaces*, MIT Press, Cambridge, Mass. (1986).

Feigl, H. and Sellars, W. (1949) *Readings in Philosophical Analysis*, Appleton Century Crofts, New York.

Field, H. (1972) 'Tarski's theory of truth', *Journal of Philosophy*, 69.

Field, H. (1977) 'Logic, meaning, and conceptual role', *Journal of Philosophy*, 74.

Field, H. (1987) 'The deflationary conception of truth', in Wright and McDonald 1987.

Fine, K. (1975) 'Vagueness, truth and logic', *Synthese*, 30.

Fine, K. (1985) *Reasoning with Arbitrary Objects*, Blackwell-Aristotelian Society.

Fodor, J. (1975) *The Language of Thought*, MIT Press, Bradford Books, Cambridge, Mass.

Fodor, J. (1981) *Representations*, MIT Press, Bradford Books, Cambridge, Mass.

Fodor, J. (1987) *Psychosemantics*, MIT Press, Bradford Books, Cambridge, Mass.

Føllesdal, D. (1975) 'Meaning and experience', in Guttenplan 1975.

Føllesdal, D. (1983) 'Situation semantics and the slingshot argument', *Erkenntnis*, 19.

Føllesdal, D. (1986) 'Essentialism and quantified modal logic', in Vuillemin 1986.

Forbes, G. (1985) *The Metaphysics of Modality*, Oxford University Press.

Forbes, G. (1986) 'Indexicals and intentionality, a Fregean perspective', *Philosophical Review*, XCVI, I.

Forbes, G. (1987) 'Truth, correspondence and redundancy', in Wright & McDonald 1987.

Forster, J. (1976) 'Meaning and truth theory', in Evans & McDowell 1976.

Forrest (1986) *The Logic of Belief*, Blackwell, Oxford.

Frege, G. (1879) *Begriffsschrift*, Halle. English trans. in Van Heijenoort 1967.

Frege, G. (1883a) *Die Grundlagen der Arithmetik*, Koebner, Breslau, quoted after J. L. Austin's translation, *The Foundations of Arithmetik*, Blackwell, Oxford.

Frege, G. (1883b) *Grundgezetze der Arithmetik*, vol. I.

Frege, G. (1952) *Translations from the Philosophical Writings of G. Frege*, Blackwell, Oxford.

Frege, G. (1956) 'The thought', *Mind*, 65, Engl. trans by A. and M. Quinton of 'Der Gedanke', *Beitrage zur Philosophie der deutschen Idealismus*, 2.

Frege, G. (1966) *Grundgezetze der Arithmetik* (1893), Georg Olms, Hindelseins.

Frege, G. (1967) *The foundations of arithmetik*, Engl. trans. by M. Furth of Frege (1966), part I, University of California Press, Berkeley.

Frege, G. (1969) *Nachgelassene Schriften*, ed. H. Hermes, F. Kambartel and F. Kluback, F. Meiner, Hamburg; Engl. trans. by P. White and P. Long (1976) *Posthumous Writings*, Blackwell, Oxford.

Frege, G. (1976) *Wissenschaftliche Briefwechsel*, ed. G. Gabriel, H. Hermes, F. Kambartel, C. Thiel and G. Veraardt, F. Meiner, Hamburg; Engl. transl. by P. White and P. Long, (1980) *Scientific Correspondence*, Blackwell, Oxford.

Gabbay, D. and Guenthner, F. (eds) (1983), (1984), (1986), *Handbook of Philosophical Logic*, vol. I: *Elements of Classical Logic*; vol. 2: *Extensions of Classical Logic*; vol. III: *Alternatives to Classical Logic*, Reidel, Dordrecht.

Geach, P. (1962) *Reference and generality*, Cornell University Press, Ithaca (rev. edn 1968).

Geach, P. (1969) *God and the Soul*, Routledge.

Geach, P. (1968) *Logic Matters*, Blackwell, Oxford (2nd edn 1972).

Geach, P. (1975) 'Names and identity', in Guttenplan 1975.

Gentzen, G. (1969) *The Collected Papers of Gerhardt Gentzen*, ed. Fenstad, North Holland, Amsterdam.

George, A. (ed.) (1989) *Reflections on Chomsky*, Blackwell, Oxford.

Gochet, P. (1972) *Esquisse d'une théorie nominaliste de la proposition*, A. Colin, Paris. English trans., *Outline of a Theory of Proposition*, Reidel, Dordrecht.

Gochet, P. (1983) 'La sémantique des situations', *Histoire, épistémologie, langages*, 1982, 5, 2.

Gochet, P. (1986) *Ascent to Truth*, Philosophia Verlag, Munich, Vienne.

Gochet, P. and Gribomont, P. (1990) *Logique*, Hermes, Paris.

Gödel, K. (1930), 'Die Vollständigkeit der Axiome des logischen Funktionenskalküls', *Monatshefte für Mathematik und Physik*, 37. English trans. in Van Heijenoort 1967.

Gödel, K. (1931) 'Über formal unendscheidbare Sätze der Principia Mathematica und verwandter Systeme, I'. English trans. in Van Heijenoort 1967.

Gödel, K. (1933) 'Eine Interpretation des intuitionistischen Aussagenskalküls', *Ergebnisse eines mathematischen Kolloquiums*, 4, English trans. in Hintikka 1969.

Gödel, K. (1944) 'Russell's mathematical logic', in Schillp ed., *The Philosophy of B. Russell*, Open Court, La Salle, IL.

Goguen, J. (1969) 'The logic of inexact concepts', *Synthese*, 19.

Goldfarb, W. (1979) 'Logic in the twenties, the nature of the quantifier', *Journal of Symbolic Logic*.

Goldman, A. (1986) *Epistemology and Cognition*, Harvard University Press.

Gonseth, F. (1937) *Qu'est-ce que la logique?*, Hermann, Paris.

Goodman, N. (1954) *Fact, fiction and forecast*, 2nd edn, 1965, Bobbs Merrill, Indianapolis.

Gottlieb, D. (1989) *Substitutional Quantification and Ontology*, Clarendon Press, Oxford.

Grandy, R. (1977) *Advanced Logic for Applications*, Reidel, Dordrecht.

Granger, G. (1976) *La théorie aristotélicienne de la science*, Aubier-Montaigne, Paris.

Granger, G. (1979) *Langages et épistémologie*, Klincksieck, Paris.

Granger, G. (1982) 'The notion of formal content', *Social Research*, 42, 2.

Granger, G. (1984) 'Le synthétique a priori et la science moderne', *Cahiers du Groupe de recherches sur la philosophie et le langage*, 4.

Granger, G. (1987a) *Pour la connaissance philosophique*, Jacob, Paris.

Granger, G. (1987b) 'Is logic a theory of objects *überhaupt?*'.

Grayling, A. C. (1982) *An Introduction to Philosophical Logic*, Harvester, Brighton.

Grice, H. P. (1975) 'Logic and conversation', in Davidson and Harman 1975.

Grice, H. P. (1986) 'Reply to the Richards', in Grandy & Warner, *Philosophical Grounds of Rationality*, Oxford University Press.

Grice, H. P. (1989) *Studies in the Way of Words*, Harvard University Press, Harvard.

Grice, H. P. and Strawson, P. F. (1956) 'In defense of a dogma', *Philosophical Review*, LXV.

Griffin, N. (1977) *Relative Identity*, Oxford, Clarendon Press.

Grover, D., Camp, J. and Belnap, N. (1975) 'A prosentential theory of truth', *Philosophical Studies*, 27.

Guttenplan, S. (1975) *Mind and Language*, Clarendon Press, Oxford.

Guttenplan, S. (1986a) *The Languages of Logic*, Blackwell, Oxford.

Guttenplan, S. (1986b) 'Meaning and metaphysics', in Travis ed., *Meaning and Interpretation*, Blackwell, Oxford.

Haack, S. (1974) *Deviant Logics*, Cambridge University Press.

Haack, S. (1976) 'Dummett's justification of deduction', *Mind*, 85.

Haack, S. (1978) *Philosophy of Logics*, Cambridge University Press.

Haack, S. (1980) 'Is truth flat or bumpy?', in Mellor ed., *Prospects for Pragmatism*, Cambridge University Press.

Hacking, I. (1979) 'What is logic?', *Journal of Philosophy*, LXXVI, 6.

Haldane, J. and Wright, C., eds (in press) *Realism and Reason*, Blackwell, Oxford.

Hamblin, C. (1970) *Fallacies*, London, Methuen.

Harman, G. (1975) 'Logical form', in Davidson and Harman 1975.

Harman G. (1982) 'Conceptual role semantics', *Notre Dame Journal of Formal Logic*, 23.

Harman, G. (1986a) *Change in View*, MIT Press, Bradford Books, Cambridge, Mass.

Harman, G. (1986b) 'The meaning of logical constants', in Le Pore 1986b.

Hart, W. (1982) 'Prior and Belnap', *Theoria*, XLVII.

Hempel, C. G. (1935) 'On the logical positivist conception of truth', *Analysis*, 2.

Herbrand, J. (1967) *Ecrits logiques*, PUF, Paris, English trans. *Logical Writings* (1977) Reidel, Dordrecht.

Herzberger (1970) 'Paradoxes of grounding in semantics', *Journal of Philosophy*, 17; in Martin 1970.

Heyting, A. (1966) *Intuitionism*, North Holland, Amsterdam.

Higginbotham, J. (1983) 'The logic of perceptual reports: an alternative to situation semantics', *Journal of Philosophy*, 80.

Hintikka, J. (1962) *Knowledge and Belief*, Cornell University Press, Ithaca.

Hintikka, J. (1969a) 'The semantics of propositional attitudes and the indeterminacy of ontology', in *Models for modalities*, Reidel, Dordrecht.

Hintikka, J. (ed.) (1969b) *The Philosophy of Mathematics*, Oxford University Press.

Hintikka, J. (1973) *Logic, Language Games and Information*, Oxford University Press.

Hintikka, J. (1974) 'Quantifiers vs quantification theory', *Linguistic Inquiry*, 5, 153–77.

Hintikka, J. (1975) 'Quantifiers in logic and in natural language', in *Philosophy of logic*, ed. S. Körner, Blackwell, Oxford.

Hintikka, J. and Haaparanta, L. (eds) (1986) *Frege synthesized*, Reidel, Dordrecht.

Hirsch, E. (1982) *The Concept of Identity*, Oxford, Clarendon Press.

Hobbes, T. (1839–45) *The English Works of Thomas Hobbes*, ed. W. Molesworth, John Botson, London.

Hodges, W. (1978) *Logic*, Penguin Books, Harmondsworth.

Hodges, W. (1985) 'First-order logic', in Gabbay & Guenthner 1985, vol. I.

Hodges, W. (1986) 'Truth in a structure', *Proceedings of the Aristotelian Society*, LXXXVI.

Hofstadter, D. (1979) *Gödel, Escher, Bach*, Penguin, Harmondsworth.

Holtzman and Leich (eds) (1981) *Wittgenstein, to Follow a Rule*, Routledge, London.

Hookway, C. (1985) *Peirce*, Routledge and Kegan Paul, London.

Hornstein, N. (1981) *Logic as Grammar*, MIT Press, Bradford Books, Cambridge, Mass.

Hornstein, N. (1986) 'Review of Barwise & Perry 1983', *Journal of Philosophy*.

Horwich, P. (1990) *Truth*, Blackwell, Oxford.

Hughes, G. E. and Cresswell, M. J. (1968) *An Introduction to Modal Logic*, Methuen, London.

Hughes, G. E. and Cresswell, M. J. (1985) *A Companion to Modal Logic*, Methuen, London.

Hunter, G. (1971) *Metalogic*, University of California Press, Berkeley.

Husserl, E. (1970; 1900) *Logical Investigations*, Routledge, London.

Ishiguro, I. (1972) *Leibniz's Philosophy of Logic and Language*, Duckworth, London.

Jackson, F. (1987) *Conditionals*, Blackwell, Oxford.

Jacob, P. (1987) 'Thoughts and belief ascriptions', *Mind and Language*, 2, 4.

Jacob, P. (1991) 'The semantics of belief ascriptions' in Cooper and Engel (1991).

Jeffrey, R. (1965) *The Logic of Decision* (2nd edn 1980) Chicago University Press.

Jeffrey, R. (1968) *Formal Logic, its Scope and Limits* (2nd edn 1980), McGraw-Hill, New York.

Jeffrey, R. and Boolos, G. (1975) *Computability and Logic*, Cambridge University Press.

Johnson-Laird, P. (1983) *Mental Models*, Cambridge University Press.

Johnson-Laird, P. and Legrenzi, P. (1972) 'Reasoning and a sense of reality', *British Journal of Psychology*, 63, 395–400.

Johnson-Laird, P. and Wason, P. (1977) *Thinking, Readings in Cognitive Science* (5th edn 1985) Cambridge University Press.

Kahneman, D. and Tversky, A. (eds) (1982) *Judgement under Uncertainty, Heuristics and Biases*, Cambridge University Press.

Kamp, H. (1975a) 'Two theories about adjectives', in Keenan, ed., *Formal Semantics for Natural Languages*, Cambridge University Press.

Kamp, H. (1981) 'A semantic theory of truth and representation', in J. Groenendijk *et al.* (eds) *Formal Methods in the Study of Language*, reprinted in J. Groenendijk *et al.* (eds) (1984) *Truth, Interpretation and Information*, Grass series, vol. 2, Foris, Dordrecht.

Kant, E. (1979) *Logic*, Dover Books.

Kaplan, D. (1968) 'Quantifying in', in Davidson and Hintikka 1968.

Kaplan, D. (1975) 'How to Russell a Frege-Church', *Journal of Philosophy*, LXXII, 6.

Kaplan, D. (1977) 'Demonstratives', mimeo UCLA.

Kaplan, D. (1986) 'Rapport', in Vuillemin 1986.

Kaplan, D. (1989) 'Demonstratives' in J. Almog, J. Perry and H. Wettstein (eds), *Themes from Kaplan*, Oxford University Press, Oxford.

Kirk, R. (1985) *Translation Determined*, Oxford, Clarendon Press.

Kleene, S. (1952) *Introduction to Metamathematics*, North Holland, Amsterdam.

Kleene, S. (1967) *Mathematical Logic*.

Kneale, W. (1956) 'The province of logic', in H. D. Lewis, ed., *Contemporary British Philosophy*, 3rd series.

Kneale, W. (1962) 'Modality, *de dicto* and *de re'*, *Logic, Methodology and Philosophy of Science, Proceedings of the 1960 Congress*, Stanford University Press.

Kneale, W. and Kneale, M. (1962) *The Development of Logic*, Oxford University Press.

Knuuttila, S. (1981) 'Time and modality in scholasticism', in Knuuttila, ed., *Reforging the Great Chain of Being*, Reidel, Dordrecht.

Kremer, M. (1988) 'Logic and meaning: the philosophical significance of Gentzens's sequent calculus', *Mind*, 97, 51–72.

Kripke (1963) 'Semantical considerations on modal logic', *Acta Philosophica Fennica*, 16, repr. in Linsky 1971.

Kripke (1975) 'Outline of a theory of truth', *Journal of Philosophy*, repr. in Martin 1982.

Kripke (1976) 'Is there a problem about substitutional quantification?' in Evans and McDowell 1976.

Kripke (1979) 'A puzzle about belief', in A. Margalit, ed., *Meaning and Use*, Reidel, Dordrecht.

Kripke (1980) (1972) *Naming and Necessity*, Blackwell, Oxford.

Kripke (1981) *Wittgenstein on Rules and Private Language*, Blackwell, Oxford.

Lakoff, G. (1972) 'Linguistics and natural logic', in Davidson and Harman 1972.

Lambert, K. (ed.) (1969) *The Logical Way of Doing Things*, Yale University Press.

Lambert, K. (1982) *Meinong and the Principle of Independance*, Yale University Press.

Lambert, K. (ed.) (1991) *Free Logic*, Oxford University Press.

Lambert, K. and Van Fraassen, B. (1972) *Derivation and Counterexample: An Introduction to Philosophical Logic*, Dickenson, Encino, Calif.

Laurier, D. (ed.) (in press) *Essais sur le sens et la realité*, Vrin-Bellamin, Paris.

Lear, J. (1979) 'Leaving the world alone', *Journal of Philosophy*, LXXVI, 4.

Lear, J. (1982) 'Aristotle's compactness proof', *Journal of Philosophy*, LXXIX, 7.

Leeds, S. (1978) 'Theories of reference and of truth', *Erkenntnis*, 13.

Lehrer, K. (1970) *Knowledge*, Clarendon Press, Oxford.

Leibniz, G. W. (1875–90), 'Nouveaux essais sur l'entendonent humain', in C. I. Gerhard, ed., *Philosophischen Schriften*, vol. VI, Berlin; Engl. trans. by A. G. Langley (1916) *New Essays Concerning Human Understanding*, La Salle, IL.

Leibniz, G. W. (1901) *Opuscules et fragments inédits*, éd. Couturat, Olms.

Lemmon, E. J. (1966) 'Propositions, statements and sentences', in Williams & Montefiore, eds, *British Analytical Philosophy*, Routledge, London.

Lemmon, E. J. (1965) *Beginning Logic*, Nelson, London.

Le Pore, E. (1982) 'Truth and inference', *Erkenntnis*, 18.

Le Pore, E. (ed.) (1986a) *Actions and Events: Perspectives on the Philosophy of Davidson*, Blackwell, Oxford.

Le Pore, E. (ed.) (1986b) *Truth and Interpretation: Perspectives on the Philosophy of Davidson*, Blackwell, Oxford.

Lewis, C. I. (1918) *A Survey of Symbolic Logic*, University of California Press, Berkeley.

Lewis, D. (1968) 'Counterpart theory and quantified modal logic', *Journal of Philosophy*, 65.

Lewis, D. (1969) *Convention*, Harvard University Press.

Lewis, D. (1972) 'General semantics', in Davidson and Harman 1972.

Lewis, D. (1973) *Counterfactuals*, Blackwell, Oxford.

Lewis, D. (1983) *Philosophical Papers*, vol. I, Oxford University Press.

Lewis, D. (1985) *On the Plurality of Worlds*, Blackwell, Oxford.

Lewis, D. (1986) *Philosophical Papers*, vol. 2, Oxford University Press.

Lewis, H. (1978) *Unsolvable Classes of Quantificational Formulas*, Addison-Wesley, New York.

Lewis, H. and Papadimitrou, D. (1978) 'The efficiency of algorithms', *Scientific American*, 238, 96–109.

Lindström, P. (1969) 'On extensions of first order logic', *Theoria*, XXXV.

Linsky (1967) *Referring*, Routledge, London.

Linsky (ed.) (1971) *Reference and Modality*, Oxford University Press.

Linsky (1977) *Names and Descriptions*, Chicago University Press.

Lorenz, K. (1968) 'Dialogspiele als semantische Grundlage von Logikkalkülen', *Archiv für Mathematische Logik und Grundlagenforschung*, II.

Lorenzen, P. (1962) *Metamathematik*, Bibliographisches Institut, Mannheim.

Loux, M. (ed.) (1970) *Universals and Particulars*, University of Notre Dame Press.

Loux, M. (ed.) (1979) *The Possible and the Actual: Readings in the Metaphysics of Modality*, Cornell University Press, Ithaca, NY.

Lower, B. and Le Pore, E. (1981) 'Translational semantics', *Synthese*, 48.

Lukasiewicz (1920) 'On three-valued logic', in McCall, ed., *Polish Logic*, Oxford, 1967.

Luntley, M. (1988) *Language, Logic and Experience, the Case for Anti-realism*, Duckworth, London.

Lycan, W. (1985a) *Logical Form in Natural Language*, MIT Press, Bradford Books, Cambridge, Mass.

Lycan, W. (1985b) 'Tacit belief', in R. Bogdan, ed., *Belief*, Oxford University Press.

McCawley, J. D. (1972) 'A program for logic', in Davidson and Harman 1972.

McCawley, J. D. (1981) *Everything that Linguists Have Always Wanted to Know About Logic (But Were Ashamed to Ask)*, Chicago University Press.

McCulloch, G. (1984) 'Frege, Sommers, and singular reference', in Wright 1984.

McCulloch, G. (1987) *The Game of the Name*, Oxford University Press.

McDowell, J. (1976) 'Truth conditions, bivalence, and verificationism', in Evans and McDowell 1976.

McDowell, J. (1977) 'On the sense and the reference of a proper name', *Mind*, 86, 159–85, reprinted in Platts (1980) pp. 141–66.

McDowell, J. (1981) 'Anti-realism and the epistemology of understanding', in Bouveresse and Parret, eds, *Meaning and Understanding*, de Gruyter, Berlin.

McDowell, J. (1984) '*De re* senses', in Wright 1984.

McDowell, J. (1987) 'In defense of modesty', in Taylor 1977.

McGinn, C. (1980) 'Truth and use', in Platts 1980.

McGinn, C. (1982) 'The structure of content', in Woodfield 1982.

McGinn, C. (1985) *Wittgenstein on Meaning*, Blackwell, Oxford.

McNamara, J. (1986) *A Border Dispute, The Place of Logic in Psychology*, MIT Press, Bradford Books, Cambridge, Mass.

Mackie, J. (1972) *Truth, Probability and Paradox*, Clarendon Press, Oxford.

Mackie, J. (1977a) 'Problems of intentionality', in *Philosophical papers*, I, Oxford University Press, 1985.

Mackie, J. (1977b) *Ethics, Inventing Right or Wrong*, Penguin Books, Harmondsworth.

Manktelow, K. I. and Over, D. (1990) *Inference and Understanding*, Routledge, London.

Marcus, R. (1946) 'A strict functional calculus of first order based on strict implication', *Journal of Symbolic Logic*, 11.

Marcus, R. (1947) 'The identity of individuals in a strict functional calculus of second order', *Journal of Symbolic Logic*, 12.

Marcus, R. (1961) 'Modalities and intensional languages', Cohen and Wartofsky, eds, *Boston Studies in the Philosophy of Science*.

Marcus, R. (1962) 'Interpreting quantification', *Inquiry*, 5.

Marcus, R. (1967) 'Essentialism in modal logic', *Nous*, 1.

Marcus, R. (1981) 'Modal logic, modal semantics and their applications', in Floistad, ed., *Contemporary Philosophy*, vol. I, Nijhoff, La Haye.

Marcus, R. (1983) 'Rationality and believing the impossible', *Journal of Philosophy*, LXXIX.

Marcus, R. (1988) 'Possibilia and possible worlds', *Grazer Philosophische Studien*.

Martin, R. (1965) *Logique contemporaine et formalisation*, PUF, Paris.

Martin, R. L. (1970) *The Paradox of the Liar*, Ridgeview, Reseda, Calif.

Martin, R. L. (1984) *New Essays on Truth and the Liar Paradox*, Oxford University Press.

Mates, B. (1986) *The Philosophy of Leibniz*, Oxford University Press.

Mendelsson, E. (1964) *Introduction to Mathematical Logic*, Van Nostrand, New York.

Mill, J. S. (1843) *A System of Logic*, Longman's, London.

Monk, D. (1976) *Notes on Mathematical Logic*, in *Lecture Notes in Mathematics*, Springer, Berlin.

Montague, R. (1974) *Formal Philosophy*, Yale University Press.

Morris, T. V. (1984) *Understanding Identity Statements*, Aberdeen University Press.

Moser, P. K. (ed.) (1987) *A Priori Knowledge*, Oxford University Press.

Mulligan, K., Smith, B. and Simons, P. (1984) 'Truthmakers', *Philosophy and Phenomenological Research*, XLIV, 3.

Neale, S. (1990) *Descriptions*, MIT Press, Cambridge, Ma.

Nef, F. (éd.) (1985) *L'analyse logique des langues naturelles*, Éditions du CNRS, Paris.

Nef, F. (1988) *Logique et langage*, Hermès, Paris.

Newton-Smith, W. (1985) *Logic*, Routledge, London.

Nisbett, R. and Ross, J. W. (1980) *Human Inference*, Prentice Hall, Englewood Cliffs, NJ.

Nisbett, R. and Thagard, P. 'Rationality and charity', *Philosophy of Science*, 50.

Noonan, H. (1982) 'Vague objects', *Analysis* 42, I.

Nuchelmans, P. (1977) *Theories of Propositions*, Nijhoff, La Haye.

Nute, D. (1980) *Topics in Conditional Logic*, Reidel, Dordrecht.

Osherson, D. (1975) 'Logic and models of logic thinking' in R. Falmagne, ed., *Reasoning: Representation and process in children and adults*, Laurence Erlbaum, Hillsdale, NJ.

Over, D. and Manktelow (1987) 'Reasoning and rationality', *Mind and Language*, 2, 4.

Pap, A. (1958) *Semantics and Necessary Truth*, Yale University Press, New Haven, CT.

Pariente, J. C. (1982) 'Le nom propre et la prédication dans les langues naturelles', *Langages*, 66.

Parsons, C. (1978) 'A plea for substitutional quantification', in *Mathematics and Philosophy*, Cornell University Press.

Parsons, T. (1980) *Non Existent Objects*, Yale University Press.

Parsons, T. (1981) 'Frege's hierarchies of indirect sense and the paradox of analysis', *Midwest Studies in Philosophy*, VI.

Patzig, G. (1963) *Die Aristotelische Syllogistik*, Göttingen.

Patzig, G. (1975) 'Syllogistics', *Encyclopedia Britannica*.

Peacocke, C. (1976) 'What is a logical constant?', *Journal of Philosophy*.

Peacocke, C. (1981a) 'Are vague predicates incoherent?', *Synthese*.

Peacocke, C. (1981b) 'Hacking on logic; two comments', *Journal of Philosophy*, LXXVIII, 3.

Peacocke, C. (1983) *Sense and Content*, Oxford University Press.

Peacocke, C. (1986) *Thoughts, an Essay on Content*, Blackwell and Aristotelian Society, Oxford.

Peacocke, C. (1987) 'The limits of intelligibility', *Philosophical Review*.
Peacocke, C. (1988) 'Understanding logical constants', *Proceedings of the British Academy*.
Peacocke, C. (in press) 'Proof and truth', in J. Haldane and C. Wright, eds (in press).
Peirce, C. S. (1930–58) *Collected Papers*, 8 vols, ed. Hartshorne, Weiss & Burks, Harvard University Press.
Peirce, C. S. (1986) *Works, a chronological edition*, ed. Fische *et al.*, vols 1–3, Indiana University Press.
Perry, J. (1977) 'Frege on demonstratives', *Philosophical Review*, 86.
Piaget, J. (1940) *Traité de logique*, PUF, Paris.
Piaget, J. and Inhelder, B. (1955) *De la logique de l'enfant à la logique de l'adolescent*, PUF, Paris. Engl. trans. 1958, *The Growth of Logical Thinking*, Basic Books, New York.
Pitcher, G. (ed.) (1965) *Truth*, Prentice Hall, Englewood Cliffs, NJ.
Plantinga, A. (1974) *The Nature of Necessity*, Oxford, Clarendon Press.
Platts, M. (1979) *Ways of Meaning*, Routledge, London.
Platts, M. (ed.) (1980) *Reference, Truth and Reality*, Routledge, London.
Popper, K. J. (1947) 'New foundations for logic', *Mind*, 56.
Popper, K. J. (1972) *Objective Knowledge*, Oxford University Press, Oxford.
Prawitz, D. (1965) *Natural Deduction*, Almqvist and Wiskell, Stockholm.
Prawitz, D. (1975) 'Comments on Gentzen-type proof procedures and the classical notion of proof', *Proof Theory Symposium*, Kiel 1974, ed. Diller and Mueller, Springer, Berlin.
Prawitz, D. (1977) 'Meaning and proofs; on the conflict between classical and intuitionistic logic', *Theoria*, 43.
Prawitz, D. (1987) 'Dummett on a theory of meaning', in Taylor 1987.
Priest, G. (1986) 'Contradiction, belief, and rationality', *Proceedings of the Aristotelian Society*, LXXXVI, 99–117.
Prior, A. (1960) 'The roundabout inference ticket', *Analysis*, 21, repr. in Strawson 1967.
Prior, A. (1971) *Objects of Thought*, Oxford University Press.
Prior, A. (1976) *Papers in Logic and Ethics*, Duckworth, London.
Proust, J. (1986) *Questions de forme*, Fayard, Paris, English trans. *Question of Form*, University of Minnesota (1990).
Putnam, H. (1971) *Philosophy of Logic*, Prentice Hall, Englewood Cliffs, NJ.
Putnam, H. (1975) *Philosophical papers*, vols 1 & 2, Cambridge University Press.
Putnam, H. (1978) *Meaning and the Moral Sciences*, Routledge, London.
Putnam, H. (1979a) 'Analyticity and a priority: beyond Wittgenstein and Quine', *Midwest Studies in Philosophy*, 4, repr. in Moser 1987.
Putnam, H. (1979b) *Philosophical Papers*, vol. 3, Cambridge University Press.
Pylyshyn, Z. (1984) *Computation and Cognition*, MIT Press, Bradford Books, Cambridge, Mass.
Quine, W. V. O. (1940) *Mathematical Logic*, Harper and Row, New York.
Quine, W. V. O. (1950) *Methods of Logic*, 1st edn, 4th edn (1982) Harvard University Press, Harvard.
Quine, W. V. O. (1953) *From a Logical Point of View*, Harper and Row, New York.
Quine, W. V. O. (1960) *Word and Object*, MIT Press, Bradford Books, Cambridge, Mass.
Quine, W. V. O. (1963) *Set Theory and its Logic*, Harvard University Press.
Quine, W. V. O. (1969) *Ontological Relativity and Other Essays*, Harvard University Press.
Quine, W. V. O. (1970a) *Philosophy of Logic*, Prentice Hall, Englewood Cliffs, NJ, 1975.
Quine, W. V. O. (1970b) 'On the reasons for the indeterminacy of translation', *Journal of Philosophy*, LXXVII.

Quine, W. V. O. (1976) *The Ways of Paradox and Other Essays*, Harvard University Press.

Quine, W. V. O. (1981) *Theories and Things*, Harvard University Press.

Ramsey, F. (1927) 'Facts and propositions', in Mellor, ed., *Foundations*, Routledge, London, 1978.

Rawls, J. (1970) *A Theory of Justice*, Harvard University Press.

Read, S. (1988) *Relevant logic*, Blackwell, Oxford.

Recanati, F. (1986) 'Contextual dependance and definite descriptions', *Proceedings of the Aristotelian Society*, LXXXVII.

Reichenback, H. (1944) *Philosophical Foundations of Quantum Mechanics*, University of California Press, Berkeley.

Rips, L. (1982) 'Cognitive processes in reasoning', *Psychological Review*, 90.

Rosser, R. (1953) *Logic for Mathematicians*, McGraw-Hill, New York.

Rosser, R. and Turquette, A. R. (1952) *Many Valued Logics*, North Holland, Amsterdam.

Russell, B. (1903) *The Principles of Mathematics*, Allen & Unwin, London.

Russell, B. (1910) *The Problems of Philosophy*, Oxford University Press.

Russell, B. (1923) 'Vagueness', *Australasian Journal of Philosophy*, **1**.

Russell, B. (1937) *The Philosophy of Leibniz*, 2nd edn, Allen and Unwin, London.

Russell, B. (1956) *Logic and Knowledge*, Allen & Unwin, London.

Russell, B. and Whitehead, D. (1910) *Principia Mathematica*, Cambridge University Press.

Ryle, G. (1954) 'Formal and informal logic', in *Dilemmas*, Cambridge University Press, Cambridge.

Sainsbury, M. (1988a) 'Tolerating vagueness', *Proceedings of the Aristotelian Society*, LXXXIX.

Sainsbury, M. (1988b) *Paradoxes*, Cambridge University Press.

Sainsbury, M. (1991) *Logical Forms*, Blackwell, Oxford.

Salmon, N. (1982) *Reference and Essence*, Princeton University Press.

Salmon, N. (1986) *Frege's Puzzle*, MIT Press, Bradford Books, Cambridge, Mass.

Schiffer, S. R. (1978) 'The basis of reference', *Erkenntnis*.

Schiffer, S. R. (1986) 'The Fido–Fido theory of belief', in *Philosophical Perspectives*, ed. J. Tomberlin, Ridgeview, Atascadero.

Schiffer, S. R. (1987) *Remnants of Meaning*, MIT Press, Bradford Books, Cambridge, Mass.

Schlesinger, G. (1984) *The Range of Epistemic Logic*, Aberdeen University Press.

Schock, R. (1968) *Logic without Existence Assumptions*, Almqvist and Wiskells, Stockholm.

Scott, D. *et al.* (1981) *Notes of Formalization of Logic*, vols 1 & 2, Subfaculty of Philosophy, Oxford.

Seymour, M. (1988) 'Quantification et existence', *Philosophie*, 19, 29–52.

Seymour, M. (1990) 'L'indétermination de la logique', review of P. Engel, *La norme du vrai, Dialogue*, in press.

Shoenfield, R. (1967) *Mathematical Logic*, Addison Wesley, New York.

Shoesmith and Smiley (1978) *Multiple Conclusion Logic*, Cambridge University Press.

Simon, H. (1957) *Models of Man*, Wiley, New York.

Skorupski, J. (1988) 'Review of Wright 1987', *Philosophical Quarterly*.

Skorupski, J. (in press) 'Anti-realism, inference, and the logical constants', in Haldane and Wright, eds, *Reality and Reason*, Blackwell, Oxford.

Skyrms, B. (1970) 'Notes on quantification and self reference', in Martin 1970.

Smullyan, A. (1948) 'Modality and description', *Journal of Symbolic Logic*, 13.

Smullyan, R. (1968) *First-Order Logic*, Springer, Berlin.

Soames, S. (1984) 'What is a theory of truth?', *Journal of Philosophy*, LXXXI.

Sober, E. (1978) 'Psychologism', *Journal for the Theory of Social Behaviour*, 8.

Sommers, F. (1982) *The Logic of Natural Language*, Oxford University Press.

Spade, P. V. (1982) 'The logic of consequentiae', in Kenny, Kretzman & Pinborg, *Cambridge History of Later Medieval Philosophy*, Cambridge University Press.

Spencer-Smith, W. (1987) 'Discourse representation semantics, a survey', *Mind and Language*, 2, 1.

Sperber, D. and Wilson, D. (1986) *Relevance, Communication and Cognition*, Blackwell, Oxford.

Stalnaker, R. (1976) 'Propositions', in McKay, A. and Merrill, D., eds, *Issues in the Philosophy of Language*, Yale University Press.

Stalnaker, R. (1979) 'Propositions', unpublished ms., reprinted in part in 1984.

Stalnaker (1984) *Inquiry*, MIT Press, Bradford Brooks, Cambridge, Mass.

Stich, S. (1983) *From Folk Psychology to Cognitive Science*, MIT Press, Bradford Books, Cambridge, Mass.

Stich, S. (1985) 'Is man a rational animal: notes on the epistemology of rationality', *Synthèse*, 50.

Stich, S. (1990) *The Fragmentation of Reason*, MIT Press, Cambridge, Mass.

Stockmeyer, L. and Chandra, A. (1979) 'Intrinsically difficult problems', *Scientific American*, 240, 140–59.

Strawson, P. F. (1952) *Introduction to Logical Theory*, Methuen, London.

Strawson, P. F. (1971) *Logico-linguistic papers*, Methuen, London.

Strawson, P. F. (1973) *Subject and Predicate in Logic and Grammar*, Oxford University Press, Oxford.

Strawson, P. F. (ed.) (1969) *Philosophical Logic*, Oxford University Press.

Strawson, P. F. (1980) 'La logique philosophique', *Critique*, 399–400.

Strawson, P. F. (1985) *Analyse et métaphysique*, Vrin, Paris.

Strawson, P. F. (1986) 'If and →', in R. Grandy and R. Warner eds, *Philosophical Grounds of Rationality, Intentions, Categories and Ends*, Oxford University Press, pp. 229–42.

Stroud, B. (1965) 'Wittgenstein and logical necessity', *Philosophical Review*, 74, repr. in Moser 1987, ch. IV.

Stroud, B. (1979) 'Inference, belief and understanding', *Mind*, pp. 179–95.

Stroud, B. (1981) 'Evolution and the necessities of thought', in Summer, Slater and Wilson, eds, *Pragmatism and Purpose*, University of Toronto Press.

Sundholm (1981) 'Hacking's logic', *Journal of Philosophy*, LXXVIII, 3.

Sundholm (1983) 'Proof theory and meaning', in Gabbay & Guenthner 1983, vol. 3.

Suppes, P. (1950) *Introduction to Logic*, Van Nostrand, New York.

Suppes, P. (1981) *Logique du probable*, Flammarion, Paris.

Suppes, P. (1984) *Probabilistic Metaphysics*, Blackwell, Oxford.

Tarski, A. (1956) *Logic Semantics, Metamathematics*, 2nd edn 1983, Hackett, Indianapolis.

Taylor, B. (1976) 'States of affairs', in Evans & McDowell 1976.

Taylor, B. (1985) *Modes of Occurrence*, Blackwell, Oxford.

Taylor, B. (ed.) (1987) *Michael Dummett: contributions to philosophy*, Martinus Nijhoff.

Tennant, N. (1978) *Natural Logic*, Edinburgh University Press.

Tennant, N. (1986) 'The withering away of formal semantics', *Mind and Language*, 2.

Tennant, N. (1987a) *Anti-realism and Logic*, Clarendon Press, Oxford.

Tennant, N. (1987b) 'Conventional necessity and the contingency of convention', *Dialectica*.

Tennant, N. (1987c) 'Holism, molecularity, and truth', in Taylor 1987.

Thagard, P. (1988) *Computational Philosophy of Science*, MIT Press, Cambridge, Mass.

Tharp, L. (1971) 'Truth, quantification and abstract objects', *Nous*, IX.

Tharp, L. (1975) 'Which logic is the right logic?', *Synthèse*, 30.

Thom, R. (1982) 'Mathématiques et théorisation scientifique', in *Penser les mathématiques*, Seuil, Paris.

Turner, R. (1984) *Logics for Artificial Intelligence*, Ellis Horwood, Chichester.

Unger, P. (1979) 'There are no ordinary things', *Synthèse*.

Van Fraassen (1969) 'Presuppositions, supervaluations and free logic', in Lambert 1969.

Van Heijenoort, J. (ed.) (1967) *From Frege to Gödel, a source book in mathematical logic*, Harvard University Press.

Van Heijenoort, J. (1977a) *El desarollo de la teoria de la quantificación*, Mexico.

Van Heijenoort, J. (1977b) *Introduction à la sémantique des logiques non classiques*, ENS, Sèvres, Paris.

Van Heijenoort, J. (1986) *Selected Essays*, Bibliopolis, Naples.

Vendler, Z. (1967) *Linguistics and Philosophy*, Cornell University Press.

Von Neumann, J. and Morgenstern, P. (1947) *The Theory of Games and Economic behaviour*, Princeton University Press.

Vuillemin, J. (1967) *De la logique à la théologie*, Flammarion, Paris.

Vuillemin, J. (1984) *Nécessité ou contingence, l'aporie de Diodore et les systèmes philosophiques*, Minuit, Paris.

Vuillemin, J. (éd.) (1986) *Mérites et limites des méthodes logiques en philosophie*, Vrin, Paris.

Wagner, S. (1981) 'Tonk', *Notre Dame Journal of Formal Logic*.

Waismann (1945) 'Verifiability', *Proceedings the Aristotelian Society*, XIX, Suppl.

Wallace, J. (1972) 'On the frame of reference', in Davidson & Harman 1972.

Wason, P. (1968) 'Reasoning about a rule', *Quarterly Journal of Experimental Psychology*, 20.

Wason, P. and Johnson-Laird, P. (1970) 'A theoretical insight into a reasoning task', *Cognitive Psychology*, I, repr. in Wason and Johnson-Laird 1977.

Weir, A. (1986) 'Dummett on meaning and classical logic', *Mind*, 95.

Wettstein, H. (1986) 'Has semantics rested on a mistake?', *Journal of Philosophy*, LXXXIII, 4.

Wiggins, D. (1980) *Sameness and Substance*, Blackwell, Oxford.

Wiggins, D. (1981) 'What would be a substantial theory of truth?' in Z. Van Staaten, ed., *Philosophical Subjects, essays in honour of P. F. Strawson*, Oxford, Clarendon Press.

Williams, C. J. F. (1976) *What is Truth?*, Cambridge University Press.

Williams, C. J. F. (1982) *What is Existence?* Oxford, Clarendon Press.

Wittgenstein, L. (1922) *Tractatus logico-philosophicus*, ed. Pears, Routledge, London 1961.

Wittgenstein, L. (1953) *Philosophische Untersuchungen*, English trans. Blackwell, Oxford.

Wittgenstein, L. (1956) *Bermerkungen uber die Grundlagen der Mathematik*, Engl. trans. by G. E. M. Anscombe (1978), *Remarks on the foundations of mathematics*, G. H. Von Wright and R. Rhees (eds), 2nd edn, Blackwell, Oxford.

Wittgenstein, L. (1969) *Philosophische Grammatik*, ed. R. Rhees, Engl. trans by A. J. P. Kenny, *Philosophical Grammar*, Blackwell, Oxford.

Wittgenstein, L. (1971) *Carnets*, Gallimard, Paris.

Woodfield, A. (ed.) (1982) *Thought and Object*, Oxford University Press.

Wright, C. (1975) 'On the coherence of vague predicates', *Synthèse*.

Wright, C. (1976) 'Language mastery and the sorites paradox', in Evans and McDowell 1976.

Wright, C. (1980) *Wittgenstein on the Foundations of Mathematics*, Duckworth, London.

Wright, C. (1981) 'Rule following, objectivity, and the theory of meaning', in Holtzman and Leich (1981), pp. 99–117.

Wright, C. (ed.) (1984) *Frege, Tradition and Influence*, Blackwell, Oxford.

Wright, C. (1986a) *Realism, Meaning and Truth*, Blackwell, Oxford.

Wright, C. (1986b) 'Inventing logical necessity' in J. Butterfield, ed. *Language, Mind and Logic*, Cambridge University Press.

Wright, C. (1986c) 'In defense of conventional wisdom', in I. Hacking, ed., *Essays in Analysis, in Honor of C. Lewy*, Cambridge University Press.

Wright, C. (1989) 'Wittgenstein's rule-following considerations and the central project of linguistics', in George (1989), pp. 233–64.

Wright, C. and McDonald, G. (eds) (1987) *Fact, Science and Morality*, Blackwell, Oxford.

Zadeh (1965) 'Fuzzy sets', *Information and Control*, 8.

Zaslawsky, D. (1981) *Analyse de l'être*, Minuit, Paris.

GLOSSARY–INDEX

Italicised items not followed by page numbers refer to entries in this glossary.

Analytic/synthetic. In the Kantian sense, a proposition is analytic if the predicate is contained in the subject, or if its negation is contradictory. In the post-positivist sense, a proposition is analytic if it is true only in virtue of the meanings of its terms. *Conventionalism*, 42, 255, 277; *logical truth*, 220, 223–6, 234–5, 258, 268–73, 327; *syntactical criterion of analyticity*, 245–6; *a priori*, 221, 256.

Anti-realism. See *Realism*.

Argument. A set of propositions, some of which are the *premises*, and one of which is the *conclusion* derived from those premises.

A priori/a posteriori. A proposition is known *a priori* if it is known independently from experience. *A priori/metaphysical*, 166, 194; *logical truth*, 221, 250, 268–9, 279–82.

Atomic. A sentence is atomic if it does not contain any logical operator (e.g. '*p*', '*Fa*') by opposition to a molecular sentence ('*p* v *q*', '*Fa* & *Ga*'), 57–66, 81, 96, 138, 163; *Fregean Atomicity Principle* (FAP), 60–6, 82, 163; *quantification*; *singular propositions*, 57–66, *atomism*, 96, 132.

Attitude (propositional). A psychological state that has a propositional content reported by a 'that-clause' (*to believe that p, to desire that q*, etc.), 127, 161–82, 326. *Proposition*, 16, 17, 19; *Fregean propositions*; *Russellian propositions*; *reference (in contexts of propositional attitudes)*; *rationality*, 307–9, 315, 317.

Axiom. A wff is an axiom if it is a primitive proposition in a system. *Axiom schema*, 38, 68, 251, 259, 260, 263, 322; *versus inference rule*, 241–2, 299; *syntax*.

Biconditional. The truth functional connective 'if and only if' (abbreviated 'iff'): sentences formed out of this connective. *Tarskian biconditional* ('*S*' is true iff *p*').

Bivalence. The classical logical principle according to which any proposition has either the value *true* or the value *false*. *Excluded middle*, 135–6, 139, 200, 205, 207, 247, 286, 293; *realism*, 129–31, 134, 138–41, 247; *vagueness*, 140, 200, 213–15.

Charity (principle of). The principle according to which one must interpret other people's beliefs so that the number of true beliefs is maximised. *Interpretation*, 123–4; *rationality*, 307–10.

Completeness. A formal system is (i) weakly complete iff every logically true wff is a theorem of the system, or (ii) strongly complete if every independent axiom added to it does not produce any contradiction. Sometimes, a conjunction of (i) and (ii). *Consistency*, 222–3; *inconsistency*, 263–4, 265, 266; *completeness theorem*, 137, 230–3, 236, 241, 244, 263, 268; *logical truth*; *incompleteness*, 231; *Lindström's theorem*, 239–40, 244.

Conditional. The connective *if . . . then*, any statement in which such a connective figures.

371

Material conditional, 38, 40, 45–7, 255, 300, 301–2; *implication*; *counterfactual conditional*, 44–5, 133, 159.

Connective (propositional). The truth-functional operators of classical propositional calculus. Any expression forming a sentence out of a sentence. *Tonk*; *intuitionist connectives*, 135–6, 139, 245, 247; *logical constants*, 235, 249–52.

Conservative extension. A theory *T'* is an *extension* of a theory *T* if *T'* contains a new vocabulary and new theorems, and if every theorem of *T* is a theorem of *T'*. A *conservative* extension of a theory *T* is an extension *T'* of *T* such that every theorem of *T'* is also a theorem of *T*, 136–8, 145–7, 242, 244, 251, 278; *Tonk*; *holism molecularism*; *anti-realism*.

Consistency. A sentence is consistent (satisfiable) if there is at least one assignment under which it is true. Two sentences are consistent if they can be both true under an assignment of truth value, or if no contradiction can be derived from them. A formal system is consistent or non-contradictory if no wff *A* & −*A* is a theorem, or if not all the sentences of it are theorems. *Tonk*, 222–3, 244, 263, 265, 266; *principle of non-contradiction*, 222, 280, 282, 286–7, 293; *paraconsistent logic*, 286–7, 289–90.

Constant. An expression the interpretation of which is constant, by opposition to the variables, which range over a domain of objects. For example, individual constants, '*a*', '*b*', '*c*', etc., or propositional constants, such as '&', '−', 'v', etc., 155. *Variables*; *proper names*. *Logical constant*: a constant belonging to the primitive vocabulary of logic. *Propositional connectives*, 35, 235, 250–2; *tonk*; *intuitionism*, 135–6, 139; *logical truth*, 219–21, 226–9, 274; *substitution*, 225–6; *analyticity*, 111, 271, 276.

Constructionism. The thesis that logic must construct artificial languages replacing or reforming natural languages, against the *naturalist* thesis, according to which logic is 'contained' in natural language, and should be revealed from it, 56, 62, 66–7, 199–200.

Constructivism. The thesis that the only existing objects are those that are constructed by effective procedures, and that the truth of a proposition reduces to its demonstrability. Often opposed to 'platonism' in the philosophy of mathematics, and synonymous with *intuitionism*, 275–6. *Proof*; *anti-realism*; *inference*; *finitism*, 265, 291.

Contradiction. A sentence of the form '*A* & −*A*'. *Principle of non-contradiction*: the principle that no sentence can be both true and false, or (*A* & −*A*). *Inconsistency*, 222, 244, 263, 265, 266.

Contradictory. The contradictory of a sentence *A* is a sentence that must be false if *A* is true, and true if *A* is false.

Contraposition. The inference form 'from *if A then not -B*, to infer *if B then not -A*'.

Convention T. The 'material adequacy condition' for a definition of truth, according to Tarski: '*S*' is true iff *p*, 73–4, 104–5, 111–2, 114, 120, 288. *Theory of truth*; *equivalence thesis*, 95, 99, 111–2, 125; *transparency*, 99–100, 104; *theory of meaning*; *bivalence*, 214; *realism*, 138–41.

Conventionalism. The thesis that logical rules, logical laws and logical truths are conventions, or derived from conventions. *Tonk*; *logical constants*, 224–5; *logical truth*; *logical necessity*, 229, 255, 258–266, 267, 272–3, 279; *analyticity*, 41, 223–5; *moderate* *conventionalism*, 258–61, 266; *radical conventionalism*, 261–6, 267; *realism*, 255, 258, 279, 289, 292, 295, 306.

Decidability. A sentence is decidable if there is an effective procedure to determine its truth value. A system is decidable if there is an effective procedure to determine whether a wff is a theorem or a tautology, 223, 229, 233, 235, 237–8, 263; *Church's theorem*, 237–8; *Granger's criterion*, 233–41; *computational complexity*, 238.

Deduction. A sequence of sentences in a language L is a deduction in L of a conclusion B from premises $A_1, \ldots, A_n$ iff this sequence forms a valid argument; or if B is deducible from $A_1, \ldots, A_n$. *Inference*, 136, 267, 272, 303; *natural deduction rules*, 38–9, 52–5, 75, 242–6, 249, 272, 274–6, 297; *Gentzen sequent calculus*, 242–6, 248; *justification of deduction*; *analyticity*; *logical constant*; *syntax*; *semantics*; *proof*.

De dicto/de re. Medieval distinction between modalities bearing on whole propositions and modalities bearing on things. In general a quantified modal sentence is read *de dicto* when the modal operator is outside the *scope* of a quantifier, and *de re* when it is within the scope of a quantifier. A similar distinction for propositional attitude context, 153, 155, 157–8, 194–5, 257, 258, 269, 279. *Modal logic*; *quantification*; *essentialism*; *reference*; *belief*, 170–1, 175, 176–9; *singular propositions*.

Definition. An explicit definition defines an expression (*definiendum*) through another expression (*definiens*) if the second replaces the first in every occurrence. A recursive definition gives a rule to eliminate the definiens in a finite number of steps, by deriving the value of a complex expression through iterated application on the values of the primitive expressions, 41–2, 245, 250. *Theory of truth*; *logical constants*; *characterisation*, 42.

Derivation. A set of formulas is a derivation (in a system S) of a wff A from a set Γ of if it is a finite sequence of formulas of S, and A is the last formula of the sequence, and every formula of the sequence is an axiom of S or an immediate consequence, 243–4, 260, 262, 266.

Definite description. An expression of the form 'the so and so'. In Russell's theory of description, such expressions are paraphrased as 'there is exists a unique individual that is so and so', 79–81, 153, 154, 157, 165–6, 169–71, 178. *Quantification*; *identity*; *reference*; *proper names*; *singular propositions*.

Domain. The set of objects in a universe of discourse, or the set of objects that form the range of a variable or of an expression, 154–5.

Equivalence. Material equivalence. Two sentences are materially equivalent iff they have always the same truth value; logical equivalence; two sentences are logically equivalent if they can be deduced from one another, 22, 41, 54, 125.

Extension/intension. The reference or denotation of an expression/its meaning or sense. *Extensional context*: a context the truth value of which is only a function of the references of its component expressions, and where the expressions with the same reference can be mutually exchanged without altering the truth value of the whole, by opposition of an *intensional context*, in which such substitutions are not allowed, 21–5, 90, 97, 107, 124–9, 149–50, 162, 170–2. *Truth functional*; 45–6, 125; *substitution salva veritate*; (*Leibniz's law*); *extensional logic*, 145; *intensional logic*, 145–60, 163; *reference*.

Harmony. The requirement, in proof theory, that the natural deduction rules for logical constants (introduction and elimination) be harmonised, so that the conditions of assertion of a sentence and the consequences drawn from it be in accordance, 274–6, 285. *Natural deduction; molecularism; anti-realism; conservative extension.*

Holism. In the theory of meaning, the view according to which the meaning of an expression or of sentence depends on the meaning of more complex expressions or of all the sentences of the language. By opposition to *molecularism*, the view that the meaning of a complex expression is a function of the meaning of simpler expressions. *Indeterminacy of translation*, 31–2, 238; *theory of meaning*, 120; *realism; anti-realism*, 136–8 *inference; logical necessity*, 132, 264, 266–71, 273–8, 284.

Identity. The identity relation '=', 78–9, 161–2, 183–98. *Quantification; reference*, 76–9, 161; *substitutivity*, 184–7, 193; *indiscernability*, 155, 186–8; *Leibniz's law*, 184, 186–7, 189–90; *relative identity*, 187–90; *individuation*, 155–7, 184, 190–1.

Implication. A sentence *A* in *L* implies another *B* if *B* is a logical consequence of *A* from the deduction rules or axioms of *L*, or if *B* is a valid consequence of *A*. *Material implication*: the connective 'if . . . then'. *Strict implication*: necessarily if A then B, 37, 54. *Relevant implication*, 44–5, 284–5, 289, 300.

Implicature. According to Grice, the pragmatic rule allowing us to infer *A* from *B* in the presence of certain maxims of conversation and certain intentions of speakers, 48, 176.

Induction. Non-deductive inference, going from particular premises to a general, but only probable and possibly defeasible conclusion. According to some, does not exist, 136, 244, 303, 321, 355.

Inference. In a wide sense: any relationship of consequence between sentences. Set of sentences forming an argument or a reasoning, where the premises imply the conclusion. In a more particular sense, the psychological act of inferring a conclusion from premises. *Inference rules*, 220, 240-1, 246; *semantics; holism*, 136–8, 266–8; *natural deduction*, 252, 262–3, 297–302; *logical necessity*, 136–7, 256, 261–2, 271–3; *Mill's paradox; realism; anti-realism.*

Inference rule. A rule allowing us to infer a sentence from another. In a *natural deduction system*, the rules associated to each logical constant, 255, 258, 264, 270–3, 275–6, 296, 298–9, 302, 305. *Propositions; quantifiers; realism; molecularism; logical constants.*

Intension, intensionality. See extension.

Intuitionism. The view, in the philosophy of mathematics, according to which numbers are mental constructions, and truth is to be reduced to assertibility or provability. *Intuitionnist logic*: the logic that conforms to these principles, 129, 133–6, 139–40, 145, 245, 247, 265, 275–6, 287, 289–91. *Realism; anti-realism; logical necessity.*

List. A finite *sequence* of objects, in a Tarskian definition of truth.

Logical form. The form or structure of expressions and of logical inferences determined by logic, by opposition to grammatical form, 25, 51, 56–7, 59, 63, 87, 90, 127, 164, 169, 173, 226–9, 252; *Logical truth*, 221, 226–9, 233–6; *analyticity*, 221; *logical constants*, 227–9.

Logicism. The thesis that mathematics is reducible to logic, 67, 224, 231, 236, 244.

Relation. A two-place *predicate*, or the dyadic property expressed by such a predicate, 86.

Relativism. In the philosophy of logic, the thesis that there is no unique correct logical system, 281–3, 288–91. Opposed to *absolutism*.

Rigid designator. A singular term designating the same object in all possible worlds, 158–9, 195, 198. *Proper names; descriptions; essences; quantified modal logic; singular propositions*, 167.

Satisfaction. In a Tarskian definition of truth, the relationship between open sentences and sequences (or lists) of objects, 71–4, 109–12, 113, 237.

Schema. Logical expression representing a sentence or a statement without itself being a sentence. According to Quine, the propositional letters '*p*', '*q*', etc. are schemas or dummies marking an appropriate function in a sentence, 32–3.

Semantics. The set of interpretations of the expressions of a language. A logical semantics is in general a theory of truth setting the truth and reference conditions of expressions or sentences. Model theory, by opposition to proof theory, 35, 37, 49–50, 146, 220, 241, 246, 275, 278, 302–5. *Theory of truth*, 70–4, 118–41; *logical constants*, 247–52; *theory of meaning*, 121–41; *natural language*, 44–9, 50–92, 118–25, 163.

Sequence. A series of ordered objects (or list) which satisfies an open sentence or a predicate, 71–3, 109–10.

Sequent. In a natural deduction system, set of signs consisting in an antecedent set of formulas and a succedent formula tied by a consequence relationship. *Sequent calculus*: calculus of natural deduction rules (Gentzen), 242–6, 248.

Selection task. A psychological experiment about the deductive capacity of subjects for conditional reasonings.

Singular term. Term designating a unique individual. It can be either descriptive (definite description) or referential (proper name). *Proper name; descriptions; singular propositions; quantification*.

Slingshot. An argument, due to Frege, Church and Gödel, according to which the extensionality and the truth functionality of a context are equivalent, 27–30, 97, 126, 152–3, 327.

Sorite. Argument, *prima facie* paradoxical, involving a vague term and deriving a contradiction out the use of that term, 156, 202–16.

Sortal. A predicate expressing a property of a kind of object, 187–91, 192–6. *Relative identity; essence; individuation*.

Soundness. An argument is sound iff it is valid and iff all its premises are true. A logical system is sound iff all the formulas that are theorems are also tautologies or valid expressions (converse of completeness).

Statement. What is asserted or expressed by a sentence.

Structure. Set of entities determining the semantics of a language; in propositional logic, truth values; in predicate logic, domains for the individual variables and predicates. *Truth in a structure*, 74; *model theory*.

Substitution. Exchange of a symbol (term, variable, propositional letter) for another. *Substitution salva veritate*: a substitution of a symbol in a sentence that does not alter the truth value of the sentence, 33, 75, 81, 125, 162–3, 183. *Identity; extensionality; substitutional theory of logical truth*, 225–6, 230–3.

Subject. In traditional logic, the subject term of a proposition is in opposition to its predicate term. In modern logic, a term susceptible of figuring in the position of a variable of quantification, 55–66, 75, 84.

Syntax. (1) Set of the formation rules for the expressions of a logical language. (2) Set of the inference rules or of the axioms of a logical theory, 37, 70, 220, 241–7, 275, 298, 303. *Natural deduction; logical constants; logical necessity; realism; anti-realism*.

Tautology. A formula is a tautology in a logical system if it is true under all its truth value assignments to its atomic components, 136, 222, 235, 255, 259, 268. *Semantics; logical truth; inference*.

Theorem. A formula *A* is a theorem of *L* iff *A* can be derived from the axioms or the inference rules of *L*, 136, 222–3, 259, 268. *Syntax; proof theory; logical truth*.

Tonk. A weird (inconsistent) logical connective invented by A. N. Prior, 40–2, 137, 225, 242, 244, 245, 251, 263, 274, 278.

Truth. *Semantics* versus *syntax*, 15, 95, 117, 210, 241, 251, 264, 275; *truth conditional*, 117, 140, 275; *extensionality*, 37, 39, 70–4, 109–10; *theory of theory of meaning and theory of truth*, 118–41, 219–53, 256, 266, 272, 274, 279, 294; *convention T; correspondence*, 27, 96–8, 100, 107, 112–15; *coherence*, 98–9; *redundancy*, 100–4; *modest*, 96, 102, 121, 127, 133, 140; *verification*, 129–41, 247, 252, 275, 278; *realism; anti-realism*.

Vagueness. Property of a vague predicate or of a vague sentence, 140, 199–215, 290. *Identity*, 156, 196–8; *Chisholm's paradox*, 156–7, 346.

Validity. A formula is valid iff it is a tautology of *L*. An argument is valid if its conclusion follows from the premises by the axioms and/or rules of inference of a language, 53, 292, 295, 297, 300, 302. *Semantics; logical truth*, 225, 228; *logical necessity*, 267.

Variable. Expression designating an object from a domain associated with a predicate or a quantifier. *Free variable*: unbound by a quantifier. *Bound variable*: bound by a quantifier, 64, 76, 152–3, 330. *Quantification; subject; predicate; individual; reference*.

wff. Well-formed formula according to the formation rules of a language, 37.

NAME INDEX

Aristotle, 57–8, 63, 65, 304, 347, 354

Barwise, J. (and Perry, J.), 28–9, 328, 338, 341
Boolos, G., 85, 331, 332, 340, 347
Bouveresse, J., 266, 273, 329, 330, 340, 350, 351, 352, 356

Carnap, R., 21, 25, 51, 107, 146, 153, 165, 209, 224, 225–6, 235, 260, 262, 268, 327, 330, 339, 340, 350
Carroll, L., 254–6, 259, 262, 264, 266, 271, 279, 292, 300, 353
Cherniak C., 316–20, 356
Church, A., 21, 27, 29, 165, 172, 236, 237, 318, 328, 341, 347
Cohen, L. J., 311–3, 316, 355, 356

Davidson, D., 26, 87, 91, 98, 108, 113, 114, 118–28, 130–3, 140, 172–4, 179, 181, 228–9, 276–8, 288–9, 307, 311, 317, 328, 329, 332, 333, 334, 335, 341, 347, 352, 355, 356
Dennett, D. C., 307–9, 311, 317, 353, 355, 356
Dummett, M., 60, 62, 63, 86, 103–4, 112, 118–9, 122, 129–41, 203, 206, 207, 209, 213–15, 223, 232, 257, 261, 262, 263, 268, 274–7, 279, 291, 321–2, 326, 329, 330, 331, 333, 340, 345, 346, 348, 349, 352

Evans, G., 177–8, 198, 229, 326, 331–2, 335, 342, 344, 347

Field, H., 109–12, 114, 333
Fine, K., 204, 206, 209, 345
Føllesdal, D., 33, 158, 160, 328, 339, 340
Foucault, M., 205, 206
Frege, G., 18–20, 22, 24, 26–28, 29, 30, 55, 56, 60–3, 64–6, 68, 69, 81–2, 97, 100, 103, 118, 126, 130, 133, 152, 161–5, 166–9, 178, 179, 184, 186, 188, 199, 201, 206, 223, 224, 236, 257–8, 292, 294–5, 314, 320, 326, 327, 331, 332, 335, 340, 343, 350, 353

Geach, P. T., 16, 30, 58, 61, 84, 86, 187, 322, 328, 329, 344
Gentzen, G., 242–5, 247, 274–5, 298, 299, 351, 353
Gödel, K., 69, 230, 231, 327, 348
Granger, G. G., 196, 233–8, 252, 254, 279, 310, 322, 325, 326, 330, 337, 347, 348, 352, 354
Grice, H. P., 47, 50, 53, 176, 326, 329, 355

Hacking, I., 222, 242–50, 252, 254, 348, 349
Harman, G., 52–6, 302, 306, 328, 354, 355
Heijenoort, J. van, 19, 67, 281, 326, 330, 332, 344, 350–2
Hintikka, J., 89, 146, 315, 326, 331, 349, 355

Johnson-Laird, P., 50–2, 54–5, 297, 302–6, 309, 353, 354

Kant, E., 196, 224, 235, 257, 294, 353
Kripke, S., 84, 115–17, 146, 149–51, 154–5, 158–9, 166, 169, 195, 196, 263, 331, 333–4, 337, 339, 340, 342, 344, 350

Leibniz, G. W., 59–60, 63, 185–7, 224, 235, 246, 257, 326, 338, 343, 344, 350
Lewis, D., 151, 156–7, 326, 328, 335, 338, 339
Lindström, P., 241, 244

Marcus, R., 83, 155, 158, 193, 331, 340, 344, 351
McDowell, J., 121, 127, 176, 335, 336, 342
Mill, J. S., 136, 163, 175, 256, 260, 262, 266, 269, 271, 293, 326, 335, 350, 351, 353

379